Lewis Campbell
William Garnett

THE LIFE
OF
James Clerk Maxwell

WITH
SELECTIONS FROM HIS CORRESPONDENCE
AND OCCASIONAL WRITINGS

Elibron Classics
www.elibron.com

Elibron Classics series.

© 2005 Adamant Media Corporation.

ISBN 1-4021-6137-9 (paperback)
ISBN 1-4021-5415-1 (hardcover)

This Elibron Classics Replica Edition is an unabridged facsimile
of the edition published in 1884 by Macmillan and Co.,
London.

THE LIFE

OF

JAMES CLERK MAXWELL

James Clerk Maxwell

Engraved by G. J. Stodart from a Photograph by Fergus of Greenock.

THE LIFE

OF

JAMES CLERK MAXWELL

WITH

SELECTIONS FROM HIS CORRESPONDENCE
AND OCCASIONAL WRITINGS

BY

LEWIS CAMPBELL, M.A., LL.D.

PROFESSOR OF GREEK IN THE UNIVERSITY OF ST. ANDREWS

AND

WILLIAM GARNETT, M.A.

PRINCIPAL OF DURHAM COLLEGE OF SCIENCE, NEWCASTLE-UPON-TYNE

NEW EDITION, ABRIDGED AND REVISED

London

MACMILLAN AND CO.

1884

And so thou wast made perfect !   Not a friend
*   Might step between thee and the sore distress*
*   Which thou with strong and patient godliness*
Enduredst uncomplaining to the end.
Heroic saint !   Bright sufferer !   Thou dost lend
*   To science a new glory.   Midst the press*
*   Of boasters, all thy meek-eyed fame confess,*
And worldlings thine unworldliness commend.

Shine on, pure spirit !   Though we see thee not,
*   Even in thy passage thou hast purged away*
The fogs of earth-born doubt and sense-bound thought
*   From hearts that followed thine all-piercing ray.*
And while thou soarest far from human view,
*   Even thy faint image shall our strength renew.*

PREFACE.

IN adapting this volume, as we would fain hope, to the wants of that indefinite personage, the General Reader, the first aim has been to omit such matter of a technically scientific kind as appeared to be separable from the main tenor of the biography. This course is further recommended or excused by the fact that a complete edition of Clerk Maxwell's scientific writings is shortly to be published. But it is greatly to be wished that the *scientific correspondence* which Maxwell held from time to time with other eminent men might, before it is too late, be collected, sifted, and arranged. It must surely be full of interest for all who are competent to appreciate it.

It has also been thought best to print the Cambridge essays of both periods separately in an Appendix, so that the narrative might be as far as possible continuous. And the selection of poems is smaller than in the first edition, not because any of those formerly printed are wanting in interest, but it was felt that by restricting choice to those which are most characteristic and most complete in themselves, the distinctive quality of these productions, and the light which they cast on Maxwell's thoughts and feelings, would be more widely appreciated.

It remains to acknowledge the kind manner in which our previous efforts have been received ; and, in particular, to thank various correspondents who have enabled us to make important additions, to correct some errors, and to suppress some doubtful statements. We have reason to be especially grateful to Miss Barnard, who, by entrusting to us three important letters from Clerk Maxwell to her uncle, Professor Faraday, and one of Faraday's to him, has made it possible to give a degree of completeness to this part of the correspondence, which will constitute a specially valuable feature of the present edition. The letters to Dr. Huggins are also new, and will be read with interest, especially that on the Structure of Comets.

In reading the proofs I have been sadly reminded that the present tense of this narrative is already past. Two of Maxwell's early friends, C. J. Monro and H. R. Droop, have died in the short interim.

LEWIS CAMPBELL.

BOURNEMOUTH, *October 9, 1884.*

FROM THE PREFACE TO THE
FIRST EDITION.

In a work which has more than one author, it is right to distinguish as far as possible what has been contributed by each.

. . . It is due to Mr. Garnett to say that, while he had the chief share of the labour of collecting materials for the whole biography, the substance of Chapters (X. XI. XII.) is largely drawn from information obtained through him. The matter of whole pages remains almost in his very words, although for the sake of uniformity and simplicity the first person has still been used in speaking of my own reminiscences.

The narrative of Maxwell's early life has been facilitated —(1) by a diary kept by Maxwell's father from 1841 to 1847, and often referred to in these pages as "the Diary;" (2) by two albums containing a series of water-colour drawings by Maxwell's first cousin, Mrs. Hugh Blackburn (*née* Jemima Wedderburn), the value of which may be inferred from the outlined reproductions of a few of them, prepared by Mrs. Blackburn herself as illustrations for this book. They are literally *bits out of the past*, each containing an exact representation, by a most accurate observer and clever draughtswoman, of some incident which had just happened when the sketch was made. The figures, even as outlined, bring back the persons with singular vividness to the memory of those who knew them.

For these and many other advantages the thanks of the authors are due to Maxwell's relatives, but above all to his widow, not only for the free access she has given them to various documents, such as those mentioned above, but for the generous confidence she has reposed in them throughout, and for many important suggestions made by her during the progress of the work.

Their thanks are also due in an especial manner to Professor G. G. Stokes of Cambridge . . .; and to Professor P. G. Tait of the University of Edinburgh for his zealous and able assistance in many ways.

The book owes much, of course, to those who entrusted the letters here published to the authors' care. Their names are duly mentioned in the course of the work. Our task has also been lightened by the help of those friends whose contributions are inserted with their names. In describing the life of one who was so many-sided, it is no small advantage to be thus enabled to register the impression which he made on different men. Even should this occasion slight repetitions and discrepancies, the reader may thus form a fuller and, on the whole, a truer image than could be conveyed by a single narrator. Attention is here particularly directed to the statements in Chapter (XII.) by Dr. Paget, the Rev. Dr. Guillemard (of St. Mary's the Less, Cambridge), and Professor Hort.

As a general rule, no attempt has been made to weave the correspondence into the narrative. The facts relating to each period have been grouped together, and the letters have been appended to these in chronological order.

A word should be said respecting the poems. Whatever may be the judgment of critics as to the literary merits of Maxwell's occasional writings in verse, there can be no doubt of their value for the purpose of the present work. Like everything which he did, they are characteristic of him, and some of them have a curious biographical interest. Maxwell was singularly reserved in common life, but would sometimes in solitude express his deepest feelings in a copy of verses which he would afterwards silently communicate to a friend. Again, he shrank from controversy. But his active mind was constantly playing on contemporary fallacies, or what appeared so to him, and his turn for parody and burlesque enabled him to give humorous expression to his criticism of mistaken methods. Of the later pieces here reproduced, several appeared in *Nature* with the signature $\frac{dp}{dt}$ (which happens to be the analytical equivalent of the thermo-dynamical formula JCM); and one (the " Notes on the President's Address ") was published in *Blackwood's Magazine* for December 1874. The greater number are now printed for the first time.

The juvenile verses and translations have been included for the same reason which has led to the prominence given to the early life. If we are right in our estimate of Maxwell, it must be interesting to watch the unfolding of such a mind and character from the first, and this not only for the psychological student, but for all those who share Wordsworth's fondness for "days" that are "linked each to each with natural piety."

While the last sheets were being revised for the press the sad news arrived that Maxwell's first cousin, Mr. Colin Mackenzie, had died on board the *Bothnia*, on his way home from America. There was no one whose kind encouragement had more stimulated the preparation of this volume, or whose pleasure in it would have been a more welcome reward. But he, too, is gone before his time, and this book will be sent into the world with fewer good wishes. He deserves to be remembered with affection wherever the name of James Clerk Maxwell is honoured or beloved.

LEWIS CAMPBELL.

August 1882.

CONTENTS.

CHAPTER I.

PAGE

INTRODUCTORY—BIRTH AND PARENTAGE . . 1

CHAPTER II.

GLENLAIR—CHILDHOOD—1831-1841 . . . 13

CHAPTER III.

BOYHOOD—1841-1844 29

CHAPTER IV.

ADOLESCENCE—1844-1847 46

CHAPTER V.

OPENING MANHOOD—1847-1850 . . . 64

CHAPTER VI.

PAGE

UNDERGRADUATE LIFE AT CAMBRIDGE—1850-1854   .   100

CHAPTER VII.

BACHELOR-SCHOLAR AND FELLOW OF TRINITY—1854-
1856   142

CHAPTER VIII.

DEATH OF HIS FATHER—PROFESSORSHIP AT ABERDEEN
—1856, 1857   166

CHAPTER IX.

ABERDEEN—MARRIAGE—1857-1860 .   .   .   189

CHAPTER X.

KING'S COLLEGE, LONDON—GLENLAIR—1860-1870   .   230

CHAPTER XI.

CAMBRIDGE—1871-1879   264

CHAPTER XII.

ILLNESS AND DEATH—1879   313

APPENDIX.

PAGE

Essays at Cambridge 337

POEMS.

Juvenile Verses 383

Occasional Pieces 385

Serio-Comic Verse 401

Mrs Clerk Maxwell and "Boy."

Engraved by G. J. Stodart after William Dyce, R.A.

CHAPTER I.

ONE who has enriched the inheritance left by Newton and has consolidated the work of Faraday,—one who impelled the mind of Cambridge to a fresh course of real investigation,—has clearly earned his place in human memory.

But there was more in James Clerk Maxwell than is implied in any praise that can be awarded to the discoverer, or in the honour justly due to the educational reformer,—much, indeed, which his friends feel they can but partly estimate, and still less adequately describe.

We have, notwithstanding, undertaken this imperfect Memoir of him, which, in its present form, is simply an attempt to trace the growth from childhood to maturity, and to record the untimely death of a man of profound original genius, who was also one of the best men who have lived, and, to those who knew him, one of the most delightful and interesting of human beings.

If I can bring before the reader's mind, even in shadowy outline, the wise and gentle but curiously blended influences which formed the cradle of his young imagination, the channels through which ideas reached him from the past, the objects which most challenged his observation and provoked his invention, his first acquaintance with what permanently interested him in contemporary speculation and discovery, and the chief moments of his own intellectual progress in earlier years,—such record should have

B

a right to live.   And it may be that a congenial spirit here
and there may look with me into the depths of this unique
personality, and feel the value of the impulses, often seemingly wayward, and strange even to himself, with which
the young eagle "imped his wings" for flight, or taught
his eyes to bear the unclouded light.   Some, even, to whom
modern Science is a sealed book may find an interest in
observing the combination of extraordinary gifts with a no
less remarkable simplicity and strength of character.

James Clerk Maxwell was born at No. 14 India Street,
Edinburgh, on the 13th of June 1831.   His parents were
John Clerk Maxwell, one of the Clerks of Penicuik, in
Midlothian, and Frances, daughter of R. H. Cay, Esq.,
of N. Charlton, Northumberland.   Excepting a daughter,
Elizabeth, who had died in infancy, James was their only
child.

Edinburgh was at this time the natural meeting-place
for the best spirits of the North.   How much of intellect
and individuality, of genuine though often eccentric worth,
of high thinking and plain living, then foregathered in
Auld Reekie, and found ample scope and leisure there, is
known to the lovers of Sir W. Scott and to the readers of
Lord Cockburn—both prominent figures in the Edinburgh
of 1824-1831.

And the *agora* of "Modern Athens" was the Parliament House.   There the heir-presumptive could while
away his time of waiting for "dead men's shoon;" there
the laird's brother might qualify for some berth hereafter
to be provided for him ; and the son of those whose ances-
tral estates had been impaired by rashness or misfortune,
and who had perchance sought the asylum of the Abbey,
might hope through honourable industry to restore the
fallen house, or even to win new lustre for an ancient
name.

When John Clerk Maxwell, after leaving the University,
first sought those purlieus of the law, he was already a
laird, although a younger brother.   For he had inherited
the estate of Middlebie, which, by the conditions of the
entail under which it had descended from the Maxwells,

could not be held together with Penicuik, and was therefore necessarily relinquished by Sir George Clerk in favour of his brother John. This arrangement had been completed when the two brothers were boys together at the High School, and were living in George Square with their mother and their sister Isabella. Their father, James Clerk,[1] who died before his elder brother, Sir John, was a naval captain in the H.E.I.C.S., but retired early, and married Miss Janet Irving, who thus became the mother of Sir George Clerk and of John Clerk Maxwell. When Sir George had come of age, and taken up his abode at Penicuik, John Clerk Maxwell continued living with his mother, Mrs. Clerk, in Edinburgh. About 1820, in order to be near Isabella, Mrs. Wedderburn, they "flitted" to a house in the New Town, No. 14 India Street, which was built by special contract for them. Mrs. Clerk died there in the spring of 1824.

The old estate of Middlebie had been considerably reduced, and there was nothing in what remained of it to tempt its possessor, while a single man, to leave Edinburgh, or to break off from his profession at the Bar. There was not even a dwelling-house for the laird. Mr. Clerk Maxwell therefore lived in Edinburgh until the age of thirty-six, pacing the floor of the Parliament House, doing such moderate business as fell in his way, and dabbling between-whiles in scientific experiment. In vacation time he made various excursions in the Highlands of Scotland and in the north of England, and kept a minute record of his observations.

But when, after his mother's death, he had married a lady of tastes congenial to his own and of a sanguine active temperament, his strong natural bent towards a country life became irresistible. The pair soon conceived

---

[1] He is said to have played well on the bagpipes, and a set of pipes was until recently preserved at Glenlair, of which the following singular story was told :—Captain James Clerk was wrecked in the Hooghly and swam ashore, using the bag of his pipes for a float ; and when he gained the shore he "played an unco' fit," whereby he not only cheered the survivors, but frightened the tigers away.

a wish to reside upon their estate, and began to form plans
for doing so ; and they may be said to have lived thenceforth as if it and they were made for one another.   They
set themselves resolutely to the work of making that inheritance of stony and mossy ground to become one of the
habitable places of the earth.   John Clerk Maxwell had

hitherto appeared somewhat indolent ; and there was a
good deal of *inertia* in his composition.   But the latent
forces of his character were now to be developed.

He was one of a race in whom strong individuality had
occasionally verged on eccentricity.   For two centuries
the Clerks had been associated with all that was most distinguished in the Northern kingdom, from Drummond of
Hawthornden to Sir Walter Scott.   Each generation had
been remarkable for the talents and accomplishments of
some of its members ; and it was natural that a family
with such antecedents should have acquired something of
clannishness.   But any narrowing effect of such a tendency
was counteracted by a strong intellectual curiosity, which
kept them *en rapport* with the world, while they remained
independent of the world.   And as each scion of the stock
entered into new relations, the keen mutual interest, instead
of merely narrowing, became an element of width.   I speak
now of the generation preceding our own.   No house was
ever more affluent in that *Coterie-Sprache*, for which the

Scottish dialect of that day afforded such full materials. It would be pleasant, if possible, to recall that humorous gentle speech, as it rolled the cherished vocables like a sweet morsel on the tongue, or minced them with a lip from which nothing could seem coarse or broad,—caressing them as some Lady Bountiful may caress a peasant's child, —or as it coined *sesquipedalia verba*, which passed current through the stamp of kindred fancy. This quaint freemasonry was unconsciously a token not only of family community, but also of that feudal fellowship with dependents which was still possible, and which made the language and the manners of the most refined to be often racy of the soil. But Time will not stand still, and neither the delicate "couthy" tones, nor that which they signified, can be fully realised to-day. Yet we can still in part appreciate the playful irony which prompted these humorous vagaries of old leisure, wherein true feeling found a modest veil, and a naïve philosophy lightened many troubles of life by making light of them.

Mr. John Clerk Maxwell's own idiosyncrasy, as has been said, was well suited for a country life. But to give a true idea of him it is necessary to be more precise. His main characteristic, beyond a warm, affectionate heart, the soundest of sound sense, and absolute sincerity, was a persistent practical interest in *all useful processes*.[1] When

---

[1] He never lost an opportunity of inspecting manufactures, or of visiting great buildings, ecclesiastical or otherwise, and he impressed the same habit upon his son. The "works" they "viewed" together were simply innumerable, but it will be sufficient to cite one crowning instance. When James Clerk Maxwell was in the midst of his last year's preparation for the Cambridge Tripos, he proposed to spend the few days of Easter vacation which the pressure of his work allowed to him, in a visit to a friend at Birmingham. His father had seen Birmingham in his youth, and gave him the following instructions, which were mostly carried out :—" View, if you can, armourers, gunmaking and gunproving—swordmaking and proving—*Papier-mâché* and japanning—silver-plating by cementation and rolling—ditto, electrotype, Elkington's works—Brazier's works, by founding and by striking out in dies—turning—spinning teapot bodies in white metal, etc.—making buttons of sorts, steel pens, needles, pins, and any sorts of small articles which are curiously done by subdivision of labour and by ingenious tools—glass of sorts is among the works of the place, and all kinds of foundry works—engine-making—tools and instru-

spending his holidays at Penicuik as a boy from the Edinburgh High School (as well as long afterwards), he took delight in watching the machinery of Mr. Cowan's paper-mill, then recently established in that neighbourhood. And Mr. R. D. Cay remembers him, when still a young man living in India Street with his mother (about 1821-24), to have been engaged, together with John Cay, who was afterwards his brother-in-law, in a series of attempts to make a bellows that should have a continuous even blast. We can readily imagine, therefore, how closely he must have followed every step in the gradual application of steam to industry, and the various mechanical improvements which took place in his youth and early manhood.[1]

His practical thoroughness was combined with a striking absence of conventionality and contempt for ornament. In matters however seemingly trivial—nothing that had to be done was trivial to him—he considered not what was usual, but what was best for his purpose. In the humorous language which he loved to use, he declared in favour of doing things with *judiciosity*. One who knew him well describes him as always balancing one thing with another —exercising his reason about every matter, great or small. He was fond of remarking, for example, on the folly of coachmen in urging a horse to speed as soon as they saw the top of a hill, when, by waiting half a minute until the summit was really attained, they might save the animal. " A sad waste of work," he would say. Long before the days of " anatomical " bootmaking, he insisted on having ample room for his feet. His square-toed shoes were made by a country shoemaker under his direction on a last of

---

ments (optical and philosophical), both coarse and fine. If you have had enough of the town lots of Birmingham, you could vary the recreation by viewing Kenilworth, Warwick, Leamington, Stratford-on-Avon, or such like." James began with the glassworks.

[1] In 1831 he contributed to the *Edinburgh Medical and Philosophical Journal* (vol. x.) a paper entitled, " Outlines of a Plan for combining Machinery with the Manual Printing Press." His acme of festivity was to go with his friend John Cay (the " partner in his revels ") to a meeting of the Edinburgh Royal Society. See p. 149.

his own and out of a piece of leather chosen by himself.
This is only one example of the manner in which he did
everything. It was thought out from the beginning to the
end, and so contrived as to be most economical and service-
able in the long run. In his Diary (1841) we find him
cutting out his own and his son's shirts, while planning
the outbuildings which still exist at Glenlair. And he not
only planned these, but made the working plans for the
masons (1842) with his own hand.[1] This habitual careful
adaptation of means to ends was the characteristic which
(together with profound simplicity) he most obviously transmitted to his son. Its effect, heightened by perfect science,
is still apparent in the construction and arrangement of the
Cavendish Laboratory at Cambridge.

While thus unostentatious and plain in all his ways, he
was essentially liberal and generous. No one could look
in his broad face beaming with kindliness and believe
otherwise. But his benevolence was best known nearest
home. And in caring for others, as in providing for his
own house, his actions were ruled, not by impulse, but
persistent thoughtfulness. By his ever-wakeful consideration, he breathed an atmosphere of warm comfort and quiet
contentment on all (including the dumb animals) within his
sphere. Whoever had any claim upon his affectionate
heart, whether as an old dependant, or as a relation or
friend, might command from him any amount of patient
thought, and of pains given without stint and without
complaint. His "*judiciosity*" was used as freely for them
as for himself.[2] And where need was he could be an
effectual peacemaker.

He was assiduous also in county business (road meetings,

---

[1] The following entry from the Diary (1842) will be appreciated by
those who are interested in the country life of a past generation:—
"Wrote to Nanny about check of the yarn of the dead Hogs, to make
trowser stuff or a plaid."

[2] Mr. Colin Mackenzie says :—"He was the confidential friend of his
widowed sister Mrs. Wedderburn's children, who were in the habit of
referring to him in all their difficulties in perfect confidence that he would
help them, and regarded him more as an elder brother than anything
else." This is abundantly confirmed by various entries in the Diary.

prison boards, and the like), and in his own quiet way took his share in political movements, on the Conservative side.

There was a deep unobtrusive tenderness in him, which in later years gave a touching, almost feminine, grace to his ample countenance, and his portly, even somewhat unwieldy, frame.[1] He was a keen sportsman (unlike his son in this), and an excellent shot; but it was observed that he was above all careful never to run the risk of wounding without killing his game.

His temper was all but perfect; yet, as "the best laid schemes o' mice and men gang aft agley," the minute care with which he formed his plans sometimes exposed him to incidents which showed that his usual calm self-possession was not invulnerable. At such times he would appear not angry, only somewhat discomposed or "vexed," and, after donning his considering-cap for a little while, would soon resume his benign equanimity.

An interesting trait is revealed to us by the Diary. Minute as the entries are for day after day, things which, if mentioned, might reflect unfavourably upon others, are invariably omitted. They have come down through other channels, but in this scrupulous record they have left no trace.

His otherwise happy life was crossed with one deep, silent sorrow,—but was crowned with one long comfort in the life of his son. They were bound together by no ordinary ties, and were extremely like in disposition, in simplicity, unworldliness, benevolence, and kindness to every living thing. Those who knew Maxwell best will be least apt to think irrelevant this somewhat lengthy description of his father.

The portrait of Mr. John Clerk Maxwell by Watson Gordon is a faithful representation of a face which returns more vividly than most others to the eye of memory, but no portrait can restore " the busy wrinkles round his eyes," or give back to them their mild radiance—

---

[1] Entry in Diary, Nov. 9, 1844.—Weighed 15 st. 7 lbs.

"Gray eyes lit up
With summer lightnings of a soul
So full of summer warmth, so glad,
So healthy, sound and clear and whole,
His memory scarce can make me sad."

He lived amidst solid realities, but his vision was neither shallow nor contracted. And his sense of things beyond, if inarticulate, was, in later life at least, not the less serious and profound. Yet those who shall compare the Watson Gordon portrait with the study of Clerk Maxwell's head by Mrs. Blackburn, may detect something of the difference between the father and the son. In the one there is a grave and placid acquiescence in the nearer environment, the very opposite of enthusiasm or mysticism; in the other, the artist has succeeded in catching the unearthly look which often returned to the deep-set eyes under the vaulted brow, when they had just before been sparkling with fun,—the look as of one who has heard the concert of the morning stars and the shouting of the Sons of God.

James himself has said to me that to have had a wise and good parent is a great stay in life, and that no man knows how much in him is due to his progenitors. And yet the speculative ideal element which was so strong in him—the struggle towards the infinite through the finite —was not prominent in either of his parents. Mrs. Clerk Maxwell was, no doubt, a good and pious (not bigoted) Episcopalian; but, from all that appears, her chief bent, like that of her husband, must have been practical and matter-of-fact. Her practicality, however, was different from his. She was of a strong and resolute nature,—as prompt as he was cautious and considerate,—more peremptory, but less easily perturbed. Of gentle birth and breeding, she had no fine-ladyisms, but with blunt determination entered heart and soul into that rustic life. It is told of her that when some men had been badly hurt in blasting at a quarry on the estate, she personally attended to their wounds before a surgeon could be brought, and

generally that wherever help was needed she was full of
courage and resource. She was very intelligent and ingenious, played well on the organ, and composed some
music, but in other respects was less "accomplished" than
most of her family, except in domestic works, and above
all in knitting, which in those days was an elegant and
most elaborate pursuit.

Her father, R. Hodshon Cay, Esq., of N. Charlton, is
thus spoken of in Lockhart's *Life of Scott* (p. 86 of the
abridged edition, 1871) :—"I find him" (Scott) "further
nominated in March 1796, together with Mr. Robert Cay,
—an accomplished gentleman, afterwards Judge of the
Admiralty Court in Scotland,—to put the Faculty's cabinet
of medals in proper arrangement." Mr. Cay at one time
held the post of Judge-Admiral and Commissary-General,
and while thus dignified in his profession used to reside
for part of the year on his hereditary estate of Charlton,
which had been freed from certain burdens[1] upon his
coming of age.

He married Elizabeth Liddell, daughter of John Liddell,
Esq., of Tynemouth, about the year 1789.   The eldest son,
John, has been already mentioned as an early companion
of John Clerk Maxwell's, and both his name and those of
Jane and R. D. Cay will reappear in the sequel.   Between
Frances (Mrs. Clerk Maxwell) and her sister Jane, who
was never married, there existed a very close affection.
There is a picture of them both as young girls (a three-
quarter length in water-colours) done by their mother, who
was an accomplished artist.   Her gift in this way, which
was very remarkable, and highly cultivated for an amateur,
was continued in Jane and Robert, and has been transmitted to the succeeding generation.   Miss Jane Cay was
one of the warmest-hearted creatures in the world ; somewhat wayward in her likes and dislikes, perhaps somewhat
warm-tempered also, but boundless in affectionate kindness
to those whom she loved.   Mr. R. D. Cay, W.S., married

---

[1] Incurred by his father in successfully resisting some manorial claims.
These debts had brought the family to Edinburgh.

a sister of Dyce the artist, and, after acting for some time
as one of the Judge's clerks, proceeded in 1844 to Hong-
Kong, where he had an appointment. His wife joined
him there in 1845, and died in 1852. In two of their
sons, besides the artistic tastes which they inherited
through both parents, there was developed remarkable
mathematical ability. It should be also noticed that Mr.
John Cay, the Sheriff of Linlithgow, though not specially
educated in mathematics, was extremely skilful in arithmetic and fond of calculation as a voluntary pursuit. He
was a great favourite in society, and full of general information. We have already seen him assisting at experiments which might have led to the invention of "blowing
fans," but seem to have produced no such profitable result.
And we shall find that his interest in practical Science
was continued late in after life.[1]

In speaking of the Cay family it has been necessary to
anticipate a little, in order to advert to some particulars
which, although later in time, seemed proper to an introduction. Having departed so far from the order of events,
I may before concluding this chapter make explicit mention
of the loss which coloured the greater part of James Clerk
Maxwell's existence, by leaving him motherless in his ninth
year. Mrs. Clerk Maxwell died on the 6th of December
1839. There was extant until after Professor Maxwell's
death a memorandum or diary kept at the time by her
husband, describing the heroic fortitude which she had
shown under the pain of her disease, and of the operation
by which they had attempted to save her. Anæsthetics
were then unknown. She had nearly completed her forty-
eighth year, having been born on the 25th of March 1792,
and married at the age of 34 (October 4, 1826). Mr.
Maxwell was aged fifty-two at the time of his wife's death.
He did not marry again.

We now return from this sad record to the birth of

---

[1] It should be remembered that in the early years of the century considerable interest in experimental science had been awakened in Edinburgh
through the teaching of Professors Playfair and Hope.

the son and heir, which was the more welcome to the parents after the loss of their first-born child.   At this joyful epoch Mr. and Mrs. Clerk Maxwell, though retaining the house in India Street, had been already settled for some years in their new home at Glenlair.

CHAPTER II.

GLENLAIR—CHILDHOOD—1831 TO 1841.

THAT part of the old estate of Middlebie which remained to the heirs of Maxwell was situate on the right or westward bank of the Water of Orr, or Urr, in Kirkcudbrightshire, about seven miles from Castle-Douglas, the market-town, ten from Dalbeattie, with its granite quarries, and sixteen from Dumfries. It consisted chiefly of the farm of Nether Corsock, and the moorland of Little Mochrum. But, before building, Mr. Clerk Maxwell, by exchange and purchases, had added other lands to these, including the farm of Upper Glenlair. The site chosen for the house was near to the march of the original estate, where a little moor-burn from the westward falls into the Urr. The two streams contain an angle pointing south-east, opposite the heathery brae which hides the village of Kirkpatrick Durham. There, on a rising ground above the last descent towards the river and the burn, a mansion-house of solid masonry, but of modest dimensions, had been erected. It was built of dark-gray stone, with a pavement and a "louping-on-stane" of granite before the front door. On the southward slope, towards the burn, was a spacious garden-ground and a plantation beyond it, occupying the den or dingle on either side the burn, and coming round to westward of the house and garden, where it ended in a shrubbery, by which the house was approached from the north. On the eastward slope, towards the Water of Urr, was a large undivided meadow for the "kye" and the ponies. To the northward was a yard with a duck-pond, and some humble "offices" or farm-buildings, which were

displaced by the new erection of 1843. At the foot of
the meadow, near the mouth of the burn, was a ford with
stepping-stones, where the bridge was afterwards to be
built, and the regular approach to the completed house
was to be constructed. But this was far in the future,
for in his building projects the laird would not trench
upon the resources that were needed for the land. At
the foot of the garden a place was hollowed out in the
bed of the burn, which has often proved convenient for
bathing. The rocky banks of the Urr, higher up, were
fringed with wood, and on the upland, on either side the
moor, there were clumps of plantation, giving cover to the
laird's pheasants, and breaking the force of the winds coming
down from the hill of Mochrum (N.W.) Glenlair was the
name ultimately appropriated to the "great house" of
Nether Corsock.

Every detail of these arrangements had been planned
by the laird himself, and may be said to have been executed under his immediate supervision. The house was
so placed and contrived as to admit of enlargement ; but,
in the first erection of it, space was economised as in the
fitting up of a ship. And while it was building, the owners
were contented with still narrower accommodation, spending
one if not two whole summers in what was afterwards the
gardener's cottage. For the journey from Edinburgh was
no light matter, even for so experienced a traveller as John
Clerk Maxwell. Coming by way of Beattock, it occupied
two whole days, and some friendly entertainment, as at
the Irvings' of Newton (his mother's half-sisters),[1] had to
be secured on the way. Carriages, in the modern sense,
were hardly known to the Vale of Urr. A sort of double-
gig with a hood was the best apology for a travelling
coach, and the most active mode of locomotion was in a
kind of rough dog-cart, known in the family speech as a
"hurly." A common farmer's cart has been seen carrying
the laird to church, or to a friend's hall-door.

Glenlair was in the parish of Parton, of which the kirk

---

[1] See above, p. 3.

is by Loch Ken. Mr. Clerk Maxwell was one of the
elders there. (The little church of Corsock, about three
miles up the Urr, was not yet thought of; for it was built
in 1838, and not completely endowed until 1862.) About
seven miles of hilly road lead from the Urr to Loch Ken
and the Dee, which is reached at a point near Cross-Michael,
about half-way between New Galloway in one direction
and Kirkcudbright and St. Mary's Isle[1] in the other. On
the high ground between the Urr and the Dee is Loch Roan,
a favourite point for expeditions from Glenlair.

In a letter dated "Corsock, 25th April 1834" (the Boy _Æt._ 2 yrs.
being then aged two years and ten months), Mr. Clerk Max- 10 mo.
well writes to Jane Cay, his sister-in-law, in Edinburgh :—

To Miss Cay, 6 Great Stuart Street, Edinburgh.

Corsock, 25th April 1834.

This has been a great day in Parton. Your humble servant
and his better half, Ned,[2] and Davie took their departure an
hour and a half after screigh[3] for Parton, to appropriate the
seats of the new kirk, which was successfully atchieved in four
hours' work to the satisfaction of all concerned, by a grand
assemblage of the Magnates of the Parochin, who adjourned to
a feast at the Manse. Master James is in great go, but on this
subject I must surrender the pen to abler hands to do justice
to the subject.

Instead of attempting to paraphrase a mode of speech
which must be studied in and for itself, I will now give
the continuation, written on the same sheet of paper by
the "abler pen."

He is a very happy man, and has improved much since the
weather got moderate ; he has great work with doors, locks,
keys, etc., and "Show me how it doos" is never out of his
mouth. He also investigates the hidden course of streams and
bell-wires, the way the water gets from the pond through the
wall and a pend or small bridge and down a drain into Water

---

[1] The seat of the Earl of Selkirk.
[2] The laird's horse.
[3] *i.e.* Daybreak ; but in the laird's vocabulary, 9 A.M.

Orr, then past the smiddy and down to the sea, where Maggy's
ships sail.   As to the bells, they will not rust ; he stands sentry
in the kitchen, and Mag runs thro' the house ringing them all
by turns, or he rings, and sends Bessy to see and shout to let
him know, and he drags papa all over to show him the holes
where the wires go through.   We went to the shop and ordered
hats and bonnets, and as he was freckling with the sun I got
him a black and white straw till the other was ready, and as
an apology to Meg said it would do to toss about ; he heard me,
and acts accordingly.   His great delight is to help Sandy Frazer
with the water barrel.   I sent the fine hat to Mrs. Crosbie [1] for
her babe, which is well bestowed. . . . You would get letters
and violets by a woman that was going back to her place ; the
latter would perhaps be rotten, but they were gathered by James
for Aunt Jane.

Not much dragging was needed, either then or afterwards, to get Mr. Clerk to explain any mechanism to
"boy," and "show him how it doos."   Henceforward
this was the chief pleasure of his life, until the order was
reversed, and the son took an equal delight in explaining
Nature's Mechanics to the father.

Before seeing this letter, I had been told by his cousin,
Mrs. Blackburn, that throughout his childhood his constant question was, "What's the go o' that ?   What does
it do ?"   Nor was he content with a vague answer, but
would reiterate, "But what's the *particular* go of it ?"
And, supported by such evidence, I may hope to win
belief for a reminiscence which I might else have shrunk
from mentioning.   I distinctly remember his telling me,
during his early manhood, that his first recollection was
that of lying on the grass before his father's house, and
looking at the sun, and *wondering*.   To which may be
added the following anecdote, which has been communicated to me by Mrs. Murdoch,[2] the " Meg " of the preceding
letter.   "When James was a little boy of two years and
a half old, I had given him a new tin plate to play with.
It was a bright sunny day ; he held it to the sun, and the

---

[1] Wife of the minister at Parton.
[2] She was distantly connected with the Liddells (above, p. 10).

reflection went round and round the room. He said, 'Do look, Maggy, and go for papa and mamma.' I told them both to come, and as they went in James sent the reflection across their faces. It was delightful to see his papa; he was delighted. He asked him, 'What is this you are about, my boy?' He said, 'It is the sun, papa; I got it in with the tin plate.' His papa told him when he was a little older he would let him see the moon and stars, and so he did." Methinks I see the laird in those happiest days, standing on some moonlit night on the pavement at the door, pointing skywards with one hand, while the small astronomer is peering from a plaid upon the other arm, and the glad wife is standing by.[1]

In Mr. Dyce's picture of the mother and child we see this open-eyed loving intercourse with the visible universe already begun. And in the accompanying woodcut (p. 18), taken from a contemporary sketch of a "barn ball" or "kirn" in Harvest-time 1837, the boy of six years old (instead of looking at the dancer) is totally absorbed in watching the bow of the " *violino primo*," unshakably determined to make out "the go of that" some day or other. The spirit which afterwards welcomed the acoustic discoveries of Helmholtz was already at work.[2]

---

[1] There has been preserved amongst the Glenlair papers a chart of the celestial globe, cut out into constellations, which fit each other like the pieces of a child's puzzle. A round hole is made in the cardboard for every star, differing in size so as to show the magnitude of each. The whole is executed with laborious neatness, and it seems probable that we have here the means (whether purchased or made at home) whereby the configuration of the starry heavens was still further impressed on "Jamsie's" mind.

[2] From his earliest manhood his ear for music was remarkably fine and discriminating, a fact (though in strict accordance with "heredity") which surprised some of those who had known him as a boy. He has told me that he remembered a time when it was exquisitely painful to him to hear music. This time must clearly have been subsequent to 1837. The truth seems to be that his naturally keen perception of sounds was interfered with by a tendency to inflammation in the ear, which came to a crisis in his sixteenth year, but that having outgrown this, together with other signs of delicacy, his powers in this respect also were developed with striking rapidity. On the other hand, his short-sightedness seems hardly to have been noticed till he was fourteen or fifteen.

In still earlier childhood, when he returned from walking with his nurse, she had generally a lapful of curiosities
(sticks, pebbles, grasses, etc.) picked up upon the paths
through the wood, which must be stored upon the kitchen
dresser till his parents had told him all about each one.

Kirn 1837

In particular, she remembers his interest in colours—"that
(sand) stone is red; this (whin) stone is blue." "But how
d'ye know it's blue?" he would insist. He would catch
insects and watch their movements, but would never hurt
them. His aunt, Miss Cay, used to confess that it was
humiliating to be asked so many questions one could not
answer "by a child like that."

But the child was not always observing or asking questions. Ever and anon he was engaged in *doing*, or in
making, which he liked better still. And here his inven-
tiveness soon showed itself. He was not long contented
with "tossing his hat about," or fishing with a stick and a
string (as in an early picture of Miss Cay's); but whenever
he saw anything that demanded constructive ingenuity in
the performance, that forthwith took his fancy, and he must

work at it. And in the doing it, it was ten to one but he must give it some new and unexpected turn, and enliven it with some quirk of fancy. At one time he is seated on the kitchen table, busily engaged in basket-making, in

which all the domestics, probably at his command, are also employed. At another he is "making seals"[1] with quaint devices, or improving upon his mother's knitting. For he must early have attained the skill, of which an elaborate example still exists in "Mrs. Wedderburn's Abigail," which will be described in the next chapter, and was worked by him in his twelfth year.

Of his education in the narrower sense during this period little is known, except that his mother had the principal charge of it until her last illness in 1839, and that she encouraged him to "look up through Nature to Nature's God."[2] She seems to have prided herself upon his wonderful memory, and it is said that at eight years old he could repeat the whole of the 119th Psalm. His

---

[1] As mentioned in his letter to Miss Cay of 18th January 1840.

[2] When James, being eight years old, was told that his mother was now in heaven, he said, "Oh, I'm so glad! Now she'll have no more pain." Already his first thought was for another.

knowledge of Scripture, from his earliest boyhood, was
extraordinarily extensive and minute; and he could give
chapter and verse for almost any quotation from the
Psalms. His knowledge of Milton also dates from very
early times. These things were not known merely by rote.
They occupied his imagination, and sank deeper than anybody knew.

But his most obvious interests were naturally out of
doors. To follow his father "sorting" things about the
farm, or "viewing" recent improvements; by and by, at
ten years old, to ride his pony after his father's phaeton;
to learn from the men "how to pickfork the sheaves into
the cart,"[1] to witness a ploughing-match, to slide on the
Urr in time of frost (January 7, 1841), to leap ditches, to
climb trees "of sorts," to see them felled and "have grand
game at getting upon them when falling,"[1] to take wasps'
nests on hot days in July;[2] to blow soap bubbles and
marvel at their changing hues; to scramble up the bed
of the eddying stream that "flowed past the smiddy to
the sea," and mark the intricate tracery of holes and
grooves which, in rolling the shingle, it had worn and
carved in the hard rock; or to watch the same river in a
"spate," rushing and whirling over those "pots" which it
had wrought, and piling up the foam into mimic towers,
like the cumuli of the sky; or to gaze into the wan water
when in a milder mood, and drink in the rich brown colour
tinged with green reflections from the trees;—such were
some of his delights, as I may confidently infer from what
he loved to show me afterwards. For in that constant
soul the impression once made was that which remained
and went on deepening—"as streams their channels deeper
wear." I well remember with what feeling he once repeated to me the lines of Burns—

> "The Muse, nae poet ever fand her,
> Till by himsel' he learn'd to wander,

---

[1] From a letter of J. C. M. to his aunt, Miss Cay, of 18th January
1840 (Æt. 8½).

[2] At ten years old this *animosus infans* took four in one day.

Adown some trottin' burn's meander,
An' no think lang."[1]

There were living companions of his solitude besides those at home, for no live thing escaped his loving observation. And chief among these was that " child of the mossy pool," the frog,—nay, humbler still, the tadpole. The marvel of that transformation has engrossed many a child; but in none, unless in some great naturalist, has it awakened such a keen, continuous interest. And it may be here observed, as a trait not to be dissociated from his intimacy with Nature as one of her familiars, that Maxwell never had a "horror" of any creature. "Clean dirt" was a favourite expression, though no one was ever more cleanly. He would pick up a young frog, handle him tenderly, as loving him (not "as if he loved him!"), listen for his scarcely audible voice ("hear him squeak!" he would say), put him into his mouth and let him jump out again! The movements of the frog in swimming were long a favourite study, and to jump like a frog was one of the pranks with which he astonished his companions when he "put an antic disposition on" at school; but of these there will be a time to speak hereafter. It was also at a later time that he was told of Galvani's discoveries; but the recital had the more vivid interest for him because of this childhood fancy.

With eminent "judiciosity," Mr. Clerk Maxwell had furnished his son with a leaping-pole. This long staff, which appears in many of the early drawings, had at least one excellent effect. Few civilised men have had such perfect use of hands and arms as Maxwell always had. (His hand was the model of a hand, at once effective and refined looking.) Thus equipped, he went across country anywhere and everywhere, with an eye for all he saw, and pluck enough to meet any emergency. One who knew him as a child, and who is fond of animals, says that he was

---

[1] From the Epistle to William Simpson, the schoolmaster of Ochiltree, May 1785.

extraordinarily "game." His endurance, both physical
and mental, was always most remarkable.

He was sometimes taken to share in the simple daylight
festivities of the neighbourhood (perhaps also to the New
Year's gathering at Largnane, where the gifts were dispensed by a Fairy from her grotto), and it is still remembered, how at an archery picnic,[1] when an elaborate pie
from Glenlair was being opened by the member of another
house, the sturdy scion of Middlebie, who had not yet
learned the meaning of Erănos,[2] and had doubtless been
at the making and baking, bounded over the cloth just
laid upon the turf, and laid his hand upon the dish, crying
eagerly, "That's oor's!" "That's oor pie!"

His resources on wet days were—first, reading voraci-
ously every book in the house, except what his mother
kept out of his reach ; and secondly, drawing, which was
begun at a very early age. Not that he ever showed the
highest order of artistic talent (though his young perform-
ances are full of spirit); but he had great accuracy of eye,
and any singular arrangement either of form or colour had
always a fascination for him. Besides his mother's knitting,
already mentioned, his Aunt Jane's Berlin-wool work, and
her landscape drawings, early sent him inventing curious
patterns and harmonising colours. And there were two
other frequent visitants at Glenlair, whom it is now time
formally to introduce. These were Mr. Clerk Maxwell's
sister Isabella, the widow of James Wedderburn, Esq., at
one time Solicitor-General for Scotland, and her daughter
Jemima, who was still a young girl, though some years
older than her cousin.

Mrs. Wedderburn had been an ornament of Edinburgh
society in the days of her youth,[3] combining beauty of an
elegant and piquant kind with great sprightliness and

---

[1] About 1838. This was graced by the presence of three persons
then in the fulness of life, who were not destined to outlive the next
fifteen years—Mrs. Clerk Maxwell, Miss Dyce (Mrs. Robert Cay), and
Isabella Wedderburn (Mrs. Mackenzie).

[2] Ἔρανος, i.e. a feast to which all contribute, and which all sb
See below, chap. xii.

[3] She was known as the " Pentland Daisy."

originality, and the staunchest loyalty to her kin. In spite of her early widowhood and of some long illnesses, she retained much of her spirit, together with her erect, lightsome figure, to the last, and danced a reel at James's wedding with the utmost sprightliness though at the age of seventy. Her daughter, now Mrs. Hugh Blackburn, was only eight years older than her cousin James; but her rare genius for pictorial delineation, especially of animals, was already manifest. It is obvious how this companionship of genius must have influenced the child's indoor pursuits.

A scientific toy had recently come into vogue, an improvement on the thaumatrope, called variously by the names "phenakistoscope," "stroboscope," or "magic disc." Instead of turning on its diameter, as in the thaumatrope, it was made to revolve on a transverse axis, before a mirror, at which the eye looked through apertures cut at equal distances near the rim of the disc. And the figures drawn upon it were so contrived, by being placed in carefully graduated positions, as thus to produce the impression of a continuous movement.[1] This was a source of endless amusement to the two cousins, the younger generally contriving, and in part executing, the elder giving life and spirit to the creatures represented. Through Mrs. Maxwell's kindness, I have in my possession some of these early works, in which the ingenuity of the contriver is everywhere manifest, the hand of the artist only here and there. The cow jumping over the waxing and waning moon, the dog pursuing the rat in and out of his hole, the circus horse, on which the man is jumping through the hoop, have the firmness and truth of touch, the fulness of life, familiar to the many admirers of J. B. The tumbler under the horse's feet; the face in which the pink and white, drawn separately, are made to blend; the tadpole

---

[1] This was afterwards developed into the "zoëtrope" or "wheel of life,"—how far through suggestions of Clerk Maxwell's, or otherwise, I am unable to say. The lenses which perfect the illusion were certainly added by Maxwell himself. See Problem xx. of Cambridge Tripos Examination, 1869, Thursday, January 7.

that wriggles from the egg and changes gradually into a swimming frog; the cog-wheels moved by the pendulum, and acting with the precision of clockwork (showing, in fact, the working of an escapement);—these display, with less power of execution, the quaint fancy and observation, and the constructive ingenuity of the young Clerk Maxwell. There are also intricate coloured patterns, of which the hues shift and open and close as in a kaleidoscope. I

would not venture to affirm that all these belong to the very earliest period.[1] But I believe that the magic disc was in full operation before 1839, and that it has a real connection not only with the "wheel of life," but also with the "colour-top" of after years.

---

[1] As late as Feb. 27, 1847, on a Saturday half-holiday, when kept in by weather, he was employed with his father in making a magic disc for a young cousin.

Another playmate and partaker of his whims must be remembered here. This was a terrier of the "Mustard" kind, called Toby, Tobin, Tobs, or Tobit, according to the moment's humour. Toby was always learning some new trick (performed for his wages of home-made biscuit after dinner), and neither he nor James were ever tired of repeating the old ones. To mention this is not mere trifling, for his power over animals and perception of their ways[1] was a permanent characteristic, and he found a scientific use for it at a later time in inspecting the eyes of dogs with a view to certain optical investigations.[2]

He does not seem to have been particularly fond of riding at an early age, though in later life it was his favourite recreation ; but at ten years old, as has been said, he used to ride his pony behind his father's "phaeton."

Lastly, amongst the constant surroundings of the boy's early years, the "vassals" must not be forgotten. Davie M'Vinnie and his family—Sandy Fraser the gardener, and his — the Murdochs, who were the kindred of Maggie, James's nurse,—were the objects of a continuous kindly interest and friendly companionship, which had a genial effect on the heart of the child. And by those of them whom I have been able to see, he is still remembered, notwithstanding many years of inevitable silence, with undoubting affection. The very names of the places where they lived are suggestive of quaintness and singularity, as were most things in the Galloway of that day, where it was supposed that the devil had come after the Creation, with the riddlings of the universe, and had begun "couping his creels" at Screels, till creel and all fell at Criffel. Tor-holm, Tor-knows, Tor-brae, Paddock Hall, Knock-vinney, the Doon of Urr, High Craigs of Glenlair—such were some of the immediately surrounding names, sorting well with the homely, yet unusual scenery, and with the picturesque

---

[1] "He seemed to get inside them more than other people."—J. B.

[2] "Coonie," a favourite terrier in later years, had a trick of howling unmercifully whenever the piano was played. He was completely cured of this, and Maxwell told a friend, in his grave way, that he had taken "Coonie" to the piano and explained to him how it went. That was all.

Gallowegian dialect, which, like everything that struck the boy's fancy, laid a strong and lasting hold upon his mind.

In speaking of his own childish pursuits, it is impossible not to recall the ready kindliness with which, in later life, he would devote himself to the amusement of children. There is no trait by which he is more generally remembered by those with whom he had private intercourse; and, indeed, in this also it appears that the boy was father to the man. An early drawing shows him at the age of twelve, with his father's help, good-naturedly guiding the constructive efforts of a still younger boy.[1]

As the months went on after Mrs. Maxwell's death, the question of education began to press. The parents had thought it possible that under their own close surveillance the boy's lessons might be continued at home until, being of the ripe age of thirteen or so, he might be entered as a student of Edinburgh University! For this purpose a lad of sixteen, who had been highly recommended, was induced to post-

---

[1] The scene is at St. Mary's Isle, and the younger boy is Lord Charles Scott, then four years old (September 1843).—Mr. A. Macmillan, the publisher, in particular, has a vivid recollection of Maxwell's ingenious ways of entertaining children, exhibiting his colour-top, showing them how to make paper boomerangs, etc.

pone the completion of his own college course, and to reside at Glenlair. The experiment was continued until November 1841, but by that time, under the altered circumstances, the plan had proved unworkable. Meanwhile the boy was getting to be more venturesome, and needed to be—not driven, but led.

There is one of Mrs. Blackburn's drawings which throws a curious light on the situation at this juncture. Master James is in the duck-pond, in a wash-tub, having ousted the ducks, to the amusement of the young "vassals," Bobby and Johnny, and is paddling himself (with some implement from the dairy, belike) out of reach of the tutor, who has fetched a rake, and is vainly trying to bring him in. Mr. Clerk Maxwell has just arrived upon the scene with Mrs. Wedderburn, and is looking on complacently, though not without concern. Cousin Jemima has been aiding and abetting, and is holding the leaping-pole, which has probably served as a boat-hook in this case.

Glenlair
1841

The achievement of sailing in the tub was one in which James gloried scarcely less than Wordsworth's Blind Highland boy in his tortoise shell. It is referred to in the following letter, written by the boy of ten years old to his father, who had gone for a short visit to St. Mary's Isle :—

> *Glenlair House,*
> *[Friday], 29th October 1841.*
>
> DEAR PAPA—We are all well. On Tuesday we[1] sailed in the tub, and the same yesterday, and we are improving, and I can make it go without spinning ;[2] but on Wednesday they were washing, and we could not sail, and we went to the potatoes. Yesterday they took up the Prince Regents, and they were a good crop. Mr. —— and I went to Maggy's, but she was away at Brooklands, and so I came back and sailed myself, for Nanny said Johnny was not to go in, and Bobby was away. Fanny was there, and was frightened for me, because she thought I was drowning, and the ducks were very tame, and let me go quite close to them. Maggy is coming to-day to see the tubbing. I have got no more to say, but remain your affectionate son,
>
> JAMES CLERK MAXWELL.

Through the influence of his wife's sister, Miss Jane Cay,[3] added to his own observation, Mr. Clerk Maxwell was at length roused to carry into effect what had been for some time in debate, viz. to take his son to Edinburgh and put him to school.

---

[1] From the context "we" seems to include "Bobby," one of the young "vassals."

[2] To enable him to "trim the vessel," he had put a block of wood in the centre. Sitting on this, and tucking his legs on either side, he could paddle about steadily and securely. Mrs. Blackburn tells me that years afterwards at Ruthven, in Forfarshire, being desirous of inspecting a water-hen's nest on a deep pond where there was no boat, she adopted the same method, and made the voyage both ways alone without the slightest uneasiness.

[3] Two letters from Miss Cay to James, one dated September 1, the other October 21, 1841, were kept by Mr. Clerk Maxwell, and have been preserved. Although not significant enough to be inserted here, they show the confidential intercourse which had sprung up between "Aunt Jane" and her sister's son. She writes of theological and other matters which would not generally be thought interesting to a boy of ten, thanks him for his thoughtfulness in getting ferns for her, and says, "I was glad to hear you were happy, with all your experiments and adventures." There had been a visit to Edinburgh that summer, and she writes as if anticipating that it would be soon repeated. There is also a reference to an elaborate set of Berlin-wool work for the furniture of the drawing-room at Glenlair, which had been begun in Mrs. Maxwell's lifetime, and was afterwards completed by Miss Cay.

CHAPTER III.

BOYHOOD——EDINBURGH ACADEMY——"OLD 31"——HOLI-
DAYS AT GLENLAIR——1841 TO 1844——ÆT. 10-13.

THE first school-days are not always a time of progress.
For one whose home life has been surrounded with an
atmosphere of genial ideas and liberal pursuits, to be
thrown, in the intervals of "gerund-grinding," amongst a
throng of boys of average intelligence and more than average boisterousness, is not directly improving at the outset.
Not that Maxwell ever retrograded——for his spirit was
inherently active; but where the outward environment
was such as awakened no response in him, he was like an
engine whose wheels do not bite——working incessantly, but
not advancing much. If the Scottish day-school system
had not still been dominated by a tyrannous economy, and
by that spirit of *laisser faire* which in education is apt to
result in the prevalence of the worst, much that was in
Maxwell would earlier have found natural vent and growth.
As it was, he was of course storing up impressions, as
under any circumstances he would have been; but his
activities were apt for the time to take odd shapes, as in
a healthy plant under a sneaping wind. Or, to employ
another metaphor, the light in him was still aglow, but in
passing through an alien medium its rays were often refracted and disintegrated. The crowd of "aimless fancies,"
whose influence upon his life he so touchingly deprecated
at a later time,[1] were now most importunate; and, bright
and full of innocence as they were, they produced an effect

---

[1] In the poem written after his father's death in 1856.

of eccentricity on superficial observers which he afterwards
felt to have been a hindrance to himself. His mother's
influence, had she lived, would have been most valuable to
him at this time.

The journey from Glenlair had been broken at Newton[1]
and at Penicuik, where a halt of some days was made.   It
was the middle of November, and a season of snow and

18° Nov.ʸ 1841

Edinburgh.

1841.   frost.   Soon after dusk on the 18th of November, the
Æt. 10. whole family party, including the faithful domestic, Lizzy
Mackeand,[2] arrived at the door of No. 31 Heriot Row,
Mrs. Wedderburn's house in Edinburgh.   This (with oc-
casional intervals, when he was with Miss Cay) was to be
James Clerk Maxwell's domicile for eight or nine years to
come.

The "White Horse" seen through a lunette above the
doorway, the quaint figure of the butler (nicknamed

---

[1] Above, p. 14.
[2] Now Mrs. MacGowan, Kirkpatrick-Durham.

"Hornie" from the way he dressed his hair[1]), and other noticeable features of this dwelling, appear and reappear in the boy's letters to his father, which now become more frequent. For, although not choosing to be much separated from James, Mr. Clerk Maxwell could not be long absent from Glenlair, and henceforward he lived a divided life between the two, spending most of the winter evenings by his sister's fireside in Edinburgh, and during most of the spring and summer attending personally to the improvement of his estate.

The Edinburgh Academy, which had been founded in 1824, was in high favour with the denizens of the New Town. Lord Cockburn was one of the directors. The Rector, Archdeacon Williams, was an Oxford first-classman, a College acquaintance of John Lockhart's,[2] and an admirable teacher. He had at one time been an assistant master at Winchester, and had subsequently, at Lockhart's recommendation, been tutor to Charles, Sir W. Scott's second son. The boys in the junior classes, however, knew little

---

[1] His real name was James Craigie.

[2] The inscription beneath his bust in Balliol College, Oxford, is a just tribute to the memory of one who, though he had his foibles, was a born educator, and no ordinary man :

JOHN WILLIAMS, M.A.,

Archdeacon of Cardigan—1835-1858 ;

Rector of the Edinburgh Academy—1824-1847 ;

Warden of Llandovery College—1848-1853 ;

Who, by the geniality of his Character

And the vigour of his Intellect,

Won the hearts of his Pupils,

And gave his life to the study of the Classics in Scotland :

A Celtic Scholar,

An ardent lover of Wales and of the Welsh People,

After a long absence

He returned to his Native Land,

And devoted his great talents

To the instruction of his Countrymen :

Born 1792 ; Died 1858.

He resided at this College

Between the years 1810 and 1814.

See also Lockhart's *Life of Scott*, small edition of 1871, pp. 484, 744, 781.

of him except by report, for the assistant masters were jealous of their independence.

Various entries in his Diary testify to the father's deliberate care in placing his son at the Academy. Everything which seemed material to the boy's advantage had no doubt been carefully considered; but there was one serious omission, arising from Mr. Clerk Maxwell's inveterate disregard of appearances. The boy was taken to school in the same garments in which we have seen him at Glenlair. No dress could be more sensible in itself. A tunic of hodden gray tweed is warmer than a round cloth jacket for winter wear, and the brazen clasps were a better fastening for the square-toed shoes than an adjustment of black tape, which is always coming undone. But round jackets were *de rigueur* amongst the young gentlemen; while it must be admitted that they were equally intolerant of dandyism. A frill for a round collar was of course unendurable, and the Gallovidian clasps—not to mention the square toes—were an unheard-of novelty. A new boy, coming in the second month of the second year, must in any case have had something to undergo; but here was evident provocation to "a parcel of boys in their teens."[1]

What happened in the interval after the first lesson (in the space behind the second classroom) is best indicated in the words of the Psalmist :—"They came about me like bees."

"Who made those shoes?" was the first question; but it was never easy to get a direct answer from Maxwell, least of all on compulsion. Brought thus to bay, he had

---

[1] "I do believe the veriest fien's
       In the world is a parcel of boys in their teens."
                                        Fo'c's'le Yarns.
The palinode should also be quoted :—
         " ' Fiends' I called them, did I ?   Well,
           I shouldn then.   It's hard to tell;
           And it's likely God has got a plan
           To put a spirit in a man
           That's more than you can stow away
           In the heart of a child.   But he'll see the day
           When he'll not have a bit too much for the work
           He's got to do."   *Ibid.*

recourse to his natural weapon—irony. His answer was
soon ready, and his tormentors might make of it what
they list.   In the broadest tones of his Corsock *patois* he
replied to one of them,

> " Div ye ken, 'twas a man,
> And he lived in a house,
> In whilk was a mouse."

He returned to Heriot Row that afternoon with his
tunic in rags and "wanting" the skirt; his neat frill
rumpled and torn;—himself excessively amused by his
experiences, and showing not the smallest sign of irritation.
It may well be questioned, however, whether something
had not passed within him, of which neither those at home
nor his schoolfellows ever knew.

The nickname of "Dafty" which they then gave him
clung to him while he remained at school, and he took no
pains to get rid of it. His " quips and cranks " were taken
for "cantrips;" his quick, short, elfin laughter (the only
sign by which he betrayed his sensitiveness) was construed
into an eldritch noise. Never was cygnet amongst goslings
more misconstrued. Within the class-rooms things were
not much more prosperous at first. Our master, Mr. A.
N. Carmichael, was a good and experienced teacher, and
an excellent scholar, in a dryish way. He was the author
of the *Edinburgh Academy Greek Grammar* and of an
Account of the Irregular Greek Verbs, which has now
been superseded, but was justly respected in its day. He
was a good disciplinarian; but those junior classes of sixty
and upwards were too large and miscellaneous for real
teaching. He had an eye for talent, too, where it was
shown. But his first business was to hear our tasks, and
to let us take places in the class in proportion to the
accuracy and readiness with which we said them. Maxwell
did not at once enter into the spirit of this contest, in
which the chief requisites, next to average talent and intelligence, were push and promptitude. His first initiation
in Latin had not been pleasant to him, and the repetition
ad nauseam of " *di, do, dum,*" by his new acquaintances,

D

varied with the sound of the tawse, did not make the
subject more attractive. Like the boy Teufelsdröckh, he
seemed to hear at school innumerable dead vocables, but
no language. His hesitation got worse and worse, and as
his place in the class was not amongst the "best boys,"
some of his neighbours willingly did their utmost to dis-
concert him. On one occasion we shall find him humorously retaliating. He was not in the least inwardly perturbed by all this, nor bore any one the slightest malice.
It was a new scene of life, which he contemplated with
amused curiosity. But it was natural that his chief interest
should not lie there. He seldom took part in any games,
though he was loyally proud of the success of his school in
them, and characteristically took some interest in the
spinning of "pearies" (pegtops), and the collision of
"bools" (marbles); but, when he could, preferred wandering alone, sometimes imprisoning the humble-bees on the
green slope at the back and letting them go again, sometimes doing queer gymnastics on the few trees that were
left,—availing himself, in short, of the scanty inlets by
which Nature visited that shingly ground.[1] For his heart
was at Glenlair, even when he made sport for the young
Philistines of the Academy "yards." It should be added
that his attendance was a good deal interrupted by delicate
health.

1842-43.   His life during this period was really centred in "Old
Æt. 10-12. 31." He was presently allowed to have a room to himself,
in which he could read and draw and write, besides preparing for school. His cousin Jemima was at this time
learning the art of woodcutting, and he was permitted
sometimes to dig away with her tools. The result was a
series of rude engravings, to which allusions occur in his
letters to his father; and a woodcut of his, representing
the head of an old woman, still remains, with the date
1843 engraved on it. In the previous year he produced
more than one elaborate piece of knitting. One of these,
a sort of sling for holding a work-basket, with its proper

---

[1] Things are altered now. For years past an ample recreation-
ground has been provided for the boys of the Academy.

name, "Mrs. Wedderburn's Abigail," worked into it, has been preserved by Mrs. Blackburn. The library at his new home was more extensive than at Glenlair. He came to know Swift and Dryden, and after a while Hobbes, and Butler's *Hudibras*. Then if his father was in Edinburgh they walked together, especially on the Saturday half-holiday, and "viewed" Leith Fort, or the preparations for the Granton railway, or the stratification of Salisbury Crags; always learning something new, and winning ideas for imagination to feed upon.[1] One Saturday, February 12, 1842, he had a special treat, being taken "to see electro-magnetic machines." *Æt.* 10.

Mr. Clerk Maxwell was much more like an elder brother than a "governor" to James, and there was nothing the boy could not or did not tell him,—none of his whimsical vagaries in which the father did not take delight. And when "his papaship" was alone at Glen-lair, James would strive to cheer him in his solitude by concocting the wildest absurdities, inventing a kind of cypher to communicate some airy nothing, illuminating his letters after the fashion of his school copy-books, and adding sketches of school-life (*e.g.* the class-room in the absence of the teacher), et cetera. His father carefully preserved those letters, and several of them still exist. Full of extravagant nonsense and boyish fun as they are, they abound also with ingenuity, and the illustrations have a curious interest, as showing his love of drawing complicated patterns and arranging colours, and as marking the early and spontaneous development of "the habit of constructing a mental representation of every problem," [2] which was in 1842-43. *Æt.* 10-12.

---

[1] Less frequently, he would rove about alone. Professor Fleeming Jenkin remembers hearing him say that when he first saw the twisted piles of candles with which grocers decorate their windows, he was struck by the curious and complex curves resulting from the combinations of these simple cylinders, and was resolved to understand all about that some day.

[2] The words are Professor Tait's. In the letter of January 18, 1840 (above, p. 20), in his ninth year, when in speaking of his amusement of seal-engraving he says, "I made a bird and a beast," the words "bird" and "beast" are each accompanied with a sort of hieroglyphic representing the figure he had made upon the seal.

some degree an hereditary proclivity. In order, however, to judge fairly of these *enfantillages*, the reader must take into account the boy's affectionate solicitude to amuse his father, who was accustomed to receive whimsical familiarities from his young relatives in "Old 31."[1]

In Edinburgh, as at Glenlair, he was allowed to participate in the amusements of his elders. It is just worth mentioning that his first play was *As You Like It*, with Mrs. Charles Kean as Rosalind; and more important to observe that on December 18th, 1843, his father took him to a meeting of the Edinburgh Royal Society.

Æt. 12.

But at school also he gradually made his way. He soon discovered that Latin was worth learning, and the Greek Delectus interested him, when we got so far.[2] And there were two subjects in which he at once took the foremost place, when he had a fair chance of doing so; these were Scripture Biography and English. In arithmetic, as well as in Latin, his comparative want of readiness kept him down.

On the whole he attained a measure of success which helped to secure for him a certain respect, and, however strange he sometimes seemed to his companions, he had three qualities which they could not fail to understand—agile strength of limb, imperturbable courage, and profound good nature. Professor James Muirhead remembers him as "a friendly boy, though never quite amalgamating with the rest." And another old class-fellow, the Rev. W. Macfarlane of Lenzie, records the following as his impression:—"Clerk Maxwell, when he entered the Academy, was somewhat rustic and somewhat eccentric. Boys called him 'Dafty,' and used to try to make fun of him. On one occasion I remember he turned with tremendous vigour, with a kind of demonic force, on his tormentors. I think he was let

---

[1] This is clearly proved by a set of delightful rhyming epistles addressed to him by his niece, Isabella Wedderburn, afterwards Mrs. Mackenzie, then a bright young girl, between the years 1825 and 1827.

[2] The *Academy Greek Rudiments* was purchased before leaving Edinburgh for the holidays, July 28, 1842.

alone after that, and gradually won the respect even of the most thoughtless of his schoolfellows." [1]

It was on some such occasion as that to which Mr. Macfarlane here refers,—somewhere in 1843 or 1844,— that my own closer intimacy and lifelong friendship with James Clerk Maxwell began. I cannot recall the exact circumstances, only the place in the Academy yards, the warm rush of chivalrous emotion, and the look of affectionate recognition in Maxwell's eyes. However imperturbable he was, one might see that he was not thick-skinned. *1843-44. Æt. 12-13.*

Shortly after this we became near neighbours, my mother's new domicile being 27 Heriot Row, and we were continually together for about three years.

His letters now refer with more of interest to his progress at school, especially to exercises in verse, and to outdoor recreation with companions; above all to his delight in bathing and in learning to swim. In this, as in everything he did, he invented curious novelties, and was particularly fond of mimicking his old acquaintance, the frog.

On Sundays he generally went with his father to St. Andrew's Church (Mr. Crawford's) in the forenoon, and, by Miss Cay's desire, to St. John's Episcopal Chapel in the afternoon, where, also by her desire, he was for a time a member of Dean Ramsay's catechetical class. Thus, having of course learned "his questions" as a child, he became equally acquainted with the catechisms both of the Scotch and of the English Church, and with good specimens of the Presbyterian and Episcopalian styles of preaching. He also went regularly "to the dancing" at Mr. MacArthur's, where he was distinguished for the neatness of his reel-steps, especially of those curious ones which some of us found most difficult, such as the "lock-step."

But more delightful than bathing, and more interesting even than writing English verse, was the achievement of

---

[1] "One hautboy will," etc. From an entry in his father's Diary of May 19, 1847, it appears that he was even then not free from annoyance. And I can bear witness to the fact.

which he writes casually to his father very shortly after his thirteenth birthday. After describing the Virginian Minstrels, and betwixt inquiries after various pets at Glenlair, he remarks, as if it were an ordinary piece of news, " I have made a tetrahedron, a dodecahedron, and two other hedrons, whose names I don't know." We had not yet begun geometry, and he had certainly not at this time learnt the definitions in Euclid ; yet he had not merely realised the nature of the five regular solids sufficiently to construct them out of pasteboard with approximate accuracy, but had further contrived other symmetrical polyhedra derived from them,[1] specimens of which (as improved in 1848) may be still seen at the Cavendish Laboratory.

Who first called his attention to the pyramid, cube, etc., I do not know. He may have seen an account of them by chance in a book. But the fact remains that at this early time his fancy, like that of the old Greek geometers, was arrested by these types of complete symmetry ; and his imagination so thoroughly mastered them, that he proceeded to make them with his own hand. That he himself attached more importance to this moment than the letter indicates, is proved by the care with which he has preserved these perishable things, so that they (or those which replaced them in 1848) are still in existence after thirty-seven years.

LETTERS, 1842 to 1844.

[April 1842.]

MY DEAR PAPA—The day you went away Lizzy and I went to the Zoological Gardens, and they have got an elephant, and Lizzy was frightened for its ugly face. One gentleman had a boy that asked if the Indian cow was he.

Asky[2] thinks he is a scholar, and was for going with me to the school, and came into the dancing to-day.

---

[1] By producing the facets until their alternate planes intersected. In the specimens still extant, the facets belonging to each plane of the original polyhedron are distinguished by specific colouring.
[2] Pet name of a dog. See illustration on p. 30.

On Friday there was great fun with Hunt the Gowk;[1] we could believe nothing, for the clocks were all "stopped," and everybody had a "hole in his jacket." Does Margaret[2] play on the trump[3] still? and what are the great works? Does Bobby sail in the tub?—I am, your obedient servant,

JAMES CLERK MAXWELL.

[Illuminated letters at beginning, and border after.]   Æt. 11.

MY DEAR MR. MAXWELL—I saw your son to-day, when he told me that you could not make out his riddles. Now, if you mean the Greek jokes, I have another for you. A simpleton wishing to swim was nearly drowned. As soon as he got out he swore that he would never touch water till he had learned to swim; but if you mean the curious letters on the last page, they are at Glenlair.—Your aff. Nephew,

JAMES CLERK MAXWELL.

I have cut a puggy[4] nut, and some of the oil came upon my fingers, and it smelt like linseed Oil, but it did not hurt. There was a boy that brought Sea fyke[5] to the school, and put it down the boys' backs, for which he was condemned to learn 12 lines for 3 days. Talking about places, I am 14 to-day, but I hope to get up. Ovid prophesies very well when the thing is over, but lately he has prophesied a victory which never came to pass. I send you a Bagpiper to astonish the natives with.[6] I have got a jumping paddock and a boortree gun.[7] When are you coming?—Your most obedient Sarvent,

JAS. ALEX. M'MERKWELL.[8]

---

[1] Scotch name for the license of April Fool's day.

[2] A daughter of his nurse.   [3] The Jew's harp.

[4] Cashew nut.

[5] A substance often found on the sea-shore. It is of a honey-combed structure, and consists, in fact, of the egg-capsules of the common whelk (*Buccinum undatum*). When dried and pulverised, it has an irritating effect upon the skin. Hence the local name:—"Fyke" = fidget. See Jamieson's *Dictionary*.

[6] This fantastic and elaborately-coloured illustration is certainly sufficiently astonishing.

[7] A pop-gun of elder-wood.

[8] Anagram of James Clerk Maxwell.

Æt. 12.   *Envelope of 24th June 1843—*
                        MR. JOHN CLERK MAXWELL,
                            Postyknowswere,
                        Kirkpatrick Durham,
                            Dumfries.

"*Old 31,*" *28th March 1844.*

MY DEAR FATHER—On Saturday last we went to the Marine
Villa ;[1] it had a very strong marine scent, but I suppose it is
all the better for that. I found out where shell-fish breed ;
they breed in sea fyke ; there were muscles, cocles, and oysters
no bigger than these O O O O fastned to the fyke by filaments.
Nell and Frolic were immersed in the serene bosom of Neptune,
from which with still quivering limbs they came out, but with
very different feelings ; but Nell exited the compassion of
Meddum,[2] and was carried by her. I have flitted up to the
little garret. What like is the new tadpole ? and how is Maggy
getting on with fmmm ;[3] how much more is to be done concerning O fye, says the pie. John's house is not finished yet,
I suppose. There have been letters from uncle Robert, dated
Gibber Altar, but I have not seen or heard what is in them
farther than that he was to be at Suez on Monday last. Lizzy
says that when you come back it would not be displeasing to
her if you would bring a bawl of gray worsted, which last word
I suppose means woolen thread. I have cast three seals of
lead from the life, or rather from the death ; one of a cockle
and two of muscles, one of which is, or rather will be, on this
letter ‡. If you want to know more look along from the
beginning of the letter to the mark ‡ for the red and blue
letters [4] in order.

How are all the bodies and beasts,—Praecipue, Nanny,
Maggy, Fanny, Bobby, Toby, and Marco.—Your obt. servt.,
                        JAS. ALEX. M'MERKWELL.

---

[1] Silverknowe, near Granton, which was being prepared as a residence
for Mr. and Mrs. Mackenzie (Isabella Wedderburn).

[2] Mrs. Wedderburn.   [3] The sound of the "trump."

[4] Here represented by italics and small capitals respectively. The
italics spell—*Sea fyke is a good thing for polishing with.* The small
capitals spell—I AM COPYING AN OLD PRINT OUT OF THE DELFIAN (*i.e.*
Delphin) SALLUST. It need not be observed that the capricious spelling
in these letters is merely a piece of "daftness." The spelling of the
letters of 1841 (*Æt.* 9-10) is faultless.

MY DEAR FATHER—On Wednesday I went to the Virginian minstrels, in which some of the songs were sung, the first line accompanied with clappers, the second on a tamborine, the third on a banjo, like this, . . . played like a guitar very quickly, and the fourth on the fiddle, and the chorus by all together. There were guesses [1] in abundance ; and there was an imitation of a steam onion, and other things which you will find in the bill. On Saturday, having got the play for verses on Laocoon, I went with Cha. H. Johnstone [2] so far, and then went to the murrain vile till Mrs. M'Kenzie, Ninny, and κυνη [3] went to visit Cramond, where I played with the boies till high water ; and the minister's young brother and the too boies and I doukit in C (big sea as κυνη calls it), and then dried ourselves after the manner of Auncient Greeks ; we had also the luxury of a pail of water to wash our feet in.

How is a' aboot the house now our Gudeman's at home ? How are herbs, shrubs, and trees doing ?—cows, sheep, mares, dogs, and folk ? and how did Nannie like bonny Carlisle ? Mrs. Robt. Cay was at the church on Sunday.[4]   I have made a tetra hedron, a dodeca hedron, and 2 more hedrons that I don't know the wright names for.   How do doos and Geraniums come on. —Your most obt. servt.,   JAS. ALEX. M^CMERKWELL.
1 2 5   12 7 4 13   3 6 11 8 9 10 14 15 16 17

---

[1] *i.e.* riddles or conundrums, of which the boy was fond.

[2] A son of Admiral Hope Johnstone, then living at Cramond, a scion of the Johnstones, who in 15— had a feud with the Maxwells, but in later times claimed kinship with them.

[3] "*i.e.* Coonie," viz. Mr. Colin Mackenzie, then a child of three.

[4] This helps to fix the date of this letter. Mrs. R. Cay joined her husband in China early in the spring of 1845. Her son Alexander was born May 7, and christened on Wednesday, June 26, 1844. Mr. C. Maxwell had left Edinburgh for Glenlair on June 7, taking with him six pigeons in a basket, and some cuttings of pelargonium. His first entry in the Diary after this, at Glenlair, is as follows :—"*Saturday, June 8.*— Got home to dinner, and find all well. After dinner plant cuttings of pelargonium from Killearn, and sort the doves in the new dove-cot." Now every letter received from James is recorded in the Diary, and the only such entry between the limits of June 7-26 is on June 21st.   "THE THREE PAIRS OF DOVES ALL SITTING.   Recd. letters from Mrs. Wed. and James."   It was a two-days' post.   The letter dated July 10 was received on July 12.—The "Verses on Laocoon" point to the same date. The translation from Virg. *Æn.* i. 159-169, which certainly preceded them, was given in on May 10, 1844.

10th July 1844.

DEAR FATHER—Excuse me on account of being so long of writing, because of my being totally employed about preparations of verses, English and Latin.   I made four lines of Latin one week, for which I got the play from ten ; but I am not going to try for the prize, as when I lithp in numberth it ith but a lithp, for the numberth do not come even with the help of Gradus ; but I am making English ones on the apparition of Creusa to Æneas in the end of the second book.   Besides this, I am preparing the biography,[1] and have been making a list of the kings of Israel and Judah.   I have been going to Cramond and playing with the boys every Saturday ; they went to Ray-hills on the ninth.   Dooking[2] is grown fine and warm now.

O father ! can it be that souls sublime
return to visit our terrestrial clime ?[3]

Your obt. servt. and son to you,
JAMES CLERK MAXWELL.

I have been wavering about 14 for a good while in the Latin.

HOLIDAYS AT GLENLAIR—1842 to 1844.

We can readily imagine the sense of enlargement and release with which the boy went home to Glenlair after his first long sojourn in Edinburgh.   The shadow which had fallen in 1839 was softened by time, and society in the Happy Valley[4] resumed its aspect of harmless gaiety. Cousin Jemima was again there with her pencil.   The "tubbing" was, of course, resumed, this time conjointly, and the scene of it was advanced from the duck-pond to the river, showing greatly increased confidence in navigation.[5]

There were nutting excursions, walks diversified with climbing, etc. etc.   And in August and September 1843

Æt. 12.

---

[1] Scripture History.   [2] Bathing.
[3] Dryden, Virg. vi., motto for poem on "Creüsa."
[4] This name was given to the Vale of Urr in the *Coterie-Sprache*, and adopted even by the local newspapers in their notices of various social gatherings.
[5] Long afterwards, when asked by some one ignorant of Galloway, if there was boating on the Urr, he would answer by a grave reference to this incident.

there were again archery meetings at different houses in the valley, of one of which (the last) there has been preserved the following notice from one of the local newspapers of the time :—

ARCHERY IN "THE HAPPY VALLEY."

The Toxophilite Club of the Valley of Urr held their last meeting for the season on Mrs. Lawrie of Ernespie's lawn, on Tuesday the 12th curt. The club consists of from forty to fifty members.

Their meetings this summer have been quite charming. They ranged over the whole valley, on this fair lawn to-day, and on that the next; and after their couple of hours of archery was over, a picnic took place on the spot. "God save the Queen" was invariably sung with the most graceful loyalty; and the hospitable mansion adjoining gave them music and a hall for the evening quadrille, which wound up the delights of the day.

At every meeting some little prize was proposed to give zest to the sport; Mr. Herries of Spottes, for instance, gave a case of ladies' arrows, which was shot for and gained by one of the lady competitors. Nor lacks the club its Laureate and its Painter to glorify the pastime. A scion of the House of Middlebie has lent gallantry to the archers by his spirited songs; and a fair lady, a friend of the same house, has painted a couple of pieces, and presented them, the one to Mr. Lawrence of Largnean, the president of the club, and the other to Mrs. Bell of Hillowton, the lady patroness. The former picture represents William Tell aiming at the apple on his son's head; the latter, the chaste huntress Diana piercing a stag. Both are "beautiful exceedingly."

Thus well accomplished in every point and accessory of their beautiful pastime, loyal and happy are the Bowyers of Urr.

One of James's spirited songs, a parody of Scott, beginning "Toxophilite, the conflict's o'er," still exists in Cousin Jemima's handwriting, with a sketch for the picture of William Tell, in which the features of the House of Middlebie are idealised. The artist also proved the best shot on this occasion. The poem is not worth printing, though it has characteristic touches of grotesque ingenuity and humorous observation which are very curious in a boy of twelve.

The summer of 1843 was also memorable for the com- _Æt._ 12.
pletion of the New Offices at Glenlair. Whatever he may
have intended before the death of his wife, Mr. Clerk
Maxwell made no change in the dwelling-house during his
lifetime. But these out-buildings had been designed by
himself; he had drawn the working plans for the masons;
he had acted as clerk of the works, rejecting unfit material,
etc., and every detail had been executed under his own eye.
So absorbed was he in the supervision, that he omitted his
usual visit to Edinburgh in July. In one of Mrs. Blackburn's drawings of the previous year, he is seen laying
out the ground for the new offices, with James beside him
intently contemplating his father's work. We may be sure
that Mr. Maxwell had explained every step in the whole
procedure, and equally sure that his son laid the lesson
well to heart.

Soon after this he was provided with a new source of
endless amusement in the "devil-on-two-sticks," which
thenceforth became inseparable from the home life at
Glenlair, and the companion of his holidays at Glasgow
and elsewhere, even in the Cambridge time. In the family
dialect it was humorously referred to, _sotto-voce_, as "the
deil." There was nothing he could not do with that
d—l. No performer on the slack or tight rope ever
made such intricate evolutions and gyrations. His delight
in it was like that which afterwards he used to take in the
dynamical top.

The boy now came to know his own neighbourhood 1843-44.
more widely. There were expeditions, visits, rides. The _Æt._ 12-13.
Covenanter's pool in the burn above Upper Corsock, New
Abbey, Caerlaverock, and other places of traditional interest,
were explored. And in the summer of 1844 there was a
sort of driving excursion into the Cairnsmuir country, which
is described in detail in the Diary.

It may be mentioned here in a general way that the
Christmas holidays were spent either at Penicuik (with
skating, etc.) or Killearn, and afterwards sometimes at
Glasgow with Professor and Mrs. Blackburn, or Professor
(now Sir William) Thomson.

CHAPTER IV.

ADOLESCENCE—1844 TO 1847—ÆT. 13-16.

THE commencement of the fifth year at the Academy was, for many of us boys, a time of cheerfulness and hope. The long period of mere drill and task-work was supposed to be over. We had learned the 800 irregular Greek verbs, either by our own efforts, or by hearing others say them, and had acquired some moderate skill in Latin verse composition. On entering the rector's class-room, our less mechanical faculties were at once called into play. We found our lessons less burdensome when we had not merely to repeat them, but were continually learning something also in school. And the repetition of Virgil and Horace was a very different thing from the repetition of the rules of gender and quantity. Some foretaste of this more genial method had been afforded us in the previous year, when we had been encouraged to turn some bits of Virgil into English verse. But the change was, notwithstanding, considerable, and it was accompanied with another advance, which for Maxwell was at least equally important, for it was now that we began the serious study of geometry.

In October 1844 Mr. Clerk Maxwell and his sister, Mrs. Wedderburn, were both far from well, and James was received in Edinburgh by his aunt, Miss Cay. He writes to his father, October 14, 1844 :—

I like P——[1] better than ——.[2] We have lots of jokes,

---

[1] The boys' nickname for the Rector, Archdeacon Williams. Maxwell's first interview with him was as follows :—Rector : "What part of Galloway do you come from ?" J. C. M. : "From the Vale of Urr, Ye spell it o, err, err, or oo, err, err." [2] Ditto for Mr. Carmichael.

and he speaks a great deal, and we have not so much monotonous parsing. In the English, Milton is better than history of Greece. . . . I was at Uncle John's,[1] and he showed me his new electrotype, with which he made a copper impression of the beetle. He can plate silver with it as well as copper, and he gave me a ☐ thing with which it may be done. At night I have generally made vases.

This letter is sealed with the scarabæus referred to as "the beetle."

In the next letter we have a trace of his hesitation not being yet conquered :—

P—— says that a person † of education never puts in † hums and haws ; he goes † on with his † sentence without senseless interjections.

N.B.—Every † means a dead pause.[2]

While thus privately retorting on his censor, he took a singular means for curing his own defect. He made a plan of the large window in the rector's room, and wrote the words of the lesson in the spaces of the framework. He conned his task in that setting, and, when saying it, looked steadily at the actual window, where, as he averred, the arrangement of the panes then helped to recall the order of the words. The only fear was that by changing his place in the class he might be obliged to stand sideways to the window.

Our mathematical teacher, Mr. Gloag, was a man who combined a real gift for teaching with certain humorous peculiarities of tone and manner. He was sometimes impatient, but had a kind heart, and we liked him all the better because we mimicked him.[3] Old academicians still delight in talking of him. He never allowed us to miss a step in any proof, and made us do many " deductions,"

---

[1] Mr. John Cay, Sheriff of Linlithgow. See above, p. 6.

[2] These pauses in the Rector's case were often filled, in less guarded moments, with "What you call," "Yes, yes," which he had a trick of interposing.

[3] He once said to a nervous boy who had crossed his legs and was sitting uneasily, " Ha, booy ! are ye making a basket wi' your legs."

which we puzzled out entirely without help.   It must have
been the companionship of Maxwell that made those hours
so delightful to me.   We always walked home together,
and the talk was incessant, chiefly on Maxwell's side.
Some new train of ideas would generally begin just when
we reached my mother's door.   He would stand there
holding the door handle, half in, half out, while,

> " Much like a press of people at a door
> Thronged his inventions, which should go before,"

till voices from within complained of the cold draught, and
warned us that we must part.

From some mathematical principle he would start off to
a joke of Martinus Scriblerus, or to a quotation from
Dryden, interspersing puns and other outrages on language
of the wildest kind, "humming and hawing" in spite of
P——; or in a quieter mood he would tell the story of
Southey's *Thalaba*, or explain some new invention, which I
often failed to understand.   Our common ground in those
days was simple geometry, and never, certainly, was emula-
tion more at one with friendship.   But whatever outward
rivalry there might be, his companions felt no doubt as to
his vast superiority from the first.   He seemed to be in
the heart of the subject when they were only at the
boundary; but the boyish game of contesting point by
point with such a mind was a most wholesome stimulus, so
that the mere exercise of faculty was a pure joy.   With
Maxwell, as we have already seen, the first lessons of
geometry branched out at once into inquiries which soon
became fruitful.

1844-46.   "Meantime, the rural ditties were not mute."   Besides
Æt. 13-15. a serio-comic impromptu on the grievance of a holiday task,
and other effusions concerning incidents of our school life,
there was a romantic ballad written about Christmas 1844
or 5, and in July 1845 the prize for English verse was
gained by the poem on the death of the Douglas, to which
he refers in one of his letters to Miss Cay.[1]

---

[1] His turn for versifying may be traced back to his twelfth year,

But a prize of more consequence was the mathematical medal, of which he writes to his aunt in a tone of undisguised though generous triumph. The following letters were written in June and July 1845 :—

To Miss Cay.

June 1845.

I have drawn a picture of Diana,[1] and made an octohedron on a new principle, and found out a great many things in geometry. If you make two circles equal, and make three steps with the compasses (of any size), and cut them out in card, and also three equal strips, with holes at each end, and joint them with thread to the upper side of one circle and the lower side of the other ; then if you put a pin through the centre of one and turn the other, the one will turn, and if you draw the same thing on both in the same position,—if you turn them *ever so,*—they will always be in the same position.

July 1845.

The subjects for prizes are as follows :—English Verses—The gude Schyr James Dowglas ; Latin Hexameters and Pentameters—The Isles of Greece ; Latin Sapphics—The Rhine. I have been getting information in many books for Douglas, but I found it so difficult not to Marmionise, that is, to speak in imitation of *Marmion,*—that I am making it in eight syllable lines. I have got Barbour's *Bruce*, Buke 20, which is a help in a different language, which is all fair ; my motto is :—

> "Men . may . weill . wyte . thouch . nane . them . tell .
> How . angry . for . sorrow . and . how . fell .
> Is . to . tyne . sic . a . lord . as . he .
> To . them . that . war . of . hys . mengye ."[2]

Pa and I went to your house on Saturday and watered the plants. I have got the lend of the whole of Horne's *Introduction to the Knowledge of the Scriptures*, and Prideaux's *Connection of*

---

when, in one of his quaint letters to his father, there occur some lines (profusely illustrated) on the death of a goldfinch :—

> " Lo ! Ossian makes Comala fall and die,
> Why should not you for Richard Goldie cry," etc.

And in September 1843, as above mentioned, he wrote for the Archers in the "Happy Valley" a page and more of spirited verse.

[1] *i.e.* A sketch from the antique.
[2] Barbour's *Bruce*, B. xx., ll. 507-10.

the Old and New Testaments, and Townshend's *Harmony*, which are of great use.[1]

July 1845.

Æt. 14.   I have got the 11th prize for Scholarship, the 1st for English, the prize for English verses, and the Mathematical Medal. I tried for Scripture Knowledge, and Hamilton in the 7th has got it. We tried for the Medal[2] on Thursday. I had done them[3] all, and got home at ½ past 2 ; but Campbell stayed till 4. I was rather tired with writing exercises from 9 till ½ past 2.[4]

Campbell and I went "once more unto the b(r)each" to-day at Portobello. I can swim a little now. Campbell has got 6 prizes. He got a letter written too soon congratulating him upon *my* medal ; but there is no rivalry betwixt us, as —— Carmichael says.

His aunt, Miss Cay, to whom these letters are addressed, had begun again to take more charge of him than in the preceding years. Mrs. Wedderburn's health was very uncertain. Cousin Jemima was grown-up and immersed in her own pursuits, and the companionship of his cousin, George Wedderburn, a young man about Edinburgh, and a humorist of a different order, was not in every way the most suitable for the growing boy. The Diary shows that he was continually at his aunt's house, No. 6 Great Stuart Street, and she is associated with some of my earliest recollections of him. She sought to bring him out amongst her friends, to soften his singularities, and to make him more like other youths of his age. And he would help her with patterns, arrangement of colours, etc., as well as with her flowers. One of his earliest applications of geometry was

---

[1] Viz. for a competition in Scripture Knowledge, which was open to the 5th, 6th, and 7th classes. The prize was gained that year by one of the 7th.

[2] "Mathematical Prize" is added between the lines by Mr. Clerk Maxwell, who writes a P.S. to the letter.

[3] "The trial exercises," ditto, ditto.

[4] In these competitions we seem to have been allowed to stay till we had done all we knew. Witness the following extract from the Diary :— "1847, *July, Mon.* 19.—James at Academy trial for Prize for Scripture Knowledge. Worked from 9 to 5. Lewis Campbell and W. Tait worked till 6."

to set right the perspective of a view of the interior of
Roslin Chapel on which she was engaged.

Mr. Clerk Maxwell was a frequent visitor at the Academy
at this time.   His broad, benevolent face and paternal air,
as of a gentler Dandie Dinmont, beaming with kindness for
the companions of his son, is vividly remembered by those
who were our schoolfellows in 1844-45.

The summer vacation of 1845 was spent almost wholly
at Glenlair.   James passed a day now and then at Upper
Corsock with the Fletcher boys,[1] and sometimes accompanied his father when he went out shooting; but he
must have had abundance of time for reading and for
following his own devices.   The country gentlemen were
particularly absorbed that year in political excitement, and
Mr. Clerk Maxwell was often called away.   The only event
worth mentioning was a "jaunt," evidently suggested by
Miss Cay, to Newcastle, Durham, and Carlisle, which gave
Maxwell his first direct impression of English Cathedral
Architecture.

The taste thus formed was strengthened by a visit to
Melrose in the following summer.

Saw the House of Abbotsford and antiquities in it, and go
to Melrose.   Got there about 2, and settle to remain all night.
Spend the day and also the evening about the Abbey.   Jane
Cay and James drawing.—Diary, 1846, Sept. 10.

On returning to Edinburgh for the winter, Mr. Clerk   1845.
Maxwell seems to have been roused by the expectation   *Æt.* 14.
which his son's first school distinction had awakened
amongst his kindred and acquaintance.   He became more
assiduous than ever in his attendance at meetings of the
Edinburgh Society of Arts and Royal Society, and took
James with him repeatedly to both.   And so it happened
that early in his fifteenth year the boy dipped his feet in
the current of scientific inquiry, where he was to prove
himself so strong a swimmer.   In our walks round Arthur's

---

[1] Sons of Colonel Fletcher of Upper Corsock.

Seat, etc., he had always something new to tell. For example, in February 1846, he called my attention to the glacier-markings on the rocks, and discoursed volubly on this subject, which was then quite recent, and known to comparatively few.

A prominent member of the Society of Arts at this time was Mr. D. R. Hay, the decorative painter, whose attempt to reduce beauty in form and colour to mathematical principles[1] had attracted considerable attention amongst scientific men. Such ideas had a natural fascination for Clerk Maxwell, and he often discoursed on "egg-and-dart," "Greek pattern," "ogive," and what not, and on the forms of Etruscan urns. One of the problems in this department of applied science was how to draw a perfect oval; and Maxwell, who had by this time begun the (purely geometrical) study of Conic sections, became eager to find a true practical solution of this. How completely his father entered into his pursuit may best be shown by the following extracts from Mr. Clerk Maxwell's Diary :—

Æt. 14.

1846,
February.

W. 25.—Called on . . Mr. D. R. Hay at his house, Jordan Lane, and saw his diagrams and showed James's Ovals—Mr. Hay's are drawn with a loop on 3 pins, consequently formed of portions of ellipses.

Th. 26.—Call on Prof. Forbes at the College, and see about Jas. Ovals and 3-foci figures and plurality of foci. New to Prof. Forbes, and settle to give him the theory in writing to consider.[2]

March.

M. 2.—Wrote account of James's ovals for Prof. Forbes. Evening.—Royal Society with James, and gave the above to Mr. Forbes.

---

[1] "First Principles of Symmetrical Beauty," by D. R. Hay, *Blackwoods*, 1846.

[2] Part of the entry on the same day is :—"Parliament House.—Return with John Cay, called at Bryson's and suggested to Alexander Bryson my plan for pure iron by electro-precipitation from sulphate or other salt." It is interesting to observe this revival of his youthful ardour for science in the old companionship, following upon his sympathy with the efforts of his son.

W. 4.—Went to the College at 12 and saw Prof. Forbes, about Jas. ovals. Prof. Forbes much pleased with them, investigating in books to see what has been done or known in this subject. To write to me when he has fully considered the matter.

Sa. 7.—Recd. note from Prof. Forbes :—

Edinburgh, 6th March 1846.

MY DEAR SIR—I have looked over your son's paper carefully, and I think it very ingenious,—certainly very remarkable for his years ; and, I believe, substantially new. On the latter point I have referred it to my friend, Professor Kelland, for his opinion.—I remain, dear Sir, yours sincerely,   JAMES D. FORBES.

W. 11.—Recd. note from Professor Forbes :—

3 Park Place, 11th March 1846.

MY DEAR SIR—I am glad to find to-day, from Professor Kelland, that his opinion of your son's paper agrees with mine ; namely, that it is most ingenious, most creditable to him, and, we believe, a new way of considering higher curves with reference to foci. Unfortunately these ovals appear to be curves of a very high and intractable order, so that possibly the elegant method of description may not lead to a corresponding simplicity in investigating their properties. But that is not the present point. If you wish it, I think that the simplicity and elegance of the method would entitle it to be brought before the Royal Society.—Believe me, my dear Sir, yours truly,   JAMES D. FORBES.

J. CLERK MAXWELL, Esq.

Th. 12.—Called for Prof. Forbes at the College and conversed about the ovals.

M. 16.—Went with James to Royal Society.

T. 17.—Jas. at Prof. Forbes's House, 3 Park Place, to Tea, and to discourse on the ovals. Came home at 10. A successful visit.

T. 24.—Cut out pasteboard trainers for Curves for James.

W. 25.—Call at Adie's,[1] to see about Report on D. R. Hay's paper on ovals.

Th. 26.—Recd. D. R. Hay's paper and machine for drawing ovals, etc.

M. 30.—Called on Prof. Forbes at College and saw Mr. Adie about report on Mr. Hay's paper. Jas. ovals to be at next meeting of R.S.

M. 6.—Royal Society with Jas. Professor Forbes gave acct. of James's ovals. Met with very great attention and approbation generally.

---

[1] The Optician's.

The result of the attempt thus eagerly pursued, as communicated by Professor Forbes that evening, is embodied in the *Proceedings of the Edinburgh Royal Society,* vol. ii. pp. 89-93.

MONDAY, *6th April* 1846.

SIR THOMAS M. BRISBANE, Bart., President, in the Chair.

The following communications were read :—

1. On the Description of Oval Curves, and those having a plurality of Foci.   By Mr. CLERK MAXWELL, junior, with' Remarks by Professor FORBES.   Communicated by Professor FORBES.

Mr. Clerk Maxwell ingeniously suggests the extension of the common theory of the foci of conic sections to curves of a higher degree of complication, in the following manner :—

1. As in the ellipse and hyperbola, any point in the curve has the *sum* or *difference* of two lines drawn from two points or *foci* = a constant quantity, so the author infers that curves to a certain degree analogous may be described and determined by the condition that the simple distance from one focus, *plus* a multiple distance from the other, may be = a constant quantity ; or more generally, *m* times the one distance + *n* times the other = constant.

2. The author devised a simple mechanical means, by the wrapping of a thread round pins, for producing these curves. See Figs. 1 and 2 (Plate 11).   He then thought of extending the principle to other curves, whose property should be, that the sum of the simple or multiple distances of any point of the curve from three or more points or foci, should be = a constant quantity ; and this, too, he has effected mechanically, by a very simple arrangement of a string of given length passing round three or more fixed pins, and constraining a tracing point, P. See Fig. 3.   Further, the author regards curves of the first kind as constituting a particular class of curves of the second kind, two or more foci coinciding in one, a focus in which two strings meet being considered a double focus ; when three strings meet a treble focus, etc.

Professor Forbes observed that the equation to curves of the first class are easily found, having the form—

$$\sqrt{x^2+y^2}=a+b \ \sqrt{(x-c)^2+y^2},$$

which is that of the curve known under the name of the First
Oval of Descartes. Mr. Maxwell had already observed that,
when one of the foci was at an infinite distance (or the thread
moved parallel to itself, and was confined, in respect of length,
by the edge of a board), a curve resembling an ellipse was
traced ; from which property Professor Forbes was led first to
infer the identity of the oval with the Cartesian oval, which is
well known to have this property.   But the simplest analogy of
all is that derived from the method of description, r and r' being
the radients to any point of the curve from the two foci.

$$mr + nr' = \text{constant,}$$

which, in ¦fact, at once expresses on the undulatory theory of
light the optical character of the surface in question, namely,
that light diverging from one focus F without the medium, shall
be directly convergent at another point f within it ; and in this
case the ratio $\frac{n}{m}$ expresses the index of refraction of the medium.

If we denote, by *the power of either focus*, the number of
strings leading to it by Mr. Maxwell's construction, and if one
of the foci be removed to an infinite distance,—if the powers of
the two foci be *equal*, the curve is a parabola ; if the power of
the nearer focus be greater than the other, the curve is an
ellipse ; if the power of the infinitely distant focus be the
greater, the curve is a hyperbola.   The first case evidently
corresponds to the reflection of parallel rays to a focus, the
velocity being unchanged after reflection ; the second, to the
refraction of parallel rays to a focus in a dense medium (in which
light moves slower) ; the third case, to refraction into a rarer
medium.

The Ovals of Descartes were described in his *Geometry*, where
he has also given a mechanical method of describing one of
them, but only in a particular case, and the method is less
simple than Mr. Maxwell's.   The demonstration of the optical
properties was given by Newton in the *Principia*, Book i. Prop.
97, by the law of the sines, and by Huyghens in 1690, on the
Theory of Undulations, in his *Traité de la Lumière*.   It probably
has not been suspected that so easy and elegant a method exists
of describing these curves by the use of a thread and pins whenever the powers of the foci are commensurable.   For instance,
the curve, Fig. 2, drawn with powers 3 and 2 respectively, give
the proper form for a refracting surface of glass, whose index of

Proceedings of the Edinburgh Royal Society, vol. ii.

PLATE XI.

Fig.1. Two Foci. Ratios 1:2.

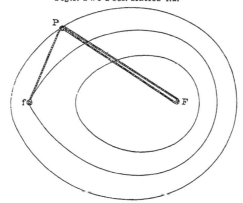

Fig.2. Two Foci. Ratios 2:3.

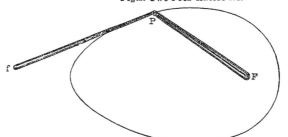

Fig.3. Three Foci. Ratios of Equality.

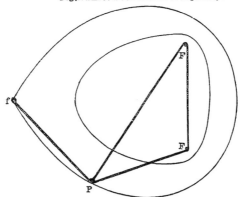

refraction is 1.50, in order that rays diverging from f may be refracted to F.

As to the higher classes of curves, with three or more focal points, we cannot at present invest them with equally clear and curious physical properties, but the method of drawing a curve by so simple a contrivance, which shall satisfy the condition,

$$mr + nr' + pr'' + \text{etc.,} = \text{constant,}$$

is in itself not a little interesting ; and if we regard, with Mr. Maxwell, the ovals above described, as the limiting case of the others by the coalescence of two or more foci, we have a further generalisation of the same kind as that so highly commended by Montucla, by which Descartes elucidated the conic sections as particular cases of his oval curves.

This was the beginning of the lifelong friendship between Clerk Maxwell and James D. Forbes. " I loved James Forbes" was his own emphatic statement to me in 1869. Maxwell's gratitude to all from whom he had received any help or stimulus was imperishable.

The curve-drawing, and the problems connected with it, *Æt.* 14-15. were by no means the only original investigations of this year. Mr. John Scott, of Scott Brothers, Greenock, re-members being in the attic of 31 Heriot Row, and seeing some preparations of jelly with which James was experi-menting there. Mr. Scott left Edinburgh in the summer of 1846. What was the exact object of these experiments and others on *gutta percha* at this time is matter of conjec-ture. There is little doubt that they prepared the way for the investigation concerning the compression of elastic solids. But it seems probable that they were immediately suggested by Forbes's *Theory of Glaciers*, which had recently called attention to the whole question of the difference between solid, liquid, and "viscous" bodies, and the different effects of gravitation and pressure as applied to them.[1] Another set of phenomena with which his mind was soon afterwards engaged, viz. those of the refraction and polarisation of light, were partly studied through similar means.

---

[1] See especially Forbes's paper on the "Viscous Theory of Glacier-Motion" in the *Philosophical Transactions* for 1846, pp. 143-210.

The work of his cousin, who was now a rising artist, still interested him. An entry in the father's Diary, December 5, 1845, has reference to this:—

Walk with Jas. and Jemima to Botanical Garden to inspect palm-trees—for her sketching for a picture.

Either in this or the following year I remember his raising the question, Whether it was not possible to determine mathematically the curve of the waves on a particular shore, so as to represent them with perfect truth in a picture.

1846-47. *Æt.* 15-16. After contributing to the *Proceedings* of the Edinburgh Royal Society, it might perhaps have been expected that Clerk Maxwell, although scarcely 15, would at least have been taken from the Academy and sent to the classes of Mathematics and Natural Philosophy at the University. Instead of this, he simply completed his course at school. His inventions may perhaps have interfered a little with his regular studies—for he missed the Mathematical medal in 1846—but he was one of the few of the class which he had joined in 1841 who continued at the Academy until 1847. And when he left, although still younger than his competitors by about a twelvemonth, he was not only first in mathematics and English, but came very near to being first in Latin. He had not yet "specialised" or "bifurcated," although the bent of his genius was manifest. Nor have I ever heard him wish that it had been otherwise. On the contrary, he has repeatedly said to me in later years that to make out the meaning of an author with no help excepting grammar and dictionary (which was our case) is one of the best means for training the mind. Some of his school exercises in Latin prose and *verse* are still extant, and, like everything which he did, are stamped with his peculiar character.[1] The first Greek play we read (the *Alcestis* of Euripides) made an impression on him to

---

[1] On his copy of Monk's *Alcestis*, which we read in the 6th class (1845-46), the owner's name is followed by an original distich:—

"Si probrum metuis, nolito tangere librum,
Nam magni domini nomina scripta vides."

which he reverted in a conversation many years afterwards.[1]
At the same time he had a quick eye for the absurdities of
pedantry. One of the teachers was apt to annoy our youthful taste by a literal exactness in translating the Greek
particles, which would have pleased some more recent
scholars. Maxwell expressed our feelings on this subject
in a few lines, of which I can only recall the beginning :—

> " Assuredly, at least, indeed,
> —*Decidedly* alsó . . ."

The frigid climax in "decidedly" is a good instance of his
roguish irony.

In September 1846 I made my first visit to Glenlair.
It was a time of perpetual gladness, but the particulars are
hardly worth recording. James used to sleep long and
soundly, and seemed to be the whole day at play, eagerly
showing me his treasures and accompanying each exhibition
with lively talk, sprinkled with innumerable puns.[2] After
such a breakfast as became that land of milk and honey,
there was a long interval, while Mr. Maxwell was attending to home business and deliberating what the "expedite"
should be. Miss Cay meanwhile was writing letters, or
finishing some drawing of Lincluden or New Abbey (where
they had lately been), and James would flit to and fro
between the little den, where his books and various
apparatus lived, and the drawing-room,[3] where his father
sat in the arm-chair, with Tobs on knee. Ever and anon
we boys would escape out of doors and have a run in the
field or the garden, or a bout with the d—l. So the
morning would pass till an early luncheon, after which

---

[1] The following bit of Diary deserves to be quoted in this connection :—"*1845, Saturday, December 27.*—Jas. dined at Miss Cay's. I
went there to tea, taking Lewis and Robert Campbell. Then we all went
to the play—'Antigone,' by Miss Faucit."

[2] I can only compare him to the fraternal spirit that William Blake
saw in vision "clapping its hands for joy" (Gilchrist's *Life of William
Blake*, vol. i. p. 59). In the talk of that period a butterfly was always
a "flutterby;" and idiotisms such as "used to could" and "be-you-have
yourself !" were in common use.

[3] The present dining-room

Tobin must do his various tricks; then, if the men were
busy, James would himself harness Meg, the Galloway
pony, for the drive of the afternoon.   After dinner and
Toby's second performance, and another turn at the deil,
there would be something more to see—Cousin Jemima's
drawings, recent diagrams or other inventions of his own,
the magic discs, etc. etc., the charm of the whole consisting in the flow of talk, incessant, but by no means
unbroken,

> " Changing, hiding,
> Doubling upon itself, dividing,"

of which neither of us ever tired.   On Sunday there was
the drive to Corsock Church (where the absolute gravity
of his countenance was itself a study),[1] and the walk home
by the river, past the Kirk pool, renowned for bathing,
with conversations of a more earnest kind, and a stroll on
the estate in the afternoon; or, if we stayed at home, he
would show his favourite books and talk about them, till
the evening closed with a chapter and a prayer, which the
old man read to the assembled household.

Æt. 15.   During the winter of 1846-47 James's health was
unusually delicate.   He was often absent from school, and
seems not to have gone to meetings of the Societies.
But of these his father was sure to give him a faithful
report.   He was certainly more than ever interested in
science.   The two subjects which most engaged his attention
were magnetism and the polarisation of light.   He was
fond of showing "Newton's rings"—the chromatic effect
produced by pressing lenses together—and of watching the
changing hues on soap bubbles.

In the spring of 1847 (somewhere in April) his uncle,
Mr. John Cay, whose scientific tastes have been mentioned
more than once above, took James and myself (with whom

---

[1] At church he always sat preternaturally still, with one hand lightly
resting on the other, not moving a muscle, however long the sermon
might be.   Days afterwards he would show, by some remark, that the
whole service, whether good or bad, had been, as it were, photographed
upon his mind.

he chose to share all such delights) to see Mr. Nicol, a friend of Sir David Brewster, and the inventor of the polarising prism.[1] Even before this James had been absorbed in "polarised light," working with Iceland spar, and twisting his head about to see "Haidinger's Brushes" in the blue sky with his naked eye. But this visit added a new and important stimulus to his interest in these phenomena, and the speculations to which they give rise.[2]

Shortly afterwards (May 25th) he went with his father to the cutler's to choose magnets suitable for experimenting.

And a little earlier in the same year (March 17) he was taken to hear a lecture[3] on another subject, which was also connected with his subsequent labours, and must have impressed him not a little at the time. This was the discovery by Adams and Leverrier simultaneously, through a striking combination of hypothesis and calculation, of the planet Neptune, which then first "swam into" human "ken."

The magnetic experiments were continued that autumn at Glenlair, as appears from two entries in the Diary :—

Sept. 3.—Walk round by smiddy ; gave steel to be made into bars for magnets for James.

Sept. 7.—James and Robert (Campbell) most of the time at the smiddy, and got the magnet bars.

My brother perfectly remembers the magnetising of these bars of steel.

Lastly, in 1847—unless my memory deceives me—James had commenced the study of chemistry, and had taken extra lessons in German.

There was an odd episode in our school life. To keep

---

[1] He lived in Inverleith Terrace, Edinburgh.

[2] So far as I can recall the order in which his ideas on this subject were developed, the phenomena of complementary colours came first, then the composition of white light, then the mixture of colours (not of pigments), then polarisation and the dark lines in the spectrum, and about the same time "the art of squinting," stereoscopic drawing, etc., then colour-blindness, the yellow spot on the retina, etc.

[3] The lecturer was Mr. Nichol, Professor of Astronomy at Glasgow, the father of the distinguished Professor of English Literature in the same University.

our education "abreast of the requirements of the day,"
etc., it was thought desirable that we should have lessons
in "Physical Science." So one of the classical masters gave
them out of a text-book. The sixth and seventh classes
were taught together; and the only thing I distinctly
remember about these hours is that Maxwell and P. G.
Tait seemed to know much more about the subject than
our teacher did.

Maxwell and Tait were by this time acknowledged as
the two best mathematicians of the school, and it was
already prophesied that Tait, who was about fifteen, would
some day be a Senior Wrangler. The two youths had
many interchanges of ideas, and Professor Tait remembers
that Maxwell had by this time proved, by purely geometrical methods, that the central tangential section of a
"tore," or anchor-ring, is a pair of intersecting equal and
similar curves, *probably circles.*

This is referred to in the following extract from Professor Tait's admirable summary :—

When I first made Clerk Maxwell's acquaintance about
thirty-five years ago, at the Edinburgh Academy, he was a
year before me, being in the fifth class while I was in the
fourth.

At school he was at first regarded as shy and rather dull.
He made no friendships, and he spent his occasional holidays in
reading old ballads, drawing curious diagrams, and making rude
mechanical models. This absorption in such pursuits, totally
unintelligible to his schoolfellows (who were then quite innocent
of mathematics), of course procured him a not very complimen-
tary nickname, which I know is still remembered by many
Fellows of this Society. About the middle of his school career,
however, he surprised his companions by suddenly becoming one
of the most brilliant among them, gaining high, and sometimes
the highest, prizes for scholarship, mathematics, and English
verse composition. From this time forward I became very
intimate with him, and we discussed together, with schoolboy
enthusiasm, numerous curious problems, among which I remember particularly the various plane sections of a ring or tore,
and the form of a cylindrical mirror which should show one his

own image unperverted. I still possess some of the MSS. we exchanged in 1846 and early in 1847. Those by Maxwell are on "The Conical Pendulum," "Descartes' Ovals," "Meloid and Apioid," and "Trifocal Curves." All are drawn up in strict geometrical form, and divided into consecutive propositions. The three latter are connected with his first published paper, communicated by Forbes to this Society and printed in our *Proceedings*, vol. ii., under the title "On the description of Oval Curves, and those having a plurality of Foci" (1846). At the time when these papers were written he had received no instruction in mathematics beyond a few books of Euclid and the merest elements of Algebra.[1]

On the whole, he looked back to his schooldays with strong affection; and his only revenge on those who had misunderstood him was that he understood them. To many of us, as we advance in life, the remembrance of our early companions, except those to whom we were specially drawn, becomes dim and shadowy. But Maxwell, by some vivid touch, has often recalled to me the image of one and another of our schoolfellows, whose existence I had all but forgotten.

Mr. Clerk Maxwell made inquiries early in the summer of 1847, with a view to placing his son at College in November. In deciding not to continue his classical training, he appears to have been chiefly guided by some disparaging accounts of the condition of the Greek and Latin classes in comparison with those of Logic, Mathematics, and Natural Philosophy. The result was that in his seventeenth year Maxwell entered the second Mathematical Class, taught by Professor Kelland, the class of Natural Philosophy under J. D. Forbes, and the Logic Class of Sir William Hamilton. Classical reading, however, was not by any means relinquished, as the correspondence of 1847-50 clearly shows.

---

[1] *Proceedings of the Royal Society of Edinburgh.* Session 1879-80, p. 332.

CHAPTER V.

OPENING MANHOOD—1847 TO 1850—ÆT. 16-19.

WHEN he entered the University of Edinburgh, James
Clerk Maxwell still occasioned some concern to the more
conventional amongst his friends by the originality and
simplicity of his ways. His replies in ordinary conversation were indirect and enigmatical, often uttered with
hesitation and in a monotonous key.[1] While extremely
neat in his person, he had a rooted objection to the vanities
of starch and gloves. He had a pious horror of destroying
anything—even a scrap of writing paper. He preferred
travelling by the third class in railway journeys, saying he
liked a hard seat. When at table he often seemed
abstracted from what was going on, being absorbed in
observing the effects of refracted light in the finger-glasses,
or in trying some experiment with his eyes—seeing round
a corner, making invisible stereoscopes, and the like. Miss
Cay used to call his attention by crying, "Jamsie, you're
in a prop."[2] He never tasted wine; and he spoke to gentle
and simple in exactly the same tone. On the other hand,
his teachers—Forbes above all—had formed the highest
opinion[3] of his intellectual originality and force ; and a few
experienced observers, in watching his devotion to his father,

---

[1] This entirely disappeared afterwards, except when ironically assumed. It was accompanied with a certain huskiness of voice, which was
observed also in later years.

[2] "Prop." here and elsewhere is an abbreviation for "mathematical
proposition."

[3] Forbes's certificate at the end of the second year goes beyond the
merely formal language of such documents :—"His proficiency gave
evidence of an original and penetrating mind."

began to have some inkling of his heroic singleness of heart.   To his college companions, whom he could now select at will, his quaint humour was an endless delight. His chief associates, after I went to the University of Glasgow, were my brother, Robert Campbell (still at the Academy), P. G. Tait, and Allan Stewart.[1] Tait went to Peterhouse, Cambridge, in 1848, after one session of the University of Edinburgh ; Stewart to the same College in 1849 ; Maxwell did not go up until 1850.

These three years—November 1847 to October 1850— *Æt.* 16-19. were impartially divided between Edinburgh and Glenlair. He was working under but slight pressure, and his originality had the freest play.   His studies were multifarious, but the subjects on which his thoughts were most concentrated during these years were—1. Polarised light, the stereoscope, etc. ; 2. Galvanism ; 3. Rolling curves ; 4. Compression of solids.   That he early felt the necessity of imposing a method on himself will appear from the letters. His paper on Rolling Curves was read before the Edinburgh Royal Society on February 19, 1849, by Professor Kelland (for it was not thought proper for a boy in a round jacket to mount the rostrum there) ; that on the Equilibrium of Elastic Solids in the spring of 1850.

With regard to his class studies, it appears that he attended Forbes for two sessions as a regular student, and occasionally as an amateur student in his third year ; Kelland for two sessions ; and Sir W. Hamilton for two. In his third session, while partially attending Forbes, he was a regular student in the Classes of Chemistry (Professor Gregory), Practical Chemistry (Mr. Kemp), and Moral Philosophy (Professor Wilson).

Mr. Macfarlan of Lenzie, in the letter already quoted, says :—" He was in the Natural Philosophy Class, Edinburgh University, the year before I was, and was spoken of by Forbes and his fellow-students as a discoverer in Natural Philosophy, and a very original worker in Mathematics."

---

[1] Allan Stewart, Esquire, of Innerhadden, Perthshire, C.E. : *Æq.* 9th Wrangler, 1853.

All scientific theories had an interest for him. It was at some time during these years that in a walk towards Arthur's Seat he discoursed to me of Owen's hypothesis of types of creation, not only with complete command of Owen's terminology, but with far-reaching views of the questions to which the theory led. On the same occasion he made some characteristic remarks on the importance of cultivating the senses, adding that he regarded dulness in that respect as a bad sign of any man.

The lectures in Mental Philosophy, which were a prominent element in the Scottish University curriculum, interested him greatly; and from Sir William Hamilton especially he received an impulse which never lost its effect. Though only sixteen when he entered the Logic Class, he worked hard for it, as his letters show; and from the Class of Metaphysics, which he attended in the following year, his mind gained many lasting impressions.[1] His boundless curiosity was fed by the Professor's inexhaustible learning; his geometrical imagination predisposed him to accept the doctrine of "natural realism;" while his mystical tendency was soothed by the distinction between Knowledge and Belief. The doctrine of a muscular sense gave promise of a rational analysis of the active powers. However strange it may appear that a born mathematician should have been thus influenced by the enemy of mathematics, the fact is indisputable that in his frequent excursions into the region of speculative thought, the ideas received from Sir William Hamilton were his habitual vantage-ground; the great difference being, that while Sir William remained for the most part within the sphere of Abstract Logic, Maxwell ever sought to bring each "concept" to the test of fact. Sir William in turn took a genial interest in his pupil, who was indeed the nephew of an old friend—Sheriff Cay having at one time been a constant companion and firm ally of

---

[1] A slight illustration of his devotion to Sir William's teaching, and also of his powers of endurance, is afforded by the following incident :— One day he sprained his ankle badly on the College staircase; but, instead of going home, he attended Sir William Hamilton's class as usual, and sat through the hour as if nothing had happened.

Sir William's.[1]   This is perhaps the most striking example
of the effect produced by Sir William Hamilton on powerful young minds,—an effect which, unless the best metaphysicians of the subsequent age are mistaken, must have
been out of all proportion to the independent value of his
philosophy.

It was impossible that young Maxwell should listen to
speculations about the first principles of things,—speculations, too, which, like all the Scottish philosophy, turned
largely on the reality of the external world, — without
eagerly working out each problem for himself.   Besides
various exercises done by him for the Logic Class, and,
like all his youthful work, preserved by him with pious
care, there is one which seems to have attracted special
attention, and was found by Professor Baynes, when he
came to assist Sir William, in the Professor's private
drawer.   This paper is so significant, and so closely related
to Maxwell's after studies, as to deserve insertion here.

ON THE PROPERTIES OF MATTER.

Æt. 17.

These properties are all relative to the three abstract entities
connected with matter, namely, space, time, and force.

1. Since matter must be in some part of space, and in one
part only at a time, it possesses the property of locality or
position.

2. But matter has not only position but magnitude ; this
property is called extension.

3. And since it is not infinite it must have bounds, and
therefore it must possess figure.

These three properties belong both to matter and to imaginary
geometrical figures, and may be called the geometric properties
of matter.   The following properties do not necessarily belong
to geometric figures.

4. No part of space can contain at the same time more than
one body, or no two bodies can coexist in the same space ; this
property is called impenetrability.   It was thought by some
that the converse of this was true, and that there was no part

---

[1] John Lockhart had made a third as the comrade of both.

of space not filled with matter. If there be a vacuum, said they, that is empty space, it must be either a substance or an accident.

If a substance it must be created or uncreated.

If created it may be destroyed, while matter remains as it was, and thus length, breadth and thickness would be destroyed while the bodies remain at the same distance.

If uncreated, we are led into impiety.

If we say it is an accident, those who deny a vacuum challenge us to define it, and say that length, breadth and thickness belong exclusively to matter.

This is not true, for they belong also to geometric figures, which are forms of thought and not of matter; therefore the atomists maintain that empty space is an accident, and has not only a possible but a real existence, and that there is more space empty than full. This has been well stated by Lucretius.

5. Since there is a vacuum, motion is possible; therefore we have a fifth property of matter called mobility.

And the impossibility of a body changing its state of motion or rest without some external force is called *inertia*.

Of forces acting between two particles of matter there are several kinds.

The first kind is independent of the quality of the particles, and depends solely on their masses and their mutual distance. Of this kind is the attraction of gravitation and that repulsion which exists between the particles of matter which prevents any two from coming into contact.

The second kind depends on the quality of the particles; of this kind are the attractions of magnetism, electricity, and chemical affinity, which are all convertible into one another and affect all bodies.

The third kind acts between the particles of the same body, and tends to keep them at a certain distance from one another and in a certain configuration.

When this force is repulsive and inversely as the distance, the body is called gaseous.

When it does not follow this law there are two cases.

There may be a force tending to preserve the figure of the body or not.

When this force vanishes the body is a liquid.

When it exists the body is solid.

If it is small the body is soft ; if great it is hard.

If it recovers its figure it is elastic ; if not it is inelastic.

The forces in this third division depend almost entirely on heat.

The properties of bodies relative to heat and light are—

Transmission, Reflection, and Destruction,

and in the case of light these may be different for the three kinds of light, so that the properties of colour are—

Quality, Purity, and Integrity ; or

Hue, Tint, and Shade.

We come next to consider what properties of bodies may be perceived by the senses.

Now the only thing which can be directly perceived by the senses is Force, to which may be reduced heat, light, electricity, sound, and all the things which can be perceived by any sense.

In the sense of sight we perceive at the same time two spheres covered with different colours and shades. The pictures on these two spheres have a general resemblance, but are not exactly the same ; and from a comparison of the two spheres we learn, by a kind of intuitive geometry, the position of external objects in three dimensions.

Thus, the object of the sense of sight is the impression made on the different parts of the retina by three kinds of light. By this sense we obtain the greater part of our practical knowledge of locality, extension, and figure as properties of bodies, and we actually perceive colour and angular dimension.

And if we take time into account (as we must always do, for no sense is instantaneous), we perceive relative angular motion.

By the sense of hearing we perceive the intensity, rapidity, and quality of the vibrations of the surrounding medium.

By taste and smell we perceive the effects which liquids and aeriform bodies have on the nerves.

By touch we become acquainted with many conditions and qualities of bodies.

1. The actual dimensions of solid bodies in three dimensions, as compared with the dimensions of our own bodies.

2. The nature of the surface ; its roughness or smoothness.

3. The state of the body with reference to heat.

To this is to be referred the sensation of wetness and dryness, on account of the close contact which fluids have with the skin.

By means of touch, combined with pressure and motion, we perceive—

1. Hardness and softness, comprehending elasticity, friability, tenacity, flexibility, rigidity, fluidity, etc.

2. Friction, vibration, weight, motion, and the like.

The sensations of hunger and thirst, fatigue, and many others, have no relation to the properties of bodies.

LUCRETIUS ON EMPTY SPACE.

Nec tamen undique corporeâ stipata tenentur
Omnia naturâ, namque est in rebus Inane.
Quod tibi cognôsse in multis erit utile rebus
Nec sinet errantem dubitare et quærere semper
De summâ rerum ; et nostris diffidere dictis.
Quapropter locus est intactus Inane Vacansque ;
Quod si non esset, nullâ ratione moveri
Res possent ; namque officium quod corporis extat
Officere atque obstare, id in omni tempore adesset
Omnibus.   Haud igitur quicquam procedere posset,
Principium quoniam cedendi nulla daret res,
At nunc per maria ac terras sublimaque cæli
Multa modis multis variâ ratione moveri
Cernimus ante oculos, quæ, si non esset Inane,
Non tam sollicito motu privata carerent
Quam genita omninô nullâ ratione fuissent,
Undique materies quoniam stipata quiesset.[1]

---

[1] Lucr. *de Rer Nat.*, i. 329-345.   The following Hamiltonian notions will be found appearing from time to time in Maxwell's correspondence and occasional writings :—

1. Opposition of Natural Realism to "Cosmothetic Idealism."

2. Unconscious Mental Modifications.

3. Distinction between Knowledge and Belief in relation to the doctrine of Perception.

4. The Infinite or Unconditioned.

The following passage is worth quoting here, although the experiment in question was probably well known to Maxwell before he went to college :—

" . . . The experiment which Sir W. Hamilton quotes from Mr. Mill, and which had been noticed before either of them by Hartley.

"It is known that the seven prismatic colours, combined in certain proportions, produce the white light of the solar ray.   Now, if the seven colours are painted on spaces bearing the same proportion to one another

In connection with his logical studies it should be mentioned that Professor Boole's attempt, made about this time, towards giving to logical forms a mathematical expression,[1] had naturally strong attractions for Clerk Maxwell.

The metaphysical writers who had received most of his attention before going to Cambridge were Descartes and Leibnitz. He knew Hobbes well also, but chiefly on the ethical side.

When, in his address to Section A of the British Association at the Liverpool meeting in 1870, Maxwell spoke of the barren metaphysics of past ages, he knew the full force of his own words. And he certainly felt that his psychological studies had given him a distinct advantage in conceiving rightly the functions of the eye.

His grasp of Moral Philosophy at the age of nineteen, —when he had been stimulated to precise thought on the subject by listening to the vague harangues of Professor Wilson (Christopher North),—appears in some of his letters, and reveals an aspect of his genius of which too little is known, and one which his subsequent career did not allow him to bring to perfection.

In the third year of his course, as above mentioned, besides attending Professor Wilson's lectures, he renewed his study of Chemistry under Professor Gregory, to whose laboratory he had unlimited access, and also to some extent continued his attendance on Professor Forbes.

It cannot be said that this period was unfruitful; yet perhaps it is to be regretted that he did not go to Cambridge at least one year earlier. His truly sociable spirit would have been less isolated, he would have gained more command over his own genius, and his powers of expression would have been more harmoniously developed.

---

as in the solar spectrum, and the coloured surface so produced is passed rapidly before the eyes, as by the turning of a wheel, the whole is seen as white."—Mill *On Hamilton* (1st edition, 1865), p. 286.

[1] Mr. George Boole's first logical treatise, "The Mathematical Analysis of Logic, being an Essay towards a Calculus of Deductive Reasoning," was published in 1847 at Cambridge, by Macmillan, Barclay, and Macmillan.

The routine of Cambridge would have been more valuable
and less irksome to him, and he would have entered
sooner and more fully upon the study of mankind, for
which he had such large capacity, and opportunities
hitherto so limited. He suffered less from isolation than
most human beings, and his spirit was deepening all the
while ; yet the freedom of working by himself during the
summer months had manifestly some drawbacks, and the
tone of his correspondence shows that he felt the disadvantages of solitude.

LETTERS, 1847 TO 1850—ÆT. 16-18.

To LEWIS CAMPBELL, Esq.

27 Heriot Row,[1]
Tuesday [16th Novr. 1847].

Æt. 16.   In Kelland we find the value of expressions in numbers as
fast as we can, the values of the letters being given ; light work.
In Forbes we do Lever, which is all in Potter ; no notes required, only read Pottery ware (light reading). Logic needs
long notes. On Monday, Wednesday, Friday, I read Newton's
Fluxions in a sort of way, to know what I am about in doing a
prop. There is no time of reading a book better than when
you need it, and when you are on the point of finding it out
yourself if you were able.

" Non usitata nec tenui ferar
Pinnâ biformi per liquida æquora
Piscis neque in terris morabor
Longius "——but I will take to swimming with
a two formed oar with blades at right angles. . . .

Yours, J. C. M., No. 2.

To THE SAME.

31 Heriot Row, Novr. 1847.

As you say, sir, I have no idle time. I look over notes and
such like till 9.35, then I go to Coll., and I always go one way
and cross streets at the same places ; then at 10 comes Kelland.
He is telling us about arithmetic, and how the common rules

---

[1] Above, p. 37.

are the best.   At 11 there is Forbes, who has now finished
introduction and properties of bodies, and is beginning Mechanics
in earnest.   Then at 12, if it is fine, I perambulate the Meadows ;
if not, I go to the Library and do references.   At 1 go to Logic.
Sir W. reads the first $\frac{1}{2}$ of his lecture, and commits the rest to
his man, but reserves to himself the right of making remarks.
To-day was examination day, and there was no lecture.   At 2
I go home and receive interim aliment, and do the needful in
the way of business.   Then I extend notes, and read text-books,
which are Kelland's *Algebra* and Potter's *Mechanics.*   The latter
is very trigonometrical, but not deep ; and the Trig. is not
needed.   I intend to read a few Greek and Latin beside.   What
books are you doing ? . . .   In Logic we sit in seats lettered
according to name, and Sir W. takes and puts his hand into a
jam pig [1] full of metal letters (very classical) and pulls one out
and examines the bench of the letter.   The Logic lectures are
far the most solid and take most notes.

Before I left home I found out a prop for Tait (P. G.) ; but
he *will* not do it.   It is "to find the algebraical equation to a
curve which is to be placed with its axis vertical, and a heavy
body is to be put on any part of the curve, as on an inclined
plane, and the horizontal component of the force, by which it is
actuated, is to vary as the nth power of the perpendicular upon
the axis."

To the Same.

Glenlair, 26th April 1848.

. . . On Saturday, the natural philosophers ran up Arthur's
Seat with the barometer.   The Professor set it up at the top
and let us pant at it till it ran down with drops.   He did not
set it straight, and made the hill grow fifty feet ; but we got it
down again.

We came here on Wednesday by Caledonian.   I intend to
open my classes next week after the business is over.   I have
been reading Xenophon's *Memorabilia* after breakfast ; also a
French collection book.   This from 9 to 11.   Then a game of
the Devil, of whom there is a duality and a quaternity of sticks,
so that I can play either conjunctly or severally.   I can jump
over him and bring him round without leaving go the sticks.
I can also keep him up behind me.

---

[1] *i.e.* Jar.

Then I go in again to science, of which I have only just got the books by the carrier. Hitherto I have done a prop on the slate on polarised light. Of props I have done several.

1. Found the equation to a square.

2. The curve which Sir David Brewster sees when he squints at a wall.

3. A property of the parabola. . . .

4. The same of the Ellipse and Hyperbola. . . .

I can polarise light now by reflection or refraction in 4 ways, and get beautiful but evanescent figures in plate glass by heating its edge. I have not yet unannealed any glass. . . .

I don't understand how you mug[1] straight on. I suit my muggery to my temper that day. When I am deep I read Xenophon's defence of Σωκ; when not I read Σωκ's witty dialogues. If I do not do this, I always find myself *reading Greek*, that is, reading the words with all their contractions, as a Jew reads Hebrew. I get on very rapidly; but know nothing about the meaning, and do not even know but that I am really translating.

Please to write about your Prizes at College, and about coming here to mug ? You must learn the D—l.

Tatties is planting.—Yours, etc.

To the Same.

Glenlair, 5/6 July 1848.

Æt. 17.   I was much glad of your letter, and will be thankful for a repetition. I understand better about your not coming. I have regularly set up shop now above the wash-house at the gate, in a garret.[2] I have an old door set on two barrels, and two chairs, of which one is safe, and a skylight above, which will slide up and down.

On the door (or table), there is a lot of bowls, jugs, plates, jam pigs,[3] etc., containing water, salt, soda, sulphuric acid, blue vitriol, plumbago ore ; also broken glass, iron, and copper wire, copper and zinc plate, bees' wax, sealing wax, clay, rosin, charcoal, a lens, a Smee's Galvanic apparatus, and a countless variety of little beetles, spiders, and wood lice, which fall into the differ-

---

[1] *i.e.* Work.

[2] In the "old house" (above, p. 14, l. 23) ; now fitted up as a gun-room.

[3] *i.e.* Jars.

ent liquids and poison themselves. I intend to get up some more galvanism in jam pigs ; but I must first copper the interiors of the pigs, so I am experimenting on the best methods of electro-typing. So I am making copper seals with the device of a beetle. First, I thought a beetle was a good conductor, so I embedded one in wax (not at all cruel, because I slew him in boiling water in which he never kicked), leaving his back out ; but he would not do. Then I took a cast of him in sealing wax, and pressed wax into the hollow, and black-leaded it with a brush ; but neither would that do. So at last I took my fingers and rubbed it, which I find the best way to use the black lead. Then it coppered famously. I melt out the wax with the lens, that being the cleanest way of getting a strong heat, so I do most things with it that need heat. To-day I astonished the natives as follows. I took a crystal of blue vitriol and put the lens to it, and so drove off the water, leaving a white powder. Then I did the same to some washing soda, and mixed the two white powders together ; and made a small native spit on them, which turned them green [1] by a mutual exchange, thus :—1. Sulphate of copper and carbonate of soda. 2. Sulphate of soda and carbonate of copper (blue or green).

With regard to electro-magnetism you may tell Bob that I have not begun the machine he speaks of, being occupied with better plans, one of which is rather down cast, however, because the machine when tried went a bit and stuck ; and I did not find out the impediment till I had dreamt over it properly, which I consider the best mode of resolving difficulties of a particular kind, which may be found out by thought, or especially by the laws of association. Thus, you are going along the road with a key in your pocket. You hear a clink behind you, but do not look round, thinking it is nothing particular ; when you get home the key is gone ; so you dream it all over, and though you have forgotten everything else, you remember the look of the place, but do not remember the locality (that is, as thus, "Near a large thistle on the left side of the road"—nowhere in particular, but so that it can be found). Next day comes a woman from the peats who has found the key in a corresponding place. This is not "believing in dreams," for the dream did not point out the place by the general locality, but by the lie of the ground.

---

[1] This is still remembered by "Lizzy," Mrs. MacGowan.

Please to write and tell how Academy matters go, if they are coming to a head. I am reading Herodotus, *Euterpe*, having taken the turn ; that is to say, that sometimes I can do props, read diff. and Int. Calc., Poisson, Hamilton's dissertations, etc. Off, then I take back to experiments, history of what you may call it, make up leeway in the newspapers, read Herodotus, and draw the figures of the curves above. O deary, 11 P.M.! Hoping to see you *before* October. . . . I defer till to-morrow.

July 6. To-day I have set on to the coppering of the jam pig which I polished yesterday.

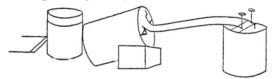

I have stuck in the wires better than ever, and it is going on at a great rate, being a rainy day, and the skylight shut and a smell of Hydrogen gas. I have left it for an hour to read Poisson, as I am pleased with him to-day. Sometimes I do not like him, because he pretends to give information as to calculations of sorts, whereas he only tells how it might be done if you were allowed an infinite time to do it in, as well as patience. Of course he never stoops to give a particular example or even class of them. He tells lies about the way people make barometers, etc.

I bathe regularly every day when dry, and try aquatic experiments.

I first made a survey of the pool, and took soundings and marked rocky places well, as the water is so brown that one cannot see one's knees (pure peat, not mud). People are cutting peats now. So I have found a way of swimming round the pool without knocking knees. The lads [1] are afraid of melting, except one. No one here would touch water if they could help it, because there are two or three eels in the pool, which are thought near as bad as adders.

I took down the clay gun and made a centrifugal pump of it ; also tried experiments on sound under water, which is very distinct, and I can understand how fishes can be stunned by knocking a stone.

---

[1] See above, p. 25.

We sometimes get a rope, which I take hold of at one end, and Bob Fraser the other, standing on the rock ; and after a flood, when the water is up, there is sufficient current to keep me up like a kite without striking at all.

The thermometer ranged yesterday from 35° to 69°.

I have made regular figures of 14, 26, 32, 38, 62, and 102 sides of cardboard.

Latest intelligence—Electric Telegraph. This is going so as to make a compass spin very much. I must go to see my pig, as it is an hour and half since I left it ; so, sir, am your afft. friend,   JAMES CLERK MAXWELL.

TO THE SAME.

Glenlair, 22d Sept. 1848.

. . . When I waken I do so either at 5.45 or 9.15, but I now prefer the early hour, as I take the most of my violent exercise at that time, and thus am *saddened down*, so that I can do as much still work afterwards as is requisite, whereas if I was to sit still in the morning I would be yawning all day. So I get up and see what kind of day it is, and what field works are to be done ; then I catch the pony and bring up the water barrel.[1] This barrel used to be pulled by the men, but Pa caused the road to be gravelled, and so it became horse work to the men, so I proposed the pony ; but all the men except the pullers opposed the plan. So I and the children not working brought it up, and silenced vile insinuators. Then I take the dogs out, and then look round the garden for fruit and seeds, and paddle about till breakfast-time. After that take up Cicero and see if I can understand him. If so, I read till I stick ; if not, I set to Xen. or Herodt. Then I do props, chiefly on rolling curves, on which subject I have got a great problem divided into Orders, Genera, Species, Varieties, etc.

One curve rolls on another, and with a particular point traces out a third curve on the plane of the first, then the problem is :—Order I. Given any two of these curves, to find the third.

Order II. Given the equation of one and the identity of the other two, find their equation.

Order III. Given all three curves the same, find them. In this last Order I have proved that the equi-angular spiral

---

[1] See above, p. 16, l. 11.

possesses the property, and that no other curve does. This is the most reproductive curve of any. I think John Bernoulli had it on his tombstone, with the motto *Eadem mutata resurgo*. There are a great many curious properties of curves connected with rolling. Thus, for example,—

If the curve A when rolled on a straight line produces a curve C, and if the curve A when rolled up on itself produces the curve B, then the curve B when rolled upon the curve C will produce a straight line.

Thus, let the involute of the circle be presented by A,

the spiral of Archimedes by B,

and the parabola by C,

then the proposition is true.

Thus the parabola rolled on a straight line traces a Catenary with its focus, an easy way to describe the Catenary. Professor Wallace just missed it in a paper in the Royal Society.

After props come optics, and principally polarised light.

Do you remember our visit to Mr. Nicol? I have got plenty of unannealed glass of different shapes, for I find window glass will do very well made up in bundles. I cut out triangles, squares, etc., with a diamond, about 8 or 9 of a kind, and take them to the kitchen, and put them on a piece of iron in the fire one by one. When the bit is red-hot, I drop it into a plate of iron sparks to cool, and so on till all are done. I have got all figures up to nonagons, triangles of all kinds, and irregular chips. I have made a pattern for a tesselated window of unannealed glass in the proper colours, also a delineation of triangles at every principal inclination. We were at Castle-Douglas yesterday, and got crystals of salt Peter, which I have been cutting up into plates to-day, in hopes to see rings. There are very few crystals which are not hollow-hearted or filled up with irregular crystals. I have got a few cross cuts like ⬡ free of irregularities and long [wedge-shaped] cuts for polarising plates. One has to be very cautious in sawing and polishing them, for they are very brittle.

I have got a lucifer match box fitted up for polarising, thus.

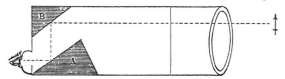

The rays suffer two reflections at the polarising angle from glasses A and B. Without the lid it does for an analysing plate. In the lid there is set a plate of mica, and so one observes the blue sky, and turns the box round till a particular colour appears, and then a line on the lid of the box points to the sun wherever he is. Thus one can find out the time of day without the sun. [*Here follow thirteen diagrams of patterns in triangles, squares, pentagons, and hexagons.*] These are a few of the figures one sees in unannealed glass.

Pray write soon and tell when, how, and where by, you intend to come, that you may neither on the other hand fall upon us at unawares, nor on the one hand break and not come at all. I suppose when you come I will have to give up all my things of my own devising, and take Poisson, for the time is short, and I am very nearly unprepared in actual reading, though a great deal more able to read it.

I hope not to write any more letters till you come. I seal with an electrotype of the young of the ephemera. So, sir, I was, etc.

To THE SAME.

Bannavie, 6th July [1849].

This being a wet night, and I, having exhausted my travelling *Æt.* 18. props, set to to write to you about what I can recollect of my past history. It is curious that though the remembrance of ploys remains longer than that of home doings, it is not so easily *imagined* after a short interval.

By *imagining* is here meant bringing up an accurate image of thoughts, words, and works, and not a mere geographical summary of voyages and travels.

But to the point. Perhaps you remember going with my Uncle John Cay (7th Class), to visit Mr. Nicol in Inverleith Terrace. There we saw polarised light in abundance. I purposed going this session but was prevented. Well, sir, I received from the aforesaid Mr. Cay a " Nicol's prism," which Nicol had made and sent him. It is made of calc-spar, so arranged as to separate the ordinary from the extraordinary ray. So I adapted it to a camera lucida, and made charts of the strains in unannealed glass.

I have set up the machine for showing the rings in crystals, which I planned during your visit last year. It answers very well. I also made some experiments on compressed jellies in illustration of my props on that subject. The principal one was this:—The jelly is poured while hot into the annular space contained between a paper cylinder and a cork : then, when cold, the cork is twisted round, and the jelly exposed to polarised light, when a transverse cross, ×, not +, appears with rings as the inverse square of the radius, all which is fully verified. Hip ! etc. Q.E.D.

But to make an *abrupt transcision*,[1] as Forbes says, we set off to Glasgow on Monday 2d ; to Inverary on 3d ; to Oban by Loch Awe on 4th ; round Mull, by Staffa and Iona, on (5th), and here on 6th. To-morrow we intend to get to Inverness and rest there. On Monday perhaps ? to the land of Beulah, and afterwards back by Caledon. Canal to Crinan Canal, and so to Arran, thence to Ardrossan, and then home. It is possible that you may get a more full account of all these things (if agreeable) when I fall in with a pen that will spell ; my present instrument partakes of the nature of skates, and I can hardly steer it.

There is a beautiful base here for measuring the height, etc., of Ben Nevis. It is a straight and level road through a moss for about a mile that leads from the inn right to the summit.

It is proposed to carry up stones and erect a cairn 3 feet high, and thus render it the highest mountain in Scotland.

During the session Prof. Forbes gave as an exercise to describe a cycloid from top of Ben Nevis to Fort William, and slide trees down it. We took an observation of the slide, but found nothing to slide but snow.

I think a body *deprived* of friction would go to Fort William in a cycloid in 49·6 seconds, and in 81 on an inclined plane. I believe I should have written the greater part of this letter to Allan Stewart, but I know not where he is, so you get it, and may read it or no as you like.

We will be at home between the 15th and 22d of this month, so you may write then, detailing your plans and specifying whether you intend to come north at all between this and November, for we would be glad if either you or Bob would disturb our solitude.

---

[1] See below, p. 92, l. 10. Forbes was extra-precise in articulation. Hence the spelling.

TO THE SAME.

Glenlair, 19th October 1849.

Here is the way to dissolve any given historical event in a mythical solution, and then precipitate the seminal ideas in their primitive form.   It is from Theodore Parker, an American, and treats of the declaration of American Independence. " The story of the Declaration of Independence is liable to many objections if we examine it *à la mode* Strauss.   The Congress was held at a mythical town, whose very name is suspicious,— Philadelphia, brotherly love.   The date is suspicious : it was the fourth day of the fourth month (reckoning from April, as it is probable that the Heraclidæ and Scandinavians, possible that the Americans, and certain that the Ebrews, did).   Now 4 was a sacred number among Americans : the President was chosen for 4 years, 4 departments of affairs, 4 political powers, etc. The year also is suspicious.   1776 is but an *ingeni[ous] ?* combination of the sacred number, thus—

$$\frac{\begin{array}{r}444\\4\end{array}}{1776}$$

Still further, the declaration is metaphysical and presupposes an acquaintance with the transcendental function on the part of the American people.   Now the *Kritik of Pure Reason* was not yet published," etc.

TO THE SAME.

October 1849.

Since last letter, I have made some pairs of diagrams representing solid figures and curves drawn in space ; of these pictures one is seen with each eye by means of mirrors, thus . . .

This is Wheatstone's Stereoscope, which Sir David Brewster has taken up of late with much violence at the Brightish Association.   (The violence consists in making two lenses out of one by breaking it.)   (See Report.)   Last winter he exhibited at the Scottish Society of Arts Calotype pictures of the statue of Ariadne and the beast seen from two stations, which, when viewed properly, appeared very solid.

Since then I have been doing practical props on compression, and writing out the same that there may be no mistake. The

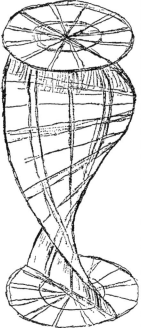

nicest cases are those of spheres and cylinders. I have got an expression for the hardness of a cricket ball made of case and stuffing. I have also the equations for a spherical cavity in an infinite solid, and this prop : Given that the polarised colour of any part of a cylinder of unannealed glass is equal to the square of the distance from the centre (as determined by observation), to find — 1st, the state of strain at each point ; 2d, the temperature of each.

.   .   .   .   .

I have got an observation of the latitude just now with a saucer of treacle, but it is very windy.

Pray excuse this wickedly perplexed letter as an effect of the paucity of our communications. If you would sharpen me a little it would be acceptable, but when there is nobody to speak to one [*loses*] the gift of speech. . . .

This is the likeness of a SKEW SCREW SURFACE.

TO THE SAME.

31 Heriot Row, Edinburgh, N.B.,
Monday, Nov. 5, 1849.

.   .   .   .   .

I go to Gregory to Chemistry at 10, Morale Phil. at 12, and Pract. Chem. at 13, finishing at 14, unless perhaps I take an hour at Practical Mechanics at the School of Arts. I do not go to Sir W. H. logic, seeing I was there before. Langhorne has got your Buchananic notes. Why do you think that I can endure nothing but Mathematics and Logic, the only things I have plenty of? and why do you presuppose my acquaintance with your preceptors, professors, tutors,[1] etc. ? . . .

I don't wonder at your failing to take interest in the exponential theorem, seeing I dislike it, although I know the use and meaning of it. But I never *would have*, unless Kelland had explained it. . . .

In your next letter you may give an abstract of Aristotle's *Rhet.*, for I do not attend Aytoun, and so I know not what Rhet. is. I know Logic only by Reid's account of it. I will tell you about Wilson's Moral Philosophy, provided always you want to know, and signify your desire.

To the Same.

[Edin.] 14th March 1850.

As I am otherwise engaged, I take this opportunity of provoking you to write a letter or two. I have begun to write Elastic Equilibrium, and I find that I must write you a letter in order *at least, indeed*,[2] to serve *on the one hand* as an excuse to myself for sticking up, and *on the other hand* as a sluice for all the nonsense which I would have written. I therefore propose to divide this letter as follows :—My say naturally breaks up into—1. Education ; 2. Notions ; 3. Hearsay.

1. Education—Public.

10-11.—Gregory is on Alloys of Metals just now. Last Saturday I was examined, and asked how I would do if the contents of a stomach were submitted to me to detect arsenic, and I had to go through the whole of the preparatory processes of chopping up the tripes, boiling with potash, filtering, boiling with $H C L$ and $K O C L O_5$, all which Kemp the *Practical* says are useless and detrimental processes, invented by chemists who want something to do. 11-12.—Prof. Forbes is on Sound and Light day about, as Bob well knows, and can tell you if he chooses. He (R. C.) has written an essay on Probabilities, with very grand props in it ; everything original, but no signs of reading, I guess. It was all written in a week. He has despaired of Optics.—12-1. Wilson, after having fully explained his own opinions, has proceeded to those of other great men : Plato, Aristotle, Stoics, Epicureans. He shows that Plato's *proof* of the immortality of the soul, from its immateriality, if it

---

[1] At Oxford.   [2] See above, p. 59.

be a proof, proves its pre-existence, the immortality of beasts and vegetables, and why not transmigration ? (Do you remember how Raphael tells Adam about meats and drinks in *Paradise Lost ?*) (Greek Iambics, if you please.) He quarrels with Aristotle's doctrine of the Golden Mean,—"a virtue is the mean between two vices,"—not properly understanding the saying. He chooses to consider it as a pocket rule to find virtue, which it is not meant to be, but an apophthegm or maxim, or dark saying, signifying that as a hill falls away on both sides of the top, so a virtue at its maximum declines by excess or defect (not of virtue but) of some variable quantity at the disposal of the will. Thus, let it be a virtue to give alms with your own money, then it is a greater virtue to pay one's debts to the full. Now, a man has so much money : the more alms he gives up to a certain point, the more virtue. As soon as it becomes impossible to pay debts, the virtue of solvency decreases faster than that of almsgiving increases, so that the giving of money to the poor becomes a vice, so that the variable is the sum given away, by excess or defect of which virtue diminishes, say I ; so that Wilson garbles Aristotle,—but I bamboozle myself. I say that some things are virtues, others are virtuous or generally lead to virtue. Substitute *goods* for virtues, and it will be more general : thus, Wisdom, Happiness, Virtue, are *goods*, and cannot be in excess ; but Knowledge, Pleasure, and— what ? (please tell me, Is it Propriety, Obedience, or what is it ?) lead to the other three, and are not so much goods as tending to good ; whereas particular knowledges, pleasures, and obediences may be in excess and lead to evils. I postpone the rest of my observations to my Collection of the Metaphysical principles of Moral Philosophy founded on the three laws of Liberty, Equality, Fraternity, thus expressed :—

1. That which can be done is that which has been done ; that is, that the possibility (with respect to the agent) of an action (as simple) depends on the agent having had the sensation of having done it.[1]

2. That which ought to be done is that which (under the given conditions) produces, implies, or tends to the greatest amount of good (an excess or defect in the variables will lessen the good and make evil).

---

[1] Maxwell often insisted on this in conversation, with especial reference to our command of the muscles depending on experience of the muscular sense.

3. Moral actions can be judged of only by the principle of exchange ; that is (1), our own actions must be judged by the laws we have made for others ; (2), others must be judged by putting ourselves in their place.

22d March.

At Practical Mechanics I have been turning Devils of sorts. For private studies I have been reading Young's *Lectures*, Willis's *Principles of Mechanism*, Moseley's *Engineering and Mechanics*, Dixon on *Heat*, and Moigno's *Répertoire d'Optique.* This last is a very complete analysis of all that has been done in the optical way from Fresnel to the end of 1849, and there is another volume a-coming which will complete the work. There is in it besides common optics all about the other things which accompany light, as heat, chemical action, photographic rays, action on vegetables, etc.

My notions are rather few, as I do not *entertain* them just now. I have a notion for the torsion of wires and rods, not to be made till the vacation ; of experiments on the action of compression on glass, jelly, etc., numerically done up ; of papers for the Physico-Mathematical Society (which is to revive in earnest next session !) ; on the relations of optical and mechanical constants, their desirableness, etc., and suspension-bridges, and catenaries, and elastic curves. Alex. Campbell, Agnew, and I are appointed to read up the subject of periodical shooting stars, and to prepare a list of the phenomena to be observed on the 9th August and 13th November. The Society's barometer is to be taken up Arthur's Seat at the end of the session, when Forbes goes up, and All students are invited to attend, so that the existence of the Society may be recognised.

I have notions of reading the whole of *Corpus Juris* and Pandects in no time at all ; but these are getting somewhat dim, as the Cambridge scheme has been howked up from its repose in the regions of abortions, and is as far forward as an inspection of the Cambridge *Calendar* and a communication with Cantabs.

Mr. Bob is choosing his college. I rejected for him all but Peter's, Caius, or Trinity Hall, the last being, though legal, not in favour, or lazy, or something. Caius is populous, and is society to itself. Peter's is select, and knows the University. Please give me some notions on these things, both for Bob and me. I postpone my answer to you about the Gorham business

till another time, when also I shall have read Waterland on
Regeneration, which is with Mrs. Morrieson, and some Pusey
books I know. In the meantime I admire the *Judgement* as a
composition of great art and ingenuity.

What cross influences had delayed his entrance at
Cambridge may be guessed at, but cannot be clearly
known. Mr. Clerk Maxwell was always slow in making
up his mind, and the habit of *inertia* had grown upon him.
There had been a lingering expectation, to which James
alludes in the preceding letter, that he would follow his
father's profession and become a member of the Scottish
Bar. And although he himself felt, as he told me at the
time, that it was "another kind of laws" he was called
upon to study, the practical result of this conviction was
slow in asserting itself. The fact that in going to Cambridge he decided against the profession which his friends
had destined for him made the step a more serious one
than it might have otherwise been. The close and constant intercourse between father and son made the parting
more difficult. James's delicate health[1] would count
heavily amongst the reasons *contra,* and certain floating
prejudices about the "dangers of the English universities,"
Puseyism, infidelity, etc., had then considerable hold, especially on the Presbyterian mind. James himself was patient,
and had hitherto decided nothing for himself. Only when
Tait and Allan Stewart were already at Cambridge, my
brother Robert destined for it, and myself at Oxford, his
own voice was added to those which had long been urging
the claims of Cambridge,[2] and then they prevailed.   There

---

[1] On this subject the following entry from Mrs. Morrieson's Diary is
of some interest :—"*5th Decr. 1846.*—L. and R. dined with Miss Cay.
James Maxwell has been under her care during his father's absence and
has been suffering very much from toothache and earache, in consequence
of cutting his eye-teeth—an extraordinary thing at 15." To which may
be added the following from his father's Diary :—"*1846, Sa., Dec. 12.*—
Jas. still affected by the tooth. . . . Took a short walk, and came back
by Mr. Nasmith (dentist), and went in, and on consultation, got the tooth
drawn at once—it was nicely and quickly done, and Jas. never winced."

[2] Amongst these may be specially mentioned Mr. Hugh Blackburn
and Dean Ramsay. Professor Forbes and Charles Mackenzie were also

had been searchings of heart on the subject as early as
April 1849, when the following entries occur in the
Diary :—

T. 17.—Called on Hugh Blackburn to talk about Cambridge.
W. 18.—Called on Capt. Wemyss to talk of Cambridge, and
Prof. Forbes called on me and had a talk on James's studies, etc.

The only other document at my command which bears
upon the point is a journal kept by my mother, then Mrs.
Morrieson, in which she occasionally noted matters relating
to her sons' friends.   She was herself at this time (1850)
making inquiries about Cambridge for my brother Robert.
The following entries may be quoted :—

1850. 1st April.—James Clerk Maxwell came in full of
Forbes's recommendation of Trinity College above all others at
Cambridge, and that Peterhouse was less expensive than Caius;
that the latter is too full to admit of rooms, and freshmen are
obliged to lodge out.

28th October.—I had a kind letter from Mr. C. M., from
Glenlair, after placing his son James at Peterhouse. He has
already distinguished himself at Edinburgh by papers on the
compression of solids, and other scientific subjects, read for him
at the Royal Society.   His manners are very peculiar ; but
having good sense, sterling worth, and good humour, the intercourse with a College world will rub off his oddities.   I doubt
not of his becoming a distinguished man.

January 1851.—James Clerk Maxwell often comes in. He
is full of genius.   He went to Cambridge with Robert in October, R. to Caius, James to Peterhouse; but he is "migrating"
to Trinity, and I have no doubt he will be a distinguished
Philosopher some day.

In concluding the account of this period, I again beg
leave to quote from Professor Tait's excellent paper:—

The winter of 1847 found us together in the classes of Forbes
and Kelland, where he highly distinguished himself. With the
former he was a particular favourite, being admitted to the free

interested in the question.   Professor Blackburn, in particular, insisted
that the mathematical discipline of Cambridge would enable him to
exercise his genius more effectively.

use of the class apparatus for original experiments. He lingered here behind most of his former associates, having spent three years at the University of Edinburgh, working (without any assistance or supervision) with physical and chemical apparatus, and devouring all sorts of scientific works in the library.[1] During this period he wrote two valuable papers, which are published in our *Transactions*, on *The Theory of Rolling Curves* and on *The Equilibrium of Elastic Solids*. Thus he brought to Cambridge, in the autumn of 1850, a mass of knowledge which was really immense for so young a man, but in a state of disorder appalling to his methodical private tutor.[2] Though that tutor was William Hopkins, the pupil to a great extent took his own way, and it may safely be said that no high wrangler of recent years ever entered the Senate-house more imperfectly trained to produce "paying" work than did Clerk Maxwell. But by sheer strength of intellect, though with the very minimum of knowledge how to use it to advantage under the conditions of the Examination, he obtained the position of Second Wrangler, and was bracketed equal with the Senior Wrangler in the higher ordeal of the Smith's Prizes. His name appears in the Cambridge *Calendar* as Maxwell of Trinity, but he was originally entered at Peterhouse, and kept his first term there, in that small but most ancient foundation which has of late furnished Scotland with the majority of the professors of mathematics and natural philosophy, in her four universities.

---

[1] "From the University Library lists for this period it appears that Maxwell perused at home Fourier's *Theorie de la Chaleur*, Monge's *Géometrie Descriptive*, Newton's *Optics*, Willis's *Principles of Mechanism*, Cauchy's *Calcul Différentiel*, Taylor's *Scientific Memoirs*, and many other works of a high order. Unfortunately no record is kept of books consulted in the reading-room."

[2] On the other hand it should be mentioned (though the statements are not contradictory) that Hopkins used to say he had never known Maxwell "make a mistake," *i.e.* he never misapprehended the conditions of any problem. Of this fact, which was communicated to me by my brother, I have since received the following confirmation from Mr. W. N. Lawson, of the Equity Bar :—Mr. Lawson quotes from a diary kept by himself at the time—"*July* 15, 1853.—He (Hopkins) was talking to me this evening about Maxwell. He says he is unquestionably the most extraordinary man he has met with in the whole range of his experience ; he says it appears impossible for Maxwell to think incorrectly on physical subjects ; that in his analysis, however, he is far more deficient ; he looks upon him as a great genius, with all its eccentricities, and prophesies that one day he will shine as a light in physical science, a prophecy in which all his fellow-students strenuously unite."

To the books mentioned by Professor Tait in his foot-note should be added Poisson's *Mechanics,* which was taken out from the Advocates' Library 6th March 1848, and carried off into the country. A copy of Fourier's *Theorie de la Chaleur* was ordered through Maclachlan, 6th April 1849, for 25s.

Letters, April to September 1850.

To Lewis Campbell, Esq.

Glenlair, 26th April 1850.

As I ought to tell you of our departure from Edinburgh and arrival here, so I ought to tell you of many other things besides. Of things pertaining to myself there are these :—The tutor of Peterhouse has booked me, and I am booked for Peterhouse, but will need a little more booking before I can write Algebra like a book.

I suppose I must go through Wrigley's problems and Paley's Evidences in the same sort of way, and be able to translate when required Eurip. *Iph. in Aulid.* In the meantime I have my usual superfluity of plans.

1. Classics—Eurip. Ἰφ. ἐν Αὐλ. for Cambridge. (I hope no Latin or Greek verses except for honours.) Greek Testament, Epistles, for my own behoof, and perhaps some of Cicero *De Officiis* or something else for Latin.

2. Mathematics—Wrigley's Problems, and Trig. for Cambridge ; properties of the Ellipsoid and other solids for practice with Spher. Trig. Nothing higher if I can help it.

3. Nat. Phil.—Simple mechanical problems to produce that knack of solving problems which Prof. Forbes has taught me to despise. Common Optics at length ; and for experimental philosophy, twisting and bending certain glass and metal rods, making jellies, unannealed glass, and crystals, and dissecting eyes—and playing Devils.

4. Metaphysics—Kant's *Kritik of Pure Reason* in German, read with a determination to make it agree with Sir W. Hamilton.

5. Moral Philosophy—Metaphysical principles of moral philosophy. Hobbes' *Leviathan,* with his moral philosophy, to be read as the only man who has decided opinions and avows them

in a distinct way.   To examine the first part of the seventh
chapter of Matthew in reference to the moral principles which
it supposes, and compare with other passages.

But I question if I shall be able to overtake all these things,
although those of different kinds may well be used as alternate
studies.

I read in Edinburgh Wilson's Poems to see what he used to
be like, and how much he had improved since then.   Did you
finish Festus ? [1]   I had only two days to read it, so that I
skipped part of the long speech and a good deal of the jollifica-
tion, which I think the dullest part of the book.

The opening makes one think that it is to be an imitation of
the book of Job, but you soon see that you have to do with a
dreamy mortal without a profession, but vain withal, and a hero
among women, a jolly companion of some men, admired of
students for talking of things which he knows not, nor can
know, having a so-called philosophy, an intuitive science, and
an underived religion, and with all these not perfect, but need-
ing more expanded views of the folly of strict virtue and outward decency, of the magnificence, nay, of the duty of sinning,
and of the identity of virtue and vice, and of all opposites.   He
takes for his friend one whom Wilson calls a very *poor devil*,
who has wonderful mechanical powers, but never attempts but
once the supposed object of his visit to earth, namely, tempta-
tion.   He takes a more rational view of affairs than Festus in
general, but is so extremely refined from ordinary devils, that
the only passage sufficiently characteristic for ordinary rapid
readers to recognise is the sermon to the crowd, as the speech
in Hell is quite raw.   He has not such an absolute and intuitive sense of things as Festus, and does not change so much
according to his company.   He seems a sincere, good-natured,
unselfish devil ; while Festus is very changeable, solemn when
alone, jolly when with the jolly, drunk with the drunk, open
with Lucifer, reserved in good company, amorous with all
women, talkative and serious with all angels and saints, stern
towards the unfortunate, and in all his affections altogether
selfish.

The book is said to have a plan, but no plot.   The plan is
an exposition of the state of a man's mind after having gone
through German metaphysics.   It was one destitute of notions,

----

[1] Festus, a poem by Philip James Bailey, 1849.

and has now been convinced that all these notions are one and
the same.   It is neither meat, nor drink, nor rank, nor money,
nor any common thing he wants : "he is sure it isn't," and he
is sore troubled for want of some great thing to do ; and when
L——r starts into proximity he is the very being he wanted to
speak to ; "he knew who it would be," and recognises him at
once.   An opportunity is thus given for showing two ways of
thinking about things, and therein lies the matter of the book.
This may be seen in L——r's sermon and Festus' prayer.   To
turn and get out of the confusion of this letter, pray let me hear
your opinion of the book.   It may be considered thus :—

1. People read the book and wonder, why ?

It is not read for the sake of the story—that is plain ; nor
for the clearness with which certain principles are developed,
nor for the consistency of the book, nor for the variety of the
characters ; there must therefore be something overpoweringly
attractive to hold you to the book.   Some say he has fine
thoughts, sufficient to set up fifty poets ; to which some may
answer, Where are they ?   Read it in a spirit of cold criticism,
and they vanish.   There is not one that is not either erroneous,
absurd, German, common, or *Daft*.   Where lies the beauty ?
In the reader's mind.   The author has evidently been thinking
when he wrote it, and that not in words, but inwardly.   The
benevolent reader is compelled to think too, and it is so great a
relief to the reader to get out of wordiness that he can put up
with insanity, absurdity, profanity, and even inanity, if by so
doing he can get into *rapport* with one who is so transcendental,
and yet so easy to follow, as the poet.   When Galileo set his
[lamp] a-swinging by breathing on it, his power lay in the relation between the interval of his breaths and the time of vibration ;
so in Festus the mind that begins to perceive that his train of
thoughts is that of the poem is readily made to follow on.   There
are some passages where one breaks loose, especially the rhyming
description of the subpœnaing of the planets, and the notion of
the angel of the earth giving Festus a pair of bracelets, and the
way in which F. improves his mind by travel.

. . . Beauty is attributed to an object when the subject
anticipates pleasure in it.   A true pleasure is a consciousness of
the right action of the faculty or function or power.   Happiness
is the integral of pleasure, as wisdom is of knowledge. . . .
Don't take all this about Festus for truth, as I don't believe

much of it, and I'll maybe tell you a new story if you tell me one.

What of St. Peter, as compared with the Keys and with Bob ?[1]

FROM PROF. FORBES.

Edinburgh, 4th May 1850.

MY DEAR SIR—Professor Kelland, to whom your paper was referred by the Council R. S., reports favourably upon it, but complains of the great obscurity of several parts, owing to the *abrupt transitions* and want of distinction between what is *assumed* and what is *proved* in various passages, which he has marked in pencil, and which I trust that you will use your utmost effort to make plain and intelligible.   It is perfectly evident that it must be useless to publish a paper for the use of scientific readers generally, the steps of which cannot, in many places, be followed by so expert an algebraist as Prof. Kelland ;—if, indeed, they be *steps* at all and not assumptions of theorems from other writers who are not quoted.   You will please to pay particular attention to clear up these passages, and return the MS. by post to Professor Kelland, West Cottage, Wardie, Edinburgh, so that he may receive it by Saturday the 11th, as I shall then have left town.—Believe me, yours sincerely,

JAMES D. FORBES.

TO L. CAMPBELL, Esq.

[June ? 1850]

As there has been a long truce between us since I last got a letter from you, and as I do not intend to despatch this here till I receive Bob's answer with your address, I have no questions to answer, and any news would turn old by keeping, so I intend briefly to state my country occupations (otherwise preparation for Cambridge, if you please).   I find that after breakfast is the best time for reading Greek and Latin, because if I read newspapers or any of those things, then it is dissipation and ruin ; and if I begin with props, experiments, or calculations, then I would be continually returning on them.   At first I had got pretty well accustomed to regular study with a Dictionary, and did about 120 lines of *Eurip.* a day, namely, 40 revised, 40 for to-day, and 40 for to-morrow, with the looking up of

---

[1] *i.e.* Is Robert Campbell going to Peterhouse or Caius ?

to-morrow's words.   As I am blest with Dunbar's *Lexicon*, it is not very highly probable that I will find my word at all ; if I do, it is used in a different sense from Dunbar's (so much the better), and it has to be made out from the context (either of the author or the Dictionary).   So much for regular study, which I have nearly forgot, for when I had got to the end of the first chorus I began to think of the rods and wires that I had in a box.   They have entirely stopped *Eurip.*, for I found that if I spent the best part of the day on him, and took reasonable exercise, I could not much advance the making of the apparatus for tormenting these wires and rods.   So the rods got the better of the Lexicon.   The observations on the rods are good for little till they are finished ; they are of three kinds, and are all distinguished for accuracy and agreement among themselves.

Thus—a rod bent by a weight at the middle takes the form of a curve, which is calculated to be one of the fourth order.   Let A C B be the rod bent by a weight at C.   Mirrors fastened to it at A and B make known the changes of the inclination of the tangent to the rod there, and a lens at C  projects an image of a copper scale of inches and parts from A to B, where it is observed, and so the deflection of the rod at C becomes known.   Now the calculated value of the elasticity deduced from the deflection differs from that deduced from the observations on the mirrors by about $\frac{1}{140}$ of either, and as the deflection at C was about $\frac{1}{4}$ inch, the difference of the observed and calculated deflections is about $\frac{1}{280}$ of an inch, which is near enough for home-made philosophical instruments to go.

Thus you see I would run on about rods and wires, and weights, angles, and inches, and copper and iron, and silvered glass, and all sorts of practicalities.   Where is now *Eurip.?*— Ay, where ?   On the top of the Lexicon, and behind bundles of observations and calculations.   When will he come out ? for he was a good soul after all, and wise (beg his pardon, *wiser*).   For the rest I have been at Shakespeare and Cowper.   I used to put Thomson and Cowper together (why?), and Thomson first ; now they are reversed and far asunder.

As I suppose my occupations are not very like yours, I pray you send me an account of what Oxford notions you have got, either from Oxonians, books, or observation ; and as, if I was to question you, you could but answer my questions, I leave you to question yourself and send me some of the answers.

The only regular College science that I have thought of lately is Moral Philosophy. Whether it is an Oxford science I know not ; but it must be, if not taught, at least interesting ; so I purpose to fill up this letter with unuttered thoughts (or crude), which, as they are crammed into words, may appear like men new waked from sleep, who leap in confusion into one another's breeches, hardly fit to be seen of decent men. Then think not my words mad if their clothes fit them not, for they have not had an opportunity of trying them on before.

There are some Moral Philosophers whose opinions are remarkable for their general truth and good sense, but not for their utility, fixity, or novelty.

They tell you that in all your actions you ought to be virtuous, that benevolence is a virtue, that lawful rulers ought to be obeyed, that a man should give ear to his conscience.

Others tell you of unalterable laws of right and wrong, of Eternal truth and the Everlasting fitnesses of things. Others of the duty of following nature, of every virtue between two vices (Aristot.), and of the golden mean. That a man should do what is best on the whole (1) for himself; (2) for other men only, and *not* himself ; (3) for the whole universe, including himself, and so on. Now I think that the answers to the following questions should be separate parts of M. Ph. :—

1. What is man ? This is the introduction, and is called statical or proper Metaphysics.

2. What are the laws of human action ? Action being all that man does—thought, word, deed.

3. What are the motives of human actions ?

4. What actions do men perform in preference to what others, and why ?

5. What is the principle by which men judge some actions right, others wrong ?

6. What do particular men think of this principle ? What are their doctrines ?

7. What is the best criticism of right and wrong, or what (to us) is absolute right ?

8. What are the best motives of human actions ?

9. How are these motives to be implanted without violating the laws of human action ?

10. What might, or rather what *will*, mankind become after this has been effected ?

Moral Philosophy differs from Nat. Phil. in this, that the more new things we hear of in Nat. Phil. the better ; but in Mor. Phil. the old things are best, so that a common objection to Mor. Phil. is that everybody knows it all before.   If a man tells you that tyranny and anarchy are bad things, and that a just and lawful government is a good thing, it sounds very fine, but only means that when men think the government bad from excess or defect they give it the name of tyranny and anarchy.   The ancient virtue of Tyrannicide was a man's determination to kill the king whenever he displeased him.   Thus it is easy to call a dog a bad name to beat him for.   But there are other parts of Mor. Phil. in which there are differences of opinion, such as the nature of selfishness, self-love, appetites, desires, and affections, disinterestedness (what a word for a rush at !), which belong to the first three questions, and so on.   I have told you something (pp. 84-85) of three laws which I had been considering.   In all parts of Mor. Phil. these three laws seem to meet one, and in each system of Morals they take a different form.   Now, that I might not deceive myself in thinking that I was safe out of the hands of the philosophers who argue these matters, I have been looking into the books of Moralists the most opposed to one another, to see what it is that makes them differ, and wherein they agree.   The three principles concerning the nature of man are continually changing their shape, so that it is not easy to catch them in their best shape.   Nevertheless :

Lemma : Metaphysics.—A man thinks, feels, and wills, and therefore Metaphysicians give him the three faculties of cognition, feeling, and conation.

Cognition is what is called Understanding, and is most thought of generally.   Feelings are pleasures, pains, appetites, desires, aversions, approval and disapproval, love, hate, and all affections.

Conations are acts of will, whatever they be.

Now to move a man's will it is necessary to move his affections.   (How ?   Wait !)   For no convictions of the understanding will do, for a man does what he likes to do, not what he believes to be best for himself or others.   The feelings can only be moved by notions coming through the understanding, for cognition is the only inlet of thoughts.   Therefore, although it can be proved that self-love leads to all goodness, or, in other words, that goodness is happiness, and *self* loves happiness, yet it can also be proved that men are not able to act rightly from pure self-love ; so that though self-love is a very fine theoretical principle, yet no man can keep it always in view, or act reasonably upon it. Now, most moralists take for granted that the end which men, good or bad, pursue is their own happiness, and that happiness, false or true, is the motive of every action, and that it is the only right motive. Others say that benevolence is the only virtue, and that any action not done expressly for the good of others is entitled to no praise. .

Most of the ancients, and Hobbes among the moderns, are of the first opinion. Hutcheson and Brown (I think) are of the second, and call the first selfish Philosophers and the selfish school. A few consider benevolence to the whole universe as the proper motive of every action, but they all (says Macintosh) confound men's motives with the criterion of right and wrong, the reason why a thing is right, and that which actually causes a man to do it. In every book on Moral Philosophy some reference is made to that precept or maxim, which is declared to be the spirit of the law and the prophets (see Matt. vii. 12), and the application of it is a good mark of the uppermost thoughts or mode of thinking of the author.

Hobbes lays down as the first agreement of men to secure their safety, that a man should lay down so much of his natural liberty with respect to others, as he wishes that other men should to him. Hobbes having shown that men, in what the poets and moralists call a state of nature (that is, of equality and liberty, and without government), must be in a state of war, every man against every other, and therefore of danger to every man, deduces the obligation of obeying the powers that be from the necessity of Power to prevent universal war. Adam Smith's theory of Moral Sentiments (which is the most systematic next to Hobbes) is that men desire others to sympathise with them, and therefore do those things which may be sympathised with ; that is, as Smith's opponents say, men ought to be guided by the desire of esteem and sympathy. Not so. Smith does not leave us there, but I suppose you have read him, as he is almost the only Scotch Moral Philosopher.

As it is Saturday night I will not write very much more. I was thinking to-day of the duties of [the] cognitive faculty. It is universally admitted that duties are voluntary, and that the will governs understanding by giving or withholding Attention. They say that Understanding ought to work by the rules of right reason. These rules are, or ought to be, contained in Logic ; but the actual science of Logic is conversant at present only with things either certain, impossible, or *entirely* doubtful, none of which (fortunately) we have to reason on. Therefore the true Logic for this world is the Calculus of Probabilities, which takes account of the magnitude of the probability (which is, or which ought to be in a reasonable man's mind). This branch of Math., which is generally thought to favour gambling, dicing, and wagering, and therefore highly immoral, is the only "Mathematics for Practical Men," as we ought to be. Now, as human knowledge comes by the senses in such a way that the existence of things external is only inferred from the harmonious (not similar) testimony of the different senses, Understanding, acting by the laws of right reason, will assign to different truths (or facts, or testimonies, or what shall I call them) different degrees of probability. Now, as the senses give new testimonies continually, and as no man ever detected in them any real inconsistency, it follows that the probability and *credibility* of their testimony is increasing day by day, and the more a man uses them the more he believes them. What is believing ? When the probability (there is no better word found) in a man's mind of a certain proposition being true is greater than that of its being false, he believes it with a proportion of faith corresponding to the probability, and this probability may be increased or diminished by new facts. This is faith in general. When a man thinks he has enough of evidence for some notion of his he sometimes refuses to listen to any additional evidence *pro* or *con*, saying, " It is a settled question, *probatis probata ;* it needs no evidence ; it is certain." This is knowledge as distinguished from faith. He says, " I do not believe ; I know." " If any man thinketh that he knoweth, he knoweth yet nothing as he ought to know." This knowledge is a shutting of one's ears to all arguments, and is the same as " Implicit faith " in one of its meanings. "Childlike faith," confounded with it, is not credulity, for children are not credulous, but find out sooner than some think that many men are liars. I must now to bed, so good night ; only please to write when you get this, if convenient, and state the probability of your coming here. We perhaps will be in Edinburgh when the Wise men are there. Now you are invited in a corner of a letter by

JAMES CLERK MAXWELL.

H

Glenlair, 16th September 1850.

Professor W. Thomson has asked me [1] to make him some magne-crystallic preparations which I am now busy with. Now, in some of these bismuth is required, which is not to be found either in Castle-Douglas or Dumfries. I have, therefore, thought fit to request you, and do now request you, during your transit through Edinburgh on your way here, to go either to Mr. Kemp's establishment in Infirmary Street, beside the College, or to some other dealer in metals, and there purchase and obtain two ounces of metallic bismuth (called Regulus of Bismuth), either powder or lumpish—all one. Thus you may perceive that the end of this letter is in two ounces of Regulus of Bismuth, that is, the metal bismuth, which if you do bring it with you, will please me well. Not that I am turned chemist. By no means ; but common cook. My fingers are abominable with glue and chalk, gum and flour, wax and rosin, pitch and tallow, black oxide of iron, red ditto and vinegar. By combining these ingredients, I strive to please Prof. Thomson, who intends to submit them to Tyndall and Knoblauch, who, by means of them, are to discover the secrets of nature, and the origin of the magne-crystallic forces.

Now, if by coming here you could turn me from a cook to a grammarian by an irresistible influence you would do well ; but if you remember the way I used to translate at the Academy, distorting the Latin of Livy to mean what I had preconceived, you will understand that at first I had not only to find out what the author meant, but to become convinced that it could not be what I thought it was.

John Wilson's lectures on Moral Philosophy do not improve on reconsideration ; they become indistinct and are resolved into the excellence of happiness, the acquiredness of conscience, and general good-humour, philanthropy and φιλαγαθια. Here is an outline of Abstract Mor. Phil.—

1. The principles of the growth of the mind (that is, the acquisition of opinions, propensities, and abilities).

2. The principles of government (the governor suits his actions to the laws of the thing governed).

---

[1] This request had probably some connection with the meeting of the "wise men" in Edinburgh. Maxwell had been present, and had spoken in Section A. Professor Swan remembers the surprise felt by all but Forbes at seeing the beardless stripling rise to dispute some point in the colour theory with Sir David Brewster.

3. The principle of sympathy (sauce for goose is sauce for gander).

Out of these heads may one make something ?

As it is bed-time, and I have to put the glue and oxide of iron into shape to-night, I must stop here, and remain in hope of seeing you soon (say when).

CHAPTER VI.

UNDERGRADUATE LIFE AT CAMBRIDGE—OCTOBER 1850 TO JANUARY 1854—ÆT. 19-22.

BEFORE placing his son at Cambridge Mr. Clerk Maxwell had, as was usual with him, consulted various persons, including Professor James Forbes and Professor Kelland of Edinburgh, Professors Thomson and Blackburn of Glasgow, and Charles Mackenzie, afterwards Archdeacon of Natal and Missionary Bishop for Central Africa, then a Lecturer of Caius College, Cambridge.[1] Forbes strongly advised Trinity, and offered an introduction to Whewell; but after various reasons urged for Trinity, Caius, and Peterhouse, the decision was in favour of Peterhouse.

Maxwell's first impression of college life, like that of some other clever freshmen, was not one of unalloyed satisfaction. He was transplanted from the rural solitudes of Galloway into the midst of a society which was of curious interest to him, but did not make him feel immediately at home. He found himself amongst the freshmen spelling out Euclid again, and again "monotonously parsing" a Greek play. He had brought with him his scraps of gelatine, gutta-percha, and unannealed glass, his bits of magnetised steel, and other objects, which were apt to appear to the uninitiated as "matter in the wrong place." And this in the home of science! Nor were his experiments facilitated by the casual "dropping-in" of the average undergraduate.

His boyish spirits and his social temper, together with

---

[1] He was the younger brother of Mr. Mackenzie of Portmore, who lived at Silverknowe, and had married Isabella Wedderburn.

the novelty of the scene, and a deep-rooted presentiment
of the possibilities of Cambridge, no doubt made even his
first term a happy one.   But there was an undercurrent
of restlessness and misgiving.   And this made him lend a
readier ear to the advice which was pressed upon him
from various quarters, that he should migrate to Trinity.

The ground of this advice was simply that from the
large proportion of high wranglers at Peterhouse, and the
smallness of the foundation, the chances of a fellowship
there for a mathematical man were less than at Trinity
College.   And this was the reason which, together with
his son's evident wish, most weighed with Mr. Clerk
Maxwell.   He was also struck with the fact that "Porter
senior," who about this time became Maxwell's private
tutor, recommended the change, although he himself
belonged to Peterhouse.   But the friend whose counsel in
this whole matter was most prized both by father and son
was Charles Mackenzie, of whom one who was his colleague
at Caius has been heard to say that he was "the best of all
men whom he had known."

On Maxwell's own mind, it need hardly be said, the
prospect of a fellowship had little or no influence, except
in so far as he desired to please his father.   His own
prime motive was undoubtedly the hope, in which he was
not disappointed, that the larger College would afford him
ampler opportunities for self-improvement.

To Lewis Campbell, Esq.

St. Peter's College, 18th Oct. 1850.

You tell me to lay my account with being dull at first, and *Æt.* 19.
to condole with Robert, whereas there is continual merriment
(stop it !), and Robert is not settled yet.   As for secrets of
nature, they are not for Freshmen even to think of.   Now for
personal journal, with observations on the manners and customs,
etc. . . .

We spent the night at Peterborough, and saw the Cathedral
in the morning.   Very grand outside.   West end a fine
subject for calotype seen right perpendicular, and the
point P for a picture made by hand, fine weeping
willows, etc.

Proceeded to Ely with some Gloucester people we met in the Cathedral, and inspected Ely Cathedral like regular Archbishops. Went up the steeple to see land like sea. Heard all the people talking of the enclosure of the Wash to be called Victoria county, and to be worth 30s. per acre. Got to Cambridge, and called on Mr. Fuller,[1] after getting room for my father (as the Bull was full) in a lodgment. Got rooms in College, sitting and bed, six paces from Chapel, and good light. Had Tait to tea. Next day breakfast with Tait and Steele (of Glasgow and Ireland, and a future wrangler), and so on in detail.

M'Kenzie came up to-day. He took us to most of the colleges. Saw Newton and Bacon in Trin. Chapel. At Hall there was a proclamation to this effect nearly :—Whereas (on the — day of —, 1850), application was made to the Syndicate (or Senate or something), by William Cooke, for leave to erect his equestrian establishment ; and whereas, considering the immoral nature of said establishment, it was unanimously resolved to refuse leave. And whereas, notwithstanding said refusal, said W. C. did publicly notify his intention of putting up said estab. : Be it known, etc., that it is resolved and enacted, that if any undergraduate or graduate *in statu pupillari*, or tutor, or fellow, or master, etc., be caught at said establishment, he will be punished with expulsion, rustication, Castigation, or such other punishment as the case may require.[2]

So there is to be a quarrel between the Town and University about this, and also about whether they are to pay poor rate, as the University is supposed to be extra-parochial.

Prelim. exam. to-morrow at 9. Peter can't afford to pluck at it. C. H. Robertson has passed *his* at Trin. He is in Ling's lodgings. He wants to keep quiet and to read by himself, and have only old acquaintances.

To a Friend suffering from Depression.

Hope to write you more again ; but to conclude and get to bed : You are always talking of your withering up, awful change, etc. Now I have not a sermon on this subject by me, neither will I deliver an *extempore* one ; but though I do not

---

[1] Then Tutor of Peterhouse, now Professor Emeritus of Aberdeen.

[2] Contrast with this the following entry in the Diary :—"1842, *Feb.* 19, *Saturday*.—Go with James to Cooke's Circus at 2 P.M. at York Hotel, Arena—being James's first time of seeing such entertainments."

pretend to have examined you in all the branches, yet I would take the liberty to say that with respect to intellect, as the Laird of Dumbiedykes said, "It'll be growing when ye're sleeping,"—that is to say, what you take for corruption and decay is only stratification.[1]

The letters written to his father by Maxwell while an undergraduate at Cambridge have unfortunately disappeared. But something of their tenor may be gathered from Mr. Maxwell's letters to his son. The following extracts are related to his first term at college :—

FROM HIS FATHER.

Glenlair, 22d October 1850.

Did Prof. Thomson catch you, and view your "dirt ;"[2] and if so, what thought he thereof ?

Glenlair, 30th October 1850.

Who is the lecturer in the Greek play ? Did I see him while at Cambridge ? I am sorry to hear the Greek class is a bad one, for you would have got more good of it if [it] had required you to work to maintain a good position in it ; but you should study your part well, for it is not comparative excellence, but absolute, that will be of use in University competitions.

Glenlair, 8th Novr. 1850.

You say your lecturer in Greek is good, so I hope you profit accordingly, altho' your class-fellows are not great scholars. . . . . It would be necessary to take care there are no mouse-holes. A very hungry Chapel mouse might come through. There had been an entrance that way to the Chapel. It would be to the organ loft.

Have you called on Profs. Sedgwick at Trin., and Stokes at Pembroke ? If not, you should do both. Stokes will be most in your way if he takes you in hand at all. Sedgwick is also a great Don in his line, and if you were entered in Geology would be a most valuable acquaintance ; and, besides, not going to him would be uncivil, both to him and to the Alisons, after

---

[1] See above, p. 70, note.
[2] "Jamsie's dirt," the disrespectful name for the bits of unannealed glass, etc. etc., in the *Coterie-Sprache.*

their having arranged the introduction.   Provide yourself
with cards.

It might be worth your while to stop at York to view it.

Glenlair, 13th Novr. 1850.

I am glad you have communication with Stokes and Mackenzie.

Is all Cambridge up in arms against the Pope and Cardinal
Wiseman ? I cannot enter into all the fuss about it. If there
is any law to hinder people calling themselves Cardinals or
Archbishops, let it be acted on ; but if there is no such law,
let the assumption of empty titles . . . be laughed at.

Men of genius are often represented by themselves and
others as owing little or nothing to their education.   This
certainly was not true of Maxwell, whose receptivity was
only less than his originality.   He laid a strong retentive
grasp on all that was given to him, and set his own stamp
on it in return.   Both what was good and what was defective in his early training had left a lasting impress on him,
and it was by no means an indifferent circumstance that,
in the maturity of his powers, he entered Trinity College,
Cambridge, at an advanced period of the long mastership
of Whewell.

I well remember my surprise, not unmixed with needless pangs of boyish jealousy, on finding in the following
summer that Maxwell had all at once made a troop of
friends.   Their names were always on his lips, and he
loved by some vivid trait to indicate the character of each.
His acquaintance was multifarious, and he had many pithy
anecdotes to relate of other than his own particular
associates.

He was at first in lodgings in King's Parade, where he
" chummed " with an old Edinburgh schoolfellow, Charles
Hope Robertson.[1]   It appears that the college lectures in
mathematics were still felt to be rather elementary, but
that he worked harder problems (some were of his own
invention) with Tait and with Porter of Peterhouse, who

---

[1] Now Rector of Smeeth, near Ashford, in Kent.

was still his private tutor.   A certain amount of classical reading was required of freshmen, and he still took his classics seriously.   There is an allusion to the Ajax in one of his letters, and he makes critical remarks upon Demosthenes.   There was also a lecture on Tacitus by a "deep, half-sentence lecturer."   Either now or in the following year—at some time before the little-go examination of March 1852—he translated the choral odes of the Ajax into rhymed English verse,[1] and made a rough caricature of Ajax slaughtering the oxen.

His chief outdoor amusements were walking, bathing, and sculling.   He was upset in his "funny" in May 1851 —a trifling accident to so expert a swimmer.   "But," writes a contemporary Cantab, "he richly deserved it. For he tried to take off his jersey after 'shipping' his oars. The oscillations of the funny became rapidly more extensive, in spite of his violent efforts at equilibrium."   For winter recreation he ordered a pair of basket-sticks to be made at home.

He tried some odd experiments in the arrangement of his hours of work and sleep.   But his father disapproved of such vagaries, and they were not continued long— although not entirely abandoned even when he had rooms in college.   The authority just quoted says, "From 2 to 2.30 A.M. he took exercise by running along the upper corridor, *down* the stairs, along the lower corridor, then *up* the stairs, and so on, until the inhabitants of the rooms along his track got up and lay *perdus* behind their sporting-doors to have shots at him with boots, hair-brushes, etc., as he passed."

Intellectual interests of all kinds surrounded him, and he soon began to lend new life to all.   There were also in the Cambridge of this period religious influences of a remarkable kind.   Apart from the Simeonite tradition which still lingered, there was a class of younger men, who, while faithful to a pious evangelical upbringing, had open and inquiring minds.   The names of Henry and Frank

---

[1] I did not know of this until the present year, 1881.

Mackenzie of Trinity, the one senior to Maxwell, the other junior to him,[1] may be mentioned in particular. To such men, and to many others, the preaching of Harvey Goodwin, now Bishop of Carlisle, but at that time chiefly known as a mathematical authority, was full of interest.

1851.   Two events of some importance to the scientific world were the introduction of Foucault's pendulum experiment for proving the rotation of the earth, and the Great Exhibition of 1851.

Maxwell saw the pendulum experiment in Mr. Thacker's (the tutor's) rooms at Trinity in April or May, and wrote an account of it to his father, which has been lost.

The "viewing" of the Crystal Palace, although a thing to be done, was made less exciting than it would otherwise have been by the constant habit of visiting all manufactures according to opportunity. Maxwell disclaims all "fanaticism" on the subject, and his father writes that while a fortnight would be required to see it properly, a great deal of it must be already familiar to them both.

Æt. 20.   In the October term he joined the "team" of Hopkins, the great private tutor, as a fifteenth pupil.

He also became a regular attendant of Professor Stokes's lectures, and commenced his lifelong friendship with one whose original investigations were so closely akin to some of his own.

Professor Stokes's kindness was greatly valued even in those old days, and much more afterwards. The young man's happiness in all ways at Trinity is manifested by the reappearance of the poetic vein, about the time of the junior sophs' examination, in the *Lay of King Numa*, dated 13th December 1851.

To this sketch of his first year at college there must be appended one more reminiscence of Glenlair. We met

---

[1] In 1852 H. M. had left Cambridge. F. M. went as a freshman to Trinity in October 1852. See a book named *Early Death not Premature*, being a Memoir of Francis L. Mackenzie, late of Trinity College, Cambridge. With Notices of Henry Mackenzie, B.A. By the Rev. Charles Popham Miles, M.A., M.D., F.L.S., Glasgow. Nisbet and Co. Fourth Edition. 1861.

there in the autumn of that year, and I remember that either then or in the previous year, he put into my hands Carlyle's translation of Goethe's *Wilhelm Meister*, remarking that it was a book to be read with discretion.

In the autumn of 1850 the neighbouring estate of Upper Corsock had been let to a shooting-party,[1] one of whom remarked to me what a pity it was that young Mr. Clerk Maxwell was "so little suited for a country life." I clearly recollect his look of exulting mirth when this was repeated to him. His disinclination to field sports was certainly not due to any lack of activity, nor even to his shortsightedness, which for other purposes was easily overcome, but simply to his love for animals. The moral of Wordsworth's *Hart-Leap Well* was not so much a principle as an instinct with him.[2] I remember his once speaking to me on the subject of vivisection. He did not condemn its use, supposing the method could be shown to be fruitful, which at that time he doubted, but—"Couldn't do it, you know," he added, with a sensitive wistful look not easy to forget. This is all I ever heard him say on the subject.

LETTERS, 1851.

To LEWIS CAMPBELL, Esq.

11th March 1851.
Lings, King's Parade, Cambridge.

. . . Have you read Soph. *Ajax*, or would you like to do it then?[3]

1851.
Æt. 19.

I have been trying an experiment of sleeping after hall. Last Friday I went to bed from 5 to 9.30, and read very hard from 10 to 2, and slept again from 2.30 to 7.

I intend some time to try for a week together sleeping from 5 to 1, and reading the rest of the morning. This is practical scepticism with respect to early rising.

An Oxford man is reported to have complained of the lateness of morning chapel; he could not sit up for it. I will have the most of my reading over by that time. . . .

---

[1] Including the present Earl Cairns.
[2] His uncle, Sir G. Clerk, is said to have had the same peculiarity.
[3] Viz. at the time of my proposed visit to Cambridge.

Demosthenes goes on.   I begin to see what may be written in prose, and how ill it may be translated.

It is a γραφη παρανομων, so there is less declamation and more demonstration ; but the arguments, small at first, are added as they proceed, and never left behind, so by oft repetition they seem stronger than they are.

Last night I searched for difficult problems to puzzle Steele and Porter junior with.   Here are some much more mild, which we freshmen get. . . .

It is twelve o'clock, and I have to do Demosthenes to-morrow before breakfast.   This implies Chapel, therefore bed, therefore I shut up.

FROM HIS FATHER.

Glenlair, 6th March 1851.

Simpson rages at present in the Electro-biology.   Dr. Alison is very wroth about it.   He says he has known two cases of nervous people whose minds were quite disordered by it.   I hope it is not in fashion at Cambridge, and at any rate that you do not meddle with it.   If it does anything, it is more likely to be harm than good ; and if harm ensue, the evil might be irreparable, so let me hear that you have dismissed it ; you have plenty better things in hand where you are.[1]

Glenlair, 29th April 1851.

Explain the pendulum experiment to me.   You used often to speak of the retardation of the Rotation of the Earth by the friction of the tides.

What is the Phosphate of Lime theory of mental progress ?

Glenlair, 18th May 1851.

Do you like the Trig. lectures A ?[2]   Tacitus is not new to you.   His style must be congenial to a deep, half-sentence lecturer.

Were you carrying your watch when you were upset in your funny ? and if so, how did it agree with the douking ?[3]

I shall be glad to hear about the Pendulum.   Who is Thacker, who asked you to his rooms to see it ?

---

[1] In the preceding Christmas vacation I was at a private "séance" in Edinburgh, where Maxwell—whether he shammed or not who can tell ? —was selected by the operator (a man named Douglas, I think), who vainly tried to make him seem to forget his name.

[2] Mr. Mathison's lecture on trigonometry.

[3] *i.e. Anglicè,* "How did the dip agree with it ?"

To Lewis Campbell, Esq.

Cambridge, 9th June 1851.

I find I owe you one letter this term. I intended to write three days ago, but I am now refreshed by classical papers, and disburdened of half the subjects of examination.

On Friday we had Euclid, on Saturday Greek,—cram on both subjects ; to-day Ajax and Tacitus translations. I did no composition, but did various readings, strongly preferring certain of them for obvious reasons.

I find that 4 hours Euclid is worse than 2 3-hour papers of cram, though I sent up much more cram than Euclid. This of itself shows that disburdening cram is not like grinding out Mathematics. M—— in the Plato cram, writing a comparison of Cynics and Platonists, said that Platonism was a real live thing, but Cynicism was sleepy, and that even in its greatest ornament, Diogenes, the view of the universe was contracted to a front look-out from a wash-tub, and the *summum bonum* reduced to sunning one's self with eyes shut and buttons open. This was to let off his jaw on first setting down, but he let it in among his papers, and could not get it out again.

Excuse my square sentences. I have spent my curves on Tacitus, and I must now proceed to Trig. Write.—Yrs.

To the Same.

8 King's Parade, 9th Nov. 1851.

I began a letter last week, but stopped short for want of matter. I will not send you the abortion. Facts are very scarce here. There are little stories of great men for minute philosophers. Sound intelligence from Newmarket for those that put their trust in horses, and Calendristic lore for the votaries of the Senate-house. Man requires more. He finds x and y innutritious, Greek and Latin indigestible, and undergrads. nauseous. He starves while being crammed. He wants man's meat, not college pudding. Is truth nowhere but in Mathematics ? Is Beauty developed only in men's elegant words, or Right in Whewell's *Morality ?* Must Nature as well as Revelation be examined through canonical spectacles by the dark-lantern of Tradition, and measured out by the learned to the unlearned, all second-hand. I might go on thus. Now do not rashly say that I am disgusted with Cambridge and meditating a retreat. On the contrary, I am so engrossed with

Æt. 20.

shoppy things that I have no time to write to you. I am also persuaded that the study of x and y is to men an essential preparation for the intelligent study of the material universe. That the idea of Beauty is propagated by communication, and that in order thereto human language must be studied, and that Whewell's *Morality* is worth reading, if only to see that there *may be* such a thing as a system of Ethics.

That few will grind up these subjects without the help of rules, the awe of authority, and a continued abstinence from unripe realities, etc.

I believe, with the Westminster Divines and their predecessors *ad Infinitum* that "Man's chief end is to glorify God and to enjoy him for ever."

That for this end to every man has been given a progressively increasing power of communication with other creatures. That with his powers his susceptibilities increase.

That happiness is indissolubly connected with the full exercise of these powers in their intended direction. That Happiness and Misery must inevitably increase with increasing Power and Knowledge. That the translation from the one course to the other is essentially *miraculous*, while the progress is natural. But the subject is too high. I will not, however, stop short, but proceed to Intellectual Pursuits.

It is natural to suppose that the soul, if not clothed with a body, and so put in relation with the creatures, would run on in an unprogressive circle of barren meditation. In order to advance, the soul must converse with things external to itself.

In every branch of knowledge the progress is proportional to the amount of facts on which to build, and therefore to the facility of obtaining data. In the Mathematics this is easy. Do you want a quantity? Take x; there it is !—got without trouble, and as good a quantity as one would wish to have. And so in other sciences,—the more abstract the subject, the better it is known. Space, time, and force come first in certainty. These are the subjects in Mechanics.

Then the active powers, Light, Heat, Electricity, etc. = Physics.

Then the differences and relations of Matter = Chemistry, and so on.

Here the order of advancement is just that of abstractedness and inapplicability to the actual. What poor blind things we Maths. think ourselves ! But see the Chemists ! Chemistry is a pack of cards, which the labour of hundreds is slowly arranging ; and one or two tricks,—faint imitations of Nature,—have been played. Yet Chemistry is far before all the Natural History sciences ; all these before Medicine ; Medicine before Metaphysics, Law, and Ethics ; and these I think before Pneumatology and Theology.

Now each of these makes up in interest what it wants in advancement.

There is no doubt that of all earthly creatures Man is the most important to us, yet we know less of him than any other. His history is more interesting than natural history ; but nat. history, though obscure, is much more intelligible than man's history, which is a tale half told, and which, even when this world's course is run, and when, as some think, man may compare notes with other rational beings, will still be a great mystery, of which the beginning and the end are all that can be known to us while the intermediate parts are perpetually filled up.

So now pray excuse me if I think that the more grovelling and materialistic sciences of matter are not to be despised in comparison with the lofty studies of Minds and Spirits. Our own and our neighbours' minds are known but very imperfectly, and no new facts will be found till we come in contact with some minds other than human to elicit them by counterposition. But of this more anon.

FROM HIS FATHER.

Glenlair, 3d Novr. 1851.

How do you like and how do you profit by Hopkins' mode of driving ? He should get one more pupil, and drive 16 in hand like Batty or Cook.

Glenlair, 18th Novr. 1851.

You seem to have great gaieties with College Parties with Scientific Dons. Do you take notes of Stokes' experiments on the bands of the Spectrum ? Will they be suitable for repetition in the garret of the old House ?[1]

The clearing away a bank of weeds was a sly trick of the Trinity 4-oar, and I think Peterhouse and Sidney justified in protesting.[2] What tribunal is there to settle such matters ?

---

[1] See above, p. 74, l. 28.
[2] According to the "contemporary Cantab," Peterhouse and Sidney

I copied from your letters plan and section and elevation of the Baskets for single stick, and committed the same to the Davie.[1]

In the spring of 1852 he got rooms in college (Letter G, Old Court, south Attics), succeeding to his friend Blakiston, and passed his Little-go. In April of the same year he gained his scholarship, and was now launched without further necessary distraction on the long pull of preparation for the Tripos under Hopkins. But his energies were by no means absorbed in this continuous "grind." He contributed various papers to the *Cambridge and Dublin Mathematical Journal*, did not confine himself to mathematics in the May examination, and in November, besides writing the comic *Vision of a University, of Pedantry, and of Philosophy*, made elaborate preparation for a College declamation, "the Scottish Covenanters" being the subject characteristically chosen by him.

In June he had paid a short visit to Oxford, and made a trip to Lowestoft with P. G. Tait, before settling at Cambridge (to read and bathe) for the vacation term.

Æt. 21.   Living in college and dining at the scholars' table, he naturally became more intimate with the other scholars, and he appears especially to have sought contact with classical men. To the names of Cracroft, Whitt, and Blakiston, amongst his newer friends are now added in his correspondence those of "Droop the ingenuous," Gedge, Howard Elphinstone, Isaac Taylor, Maclennan,[2] and Vaughan Hawkins.

The idea of self-improvement in society had taken a firm hold of him, and he was conscious of the difficulty of guiding himself among so many cross influences. He knew that he was involuntarily different with different men, and there are curious traces in his correspondence of the struggle to make the highest use of social circumstances. Those who

---

really won the race, in spite of the removal of the bank of weeds. The reason why Trinity got the cups was that the pistol of P. and S.'s umpire *missed fire*.

[1] David M'Vinnie, see above, p. 25.

[2] The late J. F. Maclennan, author of *Primitive Marriage*, etc.

saw him about this time after an interval were struck by
a marked change in his countenance, which, as compared
with the Edinburgh days, had very distinctly gained in
manliness and gravity, and showed a certain massiveness
in its proportions which they had not previously noticed.
His dark brown eye seemed to have deepened, some parts
of the iris being almost black. A slight contraction of the
chest, and a stature which, although above the average,
was not tall enough to carry off the weight of his brow,
made him less handsome standing than sitting. But his
presence had by this time fully acquired the unspeakable
charm for all who knew him, which made him insensibly
become the centre of any circle, whether large or small,
consisting of his friends or kindred. His hair and incipient
beard were raven black, with a crisp strength in each particular hair, that gave him more the look of a Nazarite
than of a nineteenth century youth. His dress was plain
and neat, only remarkable for the absence of everything
adventitious (starch, loose collars, studs, etc.), and an
"æsthetic" taste might have perceived in its sober hues
the effect of his marvellous eye for harmony of colour.[1]

The impression he made on older persons with whom
he was less intimate may be gathered from the remarks of
Dean Ramsay in a note to Miss Cay:—

I had great pleasure in seeing your nephew, young Clerk
Maxwell. He is shrewd and cautious. He seems to like Cambridge, and I doubt not will distinguish himself. He is sparing
in his words, but what he says is to the point.

The following contribution from the Rev. Charles Hope
Robertson, the Rector of Smeeth (above, p. 104), throws
light on more than one aspect of his life at this period:—

I was at Trinity College, Cambridge, in the same years as

---

[1] He was the first who spoke to me (about 1865) of the principles of
coloured glass, which have since become fashionable ; observing that it
should be rich in sea-green, and not, "like the banners of the Assyrian,
gleaming with purple and gold." In his critical studies of modern poets
he used to note their fondness for particular colours,—*e.g.*, the uses of
"white," "red," "black," "ruby," "emerald," "sapphire," in Tennyson
and Browning.

Clerk Maxwell, and for some time had lodgings in the same house. This, as well as knowing him before in Edinburgh, led to our frequently meeting.

He was of a very kindly disposition (under a blunt exterior), of which I can give an example. I had hurt my eyes a good deal with experiments on light, while working up for a course of Professor Forbes's lectures at Edinburgh College, and for a good part of my undergraduate course was able to use them very little. He used to find me sitting in my rooms with closed eyes, unable to prepare for next day's lectures, and often gave up an hour of his recreation time, to read out to me some of the book-work I wanted to get over. This infirmity prevented my reading for more than a moderate degree in mathematical honours ; but I should have been still worse off if he had not thus been " eyes to the blind " for me.

He had an innate reverence for sacred things, which I do not think was ever much disturbed by the scepticism fashionable among shallow scientific men. As my main object in coming to Cambridge was to prepare for holy orders, I had more interest in theological subjects than any others. He knew this, and would refer to me points of difficulty for our mutual consideration till we next met. The result was useful to us both. On one occasion an attack on the Mosaic history having perplexed him, he was glad of an idea that occurred to me, that the account of God's driving out the heathen by " sending the hornet " before the Israelites, was not an idea likely to occur in a book of human origin, where a leader would rather be apt to magnify than to diminish his own and his people's prowess. This exactly suited the sceptical state of some friend he had been conversing with. On another occasion he hit on a very beautiful mathematical illustration of St. Paul's closing view of his career, in 2 Tim. iv. 6-8 ; " St. Paul was looking backward, forward, and downwards—so the *resultant was upwards*."

As an original experimenter he was most ingenious in contriving out of simple means apparatus for delicate experiments. I have to this day some crystals for showing polarised light, which he gave me, cut and polished by most simple rubbing, mounted with cardboard and sealing-wax.

His *Essay on the Rings of Saturn*,—showing how mechanical principles required that these bodies were not solid, but formed by multitudes of small bodies revolving round Saturn, in bands of orbits,—has received abundant confirmation from recent observation with large telescopes. His own simple experiments with corks and rings suggested the idea.

But while so ingenious himself, he had great difficulty in imparting his ideas to others ; consequently was not so clear a lecturer or writer as might have been expected. It was probably this that prevented his being senior wrangler of his year.

I may mention that though not joining in the ordinary games of young fellows, such as cricket and rowing, he was very active ; and I have seen him in bathing take a running header from the bank, turning a complete somersault before touching the water.[1]

If shortly described, he might be said to combine a grand intellect with childlike simplicity of trust. He was too deep a thinker to be sceptical, but too well read not to feel for others' difficulties. All his experiments led him to greater reverence for the Great First Cause, heartily agreeing with Young's *Night Thoughts,* " An undevout astronomer is mad."

In the course of the winter he was elected a member of the Select Essay Club, the *crème de la crème* of Cambridge intellects, familiarly known (because limited to the number twelve) as "the Apostles." His contributions to this famous association still remain,[2] and present a curious reflection of the contemplative activities of his mind, which is far indeed from being engrossed with mere mathematics, but is rather, in the language of Plato, "taking a survey of the universe of things," πᾶσαν πάντων φύσιν ἐρευνωμένη τῶν ὄντων ἑκάστου ὅλου. Yet amidst this speculative ardour, and even wildness, we trace the persistence of certain root-ideas, and are often reminded of his intention (expressed with curious self-directed irony in 1850), "to read Kant's *Kritik* with a determination to make it agree with Sir William Hamilton."[3]

His coming of age, June 13, 1852, had been celebrated with a few quiet words in his father's letter of June 12, graced with the unusual addition of a Scripture text—" I

---

[1] Professor Tait says, " He used to go up on the pollard at the bathing-shed, throw himself *flat on his face* in the water, dive and cross, then ascend the pollard on the other side, project himself *flat on his back* in the water. He said it stimulated the circulation !"

[2] See chap. viii.   [3] P. 89.

trust you will be as discreet when Major as you have been while Minor (Prov. x. 1 [1])."

The six months from December 1852 to June 1853 were a time of great and varied mental activity. When the Tripos work became most exacting, he seemed to have the most spare energy. No part of the rich mental life of Trinity failed to touch and stimulate him—from the Moral Philosophy of the Master, to undergraduate discourses upon whist and chess. When most burdened with analytical book-work, he yearned the more deeply after comprehensive views of Nature and Life, and found refreshment in metaphysical discussion, and occasionally in theological controversy. Even the "occult" sciences, in the contemporary shapes of electro-biology and table-turning, had their share of ironical attention.

1853.

His relations with the dons, "scientific" and otherwise, whatever may have been their first impression of him,[2] were, for the most part, smooth, but a humorous passage of arms between him and the Senior Dean was long remembered in Trinity. The lines to J. A. Frere, although somewhat personal, are too well known to be omitted from his collected poems, and anything in them which might give offence at the time is more than redeemed by the large humanity of the concluding stanza. The following letter, addressed (but perhaps not sent) to the same personage, throws an amusing light on the circumstances under which the parody of " John Anderson " was written :—

To the Rev. John Alexander Frere.

Trin. Coll., 26th Feb. 1853.

Dear Sir—Looking back on the past week I find I have kept only seven chapels. I have no excuse to offer. The reason, however, of the deficiency is this. Unaware that a Saint's Day would occur in the course of the week I parted with

---

[1] "A wise son maketh a glad father."

[2] His native tones in reading the lessons in chapel seem at first to have surprised every one, from the Master downwards. And once during service his eyes were seen to move strangely, while his mouth retained its gravity. He was "measuring the angular distance between the dons."

my surplice on Monday in order to have it washed.   I was
thus prevented from appearing in chapel on the evenings of
Wednesday and Thursday, as otherwise I would have done.   I
might even after this have completed the requisite number ; but,
unfortunately, reading till a late hour on Friday night I found
myself unable to attend chapel on Saturday morning.

I can but hope that more forethought on my part may prevent the recurrence of such accidents.

I have also to acknowledge the receipt of a small paper from
you relative to the observance of Sunday.   I have read it, and
will keep it in mind.

Trusting that my past and future regularity may atone for
my present negligence, I remain, yours sincerely,

J. C. MAXWELL.

Rev. J. A. FRERE.

It was while staying up at Easter in the spring of *Æt.* 21.
1853, and working "at high pressure," that his longing for
the untrammelled and reverent investigation of Nature's
secrets found rhythmical expression in the most serious of
his poems, the "Student's Evening Hymn," in which religious and philosophical aspirations are combined.   Thus
it was always with him ; when most plunged in the minute
investigation either of phenomena or of abstract ideas, he
was most eager to rebound towards the contemplation of
the whole of things, and that which gives unity to the
whole.   Yet no mind could be more averse from "viewi-
ness," or more determined to bring every statement to the
test of fact.

The brief remainder of that Easter vacation was spent
at Birmingham with his friend Johnson Gedge, a scholar
of Trinity, whose father was second master of King
Edward's School.   The exactions of Trinity and Hopkins
had only left him a few days of holiday, and these were
passed in the manner already mentioned,[1] in viewing the
manufactures of Birmingham.   Mr. Clerk Maxwell's own
delight in such things prevented him from realising how
laborious a programme he had suggested for the interval

---

[1] Above, p. 5, note 1.

between two long spells of severe head-work.   Yet in the
midst of it Maxwell seems to have found time to contribute an elaborate piece of humorous correspondence to the
King Edward's School Chronicle.

When working hardest he was never a recluse, nor was
he ever more sociable than in his third year at college.
He seems to have had some difficulty even in avoiding
supper parties, and one of his most brilliant metaphysical
jeux d'esprit purports to be a mode of escaping from them.
To the names already mentioned as amongst his intimate
friends, those of Farrar[1] and Butler[2] are now added.
Besides the metaphysical discussions, there were Shakespeare readings, of which he was an auditor sometimes, if
not an actor in them.

Whilst speaking of these side-sparks from his anvil, it
is right to keep in view the loyal and trustful spirit in
which he did his regularly-appointed work.   His words on
this subject in one of the letters to Miss Cay, which will
be given presently, are well worthy of separate quotation
here :—

Trin. Coll., 7th June 1853.

If any one asks how I am getting on in Mathematics, say
that I am busy arranging everything, so as to be able to express
all distinctly, so that examiners may be satisfied now, and pupils
edified hereafter.   It is pleasant work, and very strengthening,
but not nearly finished.

As became his kindliness, he was still mindful of the
freshmen.   Amongst these, Alexander Robertson, now
Sheriff of Forfarshire, the brother of Charles, and Frank
Mackenzie, were Scotsmen and compatriots.   Another
junior with whom he became still more intimate was
"Freshman Tayler,"[3] so called, though now a junior
Soph., in contradistinction to Isaac Taylor.   Like Frank
Mackenzie and others who have been mentioned, Fresh-
man Tayler was of pious evangelical antecedents.   Max-
well's own thoughts at this time, as has been seen, were

---

[1] The Rev. F. W. Farrar, D.D., Canon of Westminster.
[2] The Rev. H. Butler, D.D., Head-Master of Harrow.
[3] The Rev. G. W. H. Tayler, now Vicar of Trinity Church, Carlisle.

taking a more decidedly religious colour, and this side also of his rich and deep nature received a fresh impulse in this critical year.

He had been persuaded to spend the short interval between the summer and vacation terms with the Rev. C. B. Tayler, rector of Otley, in Suffolk, who had been touched with Maxwell's kindness to his nephew. Here he found himself for the first time in the midst of a large and united English family, and in his half-speculative, half-emotional way, was contrasting what he saw with the experience of an only son, when he was suddenly taken ill. The long continuous strain of the past months had been too much for him, and indeed it appears that even in the early spring he had been physically below par.[1] The illness is described by Mr. Tayler as a sort of brain fever, and he was disabled by it for more than a month. The Taylers nursed him as they would have nursed a son of their own, and Maxwell, in whom the smallest kindnesses awakened lasting gratitude, was profoundly moved by this. He referred to it long afterwards as having given him a new perception of the Love of God. One of his strongest convictions thenceforward was that "Love abideth, though Knowledge vanish away." And this came to him at the very height of the intellectual struggle.[2]

1853. Æt. 22.

---

[1] See the letter of 2d February 1853, in which his father refers to Miss Cay's advice that he should take wine.

[2] At the same time, it is not to be supposed that Maxwell was ever completely identified with any particular school of religious opinion. He was too much "the heir of all the ages," and, as he himself expressed it, "his faith was too deep to be in bondage to any set of opinions." Scottish Calvinism was the theological system which had most historical interest for him, and most claim on his hereditary piety. He was learned in the writings of Owen and Jonathan Edwards. But that which his latest pastor has called "his deep though simple faith," was not enclosed in any system. Even his youthful training (which in the case of one so loyal is not to be disregarded) was favourable to a comprehensive view of Christianity. Beginning with the Bible, which he knew by heart from a child, Presbyterian and Episcopalian influence had been blended as we have already seen. Hence, when he went to Cambridge, there was nothing strange to him in the service of the English Church. His mind was always moving (*elle planait*, as the French would say) above and "beyond these voices," yet they were not indifferent to him.

It is to be regretted that a letter on the Parties in the Church of

The father was also much affected by this kindness shown to his son. Mr. Tayler had said nothing to make him anxious until the crisis of the illness was past. But when he knows all, there is something more than eloquence in his brief, inarticulate phrases of recognition :—

With yours I have Mr. Tayler's letter. I do not write to him to-day. My only subject is thanks, and these are not to be measured in words—the strongest I can use ; so at present give my respects and highest regards.

Though weakened by his illness, Maxwell was able to keep the vacation term, and profit by Hopkins's continued training, before going home for a few weeks of thorough refreshment. In the following term, with the Senate-House examination in immediate prospect, he was careful not to read inordinately hard.

In the autumn of this year the controversy which had been called forth by Professor Maurice's Theological Essays was brought to a crisis through his deprivation of his office by Principal Jelf. Disputation on this theme was nowhere more rife than amongst the scholars of Trinity, and Maxwell's remarks upon it will be read with interest even now. He was from the first strongly attracted by Maurice's combination of intense Christian earnestness with universal sympathy, and although he sometimes felt that the new teacher was apt to travesty the Popular Theology in trying to delineate it, he had a deep respect for what was positive in his doctrine. He was still more drawn to him when he came to know him personally,—no longer as a writer, but as a friend. A mention of Thomas Erskine of Linlathen in Mr. Maxwell's letter of 16th December 1853, was

England, written to his father in 1852, has not been found. His general approval of Hare's sermons, and his remarks on the Maurician controversy, indicate the direction which his thoughts on this subject must have taken. His interest in sermons, good and bad, was like Macaulay's interest in novels, or Charles Lamb's in old plays. Years after this, on board a friend's yacht one Sunday, he gave a sort of impromptu exposition of a chapter in the Book of Joshua, shouting up his remarks from below, which struck those who heard it as full of originality and wisdom.

probably occasioned by some question raised in connection with Mr. Maurice.

The following letter, addressed to me by the Rev. G. W. H. Tayler, will be read with interest in the light of the preceding narrative :—

Holy Trinity Vicarage,
Carlisle, 4th March 1882.

MY DEAR SIR—You have asked me to send you some account of James Maxwell, as I remember him during the space of three years, 1852, 1853, and 1854. My first acquaintance with him was about February 1852. I was soon attracted by the frankness of his manner and the singular charm of his quaint and original remarks in conversation.

We undergraduates felt we had a very uncommon personage amongst us ; but we did not then appreciate his rare powers. We had of course heard of the reputation which he had at Edinburgh.

But this acute mathematician, so addicted even then to *original* research, was among his friends simply the most genial and amusing of companions, the propounder of many a strange theory, the composer of not a few poetic *jeux d'esprits*.

Grave and hard-reading students shook their heads at his discursive talk and reading, and hinted that this kind of pursuits would never *pay* in the long run in the Mathematical Tripos.

I have sometimes watched his countenance in the lecture-room. It was quite a study—there was the look of a bright intellect, an entire concentration on the subject, and sometimes a slight smile on the fine expressive mouth, as some point came out clearly before him, or some amusing fancy flitted across his imagination. He used to profess a dislike to reproducing speculations from books, or hearing opinions quoted taken bodily from books.

Yet he read a good deal in other lines of study than natural philosophy. Sir Thomas Brown's *Religio Medici* was one of his favourite books. Any such author, who propounded his speculations in a quaint, original manner was sure to be a favourite with him.

But I particularly remember his attraction to Sir Thomas Brown during the long vacation, when he was laid up with severe illness (a brain fever) in my dear uncle's house in June 1853. He came to stay at Otley, near Ipswich, of which my

uncle was the rector.   For a few days he was tolerably well,
then suddenly fell ill, probably through overwork for his third
year college examination.   It was on his recovery from that
illness that I seemed to know him better than ever.   It was
then that my uncle's conversation seemed to make such a deep
impression on his mind.   He had always been a regular attendant
at the services of God's house, and a regular communicant in
our College Chapel.   Also he had thought and read much on
religious subjects.   But at this time (as it appears from his own
account of the matter) his religious views were greatly deepened
and strengthened.

I must add that I spent some little time in the long vacation
of 1854 with Maxwell at Glenlair.   His father was then living,
and it was touching to witness the perfect affection and confidence which subsisted between father and son : the joy and
satisfaction and exulting pride which the father evidently felt
in his son's success and well-earned fame ; and, on the other
hand, the tender, thoughtful care and watchfulness which James
Maxwell manifested towards his father.

Maxwell has indeed left a very bright memory and example.
We, his contemporaries at college, have seen in him high powers
of mind and great capacity and original views, conjoined with
deep humility before his God, reverent submission to His will,
and hearty belief in the love and the atonement of that Divine
Saviour who was his Portion and Comforter in trouble and sickness, and his exceeding great reward.—I remain, my dear sir,
yours very truly,   G. W. H. TAYLER,
                              Vicar of Trinity Church, Carlisle.

Mr. Lawson of the Equity Bar, whose diary has preserved the remark quoted on p. 88, has also furnished me
with the following vivid account of his impressions of
Maxwell as an undergraduate :—

                              22 Old Square, Lincoln's Inn,
                              London, W.C., 6th January 1882.

I was in his year at Trinity, and knew him intimately, though
our ways separated after I left Cambridge, and I scarcely ever
saw him, except once or twice when he was Professor at King's
College, and later on only at very long intervals, on an occasional visit to the University.

There must be many of his quaint verses about, if one could

lay hands on them, for Maxwell was constantly producing something of the sort, and bringing it round to his friends, with a sly chuckle at the humour, which, though his own, no one enjoyed more than himself.

I remember Maxwell coming to me one morning with a copy of verses beginning—" Gin a body meet a body Going through the air," in which he had twisted the well-known song into a description of the laws of impact of solid bodies.

There was also a description which Maxwell wrote of some University ceremony, I forget what, in which somebody " went before," and somebody " followed after," and " in the midst were the wranglers playing with the symbols."

These last words, however meant, were in fact a description of his own wonderful power. I remember one day in lecture, our lecturer had filled the black board three times with the investigation of some hard problem in Geometry of Three Dimensions, and was not at the end of it, when Maxwell came up with a question whether it would not come out geometrically, and showed how with a figure, and in a few lines, there was the solution at once.[1]

Maxwell was, I daresay you remember, very fond of a talk upon almost anything. He and I were pupils (at an enormous distance apart) of Hopkins, and I well recollect how, when I had been working the night before and all the morning at Hopkins's problems with little or no result, Maxwell would come in for a gossip, and talk on while I was wishing him far away, till at last, about half an hour or so before our meeting at Hopkins's, he would say—" Well, I must go to old Hop's problems ;" and by the time we met there they were all done.

I remember Hopkins telling me, when speaking of Maxwell, either just before or just after his degree, " It is not possible for that man to think incorrectly on physical subjects ;" and Hopkins, as you know, had had perhaps more experience of mathematical minds than any man of his time.

Of Maxwell's geniality and kindness of heart you will have had many instances. Every one who knew him at Trinity can recall some kindness or some act of his which has left an in-

---

[1] Compare Plato, *Theæt*. 147, C D. A Cambridge friend who knew Maxwell at a later time, says of him, " One striking characteristic was remarked by his contemporaries at Hopkins's lectures. Whenever the subject admitted of it he had recourse to diagrams, though the rest might solve the question more easily by a train of analysis."

effaceable impression of his goodness on the memory—for "good" Maxwell was, in the best sense of the word.

Mr. Lawson adds the following extract from his diary :—

Under date January 1, 1854 (Sunday evening), after saying I had been at tea at a friend's rooms, and naming the men who were there, of whom Maxwell was one, there is this note :—

"Maxwell, as usual, showing himself acquainted with every subject upon which the conversation turned. I never met a man like him. I do believe there is not a single subject on which he cannot talk, and talk well too, displaying always the most curious and out-of-the-way information."

1854.   The great contests of January came at last, with the
Æt. 22. result that Maxwell was Second Wrangler, Routh of Peterhouse being the Senior, and that Routh and Maxwell were declared equal as Smith's Prizemen.

A reminiscence of Professor T. S. Baynes which has reference to this time is interesting in connection with other signs of something exceptional in Maxwell's physical state during the previous year :—

He said that on entering the Senate-house for the first paper he felt his mind almost blank ; but by and by his mental vision became preternaturally clear. And, on going out again, he was dizzy and staggering, and was some time in coming to himself.

LETTERS, 1852-53.

To LEWIS CAMPBELL, Esq.

8 King's Parade, 10th Feb. 1852.

Æt. 20. . . I was at Isaac Taylor's to-night. His father has come to see him, a little, cold man, with a tremulous voice, who talks about the weather as if he were upon oath, but who can lift up his testimony against any unwarrantable statement. Taylor junr. and Maclennan were talking about associations of workmen, Christian socialism, and so forth. T. junr. approved of the system where each workman has a share in the firm. M. liked one master better than many.

T. senr. described the inducement to hard work among engineers at Manchester ; the reward is not profit, but situation.

There are advantages in subordination, besides good direction, for it supplies an *end* to each man, external to himself.   Activity requires Objectivity.—Do you ever read books written by women about women ?   I mean fictitious tales, illustrating Moral Anatomy, by disclosing all thoughts, motives, and secret sins, as if the authoress were a perjured confessor.   There you find all the good thinking about themselves, and plotting self-improvement from a sincere regard to their own interest, while the bad are most disinterestedly plotting against or for others, as the case may be ; but all are caged in and compelled to criticise one another till nothing is left, and you exclaim :—

> " Madam ! if I know your sex,
> By the fashion of your bones."

No wonder people get hypochondriac if their souls are made to go through manœuvres before a mirror.   Objectivity alone is favourable to the free circulation of the soul.   But let the Object be real and not an Image of the mind's own creating, for Idolatry is Subjectivity with respect to gods.   Let a man feel that he is wide awake,—that he has something to do, which he has authority, power, and will to do, and is doing ; but let him not cherish a consciousness of these things as if he had them at his command, but receive them thankfully and use them strenuously, and exchange them freely for other objects.   He has then a happiness which may be increased in degree, but cannot be altered in kind.

To the Same.

8 King's Parade, 7th March 1852.

I have now nobody that I see too much of, though I have got several new acquaintances, and improved several old ones. I find nothing gives one greater *inertia* than knowing a good many men at a time, who do not know each other intimately. *N.B.—Inertia,* not = *laziness,* but *mass ; i.e.* if one knows a man, he forms an idea of your character, and treats you accordingly. If one knows a company of men, they are strong in union, and overawe the individual.   If one man only, we become mutual tyrants.   If several independently, every one plays the part of Dr. Watt's celebrated " Busy Bee," and by mixing according to every possible combination hit out the best results.   Now you see I am theorising again and preaching as of old ; but the fact is, I am always laying plans and preaching to myself till I seek for some one to whom I may disgorge without fear of an imme-

diate reply. Now, my great plan, which was conceived of old,
and quickens and kicks periodically, and is continually making
itself more obtrusive, is a plan of *Search* and *Recovery*, or Revision
and Correction, or Inquisition and Execution, etc. The Rule of
the Plan is to let nothing be wilfully left unexamined. Nothing
is to be *holy ground* consecrated to Stationary Faith, whether
positive or negative. All fallow land is to be ploughed up, and
a regular system of rotation followed. All creatures as agents
or as patients are to be pressed into the service, which is never
to be willingly suspended till nothing more remains to be done;
i.e. till A.D. $+ \infty$. The part of the rule which respects self-
improvement by means of others is :—Never hide anything, be
it weed or no, nor seem to wish it hidden. So shall all men
passing by pluck up the weeds and brandish them in your face,
or at least display them for your inspection (especially if you
make no secret of your intention to do likewise). (I speak not
here literally of the case of those who revise each other's faults
every night, and quarrel before the month is out, but you did
not so misunderstand me.) Again I assert the Right of Trespass
on any plot of Holy Ground which any man has set apart (as
the rustics did their Gude-man's Rig) to the power of Darkness.
Such places must be exorcised and desecrated till they become
fruitful fields. Again, if the holder of such property refuse
admission to the exorcist, he *ipso facto* admits that it is consecrated, and that he fears the power of Darkness. It may be
that no such darkness really broods over the place, and that the
man has got a habit of shutting his eyes in that field, which
makes him think so.

Now I am convinced that no one but a Christian can actually
purge his land of these holy spots. Any one may profess that
he has none, but something will sooner or later occur to every
one to show him that part of his ground is not open to the
public. Intrusions on this are resented, and so its existence is
demonstrated. Now, I do not say that no Christians have
enclosed places of this sort. Many have a great deal, and every
one has some. No one can be sure of all being open till all has
been examined by competent persons, which is the work, as I
said before, of eternity. But there are extensive and important
tracts in the territory of the Scoffer, the Pantheist, the Quietist,
Formalist, Dogmatist, Sensualist, and the rest, which are openly
and solemnly *Tabooed*, as the Polynesians say, and are not to be
spoken of without sacrilege.

Christianity—that is, the religion of the Bible—is the only scheme or form of belief which disavows any possessions on such a tenure. Here alone all is free. You may fly to the ends of the world and find no God but the Author of Salvation. You may search the Scriptures and not find a text to stop you in your explorations.

You may read all History and be compelled to wonder but not to doubt.

Compare the God of Abraham, Isaac, and Jacob with the God of the Prophets and the God of the Apostles, and however the Pantheist may contrast the God of Nature with the "Dark Hebrew God," you will find them much liker each other than either like his.

The Old Testament and the Mosaic Law and Judaism are commonly supposed to be "Tabooed" by the orthodox. Sceptics pretend to have read them, and have found certain witty objections and composed several transcendental arguments against "Hebrew O' Clo'," which too many of the orthodox unread admit, and shut up the subject as haunted. But a Candle is coming to drive out all Ghosts and Bugbears. Let us all follow the Light.

To Miss Cay.

8 King's Parade, 23d March 1852.

I received yours (of the 18th I suppose) on Saturday, and began to muse on the difference of our modes of life : your sickness—my health ; your kind dealings with neighbours—our utter independence of each other ; you visit without seeing people—we see without visiting each other ; you hear all about people's families and domestic concerns—we do not, but we know exactly how everybody is up in his different subjects, and what are his favourite pursuits for the time.

The Little-go is now going on, so I am taking my Easter vacation at this time. I do nothing but the papers in the Senate-house, and then spend the day in walks and company, reading books of a pleasant but not too light kind, lest I should be disgusted with recreation.

I find myself quite at grass, and am sure that in 10 days I will be reading again as if I had been rusticated for a year.

I never did such a feat as get up at 5 in the morning. I get up at 6.30 for chapel in winter, and read in the daytime, but I have now begun my summer practice of sleeping in the mornings and reading at night, save when I get up on a fine day to take a walk in the morning, which makes me idle all day, and is sometimes agreeable.

I met old Isaac Taylor in his son's rooms some time ago He began by speaking of the weather in a serious way, and went on to his Manchester concerns,—effective motives to work, actual methods adopted, and so got into the merits of socialism, joint-stock workmen's associations, and so forth, appearing all the while to say nothing, but quietly feed on the wisdom of the undergrads., as they enounced their opinions.

FROM HIS FATHER.

Glenlair, 10th April 1852.

The Ordnance Surveyors are doing Contour Lines. The line 250 feet above sea-level passes just in front of the Bees.[1]

Glenlair, 25th April 1852.

I . . . congratulate you on your scholarship. You write of entering on the duties,—what are they ? and what are the Privileges and Profits ?

Glenlair, 12th May 1852.

Is M'Millan the Publisher of the *Cambridge and Dublin*, whereof William Thomson is editor ? Have you sent him your prop. you were doing at Christmastime ?

The gold-fever of Australian type prevails in these parts.

Glenlair, 19th May 1852.

[Prop. about resistance of sides and bottom of a meal-ark.]

. . . The meal, which may be called a fluid as much as a glacier.[2]

Query : Whether by putting bars beneath the bottom at points removed from the middle of the joist, the pressure would be more advantageously distributed ?

Glenlair, 12th June 1852.

[Eve of James C. M.'s 21st birthday.]

I trust you will be as discreet when major as you have been while minor (Prov. x. 1).

Remember me to Tait. I am sorry I did not see him in Edinburgh to wish him joy of his honours.

---

[1] In the garden at Glenlair.   [2] See above, p. 57.

Glenlair, 29th June 1852.

Did you take to the Geology at all ? I suppose that the Æt. 21.
cliffs at Lowestoft are Tertiary, with plenty of fossils.

Glenlair, 9th Novr. 1852.

Nativity of the Prince of Wales.

Received yours of St. Guy and William.

The Cambridge Commission as you report of it will not
affect you in any way.

What sort of thing is "College Declamation" ? You say
you have chosen The Scottish Covenanters. Do you take the
part of Advocate or Apologist for them ? or do you try the
impartial historian ? It would be difficult to give the Scots
Prelates their due without offending some of the Order. During
the Persecutions both the civil and ecclesiastical government of
Scotland was getting ripe for the Revolution.

Glenlair, 11th Novr. 1852.

It has been said, Had there been two other Leightons instead
of Sharp of St. Andrews and —— —— of Galloway, Episcopacy
would have been securely established.

⁖ Glenlair, 2d Feb. 1853.

Aunty Jane was saying—a glass of wine daily,—port for
preference.

Glenlair, 12th Feb. 1853.

. . . *Mathematical Journal,* to which you send props. What
props. ? The one about the Pendulum ?

To LEWIS CAMPBELL, Esq.

Trin. Coll., 20th Feb. 1853.

After Chapel I was at Litchfield's, where he, Farrar, Pomeroy,
and Blakiston, discussed eternal punishment from 8 to 12. Men
fall into absurdity as soon as they have settled for themselves
the question of the origin of evil. A man whose mind is "made
up" on that subject is contradictory on every other ; one day
he says that the man that can be happy in such a world is a
brute, and the next day that if a man is not happy here he is
a moping fool. At last they assert the Cretan dilemma, that if

K

a man says that man is ignorant and foolish, it was ignorant and foolish to say so. Solomon, they say, was used up when he wrote Ecclesiastes, and said "all is vanity" in a relative sense, having himself been so. Solomon describes the search after Happiness for its own sake and for the sake of possession. It is as if a strong man should collect into his house all the beauty of the world, and be condemned to look out of the window and marvel that no good thing was to be seen. "No man can eat his cake and have it." I would add that what remains till to-morrow will stink.

As for evil being unripe good, I say nothing with respect to objective evil, except that it is a part of the universe which it may be the business of immortal man to search out for ever, and still see more beyond. We cannot understand it because it is relative, and relative to more than we know. But subjective evil is absolute ; we are conscious of it as independent of external circumstances ; its physical *power* is bounded by our finitude, bodily and mental, but within these its *intensity* is without measure. A bullet may be diverted from its course by the medium through which it passes, or it may take a wrong one owing to the unskilfulness of the shooter, or the intended victim may change his place ; but all this depends, not on the will of the shooter, but on the ignorance of his mind, the weakness of his body, the resistance of inert matter, or the subsequent act of another agent ; the bullet of the murderer may be turned aside to drive a nail, or what not, but his will is independent of all this, and may be judged at once without appeal.

> Yet still the lady shook her head,
>   And swore by yea and nay,
> My whole was all that he had said,
>   And all that he could say.

J. C. MAXWELL.

FROM HIS FATHER.

Edinburgh, 21st February 1853.

The Halo and accompaniment of the 15th had been very curious. I never saw the appearance of Mock Suns.

Lord Cockburn went in plain dress to the fancy ball. When the crowd hissed him, he said he was the minister that was to marry them all ! !

To Miss Cay.

Trin. Coll., 11th March 1853.

I was so much among the year that is now departed that it makes a great difference in my mode of life. I have been seeking among the other years for some one to keep me in order. It is easier to find instructive men than influential ones. I left off here last night to go to a man's rooms where I met several others, who had gone a-prowling like me. . . . I have been reading Archdeacon Hare's sermons, which are good.

Trin. Coll., Feast of St. Charles II.

Pomeroy's mother and sister were up here lately. They used to be at Cheltenham. From them I learnt a good deal about the systematic and uncompromising mode of thinking and speaking which marks the great Irish Giant of Trinity. Bishop Selwyn of New Zealand prought [1] here yesterday about missions. He founded the Lady Margaret boat club at John's, and got the boat to the head of the river. He was 2d Classic in 1831, and still he is too energetic for his curates to keep up with him in his own visitations about the South Pole. He made a great impression on the men here by his plainness of speech and absence of all cant, whether he spoke of the doctrines of Christianity or the history of Pitcairn's Island. I have been reading various books, but few very entertaining. They are chiefly theories about things in general which take the fancies of men nowadays. The only safe way to read them is to find out the facts first. With this precaution they are tolerably transparent. I have been attending Sir James Stephen's lectures upon the causes of the first French Revolution. They are now done, so I look in upon Stokes' dealing with light.

From his Father.

Edinburgh, 13th March 1853.

Ask Gedge to get you instructions to Brummagem workshops. View, if you can, armourers, gunmaking and gunproving—swordmaking and proving—*Papier-mâché* and japanning—silver-plating by cementation and rolling—ditto, electrotype, Elkington's Works—Brazier's works, by founding and by striking up in dies—turning—spinning teapot bodies in white metal, etc.—

---

[1] *i.e.* preached.

making buttons of sorts, steel pens, needles, pins, and any sorts
of small articles which are curiously done by subdivision of
labour and by ingenious tools—glass of sorts is among the works
of the place, and all kinds of foundry work—engine-making—
tools and instruments (optical and philosophical) both coarse
and fine.   If you have had enough of the town lots of Birmingham, you could vary the recreation by viewing Kenilworth,
Warwick, Leamington, Stratford-on-Avon, or suchlike.[1]

Glenlair, 29th April 1853.

You write (from King Edward's School, Birmingham) about
plans and visits, Freshman Tayler and two others innominate.

Glenlair, 12th May 1853.

What do you know of Henry Mackenzie? Do you find
Frank to be clever, good, agreeable, and wise, which you state
to be the desiderata for a friend ?

Here is a Prop. anent fuel.   What would be the amount of
heat evolved in the combustion of a given weight of dry wood
compared with the same weight of coal ?

*Glenlair, The Day after the Wedding,[2]
1st June (1853).*

I have yours of the day of the Restoration. . . . She (Maria
Clerk) also wrote about the new phase of animal magnetism
called Table-turning.   Do you know about that ?

Photography is also in the ascendant.   You will, no doubt,
be at Ipswich, I believe an ancient city, and hath old kirks and
sundries worthy of notice.   Is Otley towards the sea? Douking,
etc. ?

To Miss Cay.

Trin. Coll., 7th June 1853.

I have an engagement to go and visit a man in Suffolk, but
the spare bed is at present occupied by the "celebrated Dr. Ting
of America." I only wait here for his departure. I spent to-day
in a great sorting of papers and arranging of the same.   Much
is bequeathed to the bedmaker, and a number of duplicate
examination papers are laid up to give to friends.

I intend to-morrow to get up early and make breakfast for

---

[1] This letter has been quoted above, p. 5, note.
[2] Viz. of Elizabeth M'Keand (see above, p. 30).

all the men who are going down, wakening them in good time ;
then read Wordsworth's *Prelude* till sleepy ; then sally forth
and see if all the colleges are shut up for the season ; and then
go and stroll in the fields and fraternise with the young frogs
and old water-rats. In the evening, something not mathematical.
Perhaps write a biographical sketch of Dr. Ting of America, of
whom you know as much as I do. To-morrow evening, or next
day, our list comes out. You will hear of it from the Robertsons
if in town, or Mackenzie if not. I have done better papers than
those of this examination ; but if the examiners are not satisfied
with them it is not my fault, for they are better than they have
yet seen of mine. If any one asks how I am getting on in
mathematics, say that I am busy arranging everything so as to
be able to express all distinctly, so that examiners may be satisfied now and pupils edified hereafter. It is pleasant work and
very strengthening, but not nearly finished.

From his Father.

Glenlair, 24th June 1853.

I have just received your letter and Mr. Tayler's. You Æt. 22.
may be sure I am thankful to hear of your recovering, although
not previously made anxious about the illness. I cannot but
think of the fever fit you had in Edinburgh after an Academy
exam., when we had settled to go to Melrose—that was in 1846.[1]
Nothing can exceed the kindness of Mr. and Mrs. Tayler, and
I hope you will not need long nursing. If you are well and
not much hindered, you can let me know more fully how you
are getting on. Neither you nor Mr. Tayler mention the day
you were taken ill. Mr. T.'s letter is dated 22d.

Glenlair, 28th June 1853.

I am most thankful and happy to hear of your convalescence
through Mr. Tayler's most kind and daily bulletins. I know
not how sufficiently to thank Mr. and Mrs. Tayler for their very
great kindness. I think you may be best to come home, when
fit to travel, for further recreation.

---

[1] From the Diary :—"*1846, July, W., 29.*—(Day of the prize-giving
at the Edinburgh Academy.) Made all ready to start on journey to-morrow
morning. At night James complained of the light of the candle hurting
his eyes. *Th. 30.*—Bad, wet day. Jas. awoke at six ; eyes weak and
headache ; . . . seems to be a disorder from excitement of school
examinations."

Glenlair, 1st July 1853.

Mr. Tayler says, both truly and kindly, "You must be his guest till you are fit to travel." . . .

With yours I have Mr. Tayler's letter of 28th. I do not write to him to-day. My only subject is thanks, and these are not to be measured in words—the strongest that I can use ; so at present give my respects and highest regards.

To the Rev. C. B. Tayler.

Trin. Coll., 8th July 1853.
Evening Post.

My dear Friend—Your letter was handed to me by the postman as I was taking a walk after morning chapel. As I was engaged then, I thought I might wait till the evening. I breakfasted with Macmillan the publisher, who has a man called Alexander Smith with him, who published a volume of poems in the beginning of the year which have been much read here, and, indeed, everywhere, for 3000 copies have been sold already. He is a designer of patterns for needlework, and he refuses to be made celebrated or to leave his trade. He speaks strong Glasgow, but without affectation, and is well-informed without the pretence of education, commonly so called. People would not expect from such a man a book in which the author seems to transfer all his own states of mind to the objects he sees. But he is young and may get wiser as he gets older. He sees and can tell of the beauty of things, but he connects them artificially. He may come to prefer the real and natural connection, and after that he may perhaps stir us all up by bringing before us real human objects of interest he has only dimly seen in the solitude of his youth.

I told you how I meant to go to Hopkins. He was not in. I had a talk with him on Sunday ; he recommended light work for a while, and afterwards he would give me an opportunity of making up what I had lost by absence. Yesterday I did a paper of his on the Differential Calculus without fatigue, and as well as usual. Ask George how Mr. Hughes has arranged about Examinations. I will write to him soon, and send him a mass of papers in an open packet, to be taken twice a week, or not so often.

You dimly allude to the process of spoiling which has gone

on during the last 2 years. I admit that people have been kind to me, and also that I have seen more variety than in other years ; but I maintain that all the evil influences that I can trace have been internal and not external, you know what I mean—that I have the capacity of being more wicked than any example that man could set me, and that if I escape, it is only by God's grace helping me to get rid of myself, partially in science, more completely in society,—but not perfectly except by committing myself to God as the instrument of His will, not doubtfully, but in the certain hope that that Will will be plain enough at the proper time. Nevertheless, you see things from the outside directly, and I only by reflexion, so I hope that you will not tell me you have *little* fault to find with me, without finding that little and communicating it.

In the *Athenæum* of the 2d there is Faraday's account of his experiments on Table-turning, proving mechanically that the table is moved by the unconscious pressure of the fingers of the people wishing it to move, and proving besides that Table-turners may be honest. The consequence has been that letters are being written to Faraday boastfully demanding explanations of this, that, and the other thing, as if Faraday had made a proclamation of Omniscience. Such is the fate of men who make real experiments in the popular occult sciences,—a fate very easy to be borne in silence and confidence by those who do not depend on popular opinion, or learned opinion either, but on the observation of Facts in rational combination. Our anti-scientific men here triumph over Faraday.

I hope the Rectory has flourished during the absence of you and Mrs. Tayler. I had got into habits with you of expecting things to happen, and if I wake at night I think the gruel is coming.

Macmillan was talking to me to-day about elementary books of natural science, and he had found the deficiency, but had a good report of " Philosophy in Sport made Science in Earnest," which I spoke of with you. When I am settled I will put down some first principles and practicable experiments on Light for Charlie, who is to write to me and answer questions proposed ; but this in good time.—Your affectionate friend,

J. C. MAXWELL.

To LEWIS CAMPBELL, Esq.

Trin. Coll., 14th July 1853.

You wrote just in time for your letter to reach me as I reached Cambridge. After examination I went to visit the Rev. C. B. Tayler (uncle to a Tayler whom I think you have seen under the name of *Freshman*, etc., and author of many tracts and other didactic works). We had little expedites, and walks, and things parochial and educational, and domesticity. I intended to return on the 18th June, but on the 17th I felt unwell, and took measures accordingly to be well again—*i.e.* went to bed, and made up my mind to recover. But it lasted more than a fortnight, during which time I was taken care of beyond expectation (not that I did not expect much before). When I was perfectly useless, and could not sit up without fainting, Mr. Tayler did everything for me in such a way that I had no fear of giving trouble. So did Mrs. Tayler; and the two nephews did all they could. So they kept me in great happiness all the time, and detained me till I was able to walk about, and got back strength. I returned on the 4th July.

The consequence of all this is that I correspond with Mr. Tayler, and have entered into bonds with the nephews, of all of whom more hereafter. Since I came here I have been attending Hop., but with his approval did not begin full swing. I am getting on, though, and the work is not grinding on the prepared brain.

I have been reading *Villette* by Currer Bell *alias* Miss Brontë. I think the authoress of Jane Eyre has not ceased to think and acquire principles since that work left her hands.

It is autobiographic in form. The *ego* is a personage of great self-knowledge and self-restraint, strength of principle and courage when roused, otherwise preferring the station of an onlooker.

Then there is an excellent prying, upright, Jesuitical, and successful French school directress; a fiery, finical, physiognomic professor, priestridden, but taking his own way in benevolence as in other things, etc. etc.

Faraday's experiments on Table-turning, and the answers of provoked believers and the state of opinion generally, show what the state of the public mind is with respect to the *principles* of natural science. The law of gravitation and the wonderful effects of the electric fluid are things which you can ascertain by asking any man or woman not deprived by penury or exclusiveness of ordinary information. But they believe them just as they believe history, because it is in books and is not doubted. So that facts in natural science are believed on account of the number of witnesses, as they ought ! I believe that tables are turned ; yea ! and by an unknown force called, if you please, the vital force, acting, as believers say, thro' the fingers. But how does it affect the table ? By the *mechanical* action of the sideward pressure of the fingers in the direction the table ought to go, as Faraday has shown. At this last statement the Turners recoil.

To R. B. LITCHFIELD, Esq.

Coniston, 23d August 1853.

I came here with Campbell of Trin. Hall to meet his brother and another Oxford man called Christie.[1] We are all in a house[2] just above the lake, recreating ourselves and reading a little. Pomeroy is off to Ireland. I have seen a good deal of him, and we have read " at the same time successively" *Vestiges of Creation* and Maurice's *Theological Essays*. Both have excited thought and talk. . . . I was down after the Mug[3] with Tayler's uncle in Suffolk, and was taken in there. I was there made acquainted with the peculiar constitution of a well-regulated family, consisting entirely of nephews and nieces, and educated entirely by the uncle and aunt. There was plenty of willing obedience, but little diligence : much mutual trust, and little self-reliance. They did not strike out for themselves in different lines, according to age, sex, and disposition, but each so excessively sympathised (*bonâ fide*, of course) with the rest, that one could not be surprised at hearing any one take part in criticising his own action.

In such a case some would recommend " a little wholesome neglect." I would suggest something like the scheme of self-emancipation for slaves. Let each member of the family be allowed some little province of thought, work, or study, which is not to be too much inquired into or sympathised with or encouraged by the rest, and let the limits of this be enlarged till he has a wide, free field of independent action, which increases

---

[1] W. Christie, Esq., advocate.   [2] Bank-ground.
[3] Trinity College Examination.

the resources of the family so much the more as it is peculiarly his own.

I see daily more and more reason to believe that the study of the "dark sciences" is one which will repay investigation. I think that what is called the proneness to superstition in the present day is much more significant than some make it. The prevalence of a misdirected tendency proves the misdirection of a prevalent tendency. It is the nature and object of this tendency that calls for examination.

To LEWIS CAMPBELL, Esq.

Glenlair, 15th September 1853.

I see that Principal Jelf is going to "have up" Maurice for heresy published in his *Theological Essays.* The consequence will probably be that some others unconnected with Maurice will be set upon, and will perhaps join with him in self-defence, or at least be associated with him in popular opinion.

If the row becomes general it will be *the* controversy of the day. They have no firm and dogmatic statements to grapple with, but they will soon make them. All the ordinary disputes have been revivals of the *letter* of old contests. Here we have the very spirit of all reformations ; an attempt must be made to find what is requisite to a Christian system, and whether the "variables" of such a system ought to remain constant, as they were at some arbitrary epoch (that of sect-founders, Fathers, General Councils, Reformers, etc.), and not rather to be trusted to the true and approved Christians of every age.

But he that is misty let him be misty still, and the same for him that is shallow ; but let him that is active not mar his activity by "tearing his neighbours in their slime," or by ascending into the thick mist and walking with "Death and Morning on the silver horns."

FROM HIS FATHER.

Glenlair, 10th October 1853.

I have set up the rain-gauge in the middle of the garden at the crossing of the gooseberry bushes at the Camomile. I think it will do.

As to changing your rooms—I suppose from that, you have settled to continue for a time at Cambridge and to look out for a fellowship.

Glenlair, 28th October 1853.

Be sure to keep a long way within your powers of working, and then you may do well whatever you undertake.

Glenlair, 13th November 1853.

Your letter was chiefly a dissertation on the election of Examinators ; the names were all strange to me, except our old friend Charles Mackenzie.

To Miss Cay.

Trin. Coll., 12th November 1853.

I am in a regular state of health though not a very regular state of reading, for I hold that it is a pernicious practice to read when one is not inclined for it. So I read occasionally for a week and then miss a few days, always remembering to do whatsoever College and Hopkins prescribe to be done, and avoiding anything more. Allan Stewart was up a week ago to be made a bye Fellow of Peterhouse, so you may congratulate him when you see him. He is to be in Edinburgh this winter. Frank Mackenzie is up, and seems pretty well. He tells me that he does not sit up late ; but as I have not the management of his candles I do not know what that means with him. I have not been up after twelve for a long time except on Saturdays when I am not reading. . . . You will have heard how the Council of King's College have sat upon Professor Maurice and intend to turn him out of the college. So there are pamphlets and replies on the meaning of the word "Eternal," and broadsides of the Record on the SIDE of the attack. I see that the Rev. Berkeley Addison is in trouble about the Scottish Reformation Society, for associating with non-episcopal clergymen. .

To Lewis Campbell, Esq.

Trin. Coll., 3d Dec. 1853.

. . . We have the usual amount of discussion here on labour parliaments, multiplicity of votes, Eternity and Maurice and Jelf, or the contest between those who think that there is a real depth to which thought must go, though words cannot well follow it, and those who maintain that that which is not obvious to a man of sense, cannot be really connected with a religion which is not confined to deep thinkers, but professes to afford the highest principles to the simple. That is what most men

discuss. Maurice has settled it for himself, believing that the
things of which he treats do actually form the necessary thoughts
of all men whether learned or no.

FROM HIS FATHER.

Glenlair, 16th December 1853.

I knew Thomas Erskine of Linlathen very well long ago.
He and his mother and sisters lived in No. 30 Heriot Row.   He
came to the Bar in Edinburgh the year before me.   He is related
to George Dundas, and Stirlings, and Erskines, and many
families we visited.   For long he has lived at Linlathen, near
Dundee, and is author of various religious books.

Your dissertation on the parties in the Church of England
goes far beyond my knowledge.   I would need an explanatory
lecture first, and before I can follow the High, Broad, and Low,
through their ramifications.

Penicuik, 30th December /53.

You will need to get muffetees for the Senate-Room.   Take
your plaid or rug to wrap round your feet and legs.

TO MISS CAY.

Trin. Coll., 13th January 1854.

All my correspondents have been writing to me, which is
kind, and have not been writing questions, which is kinder.
So I answer you now, while I am slacking speed to get up
steam, leaving Lewis and Stewart, etc., till next week, when I
will give an account of the *five days*.   There are a good many
up here at present, and we get on very jolly on the whole, but
some are not well, and some are going to be plucked or gulphed,
as the case may be, and others are reading so hard that they are
invisible.   I go to-morrow to breakfast with shaky men, and
after food I am to go and hear the list read out, and whether
they are through, and bring them word.   When the honour list
comes out the poll-men act as messengers.   Bob Campbell comes
in occasionally of an evening now, to discuss matters and vary
sports.   During examination I have had men at night working
with gutta-percha, magnets, etc.   It is much better than reading
novels or talking after $5\frac{1}{2}$ hours' hard writing.

Hunter is up here all the vacation.   Do you know anything
of him in Edinburgh?   His father, who is dead, or his uncle,

were known in Edinburgh, but I am not up in that subject.
The present man is a freshman at Queen's, and is a thundering
mathematician, is well informed on political, literary, and speculative subjects, and is withal a jolly sort of fellow with some
human nature at the bottom, and lots of good humour all
through. He does not talk much, and when he does it is broad
Scotch and to the purpose. I hope to see more of him next
term. Old Charlie Robertson is in better case I think than
usual, and rejoices in the good opinion of several men whose
opinion is most worth having. He has become better known
and better estimated of late, especially since Sandy[1] came up.
He did pretty well in the three days, and does not fret about
anything. The snow here is nearly gone, and it looks like
frost again. I have never missed a long tramp through the
slush day by day. When one is well soaked in a snow wreath,
cleaned and dried, and put beside a good fire, with bread and
butter and problems, one can eat and grind like a miller. . . .
I have been reading a book of poems called *Benoni*, by Arthur
Munby of Trinity, which are above the common run of such
things (not *Lorenzo Benoni*, illustrated by J. B., which I have
seen but not read). Have you seen the *Black Brothers*, a small
book of Ruskin's, illustrated by Doyle ;—a good child's book,
which big people ought to read.

From his Father.

18 India St., 30th January 1854.

I heartily congratulate you on your place in the list. I
suppose it is higher than the speculators would have guessed,
and quite as high as Hopkins reckoned on. I wish you success
in the Smith's Prizes ; be sure to write me the result. I will
see Mrs. Morrieson, and I think I will call on Dr. Gloag to
congratulate him. He has at least three pupils gaining honours.

---

[1] Alexander Robertson, Esq., now Sheriff of Forfarshire.

CHAPTER VII.

BACHELOR-SCHOLAR AND FELLOW OF TRINITY— 1854 TO 1856—ÆT. 22-24.

" In the Main of Light."

1854. JAMES CLERK MAXWELL'S position as Second Wrangler
Æt. 22. and equal Smith's Prizeman, gave deep satisfaction to his
friends in Edinburgh. Any lurking wish that he had
been Senior was silenced by the examples of William
Thomson and Charles Mackenzie, as others have been since
consoled with the examples of Maxwell and Clifford. His
father was persuaded by Miss Cay to sit for his portrait to
Sir John Watson Gordon, as a gift of lasting value to his
son. James was not indifferent to these reflex aspects of
his success ; but the chief interest of the moment to him
undoubtedly was that he was now free to prosecute his
life-career, and to use his newly-whetted instruments in
resuming his original investigations. His leisure was not
absolute, for he took pupils as a matter of course, and the
Trinity Fellowship was only to be gained by examination.
But his freedom was as great as he himself desired, and it
is a fact worthy of attention from "researchers," that
Maxwell, with his heart fully set on physical inquiries,
engaged of his own accord in teaching, undertook the task
of examining Cheltenham College, and submitted to the
routine which belonged to his position at Cambridge. As
a foretaste of delights in store, he had spent the evenings
of the Senate-house days in (physico-)magnetic *séances* with
his friends. But when actually emancipated he seems to
have reverted principally at first to his beloved Optics.

He makes inquiries about a microscope manufactory at
Zurich ; reads Berkeley's *Theory of Vision*—taking up Mill's
Logic by the way, and finding there by no means the last
word on the relation of sense to knowledge ; looks up his
stock of coloured papers furnished by D. R. Hay, and sets
to work spinning and weaving the different rays ; inquires
him out colour-blind persons on all sides ; and invents an
instrument for inspecting the living retina, especially of
dogs. By and by it is the Art of Squinting which again
has charms for him, and he combines it with the teaching
of solid and spherical geometry, by drawing wonderful
stereoscopic diagrams. So far, his investigations oscillate
between colour and form. But even the fascination of the
Colour-Top [1] cannot hold him long from searching into the
more hidden things of Matter in Motion. Thus, in his
letter to his father of May 15, 1855, after describing a
successful exhibition of the Top and extemporary statement of his optical theories before the Cambridge Philosophical Society, he adds :—" I am reading Electricity and
working at Fluid Motion." And on May 23—" I am
getting on with my electrical calculations every now and
then, and working out anything that seems to help the
understanding thereof." Some days earlier, May 5, he had

---

[1] The " colour-box," though perfected only in 1862, was in full operation in the study at Glenlair several years before this—I think as early as
1850. And even then he had begun spinning coloured discs, proportion-
ately arranged, so as to ascertain the true " mixture of colours." He was
fond of insisting, to his female cousins, aunts, etc., on the truth that blue
and yellow do not make green. I remember his explaining to me the
difference between pigments and colours, and showing me, through the
" colour-box," that the central band in the spectrum was different from
any of the hitherto so-called " primary colours." His theory on this
subject was gradually formed through an immense number of ingeniously
arranged observations. See Note at end of this chapter, p. 163.

His interest in Faraday's investigations must have dated from a very
early time, certainly before 1849. And now he sought to give to these
speculations, at which his imaginative mind had long been working, precise
mathematical expression. I wish I could recall the date (1857 ?) of a
drive down the Vale of Orr, during which he described to me for the first
time, with extraordinary volubility, the swift, invisible motions by which
magnetic and galvanic phenomena were to be accounted for. It was like
listening to a fairy-tale. For the substance of it see his papers in the
Philosophical Magazine for 1861-62.

written :—"I am working away at Electricity again, and have been working my way into the views of heavy German writers. It takes a long time to reduce to order all the notions one gets from these men, but I hope to see my way through the subject, and arrive at something intelligible in the way of a theory." These brief notices obviously refer to the studies which led up to his important paper on Faraday's Lines of Force, which was put into shape in the winter of 1855-56.

The "vassals" were not forgotten by him even when most occupied at Cambridge. The choice and provision of suitable literature for the consumption of Sam Murdoch and Sandy Fraser is a frequent topic of correspondence between him and his father.

How earnestly he now set himself to make the most of life in a religious sense appears from a sort of aphorism on conduct which he wrote down originally for his own use, and afterwards communicated as a parting gift to his friend Farrar (now Canon of Westminster), who was about to become a master at Marlborough School. As a record of the spirit in which Maxwell entered at three-and-twenty on his independent career, this fragment [1] is of extraordinary value.

1854.   He that would enjoy life and act with freedom must have
Æt. 23. the work of the day continually before his eyes. Not yesterday's work, lest he fall into despair, nor to-morrow's, lest he become a visionary,—not that which ends with the day, which is a worldly work, nor yet that only which remains to eternity, for by it he cannot shape his actions.

Happy is the man who can recognise in the work of To-day a connected portion of the work of life, and an embodiment of the work of Eternity. The foundations of his confidence are unchangeable, for he has been made a partaker of Infinity. He strenuously works out his daily enterprises, because the present is given him for a possession.

---

[1] An autograph copy was found amongst his papers. Another copy, together with the interesting fact mentioned above, determining the date, has been supplied by Canon Farrar's kindness.

Thus ought Man to be an impersonation of the divine process of nature, and to show forth the union of the infinite with the finite, not slighting his temporal existence, remembering that in it only is individual action possible, nor yet shutting out from his view that which is eternal, knowing that Time is a mystery which man cannot endure to contemplate until eternal Truth enlighten it.

Meanwhile in his recreations he was as boyishly agile as ever, and his feats in bathing and gymnastics, though cautiously reported by him, somewhat alarmed his father, whose own health now showed signs of breaking.

His friendships went on multiplying. To the list already given must now be added in particular the names of Hort, V. Lushington, Pomeroy, and Cecil Monro. And his constant observation of character was gaining in fulness and precision. A letter to his father of 21st April 1855, besides referring to a pupil (Platt) who had gained a Trinity scholarship, contains a graphic delineation of several of his coevals who were going in for the first open competition for appointments in the Indian Civil Service. He confides to his father all his thoughts about them, in which speculative and personal interests are combined.

He had soon another outlet for this kind of sympathy. The children of his uncle, Mr. R. Dundas Cay, who had lately returned from Hong-Kong, were advancing in their education, and two of the boys, William and Charles, showed considerable promise in mathematics. He had spent some days with his cousins in the summer vacation of 1854 at Keswick, where there was also a Cambridge reading party under Mathison, the tutor of Trinity. After a joyous time with them he walked home to Galloway from Carlisle, and it was during this walk that he thought out certain improvements in his dynamical top. He took a continuous interest in the progress of his cousins, and prepared a special set of problems for the behoof of Willy, the eldest, who was by this time a student in Edinburgh.

Maxwell continued his contributions to the "Apostle" Essay Club, and on May 5, 1855, he read to them in his own rooms a paper on Morality, in which he summed up the principles and tendencies of the chief existing systems of moral philosophy, so resuming another thread of his earlier thought.[1]

This essay appears to have been promised early in the year, to judge from an allusion to the subject of it in a letter to C. J. Monro of February 7, which may be quoted here as showing also by what home cares his intellectual energies were interrupted or diversified. The reader of what precedes will not be misled by the light way in which he speaks of things which touched his heart so nearly.

I am at present superintending a course of treatment prac- tised on my father, for the sake of relieving certain defluxions which take place in his bronchial tubes. These obstructions are now giving way, and the medico, who is a skilful bellows- mender, pronounces the passages nearly clear.

However, it will be a week or two before he is on his pins again, so would you have the goodness to tell Freeman to tell Mrs. Jones to tell those whom it may concern, that I cannot be up to time at all. . . . I may be up in time to keep the term, and so work off a streak of Mathematics, which I begin to yearn after. At present I confine myself to Lucky Nightingale's line of business, except that I have been writing descriptions of Platometers for measuring plane figures, and privately by letter confuting rash mechanics, who intrude into things they have not got up, and suppose that their devices will act when they can't. I hope that my absence will not delay the assumption of W. D. Maclagan.[2] He has been here all the vacation, if not there and everywhere. The foundation of Ethics, though it may have tickled my core, has not germinated at my vertex. Whether it will yet be laid bare, either as a paradox or a truism, is more than I can tell. Perhaps it may be a pun. . . .

I have now to do a little cooking and buttling, in the shape of toast and beef-tea and everfizzing draught. . . . Does Pomeroy flourish, and has he Crimean letters still?

It was only because his father insisted on his doing so that he returned to Cambridge at all at this time.

At the meeting of the British Association, held at

---

[1] *Supra*, p. 71.

[2] Now Bishop of Lichfield. Maxwell had recommended him for co- optation by the "Apostles'" Club.

Glasgow in September 1855, Maxwell was present when Brewster made an attack on Whewell's optical theories, but he followed the example of the Master of Trinity, who was present, in saying nothing. He exhibited his Colour-Top, however, the same afternoon, by appointment, at Professor Ramsay's house, where Brewster had been expected, but did not appear. Maxwell at the same time renewed his intercourse with Dr. George Wilson, the Edinburgh Professor of Technology, whose likeness hung beside that of Forbes in his rooms at Trinity. Wilson brought out immediately afterwards a little book on Colour Blindness, in which the substance of his conversations with Maxwell is recorded.

In October he gained his fellowship at Trinity. It was his second trial, and his name appeared as one of three mathematicians who had been chosen from the bachelors of the second year. 1855.
Æt. 24.

He was at once appointed to lecture to the Upper Division of the third year in Hydrostatics and Optics, and, to reserve time for his own studies, he now desisted from taking private pupils. He had indeed enough to occupy him without burdening himself with them. Besides the lecture in hydrostatics and optics, for which he found it desirable to read beforehand "so as not to tell lies," he had a large share in "exercising the questionists," *i.e.* preparing pass-men for the final examination, by setting papers in arithmetic, algebra, etc., and looking them over with the writers individually.

He had also been asked to prepare a text-book[1] on optics, and made some plans for doing so, having previously resisted the solicitation of his friend Monro, who had urged upon him the task of "translating Newton." And it is a fact worthy of the attention of bachelor fellows, that young Clerk Maxwell thought it worth while to attend the lectures of the Professor of Mechanics[2] and to exchange ideas with him.

---

[1] The MS. of a considerable part of this book is still extant. There appears to have been sometimes a contest in his mind between the claims of different subjects. "I will have nothing to do with optics," he was heard once to exclaim.   [2] Professor Willis.

For Electricity and Magnetism he took out *Poisson* again, and presently began putting together more systematically his own ideas on Faraday's *Lines of Force.*

His interest in coevals and juniors, which even in his undergraduate days was often like that of an elder brother, assumed a deeper and more authoritative cast. He read more widely than ever, and nothing, from the latest novel to the newest metaphysical system, escaped his penetrating mind. He never read without criticising, and his criticisms, often quaintly expressed, were always worth attending to. "I hope that analysis of Hegel has done the writer good," "Comte has good ideas about method, but no notion of what is meant by a person," "Some people keep watertight compartments in their minds." Such were the sparks that flew about. Other examples, not less striking, will be found in the letters. His observation of social phenomena also took a new departure, and his remarks on life and manners were endlessly entertaining.

He was elected a member of the Ray Club, which he had attended as a visitor in the spring, and did not forsake the assembling of the "Apostles," as appears from at least two essays which can only be referred to this period. He also took an active interest in the scheme for the higher education of working men, which had been lately set on foot by Mr. Maurice.

Between whiles he found time for a full course of classical English reading. And as all that he read he read critically, and had it thereafter in perfect possession, his literary acquirements were by this time of no mean order. He was, at the same time, careful to maintain himself in proper physical condition, by a steady course of exercises at the new gymnasium, which proved a welcome refuge in the wet November of that year. It was an unhealthy season, and to all his other employments was now added that of helping to nurse his friend Pomeroy, who was struck down with bilious fever.

His many-sided nature was in full activity. It is most characteristic of him that at this important crisis of his intellectual life, the best hour of day after day was given ungrudgingly to the task of literally making a friend's bed in his sickness. A lighter trait of the same kind may be found in the fact that, in the midst of the fellowship examination, he had given his father detailed advice about the "vassals'" reading:—"When Sam Murdoch has finished *Arabia*, there are the volumes of the Cabinet Library, called *Drake, Cavendish, and Dampier, and Circumnavigation of the Globe*, Humboldt's *Travels and Polar Regions*, but it would be better to change and try the third volume of *Household Words*."

His thoughts turned homewards the more often, because his father's health was now becoming a matter for grave anxiety. In going up to Trinity for the fellowship trials, he had been doubtful whether in any case it would be right for him to stay up for the rest of the term. And, although this question was decided in the affirmative, every letter home bears some trace of his unceasing solicitude.

Thus, at the close of a period of manifold brightness, there was some foreshadowing of darker days shortly to come, when Death would take his father from him, and make the first breach in the circle of his friends.

LETTERS, 1854 TO 1856.

FROM HIS FATHER.

India Street, 4th Feby. 1854.

I have got yours of the 1st inst., and to-night or on Monday I will expect to hear of the Smith's Prizes. I get congratulations on all hands, including Prof. Kelland and Sandy Fraser, and all others competent.

18 India St., 6th Feby. 1854.

George Wedderburn came into my room at 2 A.M. yesterday morning, having seen the Saturday *Times*, received by the express train, and I got your letter before breakfast yesterday. As you are equal to the Senior in the champion trial, you are but a very little behind him.

I am going to dine with John Cay, and with him proceed to the Royal Society. I may perhaps catch Prof. Gregory about the microscopist.

5th March 1854.

Mrs. Morrieson told me she had a poetical epistle from you on St. David's Day.[1]

Aunt Jane stirred me up to sit for my picture, as she said you wished for it and were entitled to ask for it, quâ wrangler. I have had four sittings to Sir John Watson Gordon, and it is now far advanced ; I think it is very like.   It is Kit-cat size, to be a companion to Dyce's picture of your mother and self, which Aunt Jane says she is to leave to you.

To R. B. LITCHFIELD, Esq.

Trin. Coll., 25th March 1854.

I am experiencing the effects of Mill, but I take him slowly. I do not think him the last of his kind.   I think more is wanted to bring the connexion of sensation with Science to light, and show what it is not.   I have been reading Berkeley on the *Theory of Vision,* and greatly admire it, as I do all his other non-mathematical works ; but I was disappointed to find that he had at last fallen into the snare of his own paradoxes, and thought that his discoveries with regard to the senses and their objects would show some fallacy in those branches of high mathematics which he disliked.   It is curious to see how speculators are led by their neglect of exact sciences to put themselves in opposition to them where they have not the slightest point of contact with their systems.   In the Minute Philosopher there is some very bad Political Economy and much very good thinking on more interesting subjects.   Paradox is still sought for and exaggerated.   We live in an age of wonder still.

To MISS CAY.

Trin. Coll., Whitsun. Eve, 1854.

I am in great luxury here, having but 2 pups., and able to read the rest of the day, so I have made a big hole in some subjects I wish to know.   We have hot weather now, and I am just come from a meeting of subscribers to the Bathing Shed, which we organised into a Swimming Club so as to make it a more sociable affair, instead of mere " pay your money and use your key."

A nightingale has taken up his quarters just outside my

---

[1] Mrs. Morrieson's early home was in Montgomeryshire.

window, and works away every night. He is at it very fierce now. At night the owls relieve him, softly sighing after their fashion.

I have made an instrument for seeing into the eye through the pupil. The difficulty is to throw the light in at that small hole and look in at the same time; but that difficulty is overcome, and I can see a large part of the back of the eye quite distinctly with the image of the candle on it. People find no inconvenience in being examined, and I have got dogs to sit quite still and keep their eyes steady. Dogs' eyes are very beautiful behind, a copper-coloured ground, with glorious bright patches and networks of blue, yellow, and green, with blood-vessels great and small.

Trin. Coll., 24th Novr. /54.

I have been very busy of late with various things, and am just beginning to make papers for the examination at Cheltenham, which I have to conduct about the 11th of December. I have also to make papers to polish off my pups. with. I have been spinning colours a great deal, and have got most accurate results, proving that ordinary people's eyes are all made alike, though some are better than others, and that other people see two colours instead of three; but all those who do so agree amongst themselves. I have made a triangle of colours by which you may make out everything.

You see that W lies outside the triangle B, R, Y, so that

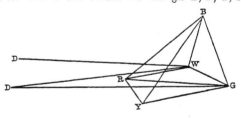

White can't be made with Blue, Red, and Yellow; but if you mix blue and yellow you don't get green, but pink—a colour between W and R. Those who see two colours only distinguish blue and yellow, but not red and green: for instance—

6 of blue and 94 of red make a red which looks to them like a gray made of 10 W and 90 Black.

40 of blue and 60 of green make 34 of W and 66 Black.

I should like you to find out if the Normans have got Bishop Percy's *Reliques of Ancient Ballad Poetry*, for if they have I would not send them a duplicate ; if not I think the book would suit one-half of that family.

If you can find out any people in Edinburgh who do not see colours (I know the Dicksons don't), pray drop a hint that I would like to see them. I have put one here up to a dodge by which he distinguishes colours without fail. I have also constructed a pair of squinting spectacles, and am beginning operations on a squinting man.

To C. J. Monro, Esq.

18 India Street, Edinburgh, 19th Feb. /55.

My steps will be no more by the reedy and crooked till Easter term. My father's recovery is retarded by the frosty weather, though we have got up an ethereal mildness here by means of a good fire and a towel hung up wet at the other end of the room, together with an internal *exhibition* of nitric ether.

I wrote to Mackenzie about putting a respectable man in my rooms as a stopper to Cat's Hall men, Manns and Boy Joneses, but I have not heard of his success. I have no time at present for anything except looking through novels, etc., and finding passages which will not offend my father to read to him. He strongly objects to new-fangled books, and knows the old by heart. But he likes the *Essays in Intervals of Business*, cause why, they have not too many words. The frost here has lasted long, and I am beginning to make use of it. I get an uncle to take my place in the afternoon, and I rush off to Lochend or Duddingston. I have not yet succeeded in skating on one foot for an indefinite time and getting up speed by rising and sinking at the bends of the path ; but I attribute my failure to want of faith, for I can get up speed for a single bend, only I always slip at a certain critical turning. However, I have only been 3 days, and I may do it yet. My plans are not fixt, but I think it will be some while before my father is on his pins again, and when he is I intend to look after him still, but do a private streak of work, for I will soon be in a too much bottled up condition of mathematics, from which even mental collapse would be a relief. I have no intention of doing a Newton or any elegant mathematics. I have a few thoughts on top-spinning and sensation generally, and a kind of dim outline of

Cambridge palavers, tending to shadow forth the influence of mathematical training on opinion and speculation.

I suppose when my father can move I will see him out of this eastern clime and safe located in Gallovidian westnesses, and so be up in Cam. before the beginning of next term.

I should like to know how many kept baccalaurean weeks go to each of these terms, and when they begin and end. Overhaul the calendar, and when found make note of.

Is Pomeroy up, or where ? This is the 2nd time of asking.

To his Father.

Trin. Coll., Saturday, 21st April 1855.
[Date in John C. M.'s hand.]

Lots of men are going in for the H.E.I.C.S. examination,—Pomeroy, B., C., D. (the best double degree for many years), E. (Senior Wrangler), etc., so I suppose the competition will be pretty active ; but it is evident that these men will be totally different judges, etc., tho' they may be all good in examination subjects.

Pomeroy is a genial giant, generous and strong, but hasty in condemnation tho' slow to wrath. B., intelligent and able to detect any humbug but his own ; but excitable, and impudent in the extreme to people he does not know. C. has strong feelings and affections, with a great amount of sympathy for all cases, but it is repressed for want of courage, and he is left with somewhat of a sneaking virtue of his own, always trying to put on the manners which suit those he is with. D. is a good man of business, using up every scrap of his time most successfully, and honest, I believe. E. is what I don't know, but I can conceive him reduced by circumstances to act the part of Sir Elijah Impey in India ; but I hope circumstances may be different, and then he may be a harmless mathematician or scientific referee, and leave a high reputation behind him.

Trin. Coll., Vesp. SS. Philipp. & S. Jac. 1855.

I have been working at the motion of fluids, and have got out some results. I am going to show the colour trick at the Philosophical on Monday. Routh has been writing a book about Newton in conjunction with Lord Brougham. Stokes is back again and lecturing as usual.

Saturday, 5th May 1855.

The Royal Society have been very considerate in sending me my paper on colours just when I wanted it for the Philosophical here. I am to let them see the tricks on Monday evening, and I have been there preparing their experiments in the gas-light. There is to be a meeting in my rooms to-night to discuss Adam Smith's "Theory of Moral Sentiments," so I must clear up my litter presently. I am working away at electricity again, and have been working my way into the views of heavy German writers. It takes a long time to reduce to order all the notions one gets from these men, but I hope to see my way through the subject and arrive at something intelligible in the way of a theory.

Trin. Coll., 15th May 1855.

The colour trick came off on Monday, 7th. I had the proof sheets of my paper, and was going to read ; but I changed my mind and talked instead, which was more to the purpose. There were sundry men who thought that Blue and Yellow make Green, so I had to undeceive them. I have got Hay's book of colours out of the Univ. Library, and am working through the specimens, matching them with the top. I have a new trick of stretching the string horizontally above the top, so as to touch the upper part of the axis. The motion of the axis sets the string a-vibrating in the same time with the re-volutions of the top, and the colours are seen in the haze pro-duced by the vibration. Thomson has been spinning the top, and he finds my diagram of colours agrees with his experiments, but he doubts about browns what is their composition. I have got colcothar brown, and can make white with it, and blue and green ; also, by mixing red with a little blue and green and a great deal of black, I can match colcothar exactly.

I have been perfecting my instrument for looking into the eye. Ware has a little beast like old Ask,[1] which sits quite steady and seems to like being looked at, and I have got several men who have large pupils and do not wish to let me look in. I have seen the image of the candle distinctly in all the eyes I have tried, and the veins of the retina were visible in some ; but the dogs' eyes showed all the ramifications of veins, with glorious blue and green net-work, so that you might copy down everything. I have shown lots of men the image in my own

---

[1] Above, p. 38.

eye by shutting off the light till the pupil dilated and then letting it on.

I am reading Electricity and working at Fluid Motion, and have got out the condition of a fluid being able to flow the same way for a length of time and not wriggle about.

Trin. Coll., Eve of H. M. Nativity.

Wednesday last I went with Hort and Elphinstone to the Ray Club, which met at Kingsley of Sidney's rooms. Kingsley is great in photography and microscopes, and showed photographs of infusoria, very beautiful, also live plants and animals, with oxy-hydrogen microscope.

. . . I am getting on with my electrical calculations now and then, and working out anything that seems to help the understanding thereof.

FROM HIS FATHER.

Glenlair, 21st May 1855.

Have you put a burn in fit condition to flow evenly, and not beat on its banks from side to side? That would be the useful practical application.

FROM PROFESSOR J. D. FORBES.

Clifton, Bristol, 4th May 1855.

I left directions with Messrs. Neill & Co. to forward proofs of your paper, by inquiring at 18 India Street, and I understand that they were sent out on the 1st May.

I am informed that my note to you about some of my experiments on colour has been printed in the *Edinburgh Philosophical Journal*. This was by no means what I intended. . . . What I thought that you might do was to introduce into that part of your paper where you speak of what has been done or written on the subject, mention of the fact that as early as January 18— (I do not at the moment recollect the year I stated to you) I had used the method of rapid motion in blending colours; that I had endeavoured to obtain an equation between certain mixed colours and pure gray; and that I had pointed out before Helmholtz, or I believe any one else, that a mixture of yellow and blue, under these circumstances at least, does not produce green; you yourself being a witness to what I then tried, though I was prevented from resuming the subject by ill health and some experimental occupations (conduction of heat) which I considered more imperative.

I hope you will continue to prosecute your interesting inquiries, and with an equal measure of success.

I address this to Cambridge, as I think you said you should be there this month.

FROM THE SAME.

Clifton, Bristol, 16th May 1855.

I am much obliged by your note mentioning your intention of referring to my experiments.

You inquire how I altered the proportions of the constituent colours. My plan was, in fact, the same as yours. I had sectors much larger than I required of each colour, making them overlap, and fixing them down by a screw at the centre, pressing a disc of indiarubber on the discs. When I got the anomalous result of blue and yellow, I got Mr. Hay to make a disc of *many* alternating narrow sectors merely to see whether it might be a physiological effect from the imperfect blending of the colours.

I still think the experiment ought to be tried *without motion*, by winding blue and yellow threads of silk or worsted round a card and looking at it at a good distance, or (as you proposed) by viewing it with a telescope out of focus.

You will recollect that I had a whirling-machine (made on purpose), in which a number of discs revolved simultaneously with equal velocities. I used black and white on one of these ; colours on another. Your teetotum, combining both, I consider preferable for experiments. By the way, I did not get the teetotum you were to leave for me.

P.S.—I hope you have got the proof of the plate as well as of the paper. If not, write to Messrs. Johnston, engravers, 4 St. Andrew Square, Edinburgh.

To R. B. LITCHFIELD, Esq.

Trin. Coll., 6th June 1855.

It is hard work grinding out "appropriate ideas," as Whewell calls them. However, I think they are coming out at last, and by dint of knocking them against all the facts and $\frac{1}{2}$-digested theories afloat, I hope to bring them to shape, after which I hope to understand something more about inductive philosophy than I do at present.

I have a project of sifting the theory of light and making everything stand upon definite experiments and definite assumptions, so that things may not be supposed to be assumptions when they are either definitions or experiments.

I have been looking into all the dogs' eyes here to see the bright coating at the back of the eye, thro' an instrument I made to that end. The spectacle is very fine. I remember the appearance of Mungo's eyes at Cheltenham. He would be the dog to sit. Human eyes are very dark and brown as to their retina, but you can see the image of a candle quite well on it, and sometimes the blood-vessels, etc.

FROM WILLIAM DYCE CAY, Esq., TO JOHN C. M.

(Glasgow, at the Meeting of the British Association.)

18th September 1855.

Sir David Brewster was upon the triple spectrum. As far as I can understand, he believes the spectrum to be composed of three colours—red, blue, and yellow; and that the intermediate colours are composed of mixtures of these, as, for example, the green from a mixture of blue and yellow, which, I think, is different from what James believes. James did not say anything in the controversy which followed his speech, as he was to meet Sir D. Brewster at the Ramsays' afterwards, where he would have his top and other apparatus to show him.

TO HIS FATHER.

(After the Meeting of the British Association at Glasgow.)

Holbrooke, by Derby, 24th Sept. 1855.

We had a paper from Brewster on the theory of three colours in the spectrum, in which he treated Whewell with philosophic pity, commending him to the care of Prof. Wartman of Geneva, who was considered the greatest authority in cases of his kind, cases in fact of colour-blindness. Whewell was in the room, but went out, and avoided the quarrel; and Stokes made a few remarks, stating the case not only clearly but courteously. However, Brewster did not seem to see that Stokes admitted his experiments to be correct, and the newspapers represented Stokes as calling in question the accuracy of the experiments.

I am getting my electrical mathematics into shape, and I
see through some parts which were rather hazy before ; but I
do not find very much time for it at present, because I am
reading about heat and fluids, so as not to tell lies in my lectures.
I got a note from the Society of Arts about the platometer,
awarding thanks, and offering to defray the expenses to the
extent of £10, on the machine being produced in working order.
When I have arranged it in my head I intend to write to James
Bryson about it.

I got a long letter from Thomson about colours and electricity.
He is beginning to believe in my theory about all colours being
capable of reference to three standard ones, and he is very glad
that I should poach on his electrical preserves.

Trin. Coll., 27th Sept. 1855.

. . . It is difficult to keep up one's interest in intellectual
matters when friends of the intellectual kind are scarce.[1] However, there are plenty friends not intellectual, who serve to bring
out the active and practical habits of mind, which overly-intel-
lectual people seldom do. Wherefore, if I am to be up this
term, I intend to addict myself rather to the working men who
are getting up classes, than to pups., who are in the main a
vexation. Meanwhile there is the examination [2] to consider.

Trin. Coll., 5th October 1855.

You say Dr. Wilson has sent his book. I will write and
thank him. I suppose it is about colour-blindness. I intend
to begin Poisson's papers on electricity and magnetism to-morrow.
I have got them out of the library ; my reading hitherto has
been of novels,—*Shirley* and *The Newcomes*, and now *Westward
Ho.*

Trin. Coll., 10th October 1855.

Macmillan proposes to get up a book of optics, with my
assistance, and I feel inclined for the job. There is great
bother in making a mathematical book, especially on a subject
with which you are familiar, for in correcting it you do as you
would to pups.—look if the principle and result is right, and
forget to look out for small errors in the course of the work.
However, I expect the work will be salutary, as involving hard

---

[1] This is said *à propos* of a recent visit to a college friend who. was
settled as a clergyman in the country.

[2] For the Trinity College Fellowship.

work, and in the end much abuse from coaches and students, and certainly no vain fame, except in Macmillan's puffs. But, if I have rightly conceived the plan of an educational book on optics, it will be very different in manner, though not in matter, from those now used.

From his Father.

Glenlair, 10th October 1855.

The book sent by Dr. Wilson is the full edition about colour-blindness, with notes and appendices, containing your letter to him and notices of your communications to him on the subject.

To Lewis Campbell, Esq.

Trin. Coll., 17th October 1855.

I expect to be grinding this term. There are lectures on hydrostatics and optics, papers for questionists to be set and read over with the men, which is procrastinatious. Besides this I may have to lecture the working men, and what spare time I have I intend to use on various subjects, which will keep me in work for some time to come, so I do not require any pupils to keep my hand in this term. I was looking for Jowett's book in the library, but, as usual, all the new theology had been carried off in a lump by the M.A.'s, who get in the first day. I wanted Ellicott, but he was out too, so I took Carlyle on the French Revolution. I have been reading the English language, comprising Chaucer, Sir Tristram, Bacon F., Pope, Berkeley, Goldsmith, Cowper, Burns' letters, Isaac Taylor's *Saturday Night,* Carlyle, Ruskin, Kingsley, Maurice, and combining the whole with Trench on *English Past and Present,* and with all this I derive pleasure and information, but not a single glimmer of a theory about Words.

And yet I have presently to state whether words mould thought or thought brews words. Is not one theory as good as another? Faith and a dale better too, if it was not for the sake of laying them together by the ears, which is a difficult task when you have to catch both yourself.

I was staying at the Blackburns' when I was at Glasgow, but they were away, and the Ramsays fed and tended me. I found your photograph there, together with a few other pleasant recollections. I have been over to H. M. Butler, who is come up

again.   We were talking about Maurice, etc.   Maurice is a man
I am loath to say nay to, or to accuse of wilful perversion of
facts ; but in some matters I think he is in great error, especially
in his estimate of respectable ordinary Christians, as far as
regards their creed.   He cannot go too far in enforcing practice
and work on people who were bound to it before, and theoretically confess it, but he is too hard upon the theories, and totally
misrepresents them.   I would rather be taken for a Yezide than
for one of Maurice's popular religionists.

To his Father.

Trin. Coll., 17th October 1855.

The lectures were settled last Friday.   I am to do the upper
division of the third year in hydrostatics and optics, and I have
most of the exercising of the questionists.

From his Father.

Glenlair, 20th October 1855.

If you do a book for M'Millan on optics, do not let him
hurry it on.   Take full time to yourself to revise and re-revise
the MS., and let anything published be creditable.   Do nothing
in a careless manner, and so get a bad name.   A first work
especially should be very carefully got up.

When you are set to lecture on hydrostatics and optics, have
you any apparatus for illustration ?

To his Father.

Trin. Coll., 25th October 1855.

I have refused to take pupils this term, as I want to get
some time for reading and doing private mathematics, and
then I can bestow some time on the men who attend lectures.

I go in bad weather to an institution just opened for sports
of all sorts—jumping, vaulting, etc.   By a little exercise of the
arms every day, one comes to enjoy one's breath, and to sleep
much better than if one did nothing but walk on level roads.

1st November 1855.

I have been lecturing two weeks now, and the class seems

improving, and they come up and ask questions, which is a good sign.

I have been making curves to show the relations of pressure and volume in gases, and they make the subject easier. I think I told you about the Ray Club. I was elected an associate last Wednesday. . . . We had a discussion and an essay by Pomeroy last Saturday about the position of the British nation in India, and sought through ancient and modern history for instances of such a relation between two nations, but found none. We seem to be in the position of having undertaken the management of India at the most critical period, when all the old institutions and religions must break up, and yet it is by no means plain how new civilisation and self-government among people so different from us is to be introduced. One thing is clear, that if we neglect them, or turn them adrift again, or simply make money of them, then we must look to Spain and the Americans for our examples of wicked management and consequent ruin.

From his Father.

11th November 1855.

The platometer will require much consideration, both by you and by any one that undertakes the making. You need hardly expect the details all rightly planned at the first ; many defects will occur, and new devices contrived to conquer unforeseen difficulties in the execution. I would suspect £10 would not go far to get it into anything like good working order. If the instrument were made, to whom is it to belong ? And if it succeeds well, for whose profit is all to be contrived ? Does Bryson so understand it as to be able to make it ? Could he estimate the cost, or would he contract to get an instrument up ? Fixing on a suitable size is very important.

To his Father.

Trin. Coll., 12th November 1855.

I attended Willis on Mechanism to-day, and I think I will attend his course, which is about the parts of machinery. I was lecturing about the velocity of water escaping from a hole this morning. There was a great noise outside, and we looked out at a magnificent jet from a pipe which had gone wrong in

M

the court. So that I was saved the trouble of making experiments.

I was talking to Willis about the platometer, and he thinks it will work. Instead of toothed wheels to keep the spheres in position always, I think watch-spring bands would be better.

Trin. Coll., 25th November 1855.

I think I told you that Pomeroy was ill. He has had rather a sharp attack of bilious fever. His mother has come up. He was getting round on Thursday, but he saw too many people, and was rather the worse of it. However, the doctor says that the recovery simply requires attention, and patience, and no hurrying.

I have been reading old books of optics, and find many things in them far better than what is new. The foreign mathematicians are discovering for themselves methods which were well known at Cambridge in 1720, but are now forgotten.

I have got a contrivance made for expounding instruments. It is a squared rod, one yard long, on which slide pieces, which will carry lenses. Each piece has a wedge which fixes it tight on the rod, and a saw-shaft, with holes through it, for fastening the pasteboard frame of the lens. By means of this I intend to set up all kinds of models of instruments.

To R. B. LITCHFIELD, Esq.

Trin. Coll., 28th November 1855.

I am busy with questionists pretty regularly just now, slanging them one after another for the same things. As they have just set upon me for the evening I must stop now and get out some optical things to show them.

To HIS FATHER.

Trin. Coll., 3d December 1855.

I had four questionist papers last week, as my subjects come thick there ; so I am full of men looking over papers. I have also to get ready a paper on Faraday's Lines of Force for next Monday.

Pomeroy is still very ill, but to-day he feels easier, and his mouth is not quite so dry and sore. He gets food every two or three hours, and port wine every time. I go up in the morning and look after the getting up and bed-making department along with the nurse, after which Mrs. Pomeroy comes, and the nurse goes to bed.

Maurice was here from Friday to Monday, inspecting the working men's education. He was at Goodwin's on Friday night, where we met him and the teachers of the Cambridge affair. He talked of the history of the foundation of the old colleges, and how they were mostly intended to counteract the monastic system, and allow of work and study without retirement from the world.

Trin. Coll., 11th December.

Last night I lectured on Lines of Force at the Philosophical. I put off the second part of it to next term. I have been drawing a lot of lines of force by an easy dodge. I have got to draw them accurately without calculation.

Pomeroy has been improving slowly, but sometimes stopping. He is so big that it requires a great deal to get up his strength again. I saw Dr. Paget at the Philosophical to-day, and he seemed to think him in a fair way to recover.

NOTE ON THE COLOUR TOP AND THE DYNAMICAL TOP.

1. The colour top was a contrivance for mixing in different proportions the light reflected from any number of coloured papers. The image of a bright object on the retina is known to last for a sensible time after the object has been removed from the field of view. Also, as Professor W. Swan has shown, if an object is exposed to view for more than a tenth of a second it appears with its proper degree of brightness, but if the exposure is less than a tenth of a second the apparent brightness of the object is proportional to the time of exposure. This so-called memory of the eye formed the fundamental principle of the colour top, which consisted of a plate of metal made to spin rapidly in its own plane, which served to carry the disks of coloured paper whose colours were to be mixed. Each disk of paper had a central hole for the spindle of the top to pass through, and had a slit from the centre to the circumference, so that two, three, or more disks could be made to overlap one another, and thus to present to the observer a corresponding

number of sectors together filling up the whole circle. By shifting them each disk could be made to present a greater or less surface in proportion to the rest. A graduated circle showed the percentage of the whole area of the circle which each coloured sector occupied. If the eye were directed towards any point of such a compound disk, while the disk was spinning with the top, it is clear that the time during which any particular colour would be passing the line of sight would be proportional to the breadth of the corresponding sector on the disk, and thus the coloured lights from the several papers would be blended on the retina in the proportion of the breadths of the corresponding sectors. By employing two sets of disks of different sizes, the smaller placed above the larger, colour *matches* could be obtained ; for the compound colour due to the smaller disks formed the central portion of the top, while that due to the larger formed a ring surrounding it, and the *match* consisted in making the two colours identical, though the coloured papers producing them were different.

If white and black only be used for the smaller disks the inner circle is always a *neutral* gray. We may then determine in what proportion other colours must be blended to produce, where possible, a match with the gray, and when this is obtained we know that the mixed coloured lights are equivalent to pure white light, though of less intensity than that from the white paper in proportion as the white sector is less than the whole circle. Now, if given colours be employed to match the gray, it appears that they must be blended in slightly different proportions for different eyes, though in the case of persons with normal vision the discrepancies are very slight. In the case of colour - blind persons, however, the matches are very extraordinary. As a rule, any amount of red light may be introduced without altering the colour apparent to a colour-blind person.

The chief results obtained by means of the top were a confirmation of the theory that normal eyes possess three, and only three, distinct colour sensations, corresponding to red, green, and blue (or violet), and that all colour-vision depends on the relative extents to which these three sensations are affected. The *colour* depends on the *ratios* of the extents to which the three sensations are affected, the *intensity* of the light on their *sum*. In most colour-blind persons the red sensation is absent, and hence with them the introduction of red light does not affect the apparent colour or intensity of a mixture. Some very interesting results with respect to the constitution of various browns and other compound colours were also obtained, and it was shown that mixtures of blue and yellow lights may produce white or pink, but never produce green.

2. The "Dynamical Top," which was invented by Maxwell to illustrate dynamical propositions, technically so-called, was, in its final form, constructed of brass by Mr. Ramage of Aberdeen. It was this top which Maxwell brought with him to Cambridge when he came up for his M.A. degree in the summer of 1857, and exhibited to a tea-party in his room in the evening. His friends left it spinning, and next morning Maxwell, noticing one of them coming across the court, leapt out of bed, started the top, and retired between the sheets. It is needless to say that the spinning power of the top commanded as great respect as its power of illustrating Poinsot's *Theorie Nouvelle de la Rotation des Corps.*

During his residence in Cambridge he endeavoured to investigate the process by which a cat is enabled invariably to alight on her feet. The mode of conducting the experiments and the impression they left on the mind of the College will appear from the following extract from a letter written to Mrs. Maxwell, from Trinity, on January 3d, 1870, when Professor Maxwell was examining for the Mathematical Tripos :—

There is a tradition in Trinity that when I was here I discovered a method of throwing a cat so as not to light on its feet, and that I used to throw cats out of windows. I had to explain that the proper object of research was to find how quick the cat would turn round, and that the proper method was to let the cat drop on a table or bed from about two inches, and that even then the cat lights on her feet.

CHAPTER VIII.

DEATH OF HIS FATHER——PROFESSORSHIP AT ABERDEEN——
1856, 1857——ÆT. 24-25.

" And yet thy heart
The lowliest duties on herself did lay."

SOON after his return to Cambridge in February 1856
(after seeing his father comfortably established in Edinburgh), Maxwell heard from his old friend Professor Forbes
that the Chair of Natural Philosophy at Marischal College,
Aberdeen, was vacant, and he shortly afterwards became a
candidate. He had never contemplated a life of entire
leisure, but it may seem strange that Cambridge, where
besides his lectureship he had various philanthropic
interests, should not have afforded him a sufficient field
for regular work. He foresaw that the Scotch appointment would please his father, and that the arrangement of
session and vacation time would enable him to spend the
whole summer uninterruptedly at Glenlair. Some expressions in his letters also seem to indicate that he rather
shrank from the prospect of becoming a Cambridge "Don."
He had observed the narrowing tendencies of college life,
and preferred the rubs of the world.

His letters to his father and others at this time sufficiently explain the course of his candidature, in which the
point most deserving notice is the generous way in which
he speaks of his rivals. While treating the whole matter
with his usual grave irony, he seems to have conducted his
part of it with considerable sagacity, and when he returned
to Edinburgh about the middle of March everything was
well in train. He had the pleasure of knowing that his

father's interest in the question was at least equal to his own, and that the old man had been roused by it to some return of his former vigour.   But the end was near. After a few days spent in Edinburgh, the father and son went home to Glenlair, as they had planned—a matter of no small anxiety and difficulty.   The short vacation had all but passed away, when, on Thursday the 2d of April, just before his son was to have returned to Cambridge, Mr. John Clerk Maxwell suddenly expired.

The outward change was not very great.   Maxwell went up to Cambridge as usual.   Glenlair was still his home.   His interest in his own subjects was undiminished. His candidature for Aberdeen continued.   But the personal loss to him was incalculable and irreparable.   Their long daily companionship had been followed by a correspondence which was all but daily, by vacations spent together, and an uninterrupted interchange, whether present or absent, of thoughts and social interests, both light and grave.   During the last six months, it is true, the old man had been failing, and, to outward observers, was considerably changed.   But the change had only called out his son's affection into more active exercise, and had never checked the flow of communication by word or letter. What depth of feeling lay beneath Maxwell's quiet demeanour at this time may be inferred from the poem written at Cambridge during that summer term, and put into my hands when we met afterwards at Glenlair.   Some lines of it may be appropriately inserted here :—

" Yes, I know the forms that meet me are but phantoms of the brain,
For they walk in mortal bodies, and they have not ceased from pain.
Oh those signs of human weakness, left behind for ever now,
Dearer far to me than glories round a fancied seraph's brow.
Oh the old familiar voices ; oh the patient waiting eyes ;
Let me live with them in dreamland while the world in slumber lies.
For by bonds of sacred honour will they guard my soul in sleep
From the spells of aimless fancies that around my senses creep.
They will link the past and present into one continuous life ;
While I feel their hope, their patience, nerve me for the daily strife.
For it is not all a fancy that our lives and theirs are one,
And we know that all we see is but an endless work begun.
Part is left in nature's keeping, part has entered into rest ;
Part remains to grow and ripen hidden in some living breast.".

Such was James Clerk Maxwell during the "years of April blood."

LETTERS, 1856.

TO HIS FATHER.

Trin., 14th Feb. 1856.

Yesterday the Ray Club met at Hort's. I took my great top there and spun it with coloured discs attached to it. I have been planning a form of top which will have more variety of motion, but I am working out the theory, so that I will wait till I know the necessary dimensions before I settle the plan.

I told Willie (Cay) how I had hung up a bullet by a combination of threads.

I have drawn from theory the curves which it ought to describe, and when I set the bullet a-going over the proper curve, it traces it out over and over again as if it were doing a pre-ordained dance and kept a steady eye on the line on the paper. I have enlarged my stock of models for solid geometry, made of coloured thread, stretched between two pasteboard ends.

FROM PROFESSOR J. D. FORBES.

Edinburgh, 13th Feb. 1856.

You may not perhaps have heard that Mr. Gray, Professor of Natural Philosophy, Marischal College, Aberdeen, is dead. He was a pleasing and energetic person, in the prime of life and health, a few months ago, when I saw him last.

I have no idea whether the situation would be any object to you ; but I thought I would mention it, as I think it would be a pity were it not filled by a Scotchman, and you are the person who occurs to me as best fitted for it.

Do not imagine from my writing that I have the smallest influence in the matter, or interest in it beyond the welfare of the Scottish Universities.

It is in the gift of the Crown. The Lord Advocate and Home Secretary are the parties to apply to. I am not acquainted with either.

In the Commissioners' Report of 1830 the emoluments are stated at about £350. But they are not always to be depended upon.

Another point.   I think you ought certainly to be a Fellow of the Royal Society of Edinburgh.   I shall be glad to propose you if you wish it.

To his Father.

Trin. Coll., 15th Feb. 1856.

Professor Forbes has written to me to say that the Professorship of Nat. Phil. at Marischal College, Aberdeen, is vacant by the death of Mr. Gray, and he inquires if I would apply for the situation, so I want to know what your notion or plan may be. For my own part, I think the sooner I get into regular work the better, and that the best way of getting into such work is to profess one's readiness by applying for it.

The appointment lies with the Crown—that is, the Lord Advocate and Home Secretary.   I suppose the correct thing to do is to send certificates of merit, signed by swells, to one or other of these officers.

I am going to ask about the method of the thing here, and Thacker has promised to get me the College Testimonials.   If you see any one in Edinburgh that understands the sort of thing, could you pick up the outline of the process ?

In all ordinary affairs political distinctions are supposed to weigh a great deal in Scotland.   The English notion is that in pure and even in mixed mathematics politics are of little use, however much a knowledge of these sciences may promote the study of politics.   As to Theology, I am not aware that the mathematicians, as a body, are guilty of any heresies, however some of them may have erred.   But these are too mysterious subjects to furnish matter for calculation, so I may tell you that the reflecting stereoscope was finished yesterday, and looks well, and that I got a Devil made at the same time, which I play at the Gymnasium for relaxation and breathing time.

Forbes also suggests my joining the Royal Society.

Trin. Coll., 20th Feb. /56.

As far as writing (Testimonials) goes, there is a good deal, and if you believe the Testimonials you would think the Government had in their hands the triumph or downfall of education generally, according as they elected one or not.

However, wisdom is of many kinds, and I do not know which

dwells with wise counsellors most, whether scientific, practical, political, or ecclesiastical. I hear there are candidates of all kinds relying on the predominance of one or other of these kinds of wisdom in the constitution of the Government.

I had a letter from Dr. Swan of Edinburgh, who is a candidate, asking me for my good opinion, which I gave him, so far as I had one. His printed papers are good, and I hear he is so himself. Maclennan is also a candidate. He has the qualification of making himself understood.

The results of this term are chiefly solid Geometry Lectures, stereoscopic pictures, and optical theorems. My lectures are to be on Rigid Dynamics and Astronomy next term, so I do not expect to be out of work by reason of Aberdeen, and I have plenty to get through in those subjects.

I have been making more stereoscopic curves for my lectures. I intend to select some and draw them very neat the size of the ordinary stereoscopic pictures, and write a description of them, and publish them as mathematical illustrations. I am going to do one now, to illustrate the theory of contour lines in maps, and to show how the rivers must run, and where the lines of watershed must be.

From his Father.

22d Feby. 1856.

. . . I believe there is some salary, but fees and pupils, I think, cannot be very plenty. But if the *postie* be gotten, and prove not good, it can be given up ; at any rate it occupies but half the year.

To his Father.

Trin. Coll., 12th March.

I was at the Working College to-day, working at decimal fractions. We are getting up a preparatory school for biggish boys to get up their preliminaries. We are also agitating in favour of early closing of shops. We have got the whole of the ironmongers, and all the shoemakers but one. The booksellers have done it some time. The Pitt Press keeps late hours, and is to be petitioned to shut up.

I have just written out an abstract of the second part of my paper on Faraday's Lines of Force. I hope soon to write properly the paper of which it is an abstract. It is four weeks since I read it. I have done nothing in that way this term, but am just beginning to ·feel the electrical state come on again, and I hope to work it up well next term.

To Miss Cay.

Glenlair, Thursday Afternoon (3d April 1856).

DEAR AUNT—My father died to-day at twelve o'clock. He was sleepless and confused at night, but got up to breakfast. He saw Sandy a few minutes, and spoke rationally, then came into the drawing-room, and sat down on a chair for a few minutes to rest, and gave a short cry and never spoke again. We gave him ether for a little, but he could not swallow it. There was no warning, and apparently no pain. He expected it long, and described it so himself.

Do you think Uncle Robert could come and help a little ? Tell Dr. Bell and other people. As it is, it is better than if it had been when I was away. He would not let me stay. I was to go to Cambridge on Friday.—Your aff. nephew,

J. C. MAXWELL.

To Mrs. Blackburn of Killearn.

Glenlair, Thursday.

DEAR MRS. BLACKBURN—My father died suddenly to-day at 12 o'clock. He had been giving directions about the garden, and he said he would sit down and rest a little as usual. After a few minutes I asked him to lie down on the sofa, and he did not seem inclined to do so, and then I got him some ether, which had helped him before.

Before he could take any he had a slight struggle, and all was over. He hardly breathed afterwards.

He used often to talk to me about this, which has come at last, and he seemed fully to have made up his mind to it and to be prepared for it. His nights have sometimes been troubled, and last night I was with him the whole time trying to get him into a comfortable sleep, which did not come till light.

Otherwise we thought him better than when in Edin^r. He was very glad to get back here again.

I write to you that you may tell Mrs. Wedderburn. She ought to know, and I trust you will let her know, that not only was there no pain or distress about my father's death, but he had often been speaking of how glad he was that he had got everything put in order, and that he was home again.

I have written to ask my Uncle Robert Cay to come and help me in various things, as I am rather alone here. Of course I have written to Sir George, and will do so to other relatives as soon as I can.—Your affte. cousin,

JAMES CLERK MAXWELL.

FROM R. DUNDAS CAY, Esq., to MISS CAY, on MR. JOHN CLERK MAXWELL'S Death.

Glenlair, 8th April 1856.

I think you will be glad to hear how we are getting on. It is very nice to see how natural James is. There is no affectation of more feeling than he really has, but he talks away upon his own subjects when not busy with the necessary preparations for to-morrow. Fortunately these occupy him a good deal, and as I think the business is of use to him, I only assist him and keep him talking. For instance, he made out all the list and directed the letters himself; I sat by and sealed them. Then my health requires a walk every day, so we go out and talk away very much as usual all the time, discussing the thinning of plantations, etc.

It is beautiful to see the feeling of all the people towards him, all thinking for him, and trying to assist him in every way, and he trying to carry on everything as before :—or when he wants to make a change, his anxiety, lest people should think he disapproves of the former customs. For instance, he wished to have the servants in for prayers every evening, instead of our reading by ourselves and reading to them separately ; he was quite afraid they should think his doing so would look as if he thought it was wrong, it not having been done before.

To LEWIS CAMPBELL, Esq.

Trin. Coll., 22d April 1856.

I have had many things to attend to lately, which have kept me from writing to you. I am glad you wrote to me. I got a very kind letter from your mother and Bob, for which you must thank them meanwhile. My uncles, Robert and Albert, stayed with me till the 15th. That day I got a letter from Cambridge about college matters, and so I had to set to work at home more vigorously. George Wedderburn came in the afternoon, and we had two hard days' work of various kinds.

On Friday he and I left Glenlair, and I got here on Saturday, and since yesterday have been lecturing.

All things are as if I had been up after a common vacation, and I see them all the same as they used to be. I have got back among chapels and halls and scholarships, and all the regular routine, with now and then some expression of condolence, which is all that strangers can or ought to afford. Neither they nor I enter on a subject which must be misunderstood ; but it seems to me that while all the old *subjects* are as interesting to me as ever, I talk about them without understanding the men I talk to.

I have two or three stiff bits of work to get through this term here, and I hope to overtake them. When the term is over I must go home and pay diligent attention to everything there, so that I may learn what to do.

The first thing I must do is carry on my father's work of personally superintending everything at home, and for doing this I have his regular accounts of what used to be done, and the memories of all the people, who tell me everything they know. As for my own pursuits, it was my father's wish, and it is mine, that I should go on with them. We used to settle that what I ought to be engaged in was some occupation of teaching, admitting of long vacations for being at home ; and when my father heard of the Aberdeen proposition he very much approved. I have not heard anything very lately, but I believe my name is not yet put out of question in the Ld Advocate's book. If I get back to Glenlair I shall have the mark of my father's work on everything I see. Much of them is still his, and I must be in some degree his steward to take care of them. I trust that the knowledge of his plans may be a guide to me, and never a constraint.

I am glad to hear of your [Oxford] W[orking Men's] Coll[ege]. The preparatory school here has at once got from seventy to ninety scholars, all in earnest, and they have had to migrate to a larger schoolhouse.

We might consider of you and Bob and W. Cay coming for a quiet week or two to Glenlair in summer, if all goes well. Bob is with Willie and Charlie now touring.

I am getting a new top turned to show my class the motion

of bodies of various forms about a fixed point.   I expect to get
very neat results from it, and agreeing with theory of course.

FROM PROFESSOR J. D. FORBES.

Bridge of Allan, 30th April 1856.

MY DEAR SIR—I have just seen in the newspaper that you
have been appointed to the Chair in Marischal College, on which
I beg sincerely to congratulate you.

I regret much that it should at the same time be my lot to
express my sympathy on the occasion of the recent death of your
father.   Such a loss occurs but once in a lifetime.   In your case
I am sure that it has the greatest alleviation which it admits of
—I mean the consciousness that you have been an affectionate
and dutiful son, and that your excellent conduct relieved your
father's mind from every shade of anxiety regarding you.—
Believe me always, yours very sincerely,

JAMES D. FORBES.

TO R. B. LITCHFIELD, Esq.

Trinity, 4th June 1856.

On Thurs. evening I take the North-western route to the
North.   I am busy looking over immense rubbish of papers,
etc., for some things not to be burnt lie among much combustible
matter, and some is soft and good for packing.

It is not pleasant to go down to live solitary, but it would
not be pleasant to stay up either, when all one had to do lay
elsewhere.   The transition state from a man into a Don must
come at last, and it must be painful, like gradual outrooting of
nerves.   When it is done there is no more pain, but occasional
reminders from some suckers, tap-roots, or other remnants of
the old nerves, just to show what was there and what might
have been.

1856.   After his father's death, Maxwell set himself anew to
Æt. 25.   the tasks before him, with a mingled sense of loss and
responsibility.   One of his first duties was to apply himself
to the management of his estate.   He remained at Glenlair
during most of the summer, only making a short excursion
to Belfast on account of his cousin, William Cay, who, in

accordance with his advice, was about to study Engineering under James Thomson, the brother of the Glasgow Professor. In the autumn, besides entertaining Charles Hope Cay, then a boy of fifteen, in his school holidays, he had various Cambridge friends to stay with him, as in former years.[1]

In November he began his work at Aberdeen. A Scotch Professor has one advantage over a College lecturer at Cambridge. If his students are less advanced, he has the entire direction of their work in his own department. It is left to him, apart from any prescribed system, to determine the order in which the parts of his subject shall be developed. His selection of topics is not dominated by the Final Examination. This peculiarity of his position was fully appreciated by Clerk Maxwell, whose experience of the course in Edinburgh under Forbes gave him a " standpoint " from which to arrange his great fund of scientific acquirement in presenting it to his students.

Had Maxwell the qualities of a teacher ? That he was not on the whole successful in oral communication is an impression too widespread to be contradicted without positive proof. Yet his letters bear sufficient evidence that in many respects he had a true vocation as an educator. The combination of keen sympathy with native authority and dignity, the intense interest in his subject, his endless power of taking trouble, his philanthropic enthusiasm, his critical study of mankind, his wide range of language and ideas, must have enabled him to make his mark as a public teacher, either at Aberdeen or Cambridge, if he had remained long enough at either place to wear off some superficial impediments, to adapt his methods to his environment, and to effect a thorough understanding with

---

[1] With one of these, who happened to be "Carlyle-mad," he drove one day on pilgrimage to Craigenputtock. The enthusiast, in his rapture, harangued an old peasant, who was hoeing "neeps," on the glorious doings of the former tenant of the farm-house. The man listened, stooping over his work till the rhapsody was over, then looked up for a moment saying, "It is aye gude that mends," and resumed his labour. Maxwell was fond of relating this.

his pupils. As it was, his lectureship at Trinity lasted
only for a year, and in the Scotch university he had only
taught for three short sessions when Marischal College was
on the point of being suppressed, and his reputation as a
teacher was, under these circumstances, brought into comparison with that of others whose strength lay in exposition.
To those who know what is implied in academical contests
and controversies, the mention of these facts will be a sufficient caution against taking the lowest estimate of Maxwell's teaching powers ; and in after years " at Cambridge,
where his class consisted of picked students," we have good
authority for saying " his lectures were listened to with an
attention and pleasure similar to that with which his books
are now read." But at this earlier time there were certainly drawbacks, of which he himself was imperfectly
conscious. Between his students' ignorance and his vast
knowledge it was difficult to find a common measure.
The advice which he once gave a friend whose duty it was
to preach to a country congregation, "Why don't you give
it them thinner ?" must often have been applicable to himself. Another hindrance lay in the very richness of his
imagination, and the swiftness of his wit. The ideas with
which his mind was teeming were perpetually intersecting,
and their interferences, like those of the waves of light,
made " dark bands" in the place of colour, to the un-
assisted eye. Illustrations of *ignotum per ignotius*, or of
the abstruse by some unobserved property of the familiar,
were multiplied with dazzling rapidity. Then the spirit
of indirectness and paradox, though he was aware of its
dangers, would often take possession of him against his
will, and either from shyness, or momentary excitement,
or the despair of making himself understood, would land
him in " chaotic statements," breaking off with some quirk
of ironical humour. Add to this his occasional hesitation,
his shortsightedness, and the long years of solitary intercourse with his father, who understood his meaning from
the slightest hint, and rather encouraged the family trick
of " calling things out of their names," and the list of
hindrances is sufficiently formidable. But he was striving

to overcome those of which he knew, and even if he had never done so completely, the weight of his character as well as the profundity of his genius, and his unvarying kindliness, must have won their way.

As marking his educational enthusiasm, it should not be forgotten here that he continued at Aberdeen the practice which he had commenced at Cambridge, of lecturing to working men.   This was entirely voluntary, and for aught I know may have been regarded as a piece of eccentricity.

A trivial incident may be recorded as throwing light on his relations to professors and students severally.   The professors had unlimited access to the library, and were in the habit of sometimes taking out a volume for the use of a friend.   The students were only allowed two volumes at a time.   Maxwell took out books for his students, and when checked for this by his colleagues explained that the students were his friends.

Amongst the human phenomena surrounding him, one which genuinely interested him was the religious "revival" which took place about that time in Scotland.   His intercourse with evangelical friends in England had prepared him to sympathise with such "experiences," and his Calvinistic reading had familiarised him with the language used. And he was less jealous of Antinomianism than of a cut and dried morality.   But he was in no wise distracted from his professional duties by this or anything else, and although he referred to it in conversation, it has left no trace in any of his remaining letters which I have seen.

LETTERS, 1856-1857.

To R. B. LITCHFIELD, Esq.

Glenlair, 4th July 1856.

I have got some prisms and opticals from Edinbro', and I am fitting up a compendious colour-machine capable of transportation.   I have also my top for doing dynamics and several colour-diagrams, so that if I come to Cheltenham I shall not be empty handed.   At the same time I should like to hear from you soon.

I have been giving a portion of time to Saturn's Rings, which I find a stiff subject but curious, especially the case of the motion of a fluid ring.   The very forces which would tend to divide the ring into great drops or satellites are made by the motion to keep the fluid in a uniform ring.

I find I get fonder of metaphysics and less of calculation continually, and my metaphysics are fast settling into the rigid high style, that is about ten times as far *above* Whewell as Mill is *below* him, or Comte or Macaulay *below* Mill, using above and below conventionally, like *up* and *down* in Bradshaw.

Experiment furnishes us with the values of our arbitrary constants, but only suggests the form of the functions.   Afterwards, when the form is not only recognised but understood scientifically, we find that it rests on precisely the same foundation as Euclid does, that is, it is simply the contradiction of an absurdity, out of which may we all get our legs at last!

To the Same.

Glenlair, 18th July 1856.

I can promise you milk and honey and mutton, with wind and water to match, a reasonable stock of natives of great diversity, and very unlike any natives I know elsewhere.   I also expect a cousin [1] here, who carries a clear and active mind in a body ditto ditto, and I hope to make them stick closer together by the material above stated.

To the Same.

Glenlair, 9th September 1856.

My only hope for Pomeroy is that he may keep his health ; if that remains I think it quite presumptuous to interfere with him by hopes or otherwise, for I would rather be interfered with by him (from which I am safe) than bother a man who steers so well himself.   You must remember that besides the clerical shell of respectability which is to be put on, there is sometimes a lay shell of $ανηριθμον$ $γελασμα$, which has in some measure to be put off, or perhaps more truly drawn in, for no

---

[1] Charles Hope Cay.

one that has once known can ever forget that instead of two
views there are three, good, bad, and grotesque ; and tho' all
things are full of jokes, that does not hinder them from being
quite full, or even more so, of more solemn matters. It also
strikes me that if we were to compare notes, the thing we would
most differ about would be the notion we have of the "standpoint" (see religious prints, *passim*) of the men whom we know
in common.

My own notion is that you see him where he ought to be
according to principle, and I see him where he acts as if he
was, that is, in the position which would naturally produce his
actual life. But I find on comparing notes with other people
that a man always shows himself up differently according to the
man who is with him. In fact I do it myself, so I must now
show up the fishing side for the benefit of Charlie (Cay).

To C. J. Monro, Esq.

Glenlair, 14th October 1856.

. . . During September I had Lushington, Maclennan, and
two cousins "Cay" here. Now I am writing a solemn address
or manifesto to the Natural Philosophers of the North,[1] which
I am afraid I must reinforce with coffee and anchovies, and a
roaring hot fire and spread coat-tails to make it all natural. By
the way, I have proved that if there be nine coefficients of
magnetic induction, perpetual motion will set in, and a small
crystalline sphere will inevitably destroy the universe by increasing all velocities till the friction brings all nature into a
state of incandescence, or as H—— would say, Terrestrial all in
Chaos shall exhibit efflorescence.

To Miss Cay.

129 Union Street, Aberdeen,
27th February 1857.

You are right about my being two letters in debt to you.   I
proceed to "post you up" to the most recent epoch. The
weather is mild and sunny, but the winter has been severe.
The planets Jupiter and Venus have been neighbours ; Saturn,
Mars, and Mercury also visible.

---

[1] His Inaugural Lecture at Aberdeen.

To descend to particulars. I find everything going on very smoothly. I never passed an equal time with less trouble. I have plenty of work but no vexation as yet. In fact, I am beginning to fear that I must get into some scrape just to put an end to my complacency.

I will begin with the College. We are having public meetings and caucuses (that is, the students are) for the election of Lord Rector. Lord Stanley won't come. Lord Elgin is doubtful. They seem to prefer Elgin to Layard. We are to have a commission consisting of Col. Mure, Cosmo Innes, and Stirling of Keir.

To-morrow I hold my second *general* examination on the subject we have done. I hope that my men of science won't have their heads turned with politics. I have all the squibs regularly presented to me. They are not very good.

I have had 13 special examinations, and the two last have been the best answered of any. I send you my paper for to-morrow to give it to Bob Campbell with my profoundest esteem.

We have been at the theory of Heat and the Steam Engine this month, and on Monday we begin Optics. I have a volunteer class who have been thro' astronomy, and we are now at high Optics. Tuesday week I give a lecture to operatives, etc., on the Eye. I have just been getting cods' and bullocks' eyes, to refresh my memory and practise dissection. The size of the cod and the ox eye is nearly the same. As this was our last day of fluids, I finished off with a splendid fountain in the sunlight. We were not very wet.

Out of College I have made the most of my time in seeing the natives. I used to walk *every day* with Professor Martin, but he was not well for some time, and we broke that habit. I get on better with people of more decision and less refinement, because they keep me in better order.

I have been keeping up friendly relations with the King's College men, and they seem to be very friendly too. I have not received any rebukes yet from our men for so doing, but I find that the families of some of our professors have no dealings, and never had, with those of the King's people. Theoretically we profess charity.

I had a glorious solitary walk to-day in Kincardineshire by the coast—black cliffs and white breakers. I took my second dip this season. I have found a splendid place, sheltered and safe, with gymnastics on a pole afterwards.

To the Rev. Lewis Campbell.

129 Union Street,
Aberdeen, 6th February 1857.

I got your letter [1] this morning at breakfast. I was some-what seedy from being up late, but the perusal seemed to clear up everything, and I got on better with explaining the properties of elastic fluids than I had any reason to hope. So when I have doubts about the best mode of explaining anything, I must consult your letter, only it will not do for ever. I must have a new one now and then.

But I have not been so glad for long. Knowing you of old, I can see how things are by the way you write, and it is not always that similar announcements have given me similar satisfaction.

So I am glad that you do not know what "it" was. Avoid the neuter pronoun. "It" is unworthy of beasts that perish. "He" and "She" are for ever and ever. What the form of the pronoun may be after this I cannot tell, but I think more is meant in the distinction than is fully expressed in this life.

The Sadducees on the one side, and the ascetics on the other, point out the errors. Solomon, Prov. viii., *et passim,* and Eph. vi., indicate matter of contemplation not unallied to action, which in good ground bears good fruit.

But as Urania remarked to Melpomene, I am but displaying the fact of my belonging to a lower stage in the scale of things, so I must for the present go down beside my native rill.

With respect to this "northern hermitage," my cell is pretty commodious. In quitting the cœnobitic cloister of Trinity for the howling wilderness of Union Street, I have not been made an anchoret. It is quite consistent with the eremitic life to modify one's fast in friends' houses 4 days per week or so.

One thing I am thankful for, though perhaps you will not believe it.—Up to the present time I have not even been tempted to mystify any one.

I have made out who were most likely to excite my passion that way, and I have avoided some, and broken the ice with others. I am glad B—— is not here; he would have ruined me. I once met him. I was as much astonished as he was

---

[1] Announcing our marriage engagement. See p. 190.

at the chaotic statements I began to make.   But as far as I can
learn I have not been misunderstood in anything, and no one
has heard a single oracle from my lips.   Of course I do not
mean that my class do not mistake my meaning sometimes.
That is found out and remedied day by day.   I speak of professors, ministers, doctors, advocates, matrons, maidens, and
phenomenal existences (Chimeræ bombylantes in vacuo).   We
are through mechanics.   I had an ex^{n} on bookwork on 24th
Jan.   I got answers to all the questions and riders, though no
one floored them all right.   I have now to be brewing experiments on Heat, as well as determining the form of doctrine to
be presented to the finite capacities of my men.

FROM C. J. MONRO, Esq.

15th February 1857.

Have you seen the Pomeroy packet ?   It has much more in
it than any travels I ever read.   Lots of phenomena, human
and otherwise, on the way out : especially the waves in a
storm. . . .

. . . They who deal in instruments of strings say that if you
strike a certain note you hear certain others above.   Is that
because of the further terms in a Fourier's integral, or because
a sympathetic vibration is excited in certain other of the strings
of the same instrument ?   I observe Weber says that it does
not occur in wind instruments.

FROM PROFESSOR J. D. FORBES.

Edinburgh, 31st March 1857.

MY DEAR MAXWELL—I have often wished to ask you to tell
me how your first session had turned out ; consequently I was
exceedingly glad to get your letter this evening, and to find
that you have not been disappointed in the results of the step
to which you kindly say that my assistance was of some use.
In what you say about the monotony of reiteration, I can confidently assure you that your conclusions are quite correct ; certain
precautions being taken which an active mind like yours is sure
to fall upon.

We shall be delighted to see you at the R. S. on the 20th,
and to have your paper, which, if convenient, please to put into
my hands, as a matter of form, when ready.

I have been at several meetings of the Society, but am feeling a little just now the effects of the season and the winter's work, so I shall not be there on the 6th. On the whole, however, I have got through the winter well.

I shall like much to see your Top, of which I read the account in the *Athenæum*.

Have you observed in that same flippant paper for last Saturday an attack upon Faraday (as it seems to me) of a most presumptuous and ignorant kind ? Though by no means as yet a convert to the views which Faraday maintains, yet I have so far a general appreciation of them as to believe that this conceited mathematician (some fifteenth Cambridge wrangler, I guess) is ignorant altogether of what Faraday wishes to prove.—Always yours sincerely,   JAMES D. FORBES.

To C. J. MONRO, Esq.

Glenlair, Springholm,
Dumfries, 20th May 1857.

I went to Old Aberdeen for Fourier, . . . but I have forgotten what was to be discovered out of him.

The session went off smoothly enough. I had Sun all the beginning of optics, and worked off all the experimental part up to Fraunhofer's lines, which were glorious to see with a water prism I have set up in the form of a cubical box, 5 inch side. The only things not generally done that I attempted last session were the undulatory medium made of bullets for advanced class, and Plateau's experiments on a sphere of oil in a mixture of spirits and water of exactly its own density.

I succeeded very well with heat. The experiments on latent heat came out very accurate. That was my part, and the class could explain and work out the results better than I expected. Next year I intend to mix experimental physics with mechanics, devoting Tuesday and THURSDAY (what would Stokes say?) to the science of experimenting accurately.

I got a glorified top made at Aberdeen. I think you saw the wooden type at Cambridge. I have made it the occasion of a short screed on rotation coming out in the Roy. Soc., Edinburgh, presently.

Last week I brewed chlorophyll (as the chemists word it), a green liquor, which turns the invisible light red. My pot of all the winter spinach that remained was portentous, so I exhibited the optical effects, which were allowed to be worth the potful.

My last grind was the reduction of equations of colour which I made last year. The result was eminently satisfactory.

To R. B. LITCHFIELD, Esq.

Glenlair, 29th May 1857.

It is with a profound feeling of pity that I write to a denizen of Hare Court after participating in the blessings of this splendid day. We had just enough of cloud to prevent scorching, and the grass seemed to like to grow just as much as the beasts to eat it.

I have not had a mathematical idea for about a fortnight, when I wrote them all away to Prof. Thomson, and I have not got an answer yet with fresh ones. But I believe there is a department of mind conducted independent of consciousness, where things are fermented and decocted, so that when they are run off they come clear.

By the way, I found it useful at Aberdeen to tell the students what parts of the subject they were *not* to remember, but to get up and forget at once as being rudimentary notions necessary to development, but requiring to be sloughed off before maturity.

I have no one with me but the domestics and dog. The valley seems deserted of its gentry; but we have one gentleman from Dumfriesshire, who is living in a hired house, and building with great magnificence an Episcopal Chapel in Castle-Douglas at his own expense. His own house is 20 miles off, a capital place, and this is perhaps the least Episcopal part of Scotland by reason of the memory of the dragoons. One old family of the Stewartry is of that persuasion, and most of the persecutors' families are now Presbyterian and Whig, so that the congregation is but feeble.

It is very different at Aberdeen, where the Presbyterians persecuted far more than the Prelatists, so there I actually found a true Jacobite (female, I could not undertake to produce a male specimen), and there are three distinct Episcopal religions in Aberdeen, all pretty lively.

Can you tell me what the illustrated Tennyson is like? I shan't see it till I go to Edinbro'. I don't mean are the prints the best possible, or impervious to green spectacles; but are

they nice diagrams as such things go ?   I should like to know
before long about it, and whether the characters are of the
Adamic type, and in reasonable condition, or pre-Rafaelitic in
all but colour, and symbolising everything except the " Arche-
typal Skeleton " and the " Nature of Limbs."

To C. J. Monro, Esq.

Glenlair, 5th June 1857.

I have not seen article seven, but I agree with your dissent
from it entirely.   On the vested interest principle, I think the
men who intended to keep their fellowships by celibacy and
ordination, and got them on that footing, should not be allowed
to desert the virgin choir or neglect the priestly office, but on
those principles should be allowed to live out their days, provided the whole amount of souls cured annually does not amount
to £20 in the King's Book.   But my doctrine is that the various
grades of College officers should be set on such a basis that,
although chance lecturers might be sometimes chosen from
among fresh fellows who are going away soon, the reliable
assistant tutors, and those that have a plain calling that way,
should after a few years be elected permanent officers of the
College, and be tutors and deans in their time, and seniors also,
with leave to marry, or rather, never prohibited or asked any
questions on that head, and with leave to retire after so many
years' service as seniors.   As for the men of the world, we
should have a limited term of existence, and that independent
of marriage or " parsonage."

I saw a paragraph about the Female' Artists Exhibition, and
that Mrs. Hugh Blackburn had her Phaethon there. . . . She
has done a very small picture of a haystack making, somewhat pre-Raphaelite in pose, but graceful withal, and such that
the Moidart natives know every lass on the stack, whether seen
behind or before.   It was at the Edinburgh Academy of
Painters.

I have done a screed of introduction to optics, and am at a
sort of general summary of mechanical principles—doctrines
relating to absolute and relative motion, analysis of the doctrine
of Force into the smallest number of independent truths, theory
of angular momentum and couples of work done, and *vis viva*, of
actual and potential energy, with continual jaw on the doctrine
of measurement by units all through.

To Rev. Lewis Campbell.

Glenlair, 7th August 1857.

Æt. 26.   I got your letter yesterday. I have oftener corresponded
with people I expected to see than with those I had just left,
so you must excuse my being rather more glad of it than if I
had expected it. So you were better than I took you for ; put
that in the Logic-mill and grind it by " Conversion of Props."
Since you left I have been stirring up old correspondents.
Poor ——— is " himself again," with not many to care about
him. He could not keep the ——— youths in order, and tried
to get his authority backed by the big authorities. Then I
suppose ensued a struggle between bodily weakness and hesitation, and mental sternness, stubbornness, and conscientiousness.
The result probably was something severe in substance and mild
in manner, or otherwise open to scorn from the youths.—I don't
know, but he has resigned his place. The youths then proceeded to express their penitence, and the authorities their
regret.   But he is now taking private pupils for that seat of
. . . learning, with not more friends and friendliness than of
old. Not exactly. I am glad to hear of his knowing some
mathematical men, actuaries, etc., and corresponding with them,
and he is much more friendly by the post than by speech and
face.

Yesterday we did our Castle-Douglas, and round by Greenlaw
(Gordon, Esq.)   Old Greenlaw impounded us at once, and em-
barked us in his boat down to Threave Castle, where some
falsified antiquity ; and some apart, behind thick woven thorns,
bathed in the black water of Dee.

Then back to dinner with another party of chance visitors,
songs both of the drawing-room and the quire and the cotton
fields, and, to conclude, the unpremeditated hop.

The thing was not destitute of its humours.   Old Greenlaw,
heir of entail, with charters in his bedroom belonging to
" Young Lochinvar " his forbear, and various Douglases, with
rights of pit and gallows, and other curious privileges, sending
all his people and visitors neck and heels in the very best
direction for themselves.   Son and daughter—mild, indefatig-
able, generally useful, doing (at home) exactly as they are bid.
One gay litter(ar)y widow, charming never so wisely, with her
hair about her ears and her elbows on her knees, on a low stool,

talking Handel, or Ruskin, or Macaulay, or general pathos of unprotected female, passing off into criticism, witticism, pleasantry, unmitigated slang, sporting, and betting.

One little Episcopal chaplain, a Celt, whom I see often, but do not quite fathom—that is, I don't know how far he respects and how far he is amused with his most patronising friends. One, mathematical teacher somewhere,—friend to chaplain. Voice. Mild, good fellow, like a grown up chorister, quite modest about everything except his voice—"What will they say in England," "The Standard Bearer," "Oh Susannah" (Chaplain leads chorus), "Courtin' down in Tenessee" (Chaplain obligato), "Yet once more" (Handel), "But who may abide" (do.), and so on.

One good old widow lady, with manners. One son to do.,—sanguine temperament, open countenance, very much run to nose, brain inactive, probably fertile in military virtue. Two daughters to do.,—healthy, physical force girls, brains more developed owing to their not having escaped in the form of nose.

Now, conceive the Voice set down beside one of the physical forces, and trying to interest her in the capacities of different rooms for singing in, she being more benevolent and horsefleshy than technically musical,—the Chaplain entertaining the other with an account of his solitary life in his rooms,—old Greenlaw hospitably entreating the mannerly widow, and trying to get the Nose to talk.

The young widow fixed on Colin, and informed him that if Solomon were to reappear with all his wisdom, as well as his glory, he would yet have to learn the polka ; and that the mode of feasting adopted by the Incas of Peru reminded her strongly of a custom prevalent among the Merovingian race of kings of France.

Living in the Pampas she regarded as an enviable lot, and she was at a loss to know the best mode of studying Euclid for the advantage of being able to teach a young brother of six (years old).

So we did not get home till near 11, and I had to be up at Glenlair at 5 this morning, the result of which is that at 12 to-night I am a little sleepy. Johnnie [1] can swim across the big pool at the Chapel, all by himself. His taste of water through

---

[1] His cousin John Cay, younger brother of William and Charles.

the nose did him great good. . . . I have had some races after stones down the water in Loch Roan. I have kept the stone in sight a good way, but it has always beaten me. I'll try some broken crockery to begin with.

I have succeeded in establishing the existence of an error in my Saturnian mazes, but I have not detected it yet. I have finished the first part of the Réligion Naturelle.[1] I am not a follower of those who believe they know what perfection must imply, and then make a deity to that pattern ; but it is very well put, and carries one through, though if the book belongs to this age at all it is eminently unlike most books of this century in England. But I only know one other book of French argument on the positive (not positiviste) side, and that also worked by " demonstration." My notion is, that reason, taste, and conscience are the judges of all knowledge, pleasure, and action, and that they are the exponents not of a code but of the unwritten law, which they reveal, as they judge by it *in presence of the facts.* The facts must be witnessed to by the senses, and cross-examined by the intellect, and not unless everything is properly put on record and proved as fact, will any question of law be resolved at headquarters.

We are only going through our Lehrjahr in the knowledge of Perfection, and we may have a Wanderjahr to complete even after getting the first diploma, which is a certificate of having eyes to see the work, a conscience to feel after Right, and faith to believe in the Word, and to reach a station thereby where both those eyes and that conscience may be satisfied, or at least appeased. I do not think it is doing Reason, etc., any injustice to say that rough dead facts are the necessary basis on which to work in order to elicit the living truth, not from the facts, but either from the utterer of facts or the giver of Reason, which two are one, or Reason would never decipher facts.

> For know, whatever was created needs
> To be sustained and fed.   Of elements
> The grosser feeds the purer, etc.
> ———— various degrees
> Of substance, and in things that live, of life
>   Meanwhile enjoy
> Your fill what happiness this happy state
> Can comprehend, incapable of more.

---

[1] By M. Jules Simon.

CHAPTER IX.

ABERDEEN——MARRIAGE——1857 TO 1860, ÆT. 26-29.

THE Glenlair letters of 1857 (see last chapter) sufficiently indicate Maxwell's mental condition in the interval between his first and second sessions at Aberdeen. His expansive sociable spirit is putting forth fresh feelers, and he has made a new beginning in his observation of man in society. But he has not yet recovered from the loss of the preceding year, and those who read between the lines cannot fail to trace here and there a touch of sadness peering from beneath the habitual buoyancy of his style.

In September of this year another loss renewed the feeling of desolation which had haunted him since his father's death. His friend Pomeroy, whom he had nursed in illness, and of whose career in India he had augured so highly, was carried off by a second attack of fever, caused by a hurried journey during the first outbreak of the Mutiny. Maxwell's letters to Mr. Litchfield show how keenly he felt this blow, and what deep thoughts on human life and destiny were once more stirred up in him.

His original work on electricity was now for a while interrupted by another laborious task, which absorbed his best energies for more than a year. The examiners for the Adams' Prize, given by St. John's College in honour of the discovery of Neptune,[1] had set as a subject, "The Motion of Saturn's Rings." To frame and test an hypothesis which should account for the observed phenomena was a problem of no ordinary complexity, and one to which the speculative imagination and mathematical ingenuity of

---

[1] See above, p. 61.

Clerk Maxwell were particularly adapted. It appears to have completely fascinated him for the time. The essay by which he gained the prize, and which he published after elaborately revising it, is well known to students, and the allusions to the subject in his letters at this time will be read with interest.

Such was the strain of feeling, and such the chief intellectual interest, with which he returned to Aberdeen, where he seems to have been once more destined, though in his native country, to understand more than he was understood ; and in his letters, together with the deepening earnestness and the unfailing humour, there is now and then mingled for the first time a grain of bitterness, or what may be taken for such. But it is rather the cry of a spirit hungering for completion. And the phase of disharmony quickly passes off, and is followed by a song of triumph.

Of his new acquaintances at Aberdeen he had become most intimate with the family of Principal Dewar of Marischal College, and he was a frequent visitor at their house. His deep and varied knowledge, not only of his own and kindred subjects, but of history, literature, and theology, his excellence of heart, and the religious earnestness which underlay his humorous "shell," were there appreciated and admired. He had been asked to join them in their annual visit to Ardhallow, the home of the Principal's son-in-law, Mr. M'Cunn, in the neighbourhood of Dunoon, and had accepted the invitation. The time of his stay there in September 1857 is marked by letters which, unlike some others of this period, reflect his brightest mood.

In February 1858 he announced his betrothal to Katherine Mary Dewar, and they were married early in the following June. In May he had made a journey to the south of England to visit me in my parish of Milford, in Hampshire, and to act as "best man" on the occasion of our marriage, which took place at Brighton. My wife and I found our way to Aberdeen in time to be present at the wedding there, and were shortly afterwards entertained at Glenlair.

The correspondence of these months and the poems then written contain the record of feelings which in the years that followed were transfused in action and embodied in a married life which can only be spoken of as one of unexampled devotion.[1]

He remained for two more sessions at Aberdeen. But in 1860 came the fusion of the colleges, and the Professorship of Natural Philosophy at Marischal College was one of those suppressed. In the same winter his old friend Professor James D. Forbes, after struggling for eight years against ill-health, resigned his Chair, and Maxwell became a candidate for the vacant post. It is enough to have alluded once for all[2] to the contest, which ended in the appointment of Professor Tait. It only remains to say that Maxwell's relations with that eminent man, who had been his companion both in Edinburgh and at Cambridge, always continued to be of the most friendly kind ; and their correspondence, often of the quaintest description, would of itself fill a volume of very entertaining reading for those possessed of a clue to the labyrinth of science, learning, wit, and frolicsome allusion, which it contains. The two men looked over proof-sheets of each other's writings, and when they most differed, Maxwell's criticism condensed in humorous verse was always understood and

---

[1] See the Poems of 1858.

[2] As this candidature was the last occasion on which Maxwell was compelled to collect testimonials, it may be well to add here to what has been said above about his teaching powers, that his success at Aberdeen was very strongly attested by his colleagues, and in particular by Thomas Clark, the Professor of Chemistry. And four years earlier, in February 1854, Professor G. G. Stokes had given this important testimony :—" . . . One thing more is wanted in a teacher, namely, a power of conveying clearly his knowledge to others. That Mr. Maxwell possesses that power I feel satisfied, having once been present when he was giving an account of some of his geometrical researches to the Cambridge Philosophical Society, on which occasion I was struck with the singularly lucid manner of his exposition." (See p. 154.)

welcomed by the Edinburgh Professor.   In the summer of
1860 the ex-professor of Aberdeen was appointed to the
vacant Professorship of Natural Philosophy in King's
College, London.

To LEWIS CAMPBELL, Esq.

Glenlair, 28th August 1857.

. . . I have been battering away at Saturn, returning to the
charge every now and then.   I have effected several breaches
in the solid ring, and now I am splash into the fluid one, amid
a clash of symbols truly astounding.   When I reappear it
will be in the dusky ring, which is something like the state of
the air supposing the siege of Sebastopol conducted from a forest
of guns 100 miles one way, and 30,000 miles the other, and
the shot never to stop, but go spinning away round a circle,
radius 170,000 miles. . . .

To THE SAME.

Ardhallow, Dunoon, 4th Sept. 1857.

The road along Loch Eck is the most glorious for shape and
colour of hills and rocks that I have seen anywhere, specially
on a fine calm day, with clouds as well as sun, and with large
patches of withered bracken mixed with green on the less steep
parts of the hills.   Then the crushing and doubling up of the
strata, and the slicing and cracking of the already doubled up
strata, quite without respect to previous torment, gives a notion
of active force, as well as passive, even to ungeological minds.
We inspected Duncan Marshall, the Hermit of these parts, and
wound up the day with a pull in the boat till dark. . . .

Mrs. Wed[derburn] professes herself ready to "follow follow
South" when asked, so when Johnny and I have done our
Moidart and Loch Aylort, we shall hoist sail or get up steam
or something, and then very likely he may reappear to his
parent and aunt, and I shall continue my road with my aunt
to wait upon the faithful Tobs, and realise Saturn's Rings, and
probably feed a few natives of the valley with the produce of
its soil.   I was writing great screeds of letters to Professor
Thomson about those Rings, and lo ! he was a-laying of the
telegraph which was to go to America, and bringing his obtrusive science to bear upon the engineers, so that they broke the

cable with not following (it appears) his advice. However, I know nothing. List to the new words to a common song, which I conceived on the railway to Glasgow. As I have only a bizzing, loose, interruption-to-talking-&-deathblow-to-general-conversation memory of the orthodox version, I don't know if the metre is correct; but it is some such rambling metre anyhow, and contains some insignificant though apparently treasonable remarks in a perfect thicket of vain repetitions. To avoid these

let　(ʊ) = "Under the sea,"

so that 2(ʊ), by parity of reasoning, represents two repetitions of that sentiment. This being granted, we shall have as follows:—

The Song of the Atlantic Telegraph Company.

I.

2(ʊ)
Mark how the telegraph motions to me,
2(ʊ)
Signals are coming along,
With a wag, wag, wag;
The telegraph needle is vibrating free,
And every vibration is telling to me
How they drag, drag, drag,
The telegraph cable along.

II.

2(ʊ)
No little signals are coming to me,
2(ʊ)
Something has surely gone wrong,
And it's broke, broke, broke;
What is the cause of it does not transpire,
But something has broken the telegraph wire
With a stroke, stroke, stroke,
Or else they've been pulling too strong.

III.

2(ʊ)
Fishes are whispering. What can it be,
2(ʊ)
So many hundred miles long?
For it's strange, strange, strange,
How they could spin out such durable stuff,
Lying all wiry, elastic, and tough,
Without change, change, change,
In the salt water so strong.

O

IV.

$2(\upsilon)$
There let us leave it for fishes to see;
$2(\upsilon)$
They'll see lots of cables ere long,
For we'll twine, twine, twine,
And spin a new cable, and try it again,
And settle our bargains of cotton and grain,
With a line, line, line,—
A line that will never go wrong.

Receive, etc.

To R. B. LITCHFIELD, Esq.

Glenlair, 23d Sept. 1857.

I have just returned from the remote Highlands, and have met all the Indian news on my way, and found your letter at home. I suppose it is best to say what I think to you, rather than what I feel, for that is confusion. You may well ask "Why?" I myself see a horrible despair waiting for us if we knew or even paid enough attention to things happening continually. Is it merely a reaction from our animal life that makes us comfortable again? or excitement of some other kind? or defective sympathy? No; I think real sympathy is the very thing we want, and we suffer more from want of union than from any other cause. I cannot make the thing clearer either to you or to myself; but as I was coming home and expecting bad news, I thought of dead and absent friends, and how they endeavoured when alive to make themselves known to us, and how the impression they had left in us remained untouched and sacred during their absence. Then I thought of those who had left the clearest impression on me,—how some were dead, and their character never known or proved to the world, and their deeds never done as they would have been if they had lived. But this secret knowledge is strengthening as well as sad, if our brother's life is an inheritance to us when he falls, and we rise (like Triamond) to fight his battle as well as our own.

Do not understand all this as a theory. I wish to say that it is in personal union with my friends that I hope to escape the despair which belongs to the contemplation of the outward aspect of things with human eyes. Either be a machine and see nothing but "phenomena," or else try to be a man, feeling your life interwoven, as it is, with many others, and strengthened by them whether in life or in death. You will say that this is what a man writes after a course of healthy exercise and boisterous health, when he suddenly feels a pull on his soul, but his body goes on as before. But though my knowledge of our friend does not reach so far back as yours, there is a great part of all my thoughts which bears the mark of his honest handling, for to me he was most liberal in communication, so that all manner of thought became our common property. When he was ill at Cambridge, my father, who was then rather better, was very much concerned about him, so that afterwards, when he was worse himself, he would speak of him from recollections of what I had told him before. So I used to think of them together,— the one guiding me along by wise plans in the ways of freedom, and the other supplying the energy of speculative honesty and the freshness of a younger mind. And is all gone? Certainly not, look at it as you will. I am not trying to persuade myself into hope. I find I cannot do otherwise. I have been miserable about these very things when there seemed no particular reason at the time, and then, when the time was worst, felt well; but that must be one's own personal affair. If we can hear the General's voice we will rise in our tears and go to our places, having conquered ourselves. Long ago I felt like a peasant in a country overrun with soldiers, and saw nothing but carnage and danger. Since then I have learned at least that some soldiers in the field die nobly, and that all are summoned there for a cause.

I am very sorry for India, and for you and poor Mrs. Pomeroy. She had a stake in him that none of us could have.

To Miss Cay.

Glenlair, 28th September 1857.

My dear friend Pomeroy died at Ghazeepore about 1st August, from overwork and forced marches. He was a civilian, and appointed assistant magistrate at Azinghur. He and the rest of the civilians proceeded thither with about 400 men. When they got there they fought about 2000 insurgents in two feet of water, and beat them off three times. Pomeroy volunteered to take in a wounded man (Lieut. Lewis, 65 N. I.) to Ghazeepore, when no one else would venture to go. He stayed there a few

days, but was unwell.   Then he went back to his post at Azinghur for about a week.   On the news of the Dinapore mutiny
they were all ordered in, and made a forced march on Ghazeepore, forty miles.

He died soon after getting in.

Of all the men I have known he was the most likely to have
done something for India.   I never knew a man more able to
see his way through difficulties, more respected by men of all
classes, or more determined that duty should be done whatever
might happen.   We have one comfort for ourselves, that few
men have made themselves more open to their friends, so that
many men may receive something of his spirit, though he is cut
off before strangers could take example by his deeds.

To R. B. Litchfield, Esq.

Glenlair, 15th October 1857.

I was glad S. sent me the letter.   Remember that besides
all the danger and distance from friends, there was the fever, of
which he had already long experience, and which in such times
he knew to be as inconvenient to his friends as himself.   But
it is no use saying this and that.   Some men redeem their
characters by their deeds, and we praise them.   Those that
merely show their character by their deeds should be remembered, not praised ; and a complete true man will live longest
in the memory, and I cannot but think will be less changed in
reality, than one who has doubtfully struggled with duplicity
in his constitution, and has walked with hesitation, though
along a good path.   I know that both do deny and renounce
themselves in favour of duty and truth, as they come to see
them ; and as they come to see how goodness, having the knowledge of evil, has passed through sorrow to the highest state of
all, they accept it as a token that they have found their true
head and leader, and so, with their eyes on him, they complete
the process called the knowledge of Good and Evil, which they
commenced so early and so ignorantly.

Now, what the "completion of the process" is I cannot
conceive, but I can feel the difference of Good and Evil in
some degree, and I can conceive the perception of that difference to grow by contemplating the Good till the confusion of
the two becomes an impossibility.   Then comes the mystery.
I have memory and a history, or I am nothing at all.   That

memory and history contain evil, which I renounce, and must still maintain that I was evil. But it contains the image of absolute good, and the fight for it, and the consciousness that all this is right.

So there the matter lies, a problem certain of solution. . . .

I am grinding hard at Saturn, and have picked many holes in him, and am fitting him up new and true. I am sure of most of him now, and have got over some stumbling-blocks which kept me niggling at calculations two years.

I am to have some artisans as weekly students this winter.

To the Same.

Lauriston Lodge,
Edinburgh, 25th October 1857.

. . . As to collecting memorials, that is a thing to do faithfully if at all. No man can write himself down wholly at once, so no one thing will give a complete autograph of the man. As for anecdotes, they are to be tolerated as the roughest way of giving to the public sketches of public men; but they will satisfy no private friend, not even him from whose memory they are drawn.

But if any essays (I know some that were not read aloud to any particular people, but were written by himself for himself) or anything else of his are to be had, they might be given to Mrs. Pomeroy with what explanation we could give, and so (not hastily but) when times occur, she might continue to learn more of him and his honestly fought and thoroughly conquered and well secured path through a land of shadows, where friends and foes seemed to exchange appearances, so that honesty and sincerity had parted with order and reverence, and indecision had passed for conscientiousness, and inquiry after truth had been taken for infidelity. A sad world to seek for truth in under any man's guiding. The exact point at which this progress has been interrupted may be disputed by men, but they have no jurisdiction, and are ignorant even of their own true faith till something bring it into action.

I could not conceive of any one undertaking to *write* a *memoir*. I am fully satisfied of the impossibility of that, with respect to any *young* man. The journal of voyage, which was meant to be read, is far the best memorial, and it is a very good one indeed for his mother and friends, for it is so wonderfully

open-hearted and unaffected.   I appreciate these qualities on
account of the force which it requires for me to say or do anything according to nature, especially in ordinary circumstances.

This spring I read a great deal of MS. at home, which gave
me much light about my father and his dealings with various
people.   There were journals of travels and adventures from
twelve years of age to thirty, and many other things.   Well, I
have found that reading profitable in making me remember
him better, and honour him more, and understand better how he
ordered his life and who were his friends.   That is the use and
intent of keeping anything belonging to our friends.   I do not
intend to advertise these things for public sale, for I doubt
whether the public would be better, and I would be worse.

The following letter from Pomeroy to his mother, of
which a copy was found in Maxwell's handwriting, throws
further light on the character of the man whose loss was
felt so deeply :—

Azingurh, July 28, 1857.

MY DEAR MOTHER—I sit down to write to you in rather a solemn
mood, partly owing to my having received yesterday a note from Mrs.
W. H. T., which I enclose, and partly because that, in this part of India,
and particularly in these outlying stations, with no European soldiers, the
lives of Englishmen more clearly lie in God's hand than on most occasions
in our sojourn on earth.

I have told you in former letters that I volunteered to go with any
civilians who reoccupied a station in the Benares district.   I did this
completely of my own responsibility, and whether I was right or wrong
God alone knows.   I was then in excellent health, and I could not bear
to think that I should be absolutely doing nothing in a safe station, when
an additional European, who could ride or use firearms, even if he could
do nothing else, was not utterly useless to the brave men who were going
out in order to make, persuade, or enable the natives to cultivate their
fields, during the three important months of the year, and so avoid a
famine.

Mr. Tucker responded immediately to my volunteering, and appointed
me "Assistant Magistrate" of Azingurh, with nearly —— a month.
You know the delay in going, and that I was ill during that time.   We
left (Benares) on the 16th, and arrived here on the 18th.   The march,
which I performed partly on horseback and partly in my buggy, did not
do me any harm, but the fatigue, excitement, and varied feelings caused
by an affray with a body of natives, led by Oude Zemindars, in which we
were finally victorious, after five hours of half fighting (not that I fought
much, but I was on horseback most of the time), rather weakened me.
Then there was a wounded man to be taken into Ghazipoor, and of those
whose duty it was to accompany him nobody who could be spared could

be induced to go, so I volunteered, whereby I pleased him, poor fellow, and his fellow-officers very much, and I believe I was of use to him. I hoped to have got three days rest at Ghazipoor, but the excitement of seeing new faces, and giving all my news over and over again, and trying to soothe angry officers whose corps had been abused, and explaining mistakes, etc. etc., made the *rest* very ambiguous ; and the journey back knocked me up. I was very feverish last night, but Home (the magistrate) took tremendous care of me, put my bed next his, and got me limes and honey, and everything he could get for cough or fever. To-day I am a great deal better, but still on rice-milk and chicken-broth, and as I have no duties but a share in the mess management, I get lots of lying down, but no absolute rest, as the nine of us, civil and military, live in one six-roomed bungalow. Don't imagine that nine (only) is the number walking about inside : everybody's bearer except mine and another's, I believe, walk about like tame dogs, bringing their masters' slightest wants, for few think of getting anything for themselves, even from across the room.

We have a very grave piece of intelligence from the neighbourhood of Legowlie, the headquarters of the 12th Irregular Cavalry. A native brought a report to a gentleman living 8 miles from Legowlie, that on the 24th of July the men of the 12th who were there left the station, and that the commanding officer (Major Holmes) and his wife, and the Doctor (Gardner), had been killed. This news has at length reached us, whom it concerns nearly, as one hundred of the same regiment are here. On the other side, it is to be said that all the principal native officers were absent from Legowlie, two being here now, and one elsewhere, so that the mutiny may not spread, and we have no treasure here to tempt them, and the Hindu Sepoys are not likely to join them, though their hatred of Mussel-mans has two or three times given way to their desire for plunder or love of Christian blood. Our position is precarious, but I can look it straight in the face, and in four days or less the crisis will, I hope, have passed.

Herne is a Poole man, with an uncle there of the name of Biddel. His wife is in the hills, and he hears from her now pretty often, but there is a month's interval between the departure and arrival of her letters. He is a decidedly religious man of a very genuine stamp. He read us last Sunday that grand sermon the Bishop of Calcutta preached towards the end of June. You should get it if it is to be had in England.

We are daily expecting to hear of the safety of Lucknow. Poor Mrs. Cooper ! She and her children must have been living in cellars for the last month, to be out of the way of cannon balls : and to live in a cellar in India must be dreadfully trying. If any children survive it will be a mercy,—a mercy indeed if they escape the awful, horrible fate of the ladies of Cawnpore. Mrs. Cave, whom I mentioned in my Journal, was, I fear, at the latter place. As a Madras fusilier said to me (in a broad Irish accent), "I don't care what they do to the likes of me—but the women—and Ladies too !"

Poor T—— writes me letters intended to be cheery, but really awfully dismal. She bears up bravely, and thinks no one sees her sorrow.

We have a picture in the house that belonged to some one who fled from this on the 3d June. It is called "Woman's Mission." You must have seen it in the print-shop windows,—two Scutari volunteer nurses attending a wounded man. A pathetic picture suits our feelings. All but two, I believe, have either wife or lover to think of ; but sorry should

I or any be that any woman should be with us. Poor Batty married a very short time ago, and had to part from his Bride almost immediately, and send her to Calcutta. He, too, has lost a Brother.

I hope the English papers will have better and truer accounts than the Indian generally have ; but you cannot follow events without some good map like Allen's £2 : 2s. one. So don't try ; it will only puzzle you, and the *Times* will give you the pith of the matter. The fire is now really being extinguished, though it will be long before stray points cease to flare up and burn those within their range.

There are two hundred of the King of Nepaul's Goorkas on the march to form part of our garrison, and on those we think we can really depend. They are very brave, and more than a match for Sepoys, and are more different in race and manners from the Hindus than we are, and very different in religion.

Urgent requisitions have been sent to Ghazipoor and Benares for Europeans, which may now at length be answered.

With regard to Mrs. T——, whom I was nearly forgetting in my egotism, I hope—if she has by the time this reaches you visited Cheltenham—that you have seen her. What a comfort it must be to her, poor thing, to think that she made him face those thoughts he had shunned and shirked so long. She left by last mail, so she will have been a fortnight in England or Ireland when this reaches you. I hope to write *you* a letter by Bombay and Marseilles of a later date, and to Editha by Calcutta and Marseilles ; so that this letter, which I confess is an alarmist one, will not arrive till you know the Event. I have written what I have that you may see I know my danger, and have, I hope, right feelings under it.—I remain, my very dear mother, your most affectionate son,

ROBERT HENRY POMEROY.

The main thread of the correspondence is now resumed with a letter addressed to Maxwell by Faraday on receiving a copy of the paper on "Lines of Force :"—

Albemarle Street, W., 25th March 1857.

MY DEAR SIR—I received your paper, and thank you very much for it. I do not say I venture to thank you for what you have said about "Lines of Force," because I know you have done it for the interests of philosophical truth ; but you must suppose it is work grateful to me, and gives me much encouragement to think on. I was at first almost frightened when I saw such mathematical force made to bear upon the subject, and then wondered to see that the subject stood it so well. I send by this post another paper to you ; I wonder what you will say to it. I hope however, that bold as the thoughts may be, you may perhaps find reason to bear with them. I hope this summer to make some experiments on the *time* of magnetic action, or rather on the time required for the assumption of the electrotonic state, round a wire carrying a current, that may help the subject on. The time must probably be short as the time of light ; but the greatness of the result, if affirmative, makes me not despair. Perhaps I had better have said nothing about it, for I am often long in realising my intentions, and a failing memory is against me.—Ever yours most truly,   M. FARADAY.

FROM THE SAME.

Albemarle Street, 7th November 1857.

I have just read and thank you heartily for your papers. I intended to send you copies of two of mine. I think I have sent them, but do not find them ticked off. So I now send copies, not because they are assumed as deserving your attention, but as a mark of my respect, and desire to thank you in the best way that I can.

FROM PROF. G. G. STOKES.

School of Mines,
Jermyn Street, 7th November /57.

I have just received your papers on a dynamical top, etc., and the account of experiments on the perception of colour. The latter, which I missed seeing at the time when it was published, I have just read with great interest. The results afford most remarkable and important evidence in favour of the theory of three primary colour-perceptions, a theory which you, and you alone, so far as I know, have established on an exact numerical basis.

FROM PROF. TYNDALL.

Royal Institution, 7th November 1857.

I am very much obliged to you for your kind thoughtfulness in sending me your papers on the Dynamical Top and on the Perception of Colour, as also for your memoir on Lines of Force, received some time ago. I never doubted the possibility of giving Faraday's notions a mathematical form, and you would probably be one of the last to deny the possibility of a totally different imagery by which the phenomena might be represented.[1]

To Professor Faraday.

129 Union Street,
Aberdeen, 9th November 1857.

DEAR SIR—I have to acknowledge receipt of your papers on the Relations of Gold to Light, and on the Conservation of Force. Last spring you were so kind as to send me a copy of the latter paper, and to ask what I thought of it.

That question silenced me at that time, but I have since heard and read various opinions on the subject, which render it both easy and right for me to say what I think. And first I pass over some who have never understood the known doctrine of conservation of force, and who suppose it to have something to do with the equality of action and reaction.

Now, first, I am sorry that we do not keep our words for distinct things more distinct, and speak of the "Conservation of Work or of Energy" as applied to the relations between the amount of "vis viva" and of "tension" in the world ; and of the "Duality of Force" as referring to the equality of action and reaction.

Energy is the power a thing has of doing work arising either from its own motion or from the "tension" subsisting between it and other things.

Force is the tendency of a body to pass from one place to another, and depends upon the amount of change of "tension" which that passage would produce.

Now, as far as I know, you are the first person in whom the idea of bodies acting at a distance by throwing the surrounding medium into a state of constraint has arisen, as a principle to be actually believed in. We have had streams of hooks and eyes flying around magnets, and even pictures of them so beset ;

---

[1] For confirmation of this, see Maxwell's (fragmentary) preface to the smaller treatise on electricity, published posthumously in 1881 ; especially these words : " In the larger treatise I sometimes made use of methods which I do not think the best in themselves, but without which the student cannot follow the investigations of the founders of the Mathematical Theory of Electricity. I have since become aware of the superiority of methods akin to those of Faraday, and have therefore adopted them from the first."

but nothing is clearer than your descriptions of all sources of force keeping up a state of energy in all that surrounds them, which state by its increase or diminution measures the work done by any change in the system.   You seem to see the lines of force curving round obstacles and driving plump at conductors, and swerving towards certain directions in crystals, and carrying with them everywhere the same amount of attractive power, spread wider or denser as the lines widen or contract.

You have also seen that the great mystery is, not how like bodies repel and unlike attract, but how like bodies attract (by gravi[ta]tion).   But if you can get over that difficulty, either by making gravity the residual of the two electricities or by simply admitting it, then your lines of force can "weave a web across the sky," and lead the stars in their courses without any necessarily immediate connection with the objects of their attraction.

The lines of Force from the Sun spread out from him, and when they come near a planet *curve out from it,* so that every planet diverts a number depending on its mass from their course, and substitutes a system of its own so as to become something like a comet, *if lines of force were visible.*

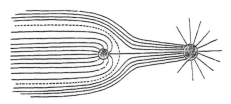

The lines of the planet are separated from those of the Sun by the dotted line.   Now conceive every one of these lines (which never interfere but proceed from sun and planet to infinity) to have a *pushing* force instead of a *pulling* one, and then sun and planet will be pushed together with a force which comes out as it ought, proportional to the product of the masses and the inverse square of the distance.

The difference between this case and that of the dipolar forces is, that instead of each body catching the lines of force from the rest, all the lines keep as clear of other bodies as they can, and go off to the infinite sphere against which I have supposed them to push.

Here then we have conservation of energy (actual and potential), as every student of dynamics learns, and besides this we have conservation of "lines of force" as to their *number* and total strength, for *every* body always sends out a number proportioned to its own mass, and the pushing effect of each is the same.

All that is altered when bodies approach is the *direction* in which these lines push. When the bodies are distant the distribution of lines near each is little disturbed. When they approach, the lines march round from between them, and come to push behind each, so that their resultant action is to bring the bodies together with a *resultant* force increasing as they approach.

Now the mode of looking at Nature, which belongs to those who can see the lines of force, deals very little with "resultant forces," but with a network of lines of action of which these are the final results, so that I, for my part, can not realise your dissatisfaction with the law of gravitation, provided you conceive it according to your own principles. It may seem very different when stated by the believers in "forces at a distance," but there can be only differences in form and conception, not in quantity or mechanical effect, between them and those who trace force by its lines.

But when we face the great questions about gravitation— Does it require time? Is it polar to the "outside of the universe" or to anything? Has it any reference to electricity? or does it stand on the very foundation of matter, mass or inertia? —then we feel the need of tests, whether they be comets or nebulæ, or laboratory experiments, or bold questions as to the truth of received opinions.

I have now merely tried to show you why I do not think gravitation a dangerous subject to apply your methods to, and that it may be possible to throw light on it also by the *embodiment* of the same ideas, which are expressed *mathematically* in the functions of Laplace and of Sir W. R. Hamilton in Planetary Theory.

But there are questions relating to the connection between magneto-electricity and certain mechanical effects which seems to me opening up quite a new road to the establishment of principles in electricity, and a possible conformation of the physical nature of magnetic lines of force. Professor W. Thomson seems to have some new lights on this subject.—Yours sincerely,

JAMES CLERK MAXWELL.

To Prof. Maxwell from Prof. Faraday.[1]

Albemarle Street,
London, 13th November 1857.

If on a former occasion I seemed to ask you what you thought of my paper, it was very wrong ; for I do not think any one should be called upon for the expression of their thoughts before they are prepared, and wish to give them. I have often enough to decline giving an opinion because my mind is not ready to come to a conclusion, or does not wish to be committed to a view that may by further consideration be changed. But having received your last letter, I am exceedingly grateful to you for it, and rejoice that my forgetfulness of having sent the former paper on conservation has brought about such a result. Your letter is to me the first intercommunication on the subject with one of your mode and habit of thinking. It will do me much good, and I shall read and meditate it again and again.

I daresay I have myself greatly to blame for the vague use of expressive words. I perceive that I do not use the word "force" as you define it, "the tendency of a body to pass from one place to another." What I mean by the word is the *source* or *sources* of all possible actions of the particles or materials of the universe ; these being often called the *powers* of nature when spoken of in respect of the different manners in which their effects are shown. In a paper which I have received at the moment from the *Phil. Mag.*, by Dr. Woods, they were called the "forces, such as electricity, heat, etc." In this way I have used the word "force" in the description of gravity which I have given as that expressing the received idea of its nature and source ; and such of my remarks as express an opinion or are critical apply only to that sense of it. You may remember I speak to labourers like myself, experimentalists on force generally, who receive that description of gravity as a physical truth, and believe that it expresses all, and no more than all, that concerns the nature and locality of the power. To these it limits the formation of their ideas, and the direction of their exertions, and to these I have endeavoured to speak ; showing how such a thought, if accepted, pledged them to a very limited and probably erroneous view of the cause of the force, and to

---

[1] This letter has already been published in the *Life of Faraday*.

ask them to consider whether they should not look (for a time
at least) to a source in part external to the particles.   I send
you two or three old printed lines *marked*, relating to this point.
To those who *disown* the definition or description as imperfect,
I have nothing to urge, as there is then probably no real difference between us.

I hang on to your words because they are to me weighty,
and where you say, " I for my part can not realise your dissatisfaction with the law of gravitation, provided you conceive
it according to your own principles," they give me great comfort.   I have nothing to say against the law of action of gravity.
It is against the law which measures its total strength as an
inherent force that I venture to oppose my opinion ; and I
must have expressed myself badly (though I do not find the
weak point) or I should not have conveyed any other impression.
All I wanted to do was to move men (not No. I. but No. II.)
from the unreserved acceptance of a principle of physical action
which might be opposed to natural truth.   The idea that we
may possibly have to connect *repulsion* with the lines of gravitation force (which is going far beyond anything my mind would
venture on at present, except in private cogitation), shows how
far we may have to depart from the view I oppose.

There is one thing I would be glad to ask you.   When a
mathematician engaged in investigating physical actions and
results has arrived at his conclusions, may they not be expressed
in common language as fully, clearly, and definitely as in mathematical formulæ ?   If so, would it not be a great boon to such
as I to express them so ?—translating them out of their hiero-
glyphics, that we also might work upon them by experiment.
I think it must be so, because I have always found that you
could convey to me a perfectly clear idea of your conclusions,
which, though they may give me no full understanding of the
steps of your process, give me the results neither above nor
below the truth, and so clear in character that I can think and
work from them.   If this be possible, would it not be a good
thing if mathematicians, working on these subjects, were to give
us the results in this popular, useful, working state, as well as
in that which is their own and proper to them ?

To H. R. DROOP, Esq.

129 Union Street,
Aberdeen, 14th November 1857.

I am very busy with Saturn on the top of my regular work. He is all remodelled and recast, but I have more to do to him yet, for I wish to redeem the character of mathematicians, and make it intelligible. I have a large advanced class for Newton, physical astronomy, the electric sciences, and high optics. What is your department by the way?

I have also a mechanics' class in the evening, once a week, on mechanical principles, such as doctrine of lever work done by machines, etc. So I have 15 hours a week, which is a deal of talking straight forward.

I am getting several tops (like the one I had at Cambridge) made here for various parties who teach rigid dynamics.

To C. J. MONRO, Esq.

129 Union Street,
Aberdeen, 26th November 1857.

The enclosed letters came from Mrs. Pomeroy to me. I think they are, one of them at least, yours. I doubt of the smaller one, but you will know. They seem dropping in still on poor Mrs. Pomeroy. Even ordinary returned letters are strange things to read again, as if you had been talking on when everybody had gone away.

I got your letter of the 6th. I have been grinding so hard ever since I came here that I left many letters unanswered. When I have time I shall write to you, and meanwhile only thank you for your letter.

I am at full college work again. A small class with a bad name for stupidity, so there was the more field for exciting them to more activity. So I have got into regular ways, and have every man *viva voce'd* once a week, and the whole class examined in writing on Tuesdays, and roundly and sharply abused on Wednesday morning; and lots of exercises which I find it advantageous to brew myself overnight.

Public Opinion here says that what our colleges want is inferior professors, and more of them for the money. Such men, says P. O., would devote their attention more to what

would pay, and would pay more deference to the authority of
the local press than superior or better paid men.   Therefore,
although every individual but one who came before the Commission was privately convinced that the best thing in itself
would be to fuse our two institutions into one, with one staff
of teachers, yet they all agreed that the public opinion of the
whole was the opposite of the private opinion of each, and that
more harm than good would result from adopting the course
which seemed good to the members, but not to the body, of the
public.   So the battle rages hot between Union (of Universities
only) and Fusion (of classes and professors).   Almost all the
professors in Arts are fusionists, and all the country south of
the Dee, together with England and the rest of Europe and the
world, but Aberdeen (on the platform), is Unionist, and nothing
else is listened to at public meetings, though perhaps a majority
of those present might be fusionists.   Such is Public Opinion ;
but we are all quiet again now, and I am working at various
high matters, for I have a very good class for Physical Astronomy,
Electricity, and Undulations, etc., and I want to do them justice.

I have had a lot of correspondence about Saturn's Rings,
Electric Telegraph, Tops, and Colours.   I am making a Collision of Bodies' machine, and a model of Airy's Transit Circle
(with lenses), and I am having students' teas when I can.   Also
a class of operatives on Monday evening, who do better exercises
than the University men, about false balances, Quantity of Work,
etc.

To Miss CAY.

129 Union Street, Aberdeen,
28th Nov. 1857.

I had a letter from Willy to-day about jet pumps to be made
for real drains, but not saying anything about the Professorship
of Engineering.

I have been pretty steady at work since I came.   The class
is small and not bright, but I am going to give them plenty to
do from the first, and I find it a good plan.   I have a large
attendance of my old pupils, who go on with the higher subjects.
This is not part of the College course, so they come merely from
choice, and I have begun with the least amusing part of what I
intend to give them.   Many had been reading in summer, for
they did very good papers for me on the old subjects at the
beginning of the month.   Most of my spare time I have been

doing Saturn's Rings, which is getting on now, but lately I have had a great many long letters to write,—some to Glenlair, some to private friends, and some all about science. . . . I have had letters from Thomson and Challis about Saturn—from Hayward of Durham University about the brass top, of which he wants one. He says that the Earth has been really found to change its axis regularly in the way I supposed. Faraday has also been writing about his own subjects. I have had also to write Forbes a long report on colours, so that for every note I have got I have had to write a couple of sheets in reply, and reporting progress takes a deal of writing and spelling. . . .

I have had two students' teas, at which I am becoming expert. I have also indulged in long walks, and have seen more of the country. The evenings are beautiful at this season. There have been some very fine waves on the cliffs south of the Dee.

To the Rev. L. Campbell.

(On taking Priest's Orders.)

129 Union Street, Aberdeen,
22d Dec. 1857.

I take for granted that sometime on Sunday last you entered the second of the ecclesiastical transformations. May your life and doctrine set forth God's glory, and be the means of setting forward the salvation of all men! Some of my friends think that the separation to a "holy function" puts a man into an artificial position with respect to the conduct of his thoughts, words, and acts, and that he is immersed in a professional atmosphere,—a *world*, in fact, differing from the world of business or of fashion only in the general colouring of its scenery. It has always seemed to me that men who have fallen into this "religious world" have completely failed in getting into the Church, seeing that the Church professes to be an escape from the world, and the only escape. And what holds of the Church ought to hold of the clergy preëminently. So far my theory of the Church not being a clerical world. Now I believe it not only as a theory, but as a fact, that a man will find the thing so if he will try it himself.

The restraints and professional stiffness of sentiment are not made for lawful members, but for those whom the truth has not yet made entirely free. I have to tell my men that all

P

they see, and their own bodies, are subject to laws which they cannot alter, and that if they wish to do anything they must work according to those laws, or fail, and therefore we study the laws. You have to say that what men are and the nature of their actions depends on the state of their wills, and that by God's grace, through union with Christ, the contradictions and false action of those wills may be settled and solved, so that one way lies perfect freedom, and the other way bondage under the devil, the world, and the flesh, and therefore you entreat them to give heed to the things which they have heard.

Now, no man accuses me of being stiff because I try to make what I say precise. Everybody knows that I believe it, whether I am stating a well-established law or only a half-verified conjecture. And I think that you have fully more right to be respected, inasmuch as the nature of your message implies the duty of *preaching* it, and the convictions that may be arrived at are as cogent, being more *clear*, if less *distinct*, than scientific truths.

I have been reading Butler's *Analogy* again, specially with reference to obscurities in style and language, and also to distinguish the merits of the man, and what habits of thought they depended on. Also Herschel's Essays, of which read that on Kosmos, and Froude's History. One night I read 160 pages of Buckle's *History of Civilisation*—a bumptious book, strong positivism, emancipation from exploded notions, and that style of thing, but a great deal of actually original matter, the true result of fertile study, and not mere brain-spinning. The style is not refined, but it is clear, and avoids fine writing. Froude is very good that way, though you can see the sort of pleasure that a University man takes in actually realising what he has talked over at Hall about showing what England was in the middle ages, and transfusing himself, style and all, thereinto, that his friends may see. A solitary student never does that sort of thing, nor can he appreciate the graces of imitation. I wish Froude would state whether he translates, and from what language, in each document.

I am still at Saturn's Rings. At present two rings of satellites are disturbing one another. I have devised a machine to exhibit the motions of the satellites in a disturbed ring ; and Ramage is making it, for the edification of sensible image worshippers. He has made four new dynamical tops, for various seats of learning.

I have set up a model of Airy's Transit Circle, and described it to my advanced class to-day. That institution is working well, with a steady attendance of fourteen, who have come of their own accord to do subjects not required by the College, *and the dryest first.*

To the present time we have been on Newton's *Principia* (that is, Sects. i. ii. iii., as they are, and a general view of the Lunar Theory, and of the improvements and discoveries founded on such inquiries). Now we go on to Magnetism, which I have not before attempted to explain.

The other class is at two subjects at once. Theoretical and mathematical mechanics is the regular subject, but two days a week we have been doing principles of mechanism, and I think the thing will work well. We now go on to Friction, Elasticity, and Breakage, considered as subjects for experiment, and as we go on we shall take up other experimental subjects germane to the regular course. I am happy in the knowledge of a good tinsmith, in addition to a smith, an optician, and a carpenter. The tinsmith made the Transit Circle.

College Fusion is holding up its head again under the fostering care of Dr. David Brown (father to Alexander of Queen's).[1] Know all men I am a Fusionist, and thereby an enemy of all the respectable citizens who are Unionists (that is, unite the three learned faculties, and leave double chairs in Arts). But there is no use writing out their theory to you. They want inferior men for professors—men who will find it their interest to teach what will pay to small classes, and who will be more under the influence of parents and the local press than more learned or better paid men would be in a larger college.

I send you a description of the Murtle Lecture delivered in our Public School :—

To those who admire the genius of the bard who sang of The Dee, the Don, Balgownie Brigg's black wall, the following lines will be welcome from their resemblance to the opening of one of his poems :—

> Know ye the Hall where the birch and the myrtle
> Are emblems of things half profane, half divine,
> Where the hiss of the serpent, the coo of the turtle,
> Are counted cheap fun at a sixpenny fine ?

---

[1] See a little book entitled *Crushed Hopes Crowned in Death,* London, 1862.

Know ye the Hall of the pulpit and form,
With its air ever mouldy, its stove never warm ;
Where the chill blasts of Eurus, oppressed with the stench,
Wax faint at the window, and strong at the bench ;
Where Tertian and Semi are hot in dispute,
And the voice of the Magistrand never is mute ;
Where the scrape of the foot and the audible sigh
In nature though varied, in discord may vie,
Till the accents of Wisdom are stifled and die ;
Where the Bajuns are dense as the cookies they chew,
And all save the Regents have something to do ;—
'Tis our Hall of Assembly, our high moral School,
Must its walls never rest from the bray of the fool ?
Oh vain as the prospect of summer in May
Are the lessons they learn and the fines that they pay.

All the public discipline, fines, etc., are arranged and levied at the Public School. The Bajuns, Semis, Tertians, and Magistrands are the four years of men. The Regents are the four Professors—Greek, Nat. Hist., Nat. Phil., and Mor. Phil.

Gaiety is just beginning here again. Society is pretty steady in this latitude,—plenty of diversity, but little of great merit or demerit,—honest on the whole, and not vulgar. . . . No jokes of any kind are understood here. I have not made one for two months, and if I feel one coming I shall bite my tongue. I shall write as soon as I hear again from you.

To the Same.

129 Union Street, 20th Jan. 1858.

I should have written to thank you for the little book,[1] but I think you will prefer my thanks now that I have read it.

What is the English book that says *dasz Wahrheit Offenbarung mache, nicht Offenbarung Wahrheit ?*

The marrow of the book lies in the man's being a Fremdling, conscious of the shell that surrounds him and divides him from others, and able neither to live in it nor to break it. But the shell is only the outer surface of a minute drop of fluid, impenetrable because minute, and arising from molecular forces in himself. But he meets with another drop, confined to one spot it is true, but a great deal larger than himself. He coalesces, and both are now larger and more fluid than before. Note that

---

[1] *Deutche Liebe.*

though he was movable and active, she fixed and ill, she knew the Hofrath; he knew no one, unless perhaps his mother. People differ in their need of knowing others, and in their power of conquering that knowledge. I have been reading Lavater and his life. He needed to know people; he was a man of a refined and tender spirit, but it was vigorous, although not very massive or powerful, and he came to know people, made friends, a few enemies, stuck to his work, and lived happy. Other men have lived well and done good without even wishing to burst the shell of separate existence, feeling it like the natural garment of a personal being.

Now I find that the transfusive tendency is not identical with personal attraction (using the last two words in anything but their newspaper sense). There are some people whom I feel disposed to love, honour, and obey, though in many things I may dislike them, and may have no wish to have a complete fusion of thought and feeling with them. There are others who are easily sympathised with, and open out willingly, but do not thereby acquire the power and authority which the first have without seeking it. Both is best, but of the two the first is more permanent than the second.

To return to the book, the different sex of the parties is treated as an accident, but by the effect on the man it certainly is not, neither is the effect of it insensible on the lady. She treats his statements with more reverence than is their due, as coming from a man, and, I think, fails entirely in framing a scheme for coalescing, without entering on that state of which marriage is the symbol, even though by accident there may be checks which may enable or compel the parties to stop short. It is not society that does it; it is a law in us. Now I must stop, or I shall be teaching my grandmother to suck eggs.

Let me try my hand on that worthy relative in her professional as well as private capacity, with respect to the Lilleshall sermon. I am sure you will be able, with pains, to put anything you have sure hold of before your hearers; but there are certain subjects which, after being handled by some of our writers, get coated over with language so tenacious that it is difficult to recognise them in plain clothes, so that you become like the "lovely song of one that hath a pleasant voice."

Now it is good to learn wisdom wherever it is to be found, but in teaching it, it must be made light, wholesome, and digestible, by being stripped of all vagueness and wordiness, and refitted with illustrations and conceptions carefully adapted to the hearers. Not but what the other method is pleasant to listen to, and not without profit (if taken with salt) ; but there are good books, out of which you may preach very bad sermons, with which your people may be as delighted as Mary Anne was with Faraday's lecture, of which she gave an account to *Punch*.

I find my principal work here is teaching my men to avoid vague expressions, as "a certain force," meaning uncertain ; *may* instead of *must; will be* instead of *is; proportional* instead of *equal*. . . .

As to yourself, I do not know whether college or parish work is best for you to be set to. I am not sorry about the rich people. They require you as much as the poor. But you must find out your own spirit, and what you were made for, and not steer by men either towards one man or from another.

Now I sent you a libellous description of our public school here last letter. Last week I was walking with the tune of the "Lorelei" running in my head, and it set itself into a "kind of allegory." The words are very crude, but that is the way they came together. I profess myself responsible for most things I say, but less for this than for most :—

> Alone on a hillside of heather,
>   I lay with dark thoughts in my mind ;
> In the midst of the beautiful weather
>   I was deaf, I was dumb, I was blind.
> I knew not the glories around me,
>   I thought of the world as it seems,
> Till a spirit of melody found me,
>   And taught me in visions and dreams.
>
> For the sound of a chorus of voices
>   Came gathering up from below,
> And I heard how all Nature rejoices,
>   And moves with a musical flow.
> O strange ! we are lost in delusion,
>   Our ways and doings are wrong,
> We are drowning in wilful confusion
>   The notes of that wonderful song.
>
> But listen, what harmony holy
>   Is mingling its notes with our own !
> The discord is vanishing slowly,
>   And melts in that dominant tone.

And they that have heard it can never
   Return to confusion again ;
Their voices are music for ever,
   And join in the mystical strain.

No mortal can utter the beauty
   That dwells in the song that they sing ;
They move in the pathway of duty,
   They follow the steps of their King.
I would barter the world and its glory,
   The vision of joy to prolong,
Or to hear and remember the story
   That lies in the heart of their song.

To the Same.

120 Union Street, 31st January 1858.

Thank you for your letter, so kind and so speedy. Now there are two of us, and I have that knowledge which is better than all advice. Not that I undervalue the advice at all, only the sense of unity between us is the main thing, whether we keep up correspondence or not. And I know that my friends are *ipso facto* your's, and your's mine, so that we are a large and influential body. . . .

But don't suppose that I intend to make you my confessor. It would not be just to you, for I do not like being confessed to myself; and I think every one should bear his own burden, though willing to lighten that of others. Besides, confession brings into set words and distinct outlines doubtful suspicions and half-formed thoughts, which would fade at once if they were not stirred up.

To do the thing adequately, without extenuation, voluntary exaggeration, or colouring of any kind, is far beyond human power. The consciousness of the presence of God is the only guarantee for true self-knowledge. Everything else is mere fiction, fancy portraiture,—done to please one's friends or self, or to exhibit one's moral discrimination at the expense of character.

.   .   .   .   .   .

And now be assured that I feel like Spenser's "Diamond," who had "Priamond's" spirit in him as well as his own. There is another human aid that is with me. The memory of my father is a great help to being practical and active. The more I think of him the better I get on, and I am the less tempted to absurdity and eccentricity in thought.

As for outward act, no one here seems to think me odd or daft. Some did at Cambridge, but here I have escaped. My rule is to avoid the company of young men whom I do not respect, unless I have the control of them.

King's College has its Senior Wrangler this year. I announced it to my class yesterday morning. Lightfoot has commissioned some more from me to be sent to Trinity.

To R. B. LITCHFIELD, Esq.

129 Union Street,
Aberdeen, 7th February 1858.

When I last wrote I was on my way here. Since then I have been at work, Statics and Dynamics ; two days a week being devoted to Principles of Mechanism, and afterwards to Friction, Elasticity and Strength of Materials, and also Clocks and Watches, when we come to the pendulum. We have just begun hydrostatics. I have found a better text-book for hydrostatics than I had thought for,—the run of them are so bad, both Cambridge and other ones,—Galbraith and Haughton's *Manual of Hydrostatics* (Longmans, 2s.) There are also manuals of Mechanics and Optics of the same set. There is no humbug in them, and many practical matters are introduced instead of mere intricacies. The only defect is a somewhat ostentatious resignation of the demonstrations of certain truths, and a leaning upon feigned experiments instead of them. But this is exactly the place where the students trust most to the professor, so that I care less about it. I shall adopt the Optics, which have no such defect, and possibly the Mechanics, next year.

My students of last year, to the number of about fourteen, form a voluntary class, and continue their studies. We went through Newton i. ii. iii., and took a rough view of the Lunar Theory, and of the present state of Astronomy. Then we have taken up Magnetism and Electricity, static and current, and now we are at Electro-magnetism and Ampère's Laws. I intend to make Faraday's book the backbone of all the rest, as he himself is the nucleus of everything electric since 1830.

So much for class work. Saturn's Rings are going on still, but this month I am clearing out some spare time to work them in. I have got up a model to show the motions of a ring of satellites, a very neat piece of work, by Ramage, the maker of the " top."

For other things—I have not much time in winter for improving my mind. I have read Froude's History, *Aurora Leigh*, and Hopkins's *Essay on Geology*, also Herschel's collected Essays, which I like much, also Lavater's life and *Physiognomy*, which has introduced me to him pleasantly though verbosely. I like the man very much, quite apart from his conclusions and dogmas. They are only results, and far inferior to methods. But many of them are true if properly understood and applied, and I suppose the rest are worth respect as the statements of a truth-telling man.

Well, work is good, and reading is good, but friends are better. I have but a finite number of friends, and they are dropping off, one here, one there. A few live and flourish. Let it be long, and let us work while it is day, for the night is coming, and work by day leads to rest by night.

To Rev. Lewis Campbell.

129 Union Street,
Aberdeen, 17th February 1858.

. . . I have not been reading much of late. I have been hard at mathematics. In fact I set myself a great arithmetical job of calculating the tangential action of two rings of satellites, and I am near through with it now. I have got a very neat model of my theoretical ring, a credit to Aberdeen workmen. Here is a diagram, but the thing is complex and difficult to draw :—

Two wheels turning on parallel parts of a cranked axle ; thirty-six little cranks of same length between corresponding points of the circumferences ; each carries a little ivory satellite.[1]

To Miss Cay.

129 Union Street,
18th February 1858.

Dear Aunt—This comes to tell you that I am going to have a wife.

I am not going to write out a catalogue of qualities, as I am not fit ; but I can tell you that we are quite necessary to one

---

[1] The sketch which follows corresponds to the model which is preserved in the Cavendish Laboratory.

another, and understand each other better than most couples I
have seen.

Don't be afraid ; she is not mathematical ; but there are other
things besides that, and she certainly won't stop the mathematics. The only one that can speak as an eye-witness is
Johnnie, and he only saw her when we were both trying to act
the indifferent. We have been trying it since, but it would not
do, and it' was not good for either.

So now you know who it is, even Katherine Mary Dewar
(hitherto). I have heard Uncle Robert speak (second-hand) of
her father, the Principal. Her mother is a first-rate lady, very
quiet and discreet, but has stuff in her to go through anything
in the way of endurance. . . . So there is the state of the case.
I settled the matter with her, and the rest of them are all
conformable.

I hope some day to make you better acquainted. I can
hardly admit that Johnnie saw her at all,—not as he will
when she appears in a true light. . . . For the present you
must just take what I say on trust. You know that I am not
given to big words. So have faith and you shall know.

. . . I don't write separately to Uncle Robert, seeing he is
with you, and I am very busy, and just now I should just write
the same thing over again, and I have not a copying press. So
good-bye.—Your affectionate nephew.

To R. B. LITCHFIELD, Esq.

129 Union Street,
Aberdeen, 5th March 1858.

My "lines" are so pleasant to me that I think that everybody ought to come to me to catch the infection of happiness.
This college work is what I and my father looked forward to
for long, and I find we were both quite right—that it was the
thing for me to do. And with respect to the particular college,
I think we have more discipline and more liberty, and therefore
more power of useful work, than anywhere else. It is a great
thing to be the acknowledged " regent " of one's class for a year,
so as to have them to one's self except in mathematics and what
additional classes they take. Then the next year I get those
that choose to come, which makes a select class for the higher
branches. They have all great power of work.

In Aberdeen I have met with great kindness from all sects

of people, and you now know of my greatest achievement in the way of discovery, namely, the method of converting friend-ship and esteem into something far better.   We are following up that discovery, and making more of it every day ; getting deeper and deeper into the mysteries of personality, so as to know that we ourselves are united, and not merely attracted by qualities or virtues, either bodily or mental.—(Don't suppose we talk metaphysics.) . . .

You will easily see that my "confession of faith" must be liable to the objection that Satan made against Job's piety. One thing I would have you know, that I feel as free from compulsion to any form of compromised faith as I did before I had any one to take care of, for I think we both believe too much to be easily brought into bondage to any set of opinions.

With respect to the "material sciences," they appear to me to be the appointed road to all *scientific* truth, whether meta-physical, mental, or social.   The knowledge which exists on these subjects derives a great part of its value from ideas suggested by analogies from the material sciences, and the remaining part, though valuable and important to mankind, is not *scientific* but aphoristic.   The chief *philosophical* value of physics is that it gives the mind something distinct to lay hold of, which if you don't, Nature at once tells you you are wrong.   Now, every stage of this conquest of truth leaves a more or less presentable trace on the memory, so that materials are furnished here more than anywhere else for the investigation of *the* great question, "How does Knowledge come ?"

I have observed that the practical cultivators of science (*e.g.*, Sir J. Herschel, Faraday, Ampère, Oersted, Newton, Young), although differing excessively in turn of mind, have all a dis-tinctness and a freedom from the tyranny of words in dealing with questions of Order, Law, etc., which pure speculators and literary men never attain.

Now, I am going to put down something on my own authority, which you must not take for more than it is worth. There are certain men who write books, who assume that what-ever things are orderly, certain, and capable of being accurately predicted by men of experience, belong to one category ; and whatever things are the result of conscious action, whatever are capricious, contingent, and cannot be foreseen, belong to another category.

All the time I have lived and thought, I have seen more and

more reason to disagree with this opinion, and to hold that all want of order, caprice, and unaccountableness results from interference with liberty, which would, if unimpeded, result in order, certainty, and trustworthiness (certainty of success of predicting). Remember I do not say that caprice and disorder are not the result of free will (so called), only I say that there is a liberty which is not disorder, and that this is by no means less free than the other, but more.

In the next place, there are various states of mind, and schools of philosophy corresponding to various stages in the evolution of the idea of liberty.

In one phase, human actions are the resultant (by par^m· of forces) of the various attractions of surrounding things, modified in some degree by internal states, regarding which all that is to be said is that they are subjectively capricious, objectively the "RESULT OF LAW,"—that is, the wilfulness of our wills feels to us like liberty, being in reality necessity.

In another phase, the wilfulness is seen to be anything but free will, since it is merely a submission to the strongest attraction, after the fashion of material things. So some say that a man's will is the root of all evil in him, and that he should mortify it out till nothing of himself remains, and the man and his selfishness disappear together. So said Gotama Buddha (see Max Müller), and many Christians have said and thought nearly the same thing.

Nevertheless there is another phase still, in which there appears a possibility of the exact contrary to the first state, namely, an abandonment of wilfulness without extinction of will, but rather by means of a great development of will, whereby, instead of being consciously free and really in subjection to unknown laws, it becomes consciously acting by law, and really free from the interference of unrecognised laws.

There is a screed of metaphysics. I don't suppose that is what you wanted. I have no nostrum that is exactly what you want. Every man must brew his own, or at least fill his own glass for himself, but I greatly desire to hear some more from you, just to get into *rapport*.

As to the Roman Catholic question, it is another piece of the doctrine of Liberty. People get tired of being able to do as they like, and having to choose their own steps, and so they put themselves under holy men, who, no doubt, are really wiser than themselves. But it is not only wrong, but impossible, to

transfer either will or responsibility to another ; and after the
formulæ have been gone through, the patient has just as much
responsibility as before, and feels it too.   But it is a sad thing
for any one to lose sight of their work, and to have to seek
some conventional, arbitrary treadmill-occupation prescribed by
sanitary jailors. . . .

With respect to the class, I send you the paper they did last
week.   Five floored it approximately, two first-rate.   I got half-
a-dozen correct answers to questions on the effects of mixtures
of ice and steam in various proportions, and on the effect of
heating and cooling on the thrust of iron beams (numerical).
From the higher class I have essay on Vision (construction of
eye, spectacles, stereoscopes, etc.) So the work done is equivalent
to the work spent.

To Rev. Lewis Campbell.

Aberdeen, 15th March 1858.

When we had done with the eclipse to-day, the next calculation was about the conjunction.   The rough approximations
bring it out early in June. . . .

The first part of May I will be busy at home.   The second
part I may go to Cambridge, to London, to Brighton, as may
be devised.   After which we concentrate our two selves at
Aberdeen by the principle of concerted tactics.   This done, we
steal a march, and throw our forces into the happy valley, which
we shall occupy without fear, and we only wait your signals to
be ready to welcome reinforcements from Brighton. . . . Good
night.—Your affectionate friend,　　　　J. C. Maxwell.

N.B.—We are going to do optical experiments together in
summer.   I am getting two prisms, and our eyes are so good as
to see the *spot* on the sun to-day without a telescope.

To Prof. J. C. Maxwell from Prof. Forbes.

Edinburgh, 16th March 1858.

I was much obliged to you for your letter, and the announce-
ment of your marriage, which I have not the smallest doubt will
add to your happiness, while at the same time I do not fear its
abstracting you from science.

Your notice of Saturn will be very acceptable.   But it

should not run to too great a length, as the 19th will probably be our last meeting, and is always a crowded billet. Give me an idea of the least time requisite to give an idea of your subject ; and more particularly try to send me a piece of the MS., so that I may legally hold it as a MS. delivered, and take precedence of some trivial communications of which I stand rather in dread.

I duly received the *Top*. I suppose it is all right, but my energies have been absorbed in Electrical experiments merely for lecture, and which have been very heavy upon me. I ought to have paid for the Top ere now, but I will soon.

We saw the Eclipse very badly, and it seems that in England it was no better. I had arranged to give a telegraphic account to R. Soc. last night, from no less than 3 points on the central line. . . .

To Rev. Lewis Campbell.

Glenlair, Springholm,
Dumfries, 28th April 1858.

. . . I wish you great joy, now and always ! I hope to certify myself ere long what sort of "friend's wife" I am to have. I have faith already, but sight is better, and you will have some pleasure in getting my verdict, though you don't need anything of the kind.

I have been very happy in observing the very admirable frame of mind in which all my friends seem disposed to regard my affairs, and yet I would rather that their opinions and sentiments had a more distinct basis of observation. But I suppose they observe me, and see I am "all right and no mistake." . . .

I tell you this . . . because you are our friend for better for worse.

I shall bring you a small pen-wiper that Katherine made for you the last day I was in Aberdeen. If you are careful in using it as it ought to be used, you will get rid of all the " odium theologicum " and other bitter principles sometimes occurring in parsons' ink, and your heart will indite good matter with the pen of a ready writer. . . .

To C. J. Monro, Esq.

Glenlair, 29th April 1858.
. . . I displayed my model of Saturn's Ring at the Edin-

burgh Royal Society on the 19th. The anatomists seemed to take most interest in the construction of it. We are going to do some experiments on colour this summer, if my prisms turn out well. I have got a beautiful set of slits made by Ramage, to let in the different pencils of light at the proper places, and of the proper breadths.

To Miss K. M. Dewar.

2d May 1858.

Now you must remember that all I say about texts and matters of that sort is only a sort of help to being together when we read, for I am not skilful to know what is the right meaning of anything so as to tell other people, only I have a right to try to make it out myself, and what I say to myself I may say to you.

To the Same.

6th May 1858.

Isaiah li. and Gal. v.—I suppose the leaven in v. 9 is the little bit of Judaism that they were going to adopt, on the plea that it is " safer " to do and believe too much than too little, and yet these little things altered the character of the whole of their religion by making it a thing of labour and wages, instead of an inward growth of faith working by love, which purifies the heart now, and encourages us to wait for the hope of righteousness. But still the desire of the spirit is contrary to the desire of the flesh, the one tending towards God, and the other towards the elements of the world, so that we are kept stretched as it were, and this is our training in this life. Our flesh is God's making, who made us part of His world ; but then He has given us the power of coming nearer to Himself, and so we ought to use the world and our bodies as means towards the knowledge of Him, and stretch always as far as our state will permit towards Him. If we do not, but wilfully seek back again to the elements as the Israelites to Egypt, then we are not like infants or even brutes, but far worse, as recoiling from God and His blessedness. Here are manifest the works of the flesh, which are not only not those of righteousness, but opposed to them ; but the fruit of the spirit comes when, like good trees, we stretch our best affections upwards till we see the sun, and breathe the air and drink the rain, and receive all free gifts, instead of sending our branches after our roots, down among things that once had life but now are decaying, and seeking there for nourishment that can only be had from above.

See the order of ripening of the fruit. Now, love brings joy to ourselves, and this, peace with others, and this, long-suffering of their attacks, for why should we be angry? Gentleness is a higher degree of this, being active. Goodness is used in a less general sense than we use it. It seems something like "good nature," only better and more manly, and refers to the good disposition of a man among men. Faith is put in here as the *result* of good living; which is true, for it is nourished thereby. Then see what comes of adding faith to a good disposition,—meekness, which we cannot afford to have without faith; and lastly, temperance or moderation, which is also founded on faith, and is a virtue that can never be perfect till all the rest are so.

To the Same.

Milford, Lymington (Hants),
9th May 1858.

To-day we were called at seven; were down soon thereafter, and had everything leisurely and comfortably till ten, when we went to school. I had a class of youths just beginning to read, and some of them knew not what swine were, still less what a herd was. At eleven to church—Lewis read prayers and lessons very well and distinctly, and Chester preached on James i. 15. Sin when it is finished bringeth forth death. He showed up sin as the universal poison, and showed how it might be seen working death in several instances, and also in all, good and bad, in this life, and then turned to the next, and finally indicated the remedy, though not so clearly as Paul in Rom. viii. 2, which he should have read.

In the afternoon Chester read prayers and Lewis preached on "Ye must be born again," showing how respectable a man it was addressed to, and how much he, and all·the Jews, and all the world, and ourselves, needed to be born *from above* (for that is the most correct version of the word translated *again*). Then he described the changes on a man new-born, and his state and privileges. I think he has got a good hold of the people, and will do them good and great good.

To the Same.

10th May 1858.

Eph. iii. 19.—Paul can express no more, but read the last

two verses and you will see this is not the crown, but only what can be asked or thought.   What a field for ambition there is,— for climbing up, or rather, being drawn up, into Christ's love, and receiving into our little selves all the fulness of God.   Let us bless God even now for what He has made us capable of, and try not to shut out His spirit from working freely.

To the Same.

13th May 1858.

I have been reading again with you Eph. vi.   Here is more about family relations.   There are things which have meanings so deep that if we follow on to know them we shall be led into great mysteries of divinity.   If we despise these relations of marriage, of parents and children, of master and servant, every-thing will go wrong, and there will be confusion as bad as in Lear's case.   But if we reverence them, we shall even see beyond their first aspect a spiritual meaning, for God speaks to us more plainly in these bonds of our life than in anything that we can understand.   So we find a great deal of Divine Truth is spoken of in the Bible with reference to these three relations and others.

To the Same.

16th May 1858.

Phil. iii.—There is great wisdom in v. 13.   Never look back with complacency on anything done, or attained, or possessed. See the description of those who mind earthly things, and let us depart from their ways.   Conversation in v. 20 means going backwards and forwards, and refers to the walking of the pre-ceding verses.   What a description of the power of Christ in the last verse, over "all things," and our vile bodies among the rest, and what a day it will be when He has done all His work and is satisfied.

I think the more we enter together into Christ's work He will have the more room to work His work in us.   For He always desires us to be one that He may be one with us.   Our worship is social, and Christ will be wherever two or three are gathered together in His name.

I have been vexed that I could not speak better to ——.   I had a long walk with him, talking of what people have believed, and what was necessary to be believed.   I hope we may come to understand each other, but more that he may come to the

clear light. I wish I could speak to him wise words. He is
so anxious to hear, and I to speak, and then the words are all
wind after all.

To PROF. J. C. MAXWELL FROM VERNON LUSHINGTON, Esq.

Ockham, 31st May 1858.

Next Wednesday is *your* second of June, after which we shall
no longer be able to think of you as one of ourselves—the youthful wanderers and seekers of the earth. So how can I better
employ the end of this Sunday evening than by bidding you
Farewell and God speed ? . . .

When Wednesday comes I hope I shall think of you. I like
thinking of you,—what you were, what you are, and what you
may be. All happiness be with you and yours !

To C. J. MONRO, Esq.

Glenlair, 24th July 1858.

. . . We are no great students at present, preferring various
passive enjoyments, resulting from the elemental influences of
sun, wind, and streams. This week I have begun to make a
small hole into Saturn, who has slept on his voluminous ring
for months.

To MRS. MAXWELL.

16th September 1859.

Mrs. Sabine learnt mathematics of her husband after she was
married, so she was not married for it. Murchison knew no
geology when he was married, but his wife did a little ; and
there was a fall of a cliff in the morning early, and her maid
told her of it, so she was for up ;[1] so Murchison got up too, and
there were the great bones of an Icthyosaurus in the broken
cliff, and he was interested and took to geology. Before that he
was an idle young officer.

To PROFESSOR FARADAY.

Marischal College, Aberdeen,
30th November 1859.

DEAR SIR—I am a candidate for the Chair of Natural

---

[1] "was for up," *i.e.* wished to get up.

Philosophy in the University of Edinburgh, which will soon be vacant by the appointment of Professor J. D. Forbes to St. Andrews. If you should be able, from your knowledge of the attention which I have paid to science, to recommend me to the notice of the Curators, it would be greatly in my favour, and I should be much indebted to you for such a certificate.

I was sorry that I had so little time in September that I could not write out an explanation of the figures of lines of force which I sent you ; but Professor W. Thomson, to whom I lent them, seems to have indicated all that was necessary, and most of them can be recognised from their resemblance to the curves made with Iron filings.

The only thing to be observed is, that these curves are due to the action either of long wires perpendicular to the paper, or of elongated magnetic poles, such as the edge of a long ribbon of steel magnetised transversely. By considering infinitely long currents or magnetic poles perpendicular to the paper we obtain systems of curves far more easily traced than in any other case, while their general appearance is similar to those produced in the ordinary experiments.

All the diagrams have two sets of lines at right angles to each other, and the width between the two sets of lines is the same, so that the reticulation is nearly square. If one system belongs to poles, the other belongs to currents, so that if the meaning of one be known, that of the other may be deduced from it.—I remain yours truly,   JAMES CLERK MAXWELL.

NOTE ON "SATURN'S RINGS."

These appendages to the planet had been seen by Galileo through his telescope in 1610, but their continually varying form met with no explanation until Huyghens in 1659 discovered that what had previously been regarded as a pair of satellites was a continuous ring. The great division between the outer and inner rings was first seen on the northern surface by William Bell in 1665, and on the southern surface by Cassini in 1675. In 1789 Herschel determined the time of rotation of the outer ring. More recent observations showed that besides the great division between the rings there is an appearance of a further subdivision, as though each ring consisted of a great number of narrow concentric rings with spaces between them. In 1850 a dark ring within the inner bright ring was discovered. This ring is transparent, so that the planet can be seen through it. By a comparison of his own measurements with those of Huyghens and Herschel, Struve concluded that the configuration of the rings is changing, their breadth continually increasing so that their inner edges are approaching the planet ; but the evidence of this change is by no means conclusive. The problem set by the Smith's Prize Examiners was to account for these appearances on mechanical principles.

If the rings were solid it is certain that the forces to which they would be exposed by the attraction of the planet would not only crush but liquify them.[1] If the rings were indefinitely narrow, the attraction of the planet might be compensated by allowing them to rotate with the proper velocity ; but in the case of a broad ring the velocity suited to the inner portions would be too great for the outer parts, while that adapted to the middle portion of the ring would suit neither the inside nor the outside. Hence it seemed to follow that if the rings were solid they must consist of a great number of very narrow rings, each rotating at its proper rate. This was shown by Laplace, who also showed that for such a system to be permanent the rings must be far from uniform. In 1851 Professor Pierce showed that the number of the rings must be much greater than Laplace supposed.

This was the condition of the question when it was taken up by Maxwell, and the gist of it is thus expressed by him in the course of his Essay :—" When we have actually seen that great arch swung over the equator of the planet without any visible connection, we cannot bring our minds to rest. We cannot simply admit that such is the case, and describe it as one of the observed facts in nature, not admitting or requiring explanation. We must either explain its motion on the prin-

---

[1] This depends on what is known to engineers as the "strength of material." For example : There is a superior limit to the span of an iron bridge, and when this limit is reached the bridge can only bear its own weight. Increasing the amount of iron would be of no use, as the weight would be increased in the same proportion as the strength, and hence this limit can never be exceeded.

ciples of mechanism, or admit that, in the Saturnian realms, there can be motion regulated by laws which we are unable to explain."

Maxwell first tried the hypothesis of Laplace and showed that to insure the permanence of the rings, the material would have to be so artificially adjusted as to be inconsistent "with the natural arrangements observed elsewhere." He found that in the case of liquid rings there would be waves set up in the system, which would increase in intensity until the rings broke up into drops. And his conclusion was that the rings must consist of independent fragments or satellites, as described in his letter of August 28, 1857 (p. 192). Sir George Airy said of this paper : " It is one of the most remarkable applications of Mathematics to Physics that I have ever seen."

CHAPTER X.

KING'S COLLEGE, LONDON, 1860 TO 1865—GLENLAIR, 1860 TO 1870—ÆT. 29-39.

FROM this point onward the interest of Maxwell's life (save things "wherewith the stranger intermeddles not") is chiefly concentrated in his scientific career. As a full account of his labours in science is beyond the scope of this volume, what remains of the present narrative will be comparatively brief.

1860-1865. The work at King's College was more exacting than Æt. 29-34. that in Aberdeen. There were nine months of lecturing in the year, and evening lectures to artisans, etc., were recognised as a part of the Professor's regular duties. Maxwell retained the post until the spring of 1865, when he was succeeded by Professor W. G. Adams, but continued lecturing to the working men during the following winter.

In June 1860 Maxwell attended the British Association's meeting at Oxford, where he exhibited his box for mixing the colours of the spectrum. He also presented to Section A a most important paper on Bernoulli's Theory of Gases; a theory which supposes that a gas consists of a number of independent particles moving about among one another without mutual interference, except when they come into collision. Maxwell showed that the apparent viscosity of gases, their low conductivity for heat, and Graham's laws of diffusion, could be satisfactorily explained by this theory, and gave reasons for believing that in air at ordinary temperature each particle experiences on an average more than 8,000,000,000 collisions per second. It is probable that the contemplation of the "flight of brick-bats" (his own vivid phrase for the constitution of Saturn's rings) led him on to his far-reaching investigations in this field of molecular physics.

On the 17th of May 1861 he delivered his first lecture before the Royal Institution. The subject was "On the Theory of the three Primary Colours."

All this while Maxwell was quietly and securely laying the foundations, deep and wide, of his great work on Electricity and Magnetism, but he had not the leisure that was requisite for bringing it to completion.

The period of his King's College Professorship was far, however, from being scientifically unfruitful. The colour-box was perfected, and many series of observations were made with it. Mrs. Maxwell's observations were found to have a special value. Through a striking discrepancy between her readings and C. H. Cay's, Maxwell discovered that the blindness of the *Foramen Centrale* to blue light, which was strongly marked in his own dark eyes, was either altogether absent from hers, or present in a very low degree. The comparison of J. C. M.'s (J.'s) eyes, and Mrs. M.'s (K.'s) forms part of this investigation.

The experimental measurements by which the present standard of electrical resistance (the Ohm) was first determined, were made at King's College by a sub-committee of the B.A., consisting of Maxwell, Balfour Stewart, and Fleeming Jenkin, in 1862-63, in accordance with a method proposed by Sir Wm. Thomson. A further experimental measurement was made next year by Maxwell, Fleeming Jenkin, and Charles Hockin (Fellow of St. John's). The importance of the work may be estimated by the fact that the system of units then determined by the B.A. Committee was, in the main, adopted by the Electrical Congress which met last year (1881) in Paris, and an International Commission has been appointed by the European Governments to make a redetermination of the standard of resistance first measured by the B.A. Committee. Maxwell's papers on this subject, with those of his fellow-workers, were republished in 1873 in a volume edited by Professor

Jenkin.[1]   Many are the references to successful or fruitless "spins" in the home letters of this period.   The following quotation will suffice :—

28th January 1864.

We are going to have a spin with Balfour Stewart to-morrow. I hope we shall have no accidents, for it puts off time so when anything works wrong, and we cannot at first find out the reason, or when a string breaks, and the whole spin has to begin again. . . . However, we hope to bring out our standards by September, and Becker [2] makes them up excellently.

A mass of correspondence, containing numerous suggestions made by Maxwell from day to day in 1863-4, has been preserved by Professor Jenkin. Two of the least technical passages will be found amongst the letters in this chapter (pp. 252, 255).

Another very important experimental investigation which was conducted by Clerk Maxwell about this period was the determination of the ratio of the electromagnetic and electrostatic units of electricity, for the purpose of comparing this quantity with the velocity of light.   With regard to this investigation, it is only necessary to say here that the experiment amounts to a comparison between the attractions of two electric currents flowing in coils of wire, and the attraction or repulsion between two metal plates which have each received a charge of electricity.   Clerk Maxwell had pointed out that, in accordance with his theory, the ratio of the units should be equal to the velocity of light, and the value obtained by him was intermediate between the extreme values obtained for that velocity by previous observers.   The experiment was the outcome of his theory of the constitution of the space in the neighbourhood of magnetic and electric currents, by which he accounted for all the then known phenomena of magnetism

---

[1] *Reports of the Committee on Electrical Standards, appointed by the British Association for the advancement of Science.*   Spon, London and New York, 1873.   [2] Of Messrs. Elliott Brothers.

and electricity, and which he published in a semi-popular
form in the *Philosophical Magazine* in 1861 and 1862.

During most of the King's College time Maxwell resided
at 8 Palace Gardens Terrace, Kensington, where he carried
on many of his experiments in a large garret which ran
the whole length of the house. When experimenting at
the window with the colour-box (which was painted black,
and nearly eight feet long), he excited the wonder of his
neighbours, who thought him mad to spend so many hours
in staring into a coffin. This was also the scene of his
well-known experiments on the viscosity of gases at different pressures and temperatures. For some days a large
fire was kept up in the room, though it was in the midst
of very hot weather. Kettles were kept on the fire, and
large quantities of steam allowed to flow into the room.
Mrs. Maxwell acted as stoker, which was very exhausting
work when maintained for several consecutive hours.
After this the room was kept cool, for subsequent experiments, by the employment of a considerable amount
of ice.

During Maxwell's residence in London his brother-in-
law, the Rev. Donald Dewar, came and stayed in his house
in order to undergo a painful operation at the hands of
Sir William Ferguson. Maxwell gave up the ground floor
of his house to Mr. Dewar and his nurse. He himself,
meanwhile, used to take his meals in a very small back
room, where frequently he breakfasted (on porridge) on
his knees, because there was no room for another chair at
the table. Maxwell acted constantly in the capacity of
nurse to Mr. Dewar, who would always look out anxiously
for his return from college, and whose face would light up
with a smile of pleasure and relief when he saw him coming.
No one else could arrange and smooth his couch for him
so perfectly.

One pleasant incident of Maxwell's stay in London was
the improvement of his acquaintance with Faraday, with
whom he seems to have dined on the occasion of his
lecture before the Royal Institution in 1861.

On one occasion he was wedged in a crowd attempting

to escape from the lecture theatre of the Royal Institution, when he was perceived by Faraday, who, alluding to Maxwell's work among the molecules, accosted him in this wise—"Ho, Maxwell, cannot you get out? If any man can find his way through a crowd it should be you."

He also renewed his personal intercourse with Litchfield, Droop, and other Cambridge friends.

His habit at this time was to do his scientific work chiefly in the mornings, unless when entertaining friends, when he would give up his days to them and take hours for work out of the night. In the afternoons he would ride with Mrs. Maxwell. She had been recommended horse exercise in 1860, when the pony "Charlie," called after Charles Hope Cay, was bought at the Rood fair. He was a high-bred, spirited, light bay Galloway, with arched neck and flowing tail. Maxwell himself broke him in, riding side-saddle, with a piece of carpet to take the place of a habit. This pony was a great favourite until the end in 1879.

About this time (between 1860 and 1865) the endowment of Corsock Church was completed, and the Manse built. Maxwell gave largely to both objects, which were promoted mainly by his zeal and energy.

At the beginning and at the close of the King's College period Maxwell suffered from two severe illnesses, both of a dangerously infectious nature, and in both of them he was nursed by Mrs. Maxwell. In September 1860 he had an attack of smallpox at Glenlair, which he was supposed to have caught at the fair, where "Charlie" was bought. During this illness his wife was left quite alone with him —the servants only coming to the door of the sick-room. He has been heard to say that by her assiduous nursing on this occasion she saved his life.

The second illness was in September 1865, also at Glenlair. Maxwell had been riding a strange horse, and got a scratch on the head from a bough of a tree; this was followed by an attack of erysipelas, which brought him very low. Mrs. Maxwell was again his nurse, and to listen, as

he insisted on doing, to her quiet reading of their usual
portion of Scripture every evening, was the utmost mental
effort which he could bear.

The years which followed the resignation of his post at 1866-1870.
King's College were spent, for the most part, at Glenlair, *Æt.* 35-39.
the house being at this time enlarged in general accordance
with his father's plan.　And Maxwell took advantage of
this retirement to embody some of the results of his investigations in substantive books.　The great work on
Electricity and Magnetism, although not published till
1873, was now taking definite shape, and the treatise on
Heat, which appeared in 1870, had been undertaken as a
by-work during the same period.

His scientific and other correspondence also absorbed a
good deal of energy.　Some measure of it is afforded by
the fact that a "pillar"-box was let into the rough stone
wall on the roadside, across the Urr, for the sole use of
Glenlair House.　Maxwell would himself carry the letters
to and from this rustic post-office in all weathers, at the
same time giving the dogs a run.

Both now and afterwards, his favourite exercise—as
that in which his wife could most readily share—was
riding, in which he showed great skill.　Mr. Fergusson
remembers him in 1874, on his new black horse,
"Dizzy," which had been the despair of previous owners,
"riding the ring," for the amusement of the children at
Kilquhanity, throwing up his whip and catching it, leaping
over bars, etc.

A considerable portion of the evening would often be
devoted to Chaucer, Spenser, Milton, or a play of Shakespeare, which he would read aloud to Mrs. Maxwell.

On Sundays, after returning from the kirk, he would
bury himself in the works of the old divines.　For in
theology, as in literature, while reckoning frankly with all
phases, his sympathies went largely with the past.　Not
that he would have checked the real progress of thought
on the subject of religion, but he did not share the sanguine
hopes of some who have sought to hasten these "slow-

paced" changes ; nor did he believe in progress by ignoring differences, or by merging the sharp outlines of traditional systems in the haze of a "common Christianity." He was one of those in whom physical studies seem to have the effect of leading the mind to dwell on the permanent aspects of thought as well as of things, thus reinforcing the instincts of conservatism. No mind ever delighted more in speculation, and yet none was ever more jealous of the practical application or the popular dissemination of what appeared to him as crude and half-baked theories about the highest subjects. He preferred resting on the great thoughts of other ages, though no man knew better wherein they (and scientific theories likewise) fell short of certainty ; and while he was anything rather than a formalist or a dogmatist, and still clung to the belief that love remains while knowledge vanishes away, he was the enemy of indefiniteness and indifferentism, as well as of a style of preaching which, as he used to say, "dings ye wi' mere morality." His theological attitude, which it would be rash to develop further here, is indicated to some extent in his letter to Bishop Ellicott, and in his reply to the Secretary of the Victoria Institute, both of which will be found in Chapter XI. (pp. 301, 312).

But he was far, indeed, from judging men by their opinions. "I have no nose for heresy," he used to say. His sympathy pierced beneath the outer shell of circumstance and association, and he hardly ever failed to discover what was best and strongest in those with whom he had to do.

His kindly relations with his neighbours and with their children may be passed without further notice after what has been said above. But it may be mentioned that he used occasionally to visit any sick person in the village, and read and prayed with them in cases where such ministrations were welcomed.

One who visited at Glenlair between 1865 and 1869 was particularly struck with the manner in which the daily prayers were conducted by the master of the household.

The prayer, which seemed *extempore*, was most impressive and full of meaning.[1]

It is right also to record briefly his continued intercourse with his cousins of the Cay family. Mr. William Dyce Cay, who had now entered on his profession as a civil engineer, was employed by him to build the bridge over the Urr, and has a vivid recollection of their intercourse, both then (1861-62) and in former years. In particular, he remembers how, on one occasion, Maxwell spent the whole time during a walk of several miles over the hill from Glenlair to Parton, "giving one example after another to explain by illustration the principle of virtual velocities." . . . "The feeling I had," says Mr. Cay, "was, that before I got to the bottom of one example he had rushed off to another."

And the reader will find in the correspondence two of Maxwell's letters to my friend Charles Hope Cay, and in an earlier letter (above, p. 178) a bright description of him. He died in 1869, at the early age of twenty-eight, the most devoted of teachers, one of the purest-hearted and most amiable of men. If he *could* have listened to his

---

[1] The following fragments have been found amongst his papers :—
"Almighty God, who hast created man in Thine own image, and made him a living soul that he might seek after Thee and have dominion over Thy creatures, teach us to study the works of Thy hands, that we may subdue the earth to our use, and strengthen our reason for Thy service; and so to receive Thy blessed Word, that we may believe on Him whom Thou hast sent to give us the knowledge of salvation and the remission of our sins. All which we ask in the name of the same Jesus Christ our Lord."

"O Lord, our Lord, how excellent is Thy name in all the earth, who hast set Thy glory above the heavens, and out of the mouths of babes and sucklings hast perfected praise. When we consider Thy heavens, the work of Thy fingers, the moon and the stars which Thou hast ordained, teach us to know that Thou art mindful of us, and visitest us, making us rulers over the works of Thy hands, showing us the wisdom of Thy laws, and crowning us with honour and glory in our earthly life; and looking higher than the heavens, may we see Jesus, made a little lower than the angels for the suffering of death, crowned with glory and honour, that He, by the grace of God, should taste death for every man. O Lord, fulfil Thy promise, and put all things in subjection under His feet. Let sin be rooted out of the earth, and let the wicked be no more. Bless Thou the Lord, O my soul, praise the Lord."

cousin's gentle warnings against excessive zeal, perhaps his
services to Clifton College, if less vividly remembered,
might have been continued longer.   But who knows?
"They whom the gods love die young."

Maxwell's retirement was not by any means unbroken.
There was a visit to London in the spring of every year.
And in the spring and early summer of 1867 he made a
_Æt._ 35. tour in Italy with Mrs. Maxwell.   They had the misfortune
to be stopped for quarantine at Marseilles, and his remarkable power of physical endurance and of ministration were
felt by all who shared in the mishap.   True to the associations of his early days (see above, pp. 16, 77), he became
the general water-carrier, and in other ways contributed
greatly to the alleviation of discomforts that were by no
means light.

We met accidentally at Florence, and I remember his
mentioning two things as having particularly struck him
amongst the innumerable objects of interest at Rome.   He
had looked at the dome of St. Peter's with an eye of sympathetic genius,[1] and his ear for melody had been satisfied
by "the Pope's band."   He acquired Italian with great
rapidity, and amused himself with noticing the different
phonetic values of the letters in Italian and English.[2]   One
of his chief objects in learning the language was to be able
to converse with Professor Matteucci, whose bust now
stands in the Campo Santo at Pisa.   During the same tour
he took special pains to improve his acquaintance with
French and German.   The only language he had any difficulty in mastering was Dutch.

In the years 1866, 1867, 1869, and 1870, he was
either Moderator or Examiner in the Mathematical Tripos
at Cambridge, where his influence was more and more felt.
His work on these occasions was, indeed, a principal factor
in the movement, to be hereafter described, which led ulti-

---

[1] The tone in which he spoke of this brought home to me, more than
anything I have seen in books, the joy of Michael Angelo in etherealising
the work of Brunelleschi.

[2] On learning from our teacher, Sign. Briganti, the pronunciation of
suolo, he said, "That is the English for _rondinella._"

mately to important changes in the Examination system; to the creation of the Cavendish Laboratory; and to the foundation of the Chair of Experimental Physics.

His paper on the Viscosity of Gases, printed in the *Phil. Trans.* for 1866, had been delivered by him as the Bakerian Lecture for that year.

He also attended several meetings of the British Association, and, in 1870, at the Liverpool meeting, was President of Section A (Mathematics and Physics). His Presidential Address was on the relation of Mathematics and Physics to each other—a theme suggested by Professor Sylvester, who had been president of the same section in the previous year. The opening passage, in which he alludes to other recent scientific addresses, is characteristic, and may be quoted here :— *Æt.* 39.

I have endeavoured to follow Mr. Spottiswoode, as with far-reaching vision he distinguishes the systems of science into which phenomena, our knowledge of which is still in the nebulous stage, are growing. I have been carried, by the penetrating insight and forcible expression of Dr. Tyndall, into that sanctuary of minuteness and of power, where molecules obey the laws of their existence, clash together in fierce collision, or grapple in yet more fierce embrace, building up in secret the forms of visible things. I have been guided by Professor Sylvester towards those serene heights

> " Where never creeps a cloud or moves a wind,
> Nor ever falls the least white star of snow,
> Nor ever lowest roll of thunder moans,
> Nor sound of human sorrow mounts, to mar
> Their sacred everlasting calm."

But who will lead me into that still more hidden and dimmer region where Thought weds Fact,—where the mental operation of the mathematician and the physical action of the molecules are seen in their true relation ? Does not the way to it pass through the very den of the metaphysician, strewed with the remains of former explorers and abhorred by every man of science ? . . .

Two important papers read by Maxwell at the same meeting were that " On Hills and Dales," to which reference will be found in the correspondence (Chap. XI. p. 292), and that " On Colour Vision at different Points of the Retina."

The Cambridge examinations were the only cause which separated him for more than a day or two from Mrs. Maxwell. When most pressed with the load of papers to be read, he would write to her daily—sometimes twice a day—in letters full of "*enfantillages*," as in his boyish endeavours to amuse his father, telling her of everything, however minute, which, if she had seen it, would have detained her eye, small social phenomena, grotesque or graceful (including the dress of lady friends), together with the lighter aspects of the examinations ; College customs, such as the "grace-cup ;" his dealings with his co-examiners, and marks of honour to himself which he knew would please her, though they were indifferent to him. And sometimes he falls into the deeper vein, which was never long absent from his communion with her, commenting on the portion of Scripture which he knew that she was reading, and passing on to general meditations on life and duty.

In November 1868 his old teacher, James D. Forbes, had resigned the principalship of the United College in the University of St. Andrews, and an effort was made by several of the professors[1] to induce Maxwell to stand for the vacant post, which was in the gift of the Crown, and had been held by Brewster and Forbes successively. He was touched by the kindness, and travelled a whole day from Galloway to confer with us, but, on mature consideration, relinquished the idea.

LETTERS, 1860 TO 1870.

TO REV. LEWIS CAMPBELL.

Marischal College,
Aberdeen, 5th January 1860.

. . . I have been publishing my views about Elastic Spheres in the *Phil. Mag.* for Jany., and am going to go on with it as I

---

[1] It is right that I should add that the suggestion did not proceed from me.—*L. C.*

get the prop^{ns.} written out. I have also sent my experiments on Colours to the Royal Society of London, so I have two sets of irons in the fire, besides class work. I hope you get on with Plato, and that your pupils are all Theætetuses, and that wisdom soaks like oil into their inwards. There is a man here who is striving after a general theory of things, but he has great difficulty in so churning his thoughts as to coagulate and solidify the vague and nebulous notions which wander in his head. He has been applying to me very steadily whenever he can pounce on me, and I have prescribed for him as I best could, and I hope his abstract of his general theory of things will be palatable to the readers of the *British Ass. Reports* for 1859.

To HIS WIFE.

Edinburgh, 13th April 1860.

Now let us read (2 Cor.) chapter xii., about the organisation of the Church, and the different gifts of different Christians, and the reason of these differences that Christ's body may be more complete in all its parts. If we felt more distinctly our union to Christ, we would know our position as members of His body, and work more willingly and intelligently along with all the rest in promoting the health and growth of the body, by the use of every power which the spirit has distributed to us.

14th April 1860.

Let us read about charity,—that love which is so perfect that it remains when that which is in part shall be done away. May God purify our love, and make it fit for eternity, by grafting upon it the love of Himself, that so both the human root and the engrafted branches and the divine fruit may be holy to Him!

To PROFESSOR FARADAY.

8 Palace Gardens Terrace, W.,
21st May 1861.

DEAR SIR—If a sphere were set in rotation about any diameter, it would continue to revolve about that diameter for ever. If the body is of unequal dimensions it will continue to revolve about the same axis, provided that axis be a principal axis of the body (of which there are always three).

R

If the original axis of rotation is not a principal axis, then the axis of rotation will change its position both in the body and in space.

In the body the extremity of the axis of rotation will describe an ellipse (or circle) about the greatest or least axis. In space it describes a complicated curve. The ellipse is described in

$$\frac{a^2}{\sqrt{b^2 - a^2} \ \sqrt{c^2 - a^2}}$$

revolutions of the body, where $\frac{1}{a^2}$, $\frac{1}{b^2}$, $\frac{1}{c^2}$ are the moments of inertia about the principal axis.

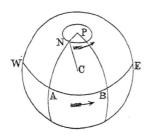

If the body be very nearly spherical like the earth, this motion is very slow. ·If P be the end of the principal axis of the earth, and N that of the actual axis of rotation, the rotation being from W to E, then N will travel round P from W to E, so as to complete its circuit in about 325·6 mean solar days. ,

This phenomenon depends only on the configuration of the earth, and its rotation round an axis which is nearly but not exactly a principal axis, and would be the same if all other bodies were absent from the sky. The position of the pole among the stars is not at all affected; but the latitude of every place on the earth is alternately increased and diminished, the maximum latitude occurring when N is in the same meridian with the place. Thus our maximum should occur sooner than that of Paris or Poulkova.

The *amount* of the variation can only be determined by observation. I have not the means at present of making reference to the statement that Peters, astronomer at Konigsberg or Berlin, has determined the amount at less than $\frac{1}{10}$ of a second, and the period about 312 days. He has also stated the epoch of maximum at his observatory, which I do not remember.

An explanation of this motion, illustrated by experiments, was published by me in the *Edinburgh Transactions*, vol. xxi., pt. iv., "On a Dynamical Top."

The motion, without reference to the earth, is described in Poinsot's treatise on Rotation.

The Astronomer Royal says he may possibly be able to test it by a long series of observations. As far as I am concerned, you are at liberty to speak to any one on the subject.

I have my dynamical top in London, and can show you the motion at any time.—I remain, yours truly,

J. C. MAXWELL.

To THE SAME.

8 Palace Gardens Terrace,
Kensington, W., 19th Oct. 1861.

DEAR SIR—I have been lately studying the theory of static electric induction, and have endeavoured to form a mechanical conception of the part played by the particles of air, glass, or other dielectric in the electric field, the final result of which is the attraction and repulsion of "charged" bodies.

The conception I have hit on has led, when worked out mathematically, to some very interesting results, capable of testing my theory, and exhibiting numerical relations between optical, electric, and electromagnetic phenomena, which I hope soon to[1] verify more completely.

What I now wish to ascertain is, whether the measures of the capacity for electric induction of dielectric bodies with reference to air have been modified materially since your estimates of them in "Series XI." either by yourself or others.

I wish to get the numerical value of the "electric capacity" of various substances, especially transparent ones, if formed into a thin sheet of given thickness, and coated on both sides with tinfoil. Sir W. Snow Harris has made experiments of this kind ; but I do not know whether I can interpret them numerically.

Another question I wish to ask is, whether any experiments, similar to those in Series XIV., on crystalline bodies, have yet led to positive results. I expect that a sphere of Iceland spar, suspended between two oppositely electrified surfaces, would point with its optic axis transverse to the electric force, and I expect soon to calculate the value of the force with which it should point. Again, I have not yet found any determination of the rotation of the plane of polarisation by magnetism, in

---

[1] *Faraday has inserted in pencil*, Magnecrystallic action.　(Ser. vi. ?) *This hardly legible.*—L. C.

which the absolute intensity of magnetism at the place of the [1]
transparent body was given.   I hope to find such a statement
by searching in libraries, but perhaps you may be able to put
me on the right track.   My theory of electrical forces is, that
they are called into play in insulating media by *slight* electric
displacements, which put certain small portions of the medium
into a state of distortion, which, being resisted by the *elasticity*
of the medium, produces an electromotive force.   A spherical
cell would, by such a displacement, be distorted thus—

where the curved lines represent
diameters originally straight, but
now curved.

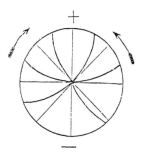

I suppose the elasticity of the
sphere to react on the electrical
matter surrounding it, and press
it downwards.   From the determination by Kohlrausch and Weber
of the numerical relation between
the statical and magnetic effects of
electricity, I have determined the
elasticity of the medium in air, and
assuming that it is the same with the luminiferous ether,
I have determined the velocity of propagation of transverse
vibrations.

The result is 193,088 miles per second (deduced from electrical and magnetic experiments).   Fizean has determined the
velocity of light = 193,118 miles per second, by direct experiment.

This coincidence is not merely numerical.   I worked out the
formulæ in the country before seeing Weber's number, which
is in millimetres, and I think we have now strong reason to
believe, whether my theory is a fact or not, that the luminiferous and the electromagnetic medium are one.

Supposing the luminous and the electromagnetic phenomena
to be similarly modified by the presence of gross matter, my
theory says that the inductive capacity (static) is equal to the
square of the index of refraction, divided by the coefficient of
magnetic induction (air = 1).

I have also examined the theory of the passage of light through
a medium filled with magnetic vortices, and find that the rotation

---

[1] *Faraday has here added in pencil,* Verdet.

of the plane of polarisation is in the same direction with that of the vortices, that it varies inversely as the *square* of the wave length (as is shown by experiment), and that its amount is proportional to the *diameter* of the vortices.

The absolute diameter of the magnetic vortices, their velocity and their density, are so involved that, though as yet they are all unknown, the discovery of a new relation among them would determine them all.

Such a relation might be obtained by the observation of a revolving electromagnet if our instruments were accurate enough. I have had an instrument made for this purpose, but I have not yet overcome the effects of terrestrial magnetism in marking the phenomena.

When I began to study electricity mathematically I avoided all the old traditions about forces acting at a distance, and after reading your papers as a first step to right thinking, I read the others, interpreting as I went on, but never allowing myself to explain anything by these forces. It is because I put off reading about electricity till I could do it without prejudice that I think I have been able to get hold of some of your ideas, such as the electrotonic state, action of contiguous parts, etc., and my chief object in writing to you is to ascertain if I have got the same ideas which led you to see your way into things, or whether I have no right to call my notions by your names.—I remain, yours truly, J. C. MAXWELL.

FROM C. J. MONRO, Esq.

Hadley, Barnet, N.
23d October 1861.

Thank you much for the papers. That about vortices I had skimmed already in the magazine. I shall now be able to do more than skim it. The coincidence between the observed velocity of light and your calculated velocity of a transverse vibration in your medium seems a brilliant result. But I must say I think a few such results are wanted before you can get people to think that every time an electric current is produced a little file of particles is squeezed along between rows of wheels. But the instances of bodily transfer of matter in the phenomena of galvanism look like it already, and I admit that the possibility of convincing the public is not the question.

To H. R. DROOP, Esq. (of the Equity Bar).

Glenlair, Dalbeattie, N.B., 28th December 1861.

I enclose a short statement of the scheme of endowing the chapel which was built near us in 1838 for this district, which is very far from any parish church. If we can raise £1000, there is a fund already raised which will contribute £2000, so as to give a salary of £120 to the minister permanently, and as the people are too poor to support the minister themselves we hope to make the chapel independent of chance contributions in this way. Great part of the funds for building the church were subscribed in London by all kinds of people who were friends of an English gentleman who then had property here ; but we have no longer any such means of drawing on the metropolis.

If you can put us in the way of diminishing the deficit we shall be grateful, and I will see that the money goes to the fund, and that the names are duly entered, however small the contributions.

. . . I have nothing to do in King's College till Jany. 20, so we came here to rusticate. We have clear hard frost without snow, and all the people are having curling matches on the ice, so that all day you hear the curling-stones on the lochs in every direction for miles, for the large expanse of ice vibrating in a regular manner makes a noise which, though not particularly loud on the spot, is very little diminished by distance. I am trying to form an exact mathematical expression for all that is known about electro-magnetism without the aid of hypothesis, and also what variations of Ampère's formula are possible without contradicting his expressions. All that we know is about the action of *closed* currents—that is, currents through closed curves. Now, if you make a hypothesis (1) about the mutual action of the elements of two currents, and find it agree with experiment on closed circuits, it is not proved, for—

If you make another hypothesis (2) which would give *no action* between an element and a *closed* circuit, you may make a combination of (1) and (2) which will give the same result as (1). So I am investigating the most general hypothesis about the mutual action of elements, which fulfils the condition that the action between an element and a closed circuit is null. This is the case if the action between two elements can be reduced to forces between the extremities of those elements depending only on the distance and $+$ or $-$ according as they act between similar or opposite ends of the elements. If the force is an attraction

$$= \phi \ (r) \ ss' \ (\cos \omega \ + \ 2 \ \cos \theta \cos \theta')$$

where ω is the angle between s and s', r the distance of s and s' and θ and θ' the angles s and s', the elements, make with r, then the condition of no action will be fulfilled.

To the Same.

8 Palace Gardens Terrace, W.,
24th January 1862.

. . . When I wrote to you about closed currents it was partly to arrange my own thoughts by imagining myself speaking to you. Ampère's formula containing n and k is the most general expression for an attractive or repulsive force in the line joining the elements ; and I now find that if you take the most general expression consistent with symmetry for an action transverse to that line, the resulting expression for the action of a closed current on an element gives a force not perpendicular to that element. Now, experiment 3d (Ampère) shows that the force on a movable element is perp. to the directions of the current, so that I see Ampère is right.

But the best way of stating the effects is with reference to " lines of magnetic force." Calculate the magnetic force in any plane, arising from every element of the circuit, and from every other magnetising agent, then the force on an element is in the line perp. to the plane of the element and of the lines of force.

But I shall look up Cellerier and Plann, and the long article in Karsten's *Cyclopædia.* I want to see if there is any evidence from the mathematical expressions as to whether element acts on element, or whether a current first produces a certain effect in the surrounding field, which afterwards acts on any other current.

Perhaps there may be no mathematical reasons in favour of one hypothesis rather than the other.

As a fact, the effect on a current at a given place depends solely on the direction and magnitude of the magnetic force at that point, whether the magnetic force arises from currents or from magnets. So that the theory of the effect taking place through the intervention of a medium is consistent with fact,

and (to me) appears the simplest in expression ; but I must prove
either that the direct action theory is completely identical in its
results, or that in some conceivable case they may be different.
My theory of the rotation of the plane of polarised light by
magnetism is coming out in the *Phil. Mag.* I shall send you
a copy.

To the Same.

8 Palace Gardens Terrace,
Kensington, London, W., 28th January 1862.

Some time ago, when investigating Bernoulli's theory of
gases, I was surprised to find that the internal friction of a gas
(if it depends on the collision of particles) should be independent
of the density.

Stokes has been examining Graham's experiments on the
rate of flow of gases through fine tubes, and he finds that the
friction, if independent of density, accounts for Graham's results,
but, if taken proportional to density, differs from those results
very much. This seems rather a curious result, and an additional phenomenon, explained by the "collision of particles"
theory of gases. Still one phenomenon goes against that theory
—the relation between specific heat at constant pressure and at
constant volume, which is in air = 1·408, while it ought to be
1·333.

My brother-in-law, who is still with us, is getting better, and
had his first walk on crutches to-day across the room.

To C. J. Monro, Esq.

8 Palace Gardens Terrace,
London W., 18th February 1862.
(Recd. 3d March.)

I got your letter in Scotland, whither we had gone for the
Christmas holidays. I have been brewing Platonic suds, but
failed, owing I suppose to a too low temperature. I had not
read Plateau's recipe then. Some of the bubbles on the surface
lasted a fortnight in the air, but they were scummy and scaly
and inelastic. I shall take more care next time. Elliot of the
Strand (30) is going to produce colour-tops, with papers from
De La Rue, and directions for use by me ; and so I shall be put
in competition with the brass Blondin and the Top on the top
of the Top. . . . With regard to Britomart's nurse—I have not

Spenser here, but I think Spenser was not a magician himself, and got all his black art out of romances and not out of the professional treatises,—the notions to be brought out were :—
1st, The unweaving any web in which B. had been caught ;
2d, Doing so in witch-like fashion ; 3d, Not like a wicked witch, but like a well-intentioned nurse, unused to the art, and therefore blunderingly.   She believes in the number three and in contrariety, and therefore says everything thrice and does everything thrice, saying inversions of sentences, and doing reversions of her revolutions, which are described in similar language.   The revolutions begin by $+ 3 (2\pi)$ against the visible motion of the sun, then by a revolution $- 6 \pi$, she returns all contrary and unweaves the first.   Then she goes round $+ 6\pi$, to make the final result contrary to the natural revolution, and to make a complete triad.   Withershins is, I believe, equivalent to wider die Sonne in High Dutch, which I am not aware is a modern or ancient idiom in that language, but it may be one in a cognate language.   If the "phamplets" have not turned up in Madeira yet, let. me know, that I may "replace" them.

I suppose in your equations, when the numbers do not amount to unity, Black has been present.

$$\cdot 841 \text{ Brunsw.} \cdot \text{G} + \cdot 159 \text{ W} = \cdot 200 \text{ V} + \cdot 423 \text{ U} + \cdot 377 \text{ Black.}$$

That is, green a little palish and dark mauve, your last equation by the young eyes.   It is something like a colour-blind eq^{n}, but all those I know say 100 Brunswick $\text{G} = 100$ Vermillion, so that this person sees the green darker than the Vermillion ; or, in other words, sees much more of the second side of the equation than a colour-blind person would.   But in twilight U comes out strong, while G does not ; so that I think the apparent equality arises from suppression of all colours but blue (in U and W) in the twilight, so that you may write—

$$\cdot 841 \text{ Black} + \cdot 159 \text{ W} = \cdot 577 \text{ Black} + \cdot 423 \text{ U.}$$

There is no use going to the $3^{\text{rd.}}$ place of decimals, unless you spend a good while on each observation, and have first-rate eyes.   But if you can get observations to be consistent to the $3^{\text{rd.}}$ place of decimals, glory therein, and let me know what the human eye can do.

Donkin gave me tea in Oxford, July 1, 1860.

I find that my belief in the reality of State affairs is no greater in London than in Aberdeen, though I can see the clock

at Westminster on a clear day.   If I went and saw the parks of
artillery at Woolwich, and the Consols going up and down in
the city, and the Tuscarora and Mr. Mason, I would know what
like they were, but otherwise a printed statement is more easily
appropriated than experience is acquired by being near where
things are being transacted.

I am getting a large box made for mixture of colours.   A
beam of sunlight is to be divided into colours by a prism, certain
colours selected by a screen with slits.   These gathered by a
lens, and restored to the form of a beam by another prism, and
then viewed by the eye directly.   I expect great difficulties in
getting everything right adjusted, but when that is done I shall
be able to vary the intensity of the colours to a great extent,
and to have them far purer than by any arrangement in which
white light is allowed to fall on the final prism.

I am also planning an instrument for measuring electrical
effects through different media, and comparing those media with
air.   A and B are two equal metal discs, capable of motion
towards each other by fine screws ; D is a metal disc suspended
between them by a spring, C ; E is a piece of glass, sulphur,
vulcanite, gutta-percha, etc.   A and B are then connected with
a source of $+$ electricity, and D with $-$ electricity.   If everything
was symmetrical, D would be attracted both ways, and would
be in unstable equilibrium, but this is rendered stable by the
elasticity of the spring C.   To find the effect of the plate E,
you work A farther or nearer till there is no motion of D consequent on electrification.   Then the plate of air between A and
D is electrically equivalent to the two plates of air and one of
glass (say) between D and B, whence we deduce the coeff^t for E.

To Rev. Lewis Campbell.

8 Palace Gardens Terrace,
Kensington, W., 21st April 1862.

It is now a long time since I wrote half a letter to you, but
I have never since had time to write or to find the scrap.   I
suppose, as it was more than a good intention but less than a
perfect act, it may be regarded as destined to paper purgatory.
This is the season of work to you, when folks visit shrines in
April and May, but I get holiday this week.   I have been
putting together a large optical box, 10 feet long, containing two
prisms of bisulphuret of carbon, the largest yet made in London,

five lenses and two mirrors, and a set of movable slits. Everything requires to be adjusted over and over again if one thing is not quite right placed, so I have plenty of trial work to do before it is perfect, but the colours are most splendid.

I think you asked me once about Helmholtz and his philosophy. He is not a philosopher in the exclusive sense, as Kant, Hegel, Mansel are philosophers, but one who prosecutes physics and physiology, and acquires therein not only skill in discovering any desideratum, but wisdom to know what are the desiderata, *e.g.*, he was one of the first, and is one of the most active, preachers of the doctrine that since all kinds of energy are convertible, the first aim of science at this time should be to ascertain in what way particular forms of energy can be converted into each other, and what are the equivalent quantities of the two forms of energy.

The notion is as old as Descartes (if not Solomon), and one statement of it was familiar to Leibnitz. It was wholly unknown to Comte, but all sorts of people have worked at it of late,—Joule and Thomson for heat and electricals, Andrews for chemical combinations, Dr. E. Smith for human food and labour. We can now assert that the power of our bodies is generated in the muscles, and is not conveyed to them by the nerves, but produced during the transformation of substances in the muscle, which are supplied fresh by the blood.

We can also form a rough estimate of the efficiency of a man as a mere machine, and find that neither a perfect heat engine nor an electric engine could produce so much work and waste so little in heat. We therefore save our pains in investigating any theories of animal power based on heat and electricity. We see also that the soul is not the direct moving force of the body. If it were, it would only last till it had done a certain amount of work, like the spring of a watch, which works till it is run down. The soul is not the mere mover. Food is the mover, and perishes in the using, which the soul does not. There is action and reaction between body and soul, but it is not of a kind in which energy passes from the one to the other,—as when a man pulls a trigger it is the gunpowder that projects the bullet, or when a pointsman shunts a train it is the rails that bear the thrust. But the constitution of our nature is not explained by finding out what it is not. It is well that it will go, and that we remain in possession, though we do not understand it.

Hr. Clausius of Zurich, one of the heat philosophers, has

been working at the theory of gases being little bodies flying about, and has found some cases in which he and I don't tally, so I am working it out again. Several experimental results have turned up lately, rather confirmatory than otherwise of that theory.

I hope you enjoy the absence of pupils. I find that the division of them into smaller classes is a great help to me and to them; but the total oblivion of them for definite intervals is a necessary condition of doing them justice at the proper time.

To FLEEMING JENKIN, Esq.[1]

27th Aug. 1863.

. . . To compare electromagnetic with electrostatic units :—

1*st*, Weber's method.—Find the capacity of a condenser in electrostatic measure (meters).

Determine its potential when charged, and measure the charge or discharge through a galvanometer.

2*d*, Thomson's.—Find the electromotive force of a battery by electromagnetic methods, and then weigh the attraction of two surfaces connected with the two poles.

3*d*, (Not tried, but talked of by Jenkin).—Find the resistance of a very bad conductor in both systems—

(1) By comparison with (4th June),

(2) By the log. decrement of charge per second.

All the methods require a properly graduated series of steps. The 1st and 2d determine V, a velocity = 310,740,000 meters per second.

The 3d method determines V^2.

The first method requires a condenser of large capacity, and the measurement of this capacity and that of the discharge by a galvanometer.

I think this method looks the best; but I would use a much larger condenser than Weber, and determine its capacity by more steps.

The chief difficulty of Thomson's method is the measurement of a very small force and a very small distance. I think these difficulties may be overcome by making the force act on a comparatively stiff spring and magnifying optically the deflection.

On the third method we require a very large condenser

---

[1] Now Professor of Engineering in Edinburgh.

indeed, also a series of resistances in steps between 4th June and that of the insulating substance of the condenser, and a galvanometer (or electrometer) to measure discharge (or tension). . . .

To C. H. CAY, Esq.

8 Palace Gardens Terrace,
18th November 1863.

We hope to hear how you are. A little literature helps to chase away mathematics from the mind. I have read *Paracelsus* in parts, but concluded that there was a great deal of poetry in it ; but Mr. Browning has written much better poems with half the quantity of poetry at his disposal. Have you seen *Pessimus, a Prose Poem in Paradox,* from Oxford, and *Sketch from Cambridge* by a Don who imagines that mathematical men are safer not to talk shop than classical. I know several men who see all nature in symbols, and express themselves conformably, whether in Quintics or Quantics, Invariants or Congruents. I send you the electric scheme.

To HIS WIFE.

22d June 1864.

May the Lord preserve you from all evil, and cause all the evil that assaults you to work out His own purposes, that the life of Jesus may be made manifest in you, and may you see the eternal weight of glory behind the momentary lightness of affliction, and so get your eyes off things seen and temporal and be refreshed with the things eternal ! Now love is an eternal thing, and love between father and son or husband and wife is not temporal if it be the right sort, for if the love of Christ and the Church be a reason for loving one another, and if the one be taken as an image of the other, then, if the mind of Christ be in us, it will produce this love as part of its complete nature, and it cannot be that the love which is first made holy, as being a reflection of part of the glory of Christ, can be any way lessened or taken away by a more complete transformation into the image of the Lord.

I have been back at 1 Cor. xiii. I think the description of charity or divine love is another loadstone for our life—to show us that this is one thing which is not in parts, but perfect in its own nature, and so it shall never be done away. It is

nothing negative, but a well-defined, living, almost acting picture
of goodness ; that kind of it which is human, but also divine.
Read along with it 1 John iv., from verse 7 to end ; or, if you
like, the whole epistle of John and Mark xii. 28.

To the Same.

23d June 1864.

Think what God has determined to do to all those who submit themselves to His righteousness and are willing to receive
His gift. They are to be conformed to the image of His Son,
and when that is fulfilled, and God sees that they are conformed
to the image of Christ, there can be no more condemnation, for
this is the praise which God Himself gives, whose judgment is
just. So we ought always to hope in Christ, for as sure as we
receive Him now, so sure will we be made conformable to His
image. Let us begin by taking no thought about worldly cares,
and setting our minds on the righteousness of God and His
kingdom, and then we shall have far clearer views about the
worldly cares themselves, and we shall be continually enabled
to fight them under Him who has overcome the world.

To the Same.

26th June 1864.

Note in (2 Cor.) ver. 10 that the judgment is according to
what we have done, so that if we are to be counted righteous we
must really get righteousness and do it. Note also that we are
to receive the things done in the body, not rewards or punish-
ments merely, but the things themselves are to be brought back
to us, and we must meet them in the spirit of Christ, who bore
our sins and abolished them, or else we must be overwhelmed
altogether.

. . . I have come from Mr. Baptist Noel. The church was
full to standing, and the whole service was as plain as large
print. The exposition was the Parable of Talents, and the
sermon was on John iii. 16. The sermon was the text writ
large, nothing ingenious or amusing, and hardly any attempt at
instruction, but plain and very serious exhortation from a
man who evidently believes neither more nor less than what
he says.

To the Same.

28th June 1864.

I can always have you with me in my mind—why should we not have our Lord always before us in our minds, for we have His life and character and mind far more clearly described than we can know any one here ? If we had seen Him in the flesh we should not have known Him any better, perhaps not so well. Pray to Him for a constant sight of Him, for He is man that we may be able to look to Him, and God, so that He can create us anew in His own image.

To C. Hockin, Esq.

Glenlair, Dalbeattie, September 7th, 1864.

. . . I have been doing several electrical problems. I have got a theory of "electric absorption," *i.e.* residual charge, etc., and I very much want determinations of the specific induction, electric resistance, and absorption of good dielectrics, such as glass, shell-lac, gutta-percha, ebonite, sulphur, etc.

I have also cleared the electromagnetic theory of light from all unwarrantable assumption, so that we may safely determine the velocity of light by measuring the attraction between bodies kept at a given difference of potential, the value of which is known in electromagnetic measure.

I hope there will be resistance coils at the British Association.

To Professor Lewis Campbell.[1]

8 Palace Gardens Terrace,
London, W., 22d November 1864.

It was very kind of you to think of me at this time, and write to me. I shall always remember your mother's kindness to me, beginning more than twenty-three years ago, and how she made me the same as you two when I came to see you. To you her memory is what you can share with none, so I can say no more except that you will continue to find that to have had a mother so devoted to her duty gives you a consciousness of your own obligations which will be strengthened whenever you think of her.

---

[1] Mrs. Morrieson died on the 17th of November 1864.

To C. H. CAY, Esq.

Glenlair, 5th January 1865.

We are sorry to hear you cannot come and see us, but you seem better by your letter, and I hope you will be able for your travels, and be better able for your work afterwards, and not take it too severely, and avoid merimnosity and taking over too much thought, which greatly diminishes the efficiency of young teachers. We have been here since 22d ult., and are in the process of dining the valley in appropriate batches. We have had very rough weather this week, which, combined with the dining, has prevented our usual airings. The ordinary outing is to the Brig of Urr, Katherine on Charlie and I on Darling. Charlie has got a fine band on his forehead, with his name in blue and white beads.

The Manse of Corsock is now finished; it is near the river, not far from the deep pool where we used to bathe.

I set Prof. W. Thomson a prop. which I had been working with for a long time. He sent me 18 pages of letter of suggestions about it, none of which would work; but on Jan. 3, in the railway from Largs, he got the way to it, which is all right; so we are jolly, having stormed the citadel, when we only hoped to sap it by approximations.

The prop. was to draw a set of lines like this

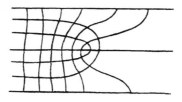

so that the ultimate reticulations shall all be squares.

The solution is exact, but rather stiff. Now I have a disc A

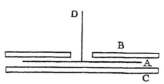

hung by a wire D, between two discs B, C, the interval being occupied by air, hydrogen, carbonic acid, etc., the friction of which gradually brings A to rest. In order to calculate the thickdom or viscosity of the gas, I require to solve the problem above mentioned, which is now done, and I have the apparatus now ready to begin. We are also intent on electrical measurements, and are getting up apparatus, and have made sets of wires of alloy of platinum and silver, which are to be sent all abroad as standards of resistance. I have also a paper afloat, with an electromagnetic theory of light, which, till I am convinced to the contrary, I hold to be great guns.

Spice[1] is becoming first-rate : she is the principal patient under the ophthalmoscope, and turns her eyes at command, so as to show the tapetum, the optic nerve, or any required part. Dr. Bowman, the great oculist, came to see the sight, and when we were out of town he came again and brought Donders of Utrecht with him to visit Spice.

To H. R. Droop, Esq.

Glenlair, Dalbeattie, 19th July 1865.

There are so many different forms in which Societies may be cast, that I should like very much to hear something of what those who have been thinking about it propose as the plan of it.

There is the association for publishing each other's productions ; for delivering lectures for the good of the public and the support of the Society ; for keeping a reading room or club, frequented by men of a particular turn ; for dining together once a month, etc.

I suppose W——'s object is to increase the happiness of men in London who cultivate physical sciences, by their meeting together to read papers and discuss them, the publication of these papers being only one, and not the chief end of the Society, which fulfils its main purpose in the act of meeting and enjoying itself.

The Royal Society of Edinburgh used to be a very sociable body, but it had several advantages. Most of the fellows lived within a mile of the Society's rooms. They did not need to disturb their dinner arrangements in order to attend.

Many of them were good speakers as well as sensible men,

---

[1] The Scotch terrier of the period.

whose mode of considering a subject was worth hearing, even if not correct.

The subjects were not limited to mathematics and physics, but included geology, physiology, and occasionally antiquities, and even literary subjects. Biography of deceased fellows is still a subject of papers. Now those who cultivate the mathematical and physical sciences are sometimes unable to discuss a paper, because they would require to keep it some days by them to form an opinion on it, and physical men can get up a much better discussion about armour plates or the theory of glaciers than about the conduction of heat or capillary attraction.

The only man I know who can make everything the subject of discussion is Dr. Tyndall. Secure his attendance and that of somebody to differ from him, and you are all right for a meeting.

If we can take the field with a plan in our head, I dare say we could find a good many men who would co-operate.

We ride every day, sometimes both morning and evening, and so we consume the roads. I have made 68 problems, all stiff ones, not counting riders.

I am now getting the general equations for the motion of a gas considered as an assemblage of molecules flying about with great velocity. I find they must repel as inverse fifth power of distance.

To C. H. CAY, Esq.

Glenlair, 14th October 1865.

. . . I hope you keep your conscience in good order, and do not bestow more labour on erroneous papers than is useful to the youth who wrote it. Always set him to look for the mistake, if he prefers that to starting fresh, for to find your own mistake may sometimes be profitable, but to seek for another man's mistake is weariness to the flesh.

There are three ways of learning props.—the heart, the head, and the fingers ; of these the fingers is the thing for examinations, but it requires constant practice. Nevertheless the fingers have a fully better retention of methods than the heart has. The head method requires about a mustard seed of thought, which, of course, is expensive, but then it takes away all anxiety. The heart method is full of anxiety, but dispenses with the thought ; and the finger method requires great labour and constant practice, but dispenses with thought and anxiety together.

We have had very fine weather since you went away, but I was laid up for more than three weeks with erysipelas all over my head, and got very shaky on my pins. But I have been out for a fortnight, and riding regularly as of old, which is good for Katherine after the nursing, and I eat about double what any man in Galloway does, and know nothing of it in half an hour; but my legs are absorbing the beef as fast as it is administered.

To the Rev. C. B. Tayler.

8 Palace Gardens Terrace, W.,
2d February 1866.

I was very glad to get your kind letter, and to be assured that you still remembered me. I thought of you when I was in Cambridge, and made up my mind to write to you and hear of you and Mrs. Tayler, and your nephew George. A nephew of yours was for a short time in my class in King's Coll., and I asked him about you, but he had not seen you lately. Is George still in Hull?

You ask for my history since I wrote to you before my marriage. We remained in Aberdeen till 1860, when the union or fusion of the Colleges took place, and I went to King's Coll., London, where I taught till last Easter, when I was succeeded by W. G. Adams, brother of the astronomer. I have now my time fully occupied with experiments and speculations of a physical kind, which I could not undertake as long as I had public duties. These are the chronological data. It is 13 years nearly since I was with you, and you carried me about when I could not move myself, but I remember everything about you and Otley much better than most things before and after that time. I got advantage from your nursing when my father was ill, and many other things have since brought you and Mrs. Tayler to mind. If you and Mrs. Tayler are to be in London during the spring we shall be exceedingly glad to see you here, or if you ever go to Scotland in summer or autumn we hope you will try and stay with us some time. My wife knows you quite well,—that is, as well as I do,—all but what can only be got by seeing and hearing directly, and it would do us both great good to see you, and open up our minds a little.

Many people's minds seem to be shut up with solemn charms, so that though they seem Christians, and know what they mean to speak about they can say nothing. At Cambridge I heard several sermons from excellent texts, but all either on other subjects or else right against the text. There is a Mr. Offord in this street, a Baptist[1] who knows his Bible, and preaches as near it as he can, and does what he can to let the statements in the Bible be understood by his hearers. We generally go to him when in London, though we believe ourselves baptized already.

Pray let me hear from you occasionally. We shall be here till the end of March, and after that address Glenlair, Dalbeattie, N.B., which is my permanent address, and is sure at all times to find me.

Mrs. Maxwell joins me in kind regards to you and Mrs. Tayler, and I remain your afft. friend,

J. CLERK MAXWELL.

To Dr. HUGGINS, F.R.S.

Ardhallow, Dunoon, Oct. 13/68.

MY DEAR SIR—I sympathise with you in your great sorrow. Though my own mother was only eight years with me, and my father became my companion in all things, I felt her loss for many years, and can in some degree appreciate your happiness in having so long and so complete fellowship with your mother. I have little fear, however, that the nearness to the other world which you must feel will in any way unfit you for the work on which you have been engaged, for the higher powers of the intellect are strengthened by the exercise of the nobler emotions.

．　　　．　　　．

Your identification of the spectrum of comet 11 with that of carbon is very wonderful. The dynamical state of comets' tails is most perplexing, but the chemistry and activity of their heads leads to new questions. With respect to the transparency of a heavenly body, I think it indicates scattered condition rather than gaseity. A cloud of large blocks of stone is much more transparent than air of the same average density. Such blocks in a nebula would never be themselves seen, but perhaps if they

---

[1] Whilst in London, Mr. and Mrs. Maxwell occasionally attended Nonconformist services, partly led, perhaps, by recollections of the simple Presbyterian worship, to which Mrs. Maxwell had been accustomed.

were often to encounter each other, the results of the collision would be incandescent gases, and might be the only visible part of the nebula.

. . . Any opinion as to the form in which the energy of gravitation exists in space is of great importance, and whoever can make his opinion probable will have made an enormous stride in physical speculation. The apparent universality of gravitation, and the equality of its effects on matter of all kinds are most remarkable facts, hitherto without exception ; but they are purely experimental facts, liable to be corrected by a single observed exception. We cannot conceive of matter with negative inertia or mass ; but we see no way of *accounting* for the proportionality of gravitation to mass by any legitimate method of demonstration. If we can see the tails of comets fly off in the direction opposed to the sun with an accelerated velocity, and if we believe these tails to be matter and not optical illusions or mere tracks of vibrating disturbance, then we must admit a force in that direction, and we may establish that it is caused by the sun if it always depends upon his position and distance. I therefore admit that the proposition that the sun repels comets' tails is capable of proof ; but whether he does so by his ordinary attractive power being changed into repulsion by a change of state of the matter of the tail is another question. Now, it seems ascertained by simple observations with telescopes that the coma is formed by successive explosions out of the nucleus, mostly on the side of the sun, and that the formation of the tail depends on the coma, though the substance is invisible in the state of passing from the coma to the tail. Then, by your observations, the nucleus and coma have light of their own, probably due to carbon in some gaseous form ; but the tail's light being polarised in the plane of the sun is due to him. Hence the head is fire and the tail smoke. The head obeys gravitation, which is exerted on it with precisely the same intensity as on all other known matter, solid or gaseous. The tail appears to be acted on in a contrary way. If the comet consisted of a mixture of gravitating and levitating matter, and is analysed by the sun, then before the emission of the tail the acceleration due to gravitation should be less than on a planet at the same distance ; the more complete the discharge of tail the greater the intensity of gravitation on the remaining head.

N.B.—To understand the dynamics of the tail, the motion in space of particular portions of it must be studied.

To Professor Lewis Campbell.

Glenlair, Dalbeattie, 3d November 1868.

I have given considerable thought to the subject of the candidature, and have come to the decision not to stand. The warm interest which you and other professors have taken in the matter has gratified me very much, and the idea of following Principal Forbes had also a great effect on my feelings as well as the prospect of residing among friends ; but I still feel that my proper path does not lie in that direction.—Your afft. friend,

J. CLERK MAXWELL.

To C. J. Monro, Esq.

Glenlair, Dalbeattie, 6th July 1870.

My question to the Mathematical Society bore fruit in various forms. . . . It would give my mind too great a wrench just now to go into elliptic integrals, but I will do so when I come to revise about circular conductors. . . . I can cut the subject short with an easy conscience, for I have no scruple about steering clear of tables of double entry, especially when, in all really useful cases, convergent series may be used with less trouble, and without any knowledge of elliptic integrals. On this subject see a short paper on Fluid Displacement in next part of the *Math. Soc. Trans.*, where I give a picture of the stream lines, and the distortion of a transverse line as water flows past a cylinder.

Mr. W. Benson, architect, 147 Albany Street, Regent Park, N.W., told me that you had been writing to *Nature*, and that yours was the only rational statement in a multitudinous correspondence on colours. Mr. Benson considers that Aristotle and I have correct views about primary colours. He has written a book, with coloured pictures, on the science of colour, and he shows how to mix colours by means of a prism. He wants to publish an elementary book with easy experiments, but gets small encouragement, being supposed an heretic. No other architect in the Architect's Society believes him. This is interesting to me, as showing the chromatic condition of architects. I made a great colour-box in 1862, and worked it in London in '62 and '64. I have about 200 equations each year, which are reduced but not published. I have set it up here this year, and have just got it in working order. I expect to get some more material, and work up the whole together. In particular, I want to find any change or evidence of constancy in the eyes of myself and wife during eight years. I can exhibit the yellow spot to all who have it,—and all have it except Col. Strange, F.R.S., my late father-in-law, and my wife,—whether they be Negroes, Jews, Parsees, Armenians, Russians, Italians, Germans, Frenchmen, Poles, etc. Professor Pole, for instance, has it as strong as me, though he is colour-blind ; Mathison, also colour-blind, being fair, had it less strongly marked.

One J. J. Müller, in *Pogg. Ann.* for March and April 1870, examines compound colours, and finds the violet without any tendency to red, or the red to blue. He also selects a typical green out of the spectrum.

CHAPTER XI.

CAMBRIDGE—1871 TO 1879.

THE Chair of Experimental Physics in the University of
Cambridge was founded by a Grace of the Senate on the
9th of February 1871.

In October 1870 the Duke of Devonshire, who was
Chancellor of the University, had signified his desire to
build and furnish a Physical Laboratory for Cambridge.
In acting as a member of the Royal Commission on
Scientific Education he had perceived how useful such an
institution might be made. It was in connection with the
acceptance of this munificent offer that the new professorship was established by the Senate.

The question, who should be the first professor? was
for some time attended with anxiety. It was understood
that Sir William Thomson had declined to stand, and it
was thought uncertain whether Clerk Maxwell could be
persuaded to leave the retirement of his country-seat.
After some hesitation, arising chiefly from genuine diffi-
dence, he was induced to become a candidate, on the understanding that he might retire at the end of a year if he
wished to do so. His candidature was announced on the
24th of February.[1] There was no opposition, and he was
appointed on the 8th of March.

The following letters indicate the part taken by different
persons in bringing about this result :—

---

[1] On February 23, Professor Stokes (who had been urgent in pressing
Maxwell to stand) wrote to him :—"I am glad you have decided to come
forward."

FROM THE HON. J. W. STRUTT (Lord Rayleigh).

Cambridge, 14th February 1871.

When I came here last Friday I found every one talking about the new professorship, and hoping that you would come. Thomson, it seems, has definitely declined. . . . There is no one here in the least fit for the post. What is wanted by most who know anything about it is not so much a lecturer as a mathematician who has actual experience in experimenting, and who might direct the energies of the younger Fellows and bachelors into a proper channel. There must be many who would be willing to work under a competent man, and who, while learning themselves, would materially assist him. . . . I hope you may be induced to come ; if not, I don't know who it is to be. Do not trouble to answer me about this, as I believe others have written to you about it.

FROM THE REV. E. W. BLORE, M.A. (now Vice-Master of Trinity).

14th February 1871.

Many residents of influence are desirous that you should occupy the post, hoping that in your hands this University would hold a leading place in this department. It has, I believe, been ascertained that Sir W. Thomson would not accept the professorship. I mention this lest you should wish to avoid the possibility of coming into the field against him.

Maxwell's usual modesty is apparent in the draft of his reply to this letter :—

Glenlair, Dalbeattie, 15th February 1871.

MY DEAR BLORE—Though I feel much interest in the proposed Chair of Experimental Physics, I had no intention of applying for it when I got your letter, and I have none now, unless I come to see that I can do some good by it.

. . . I am sorry Sir W. Thomson has declined to stand. He has had practical experience in teaching experimental work, and his experimental corps have turned out very good work. I have no experience of this kind, and I have seen very little of the somewhat similar arrangements of a class of real practical chemistry. The class of Physical Investigations, which might

be undertaken with the help of men of Cambridge education,
and which would be creditable to the University, demand, in
general, a considerable amount of dull labour which may or
may not be attractive to the pupils.

In the Grace of Senate of 9th February, it had been
enacted that it should be "the principal duty of the professor to teach and illustrate the laws of Heat, Electricity,
and Magnetism; to apply himself to the advancement of
the knowledge of such subjects; and to promote their
study in the University."

For some time after his appointment, Maxwell's principal
work was that of designing and superintending the erection
of the Cavendish Laboratory.

He inspected the Physical Laboratories of Sir William
Thomson at Glasgow and of Professor Clifton at Oxford,
in order to embody in the new structure the best features
of both of these institutions. But many of the most important arrangements were of his own invention.   An
account of the Laboratory itself will be found in *Nature*
(vol. x. p. 139); it is sufficient here to say that it would
be difficult to imagine a building better adapted to its
purpose, or one in the construction of which more provision
should be made for possible requirements.   In no case was
convenience sacrificed to architectural effect, but in both
respects the building is a decided success.   The architect
was Mr. W. M. Fawcett of Cambridge, who appears to
have fully appreciated and thoroughly carried out all Professor Maxwell's suggestions.   The contract was given to
Mr. Loveday of Kibworth, his tender being recommended
by the report of the Syndicate appointed to superintend
the building, dated 1st March 1872.

The work of arranging and furnishing the Cavendish
Laboratory occupied a considerable time.   It was not completed until the spring of 1874, when the practical work
of experimenting commenced, and on the 16th of June in
that year, the Chancellor formally presented his gift to the
University.   Sir Charles Lyell and the French astronomer

Leverrier were among those who visited the Laboratory and received the honorary degree of LL.D. from the University on that occasion.

The following draft of a letter from Maxwell to the Vice-Chancellor in the previous year affords an interesting illustration of the thorough and business-like manner in which he had addressed himself to these preliminary labours.

To the Vice-Chancellor, Cambridge.

(Draft of a Letter.)

Glenlair, 5th July 1873.

I enclose a provisional list of fixtures and apparatus required for the Laboratory.

At present I am not able to estimate the prices of many of the articles.

Some of them are in the market, and have simply to be ordered ; others require to be constructed specially for the Laboratory.

I have begun with a list arranged according to the places and rooms in the Laboratory, but, of course, all small things must be kept in cases, either in the apparatus room or in the special rooms.

The special duty of the professor of experimental physics is to teach the sciences of heat and electricity, and also to encourage physical research. The Laboratory must therefore contain apparatus for the illustration of heat and electricity, and also for whatever physical research seems most important or most promising.

The special researches connected with heat which I think most deserving of our efforts at the present time are those relating to the elasticity of bodies, and in general those which throw light on their molecular constitution ; and the most important electrical research is the determination of the magnitude of certain electric quantities, and their relations to each other.

These are the principles on which I have been planning the arrangement of the Laboratory. But if in the course of years the course of scientific research should be deflected, the plans of work must vary too, and the rooms must be allotted differently.

I agree with you that the income of the Museums must be largely increased in order to meet the demands of this and other new buildings, and I am glad that the University is able to increase it.

It is impossible to procure many of the instruments, as they are not kept in stock, and have to be made to order. Some of the most important will require a considerable amount of supervision during their construction, for their whole value depends on their fulfilling conditions which can as yet be determined only by trial, so that it may be some time before everything is in working order.

Even in 1874, however, there were still manifold desiderata, and the Duke expressed his wish to furnish the Laboratory completely with the necessary apparatus. To carry out this wish was again a work of time, for the Professor would never order an important instrument until he was satisfied that its design and construction were the best that could be obtained. In his annual report to the University in 1877 Professor Maxwell announced that the Chancellor had now "completed his gift to the University by furnishing the Cavendish Laboratory with apparatus suited to the present state of science;" but at the same time he wrote to the Vice-Chancellor stating that he should reserve to himself the privilege of presenting to the Laboratory such apparatus as the advancement of science might render it desirable for the University to possess. And during the short remainder of his tenure of the professorship he expended many hundreds of pounds in this manner. Already, in the spring of 1874, he had presented to the Laboratory all the apparatus in his own possession. The apparatus provided by the British Association for their Committee on Electrical Standards (see p. 231) was also deposited in the Laboratory, in accordance with a resolution passed at the Edinburgh Meeting of 1871—the apparatus remaining the property of the Association, and subject to the control of the Committee.

While the Laboratory was thus gradually made available, the other work of the professorship went on uninterruptedly from the first. Maxwell gave annual courses of lectures on the subjects prescribed in his commission,[1] commencing with October 1871, when he delivered his inaugural lecture. This and the lecture " On Colour Vision," given at the Royal Institution shortly after his appointment in the preceding spring, are perhaps the happiest of his literary efforts. Philosophic grasp, scientific clearness, and poetic imagination could hardly be more successfully combined.

The Cambridge lecture (October 1871) sets forth in luminous outline the meaning and tendency of the moment in the evolution of the University of Cambridge, which was marked by the institution of the course of Experimental Physics, and the erection of the Devonshire Laboratory.

The following passage is especially characteristic :—

Science appears to us with a very different aspect after we have found out that it is not in lecture-rooms only, and by means of the electric light projected on a screen, that we may witness physical phenomena, but that we may find illustrations of the highest doctrines of science in games and gymnastics, in travelling by land and by water, in storms of the air and of the sea, and wherever there is matter in motion.

This habit of recognising principles amid the endless variety of their action can never degrade our sense of the sublimity of nature, or mar our enjoyment of its beauty. On the contrary, it tends to rescue our scientific ideas from that vague condition in which we too often leave them, buried among the other products of a lazy credulity, and to raise them into their proper position among the doctrines in which our faith is so assured that we are ready at all times to act on them. Experiments of

---

[1] Throughout the tenure of his Cambridge Chair Maxwell annually delivered a course of lectures on Heat and the Constitution of Bodies during the October Term ; on Electricity in the Lent Term ; and on Electro-Magnetism in the Easter Term. The character of these lectures very much resembled that of the early chapters in the *Elementary Treatise on Electricity*, which he wrote before taking the Cavendish papers in hand, and which was published in a fragmentary form by the Delegates of the Clarendon Press in October 1881. During the first four or five years that Maxwell lectured in Cambridge, candidates for the Ordinary or Poll Degree were compelled to attend professors' lectures, and not unfrequently they would appear at the Cavendish Laboratory. Maxwell's lectures were the delight of those who could follow him in his brilliant expositions and rapid changes of thought.

illustration may be of very different kinds.   Some may be
adaptations of the commonest operations of ordinary life ; others
may be carefully arranged exhibitions of some phenomenon which
occurs only under peculiar conditions.   They all, however, agree
in this, that their aim is to present some phenomenon to the
senses of the student in such a way that he may associate with
it some appropriate scientific idea.   When he has grasped this
idea, the experiment which illustrates it has served its purpose.

In an experiment of research, on the other hand, this is not
the principal aim. . . . Experiments of this class—those in
which measurement of some kind is involved—are the proper
work of a physical laboratory.   In every experiment we have
first to make our senses familiar with the phenomenon ; but we
must not stop here,—we must find out which of its features are
capable of measurement, and what measurements are required
in order to make a complete specification of the phenomenon.
We must, then, make these measurements, and deduce from them
the result which we require to find.

This characteristic of modern experiments—that they consist
principally of measurements—is so prominent that the opinion
seems to have got abroad that, in a few years, all the great
physical constants will have been approximately estimated, and
that the only occupation which will then be left to men of
science will be to carry these measurements to another place of
decimals.

If this is really the state of things to which we are approaching, our Laboratory may perhaps become celebrated as a place
of conscientious labour and consummate skill ; but it will be
out of place in the University, and ought rather to be classed
with the other great workshops of our country, where equal
ability is directed to more useful ends.

But we have no right to think thus of the unsearchable
riches of creation, or of the untried fertility of those fresh minds
into which these riches will continually be poured. . . . The
history of science shows that even during that phase of her
progress in which she devotes herself to improving the accuracy
of the numerical measurement of quantities with which she has
long been familiar, she is preparing the materials for the subjugation of new regions, which would have remained unknown
if she had been contented with the rough methods of her early
pioneers.

The movement which was now to receive so great an impulse may be roughly dated from Sir William Thomson's first appearance as a Public Examiner in Cambridge ; and Maxwell's own influence, as Examiner and Moderator, had been mainly instrumental in promoting it. The nature of the change has been described as follows by one whose University experience reaches back into the previous time :—

The style of mathematics which was popular in Cambridge for some time before was, to say the least, one-sided, and one-sided in a somewhat unproductive direction.   There were many complaints that Cambridge was behind the rest of the scientific world, and that, whereas the students of so many other Universities were introduced to the splendid discoveries of such subjects as Electricity and Heat, the Wranglers of Cambridge spent their time upon mathematical trifles and problems, so-called, barren alike of practical results and scientific interest.   Maxwell's questions (as Moderator in 1866) infused fresh life into the Cambridge Tripos, and, therefore, into the University studies, by the number of original ideas and new lines of thought opened up by them, thus preparing for the change of system in 1873, when so many interesting subjects were added to the Examination.

Sir William Thomson gives the following important testimony to the same effect :—

The University, Glasgow,
21st January 1882.

The influence of Maxwell at Cambridge had undoubtedly a great effect in directing mathematical studies into more fruitful channels than those in which they had been running for many years.   His published scientific papers and books, his action as an examiner at Cambridge, and his professorial lectures, all contributed to this effect ; but above all, his work in planning and carrying out the arrangements of the Cavendish Laboratory. There is, indeed, nothing short of a revival of Physical Science at Cambridge within the last fifteen years, and this is largely due to Maxwell's influence.

Evidence might easily be multiplied, but it is enough

to quote the weighty words of Lord Rayleigh at a recent
public meeting at Cambridge in support of the proposed
Devonshire Memorial :—

It was no little thing to have had Professor Maxwell so
closely connected with Cambridge, for by his genius effects were
produced which could hardly have been produced in any other
way.   Before coming there to occupy the position he then held,
he (Lord Rayleigh) had not given any particular attention to
electricity, but he found Cambridge to be so saturated with the
subject that he quickly came to the conclusion that it would be
best to make it his particular study.   All this was owing to the
influence of Maxwell.[1]

While speaking of his work in lecturing, it may be well
briefly to advert to the famous " Discourse on Molecules,"
delivered before the British Association at Bradford in
September 1873, which has been more often quoted than,
perhaps, any other of his writings.   This address was
extremely rich in scientific matter, but its chief interest
lay in the concluding paragraphs, which may be said to
indicate more clearly than any other of Maxwell's writings
the position of his mind towards certain doctrines maintained by scientific men :—

In the heavens we discover by their light, and by their light
alone, stars so distant from each other that no material thing
can ever have passed from one to another ; and yet this light,
which is to us the sole evidence of the existence of these distant
worlds, tells us also that each of them is built up of molecules
of the same kinds as those which we find on earth.   A molecule

---

[1] Professor Westcott's utterance on the same occasion, though less
immediately relevant, ought not to be omitted :—" It was impossible to
think of him whom they had so lately lost, to whom first the charge of
the Cavendish Laboratory had been committed, Prof. Clerk Maxwell, and
to recollect his genius and spirit, his subtle and profound thought, his
tender and humble reverence, without being sure that that close connection
between Physics and Theology which was consecrated by the past was still
a living reality among them.   That was an omen for the future.   He felt,
as probably all present felt, that he owed a deep debt of gratitude to him,
both for his researches, and for the pregnant words in which he gathered
up their lessons."

of hydrogen, for example, whether in Sirius or in Arcturus, executes its vibrations in precisely the same time.

Each molecule therefore throughout the universe bears impressed upon it the stamp of a metric system as distinctly as does the metre of the Archives at Paris, or the double royal cubit of the temple of Karnac.

No theory of evolution can be formed to account for the similarity of molecules, for evolution necessarily implies continuous change, and the molecule is incapable of growth or decay, of generation or destruction.

None of the processes of Nature, since the time when Nature began, have produced the slightest difference in the properties of any molecule. We are therefore unable to ascribe either the existence of the molecules or the identity of their properties to any of the causes which we call natural.

On the other hand, the exact equality of each molecule to all others of the same kind gives it, as Sir John Herschel has well said, the essential character of a manufactured article, and precludes the idea of its being eternal and self-existent.

Thus we have been led, along a strictly scientific path, very near to the point at which Science must stop,—not that Science is debarred from studying the internal mechanism of a molecule which she cannot take to pieces, any more than from investigating an organism which she cannot put together. But in tracing back the history of matter, Science is arrested when she assures herself, on the one hand, that the molecule has been made, and, on the other, that it has not been made by any of the processes we call natural.

Science is incompetent to reason upon the creation of matter itself out of nothing. We have reached the utmost limits of our thinking faculties when we have admitted that because matter cannot be eternal and self-existent it must have been created.

It is only when we contemplate, not matter in itself, but the form in which it actually exists, that our mind finds something on which it can lay hold.

That matter, as such, should have certain fundamental properties,—that it should exist in space and be capable of motion, —that its motion should be persistent, and so on,—are truths which may, for anything we know, be of the kind which metaphysicians call necessary. We may use our knowledge of such truths for purposes of deduction, but we have no data for speculating as to their origin.

T

But that there should be exactly so much matter and no more in every molecule of hydrogen is a fact of a very different order. We have here a particular distribution of matter—a *collocation*—to use the expression of Dr. Chalmers, of things which we have no difficulty in imagining to have been arranged otherwise.

The form and dimensions of the orbits of the planets, for instance, are not determined by any law of nature, but depend upon a particular collocation of matter. The same is the case with respect to the size of the earth, from which the standard of what is called the metrical system has been derived. But these astronomical and terrestrial magnitudes are far inferior in scientific importance to that most fundamental of all standards which forms the base of the molecular system. Natural causes, as we know, are at work, which tend to modify, if they do not at length destroy, all the arrangements and dimensions of the earth and the whole solar system. But though in the course of ages catastrophes have occurred and may yet occur in the heavens, though ancient systems may be dissolved and new systems evolved out of their ruins, the molecules out of which these systems are built—the foundation-stones of the material universe—remain unbroken and unworn. They continue this day as they were created—perfect in number and measure and weight ; and from the ineffaceable characters impressed on them we may learn that those aspirations after accuracy in measurement, and justice in action, which we reckon among our noblest attributes as men, are ours because they are essential constituents of the image of Him who in the beginning created, not only the heaven and the earth, but the materials of which heaven and earth consist.

In 1875 he read before the Chemical Society a paper "On the Dynamical Evidence of the Molecular Constitution of Bodies."

The lecture on Thermodynamics at the Loan Exhibition of Scientific Apparatus in London in 1876 (to which he had contributed his real-image Stereoscope, etc.), was illustrated by his own model of the Thermodynamic Surface.[1]

---

[1] In the official handbook to the collection, the articles entitled "General considerations respecting Scientific Apparatus," and "Molecular Physics," were written by Professor Maxwell. When her Majesty the

The last of his public lectures was the Rede Lecture "On the Telephone," delivered at Cambridge in 1878, and illustrated with the aid of Mr. Gower's Telephonic Harp.

After pointing out the extreme simplicity as well as the absolute novelty of the invention, he made it the text of a discourse which is remarkable both for suggestiveness and discursiveness.

I shall . . . consider the telephone as a material symbol of the widely separated departments of human knowledge, the cultivation of which has led, by as many converging paths, to the invention of this instrument by Professor Graham Bell.

. . . In a University we are especially bound to recognise not only the unity of Science itself, but the communion of the workers of Science. We are too apt to suppose that we are congregated here merely to be within reach of certain appliances of study, such as museums and laboratories, libraries and lectures, so that each of us may study what he prefers. I suppose that when the bees crowd round the flowers it is for the sake of the honey that they do so, never thinking that it is the dust which they are carrying from flower to flower which is to render possible a more splendid array of flowers and a busier crowd of bees in the years to come.

We cannot therefore do better than improve the shining hour in helping forward the cross-fertilisation of the Sciences.

One great beauty of Professor Bell's invention is that the instruments at the two ends of the line are precisely alike. . . . The perfect symmetry of the whole apparatus—the wire in the middle, the two telephones at the ends of the wire, and the two gossips at the ends of the telephones—may be very fascinating to a mere mathematician, but it would not satisfy the evolutionist of the Spenserian type, who would consider anything with both ends alike, such as the Amphisbæna, or Mr. Bright's terrier, or Mr. Bell's telephone, to be an organism of a very low type, which must have its functions differentiated before any satisfactory integration can take place.

Accordingly, many attempts have been made, by differen-

Queen visited the collection Professor Maxwell, at the invitation of the Lords of the Committee of Council on Education, attended as the representative of Molecular Physics.

tiating the function of the transmitter from that of the receiver, to overcome the principal limitation of the power of the telephone. As long as the human voice is the sole motive power of the apparatus, it is manifest that what is heard at one end must be fainter than what is spoken at the other. But if the vibration set up at one end is used no longer as the source of energy, but merely as a means of modulating the strength of a current supplied by a voltaic battery, then there will be no necessary limitation of the intensity of the resulting sound, so that what is whispered to the transmitter may be proclaimed *ore rotundo* by the receiver.

He then briefly referred to Edison's loud-speaking telephone, and went on to exhibit and explain the microphone of Professor Hughes.

I have said the telephone is an instance of the benefit to be derived from the cross-fertilisation of the sciences. . . . Professor Graham Bell . . . is the son of a very remarkable man, Alexander Melville Bell, author of a book called *Visible Speech,* and of other works relating to pronunciation. In fact his whole life has been employed in teaching people to speak. He brought the art to such perfection that, though a Scotchman, he taught himself in six months to speak English, and I regret extremely that when I had the opportunity in Edinburgh I did not take lessons from him.[1] Mr. Melville Bell has made a complete analysis and classification of all the sounds capable of being uttered by the human voice, from the Zulu clicks to coughing and sneezing ; and he has embodied his results in a system of symbols, the elements of which are not taken from any existing alphabet, but are founded on the different configurations of the organs of speech.

. . . Helmholtz, by a series of daring strides, has effected a passage for himself over that untrodden wild between acoustics and music—that Serbonian bog where whole armies of scientific musicians and musical men of science have sunk without filling it up.

---

[1] Maxwell had profited not a little by his own studies in this direction. But the Gallowegian tones are hard to modify, and even in his verse such rhymes as "hasn't" = "pleasant" recall to those who knew him his peculiar mode of speech.

We may not be able even yet to plant our feet in his tracks and follow him right across—that would require the seven league boots of the German Colossus ; but to help us in Cambridge we have the Board of Musical Studies vindicating for music its ancient place in a liberal education.   On the physical side we have Lord Rayleigh laying our foundation deep and strong in his *Theory of Sound.*   On the æsthetic side we have the University Musical Society doing the practical work, and, in the space between, those conferences of Mr. Sedley Taylor, where the wail of the Siren draws musician and mathematician together down into the depths of their sensational being, and where the gorgeous hues of the Phoneidoscope are seen to seethe and twine and coil like the

> Dragon boughts and elvish emblemings

on the gates of that city, where

> An ye heard a music, like enow
> They are building still, seeing the city is built
> To music, therefore never built at all
> And therefore built for ever.

The special educational value of this combined study of music and acoustics is that more than almost any other study it involves a continual appeal to what we must observe for ourselves.

The facts are things which must be felt ; they cannot be learned from any description of them.

All this has been said more than 200 years ago by one of our own prophets, William Harvey of Gonville and Caius College :—" For whosoever they be that read authors, and do not, by the aid of their own senses, abstract true representations of the things themselves (comprehended in the author's expressions) they do not represent true ideas, but deceitful idols and phantasmas ; by which means they frame to themselves certaine shadows and chimæras, and all their theory and contemplation (which they call science) represents nothing but waking men's dreams and sick men's phrensies."

After the opening of the Cavendish Laboratory in 1874, the most continuous, as well as the most important, work of the Chair was the superintendence of various courses of experiments, undertaken by young aspirants for scientific distinction.   With characteristic loyalty and humility,

Maxwell seems often to have taken more pride in their researches than in his own. To enumerate the men who were thus favoured would be to name many who are now amongst the most efficient teachers of science in the United Kingdom. But there can be nothing invidious in making particular mention of those who are named by Maxwell himself in his correspondence, although the omission of other names may be accidental. Besides Mr. W. Garnett, who was his demonstrator in the Laboratory from first to last, he refers with especial satisfaction to the work of Mr. George Chrystal, now Professor of Mathematics in Edinburgh, and to that of Mr. W. D. Niven.

Mr. Chrystal was encouraged by him to undertake a series of experiments for verifying Ohm's Law respecting the relation between the current and the electro-motive force in a wire, on which some doubt had been thrown by Weber's theories, and, in an opposite direction, by a series of experiments reported to the British Association by Dr. Schuster in 1874.

In consequence of these doubts a committee was appointed by the British Association consisting of Professor Maxwell, Professor Everitt, and Dr. Schuster, and the report of this committee was presented to the Association at their annual meeting in Glasgow in 1876. The report consists mainly of an account of two experimental investigations planned by Professor Maxwell and carried out in the Cavendish Laboratory by Mr. Chrystal. To this report Mr. Chrystal added a brief account of his experiments on the unilateral and bilateral deflection of a galvanometer, affording a possible explanation of Dr. Schuster's result. The investigation proved that when a unit current passes through a conductor of a square centimetre section, its resistance does not differ from its value for indefinitely small currents by 0·000,000,001 per cent.

1873-79.   The scene of these congenial labours was surrounded with manifold associations, which his love for Cambridge intensified. He had pleasant intercourse with many

persons there, and after a while resumed the habit of
occasional essay writing.   Under the name of Erănus (or
pic-nic) a club of older men was formed, differing little
apparently from the "Apostles," except in the greater
seriousness of the discussions.   Dr. Lightfoot (now Bishop
of Durham) and Professors Hort and Westcott were members of this little circle of congenial spirits.   Maxwell's
contributions, containing his matured thoughts on various
speculative questions, will be found in Appendix B.   It
may be remarked generally that the most marked feature
of his later life was an ever-increasing soberness of spirit,
and a deepening inward repose, which took nothing from
the brightness of his companionship, but rather kept fresh
the inexhaustible springs of cheerfulness and humorous
mirth in him.   The beginnings of such "life in earnest"
may be traced far back, but are most obviously perceptible
in his third year at Cambridge (1853),[1] in the summer of
1856, after his father's death, and in the crisis of his life
at Aberdeen (1857-58).

This graver tone by no means checked the playful
impulses that burst forth from time to time in sparkling
jeux d'esprits.   It rather fledged his arrows, while it loaded
them, giving them a steadier aim, so that his lightest
effusions carried an unsuspected weight of meaning.   His
wit was never more brilliant, more incisive, or (it may be
added) more perfectly good-humoured, than in the verses

---

[1] How readily his thoughts took a serious turn, even in the earlier
undergraduate days, may be seen in a letter (not given above) of 26th
March 1852 :—   *Æt.* 20.

"A. was sent for by telegraph to his sister : he found her past recovery, and she is since dead.   The family is large, and till now was
entire, so that the grief is great and new.

"The attributes of man, as one of a family, seem to be more highly
developed in large families.   The pronoun 'we' acquires a peculiar
significance.   The family man has an idea of a *living* home, to which he
can in imagination retreat, and which gives him a steadiness and force
not his own.   He is one member of a naturally constituted society ; he
has protected his juniors and been protected by his seniors ; and now he
has the consciousness that he is but one of the arrows in the quiver of the
Mighty, and that it is the interest of others as well as his own that he
should succeed."

on Professor Cayley's portrait, and the "Notes of the President's Address." He found time also to indulge his old taste for reading and writing in cypher, and thus, on one occasion, considerably disconcerted a contributor to the second column of the *Times*.

His outward appearance in these later years has been well described by one who saw him first in 1866 :—

A man of middle height, with frame strongly knit, and a certain spring and elasticity in his gait ; dressed for comfortable ease rather than elegance ; a face expressive at once of sagacity and good humour, but overlaid with a deep shade of thoughtfulness ; features boldly but pleasingly marked ; eyes dark and glowing ; hair and beard perfectly black, and forming a strong contrast to the pallor of his complexion. . . . He might have been taken, by a careless observer, for a country gentleman, or rather, to be more accurate, for a north country laird. A keener eye would have seen, however, that the man must be a student of some sort, and one of more than ordinary intelligence.

In later years his hair had turned to iron gray, but until a few years before his death he retained his elasticity of step.

The picture of Maxwell, as he appeared in 1866, became afterwards perfectly familiar to residents in Cambridge. They will remember his thoughtful face as he walked in the street, revolving some of the many problems that engaged him, Toby lagging behind, till his master would suddenly turn, as if starting from a reverie, and begin calling the dog.

The same authority continues—

. . . He had a strong sense of humour, and a keen relish for witty or jocose repartee, but rarely betrayed enjoyment by outright laughter. The outward sign and conspicuous manifestation of his enjoyment was a peculiar twinkle and brightness of the eyes. There was, indeed, nothing explosive in his mental composition, and as his mirth was never boisterous, so neither was he fretful or irascible. Of a serenely placid temper, genial and temperate in his enjoyments, and infinitely patient when others would have been vexed or annoyed, he at all times opposed a solid calm of nature to the vicissitudes of life.

In performing his private experiments at the laboratory,

Maxwell was very neat-handed and expeditious. When working thus, or when thinking out a problem, he had a habit of whistling, not loudly, but in a half-subdued manner, no particular tune discernible, but a sort of running accompaniment to his inward thoughts. . . . He could carry the full strength of his mental faculties rapidly from one subject to another, and could pursue his studies under distractions which most students would find intolerable, such as a loud conversation in the room where he was at work.   On these occasions he used, in a manner, to take his dog into his confidence, and would say softly, "Tobi, Tobi," at intervals, and after thinking and working for a time, would at last say (for example), "It must be so : Plato (*i.e.* Plateau), thou reasonest well." He would then join in the conversation.

. . . His acquaintance with the literature of his own country, and especially with English poetry, was remarkable alike for its extent, its exactness, and the wide range of his sympathies.   His critical taste, founded as it was on his native sagacity, and a keen appreciation of literary beauty, was so true and discriminating that his judgment was, in such matters, quite as valuable as on mathematical writings. . . . As he read with great rapidity, and had a retentive memory, his mind was stored with many a choice fragment which had caught his fancy. He was fond of reading aloud at home from his favourite authors, particularly from Shakspeare, and of repeating such passages as gave him the greatest pleasure.[1]

Maxwell was rarely seen walking without a dog accompanying him, and, when visiting the Laboratory for a short time, Toby or Coonie, or both, would always attend him. Toby (II. or III.) came to Cambridge with Professor Maxwell in 1871, and was thoroughly conversant with the details of the Laboratory and some of its apparatus.   He always betrayed signs of uneasiness when he heard electric sparks, but when summoned to his post he would sit down

---

[1] There was found amongst his papers a scrap on which he had written, in pencil, *the whole* of Shelley's "Ode to the West Wind," in all probability from memory, and as a distraction from anxiety or from severer study.   His note-books, one of which he always carried with him, are full of the most miscellaneous jottings, plans of works, solutions of problems, extracts in prose and verse, etc.

between his master's feet and allow the electrophorus to be excited upon his back, growling all the time in a peculiar manner, as though to relieve his mind, but not evidencing any signs of real discomfort. On one occasion Toby sat quietly on an insulating support, and allowed himself to be rubbed with a cat's skin, when it was found that the dog became positively electrified, contrary to the general belief that a cat's skin is positive to everything; whereupon Professor Maxwell remarked that "a live dog is better than a dead lion." It remains for a future physicist to determine the electric relations of a live cat and dog.

One great charm of Maxwell's society was his readiness to converse on almost any topic with those whom he was accustomed to meet, although he always showed a certain degree of shyness when introduced to strangers. He would never tire of talking, with boyish glee, about the d——l on two sticks and similar topics, and no one ever conversed with him for five minutes without having some perfectly new ideas set before him; sometimes so startling as to utterly confound the listener, but always such as to well repay a thoughtful examination. Men have often asked, after listening to a conversation on some scientific question, whether Maxwell were in earnest or joking.[1] The charm of his conversation rendered it very difficult to carry on any independent work when he was present, but his suggestions for future work far more than compensated for the time thus spent.

On one occasion, after removing a large amount of calcareous deposit which had accumulated in a curiously oolitic form in a boiler, Maxwell sent it to the Professor of Geology with a request that he would identify the formation. This he did at once, vindicating his science from the aspersion which his brother professor would playfully have cast on it.

Maxwell still found occasional recreation in riding at Cambridge as well as more frequently at Glenlair, where he resided as much as he could consistently with his pro-

---

[1] For an instance of humorous mystification, see the letter to Mr. Garnett of 4th January 1877.

fessorial duties.[1]   He always arranged to leave Cambridge at the end of the Easter term, in time to officiate at the midsummer communion in the kirk at Parton, where he was an elder.   His liberality in his own neighbourhood was very great.   Besides the endowment of the church, and building of the manse at Corsock, he had planned a large contribution to the cause of primary education. When the School Board was instituted in the district, Maxwell was very anxious to keep up the school established in the reign of George III. at Merkland, in the immediate neighbourhood of the village of Kirkpatrick-Durham, in addition to the Board school at Corsock, five miles away.   When this offer was refused, he set apart a site and had plans made for a school to be erected and supported at his own expense upon his estate, but failing health prevented the accomplishment of his purpose.

The last few years of Maxwell's life were saddened by the serious and protracted illness of Mrs. Maxwell.   Notwithstanding the inexhaustible freshness of his spirit, his work could not but be somewhat modified by a cause so grave.   He was an excellent sick-nurse, and we have already seen how he attended upon Pomeroy when attacked with fever in college, how he devoted himself to his father during his illness, and how he cared for his brother-in-law when in London.   On one occasion during Mrs. Maxwell's illness he did not sleep in a bed for three weeks, but conducted his lectures and other work at the Laboratory as usual.   While attending on his wife he would continue working at his manuscripts, or would arrange a series of experiments to be carried out by one of the workers at the Cavendish Laboratory ; but the time which he could personally devote to his own experiments was very limited. The same cause prevented his attendance at meetings in London and at the British Association, for which, however, he retained his affection.   His wonderful devotion to his

---

[1] He kept up the old habit of regulating the clocks at Glenlair by the sun, which, when on the meridian, threw the shadow of a stick upon a notch cut in the stone outside the door.

wife, and the almost mystical manner in which he regarded the marriage tie, are sufficiently apparent from his letters.

The meeting of the British Association, held at Belfast in 1874 when Professor Tyndall was President, was the last which Maxwell attended. Before Section A he read a note " On the Application of Kirchhoff's Rules for Electric Circuits to the Solution of a Geometrical Problem ; " but his attendance at this meeting will be remembered chiefly on account of his paraphrase of the President's address, which was published in *Blackwood's Magazine*, and will be found reprinted amongst the poems at the end of this volume. His verses on the Red Lions, a social club consisting of members of the Association, were also written at this meeting.

In university politics Maxwell was regarded as a Conservative, and, as such, in November 1876, he was elected a member of the Council of the Senate of the University. His views respecting various questions of university reform are sufficiently indicated by his letters, especially those addressed to Mr. Monro (see p. 185). He was also a member of the Mathematical Studies and Examinations Syndicate, which was appointed on 17th May 1877, and which sat every week during term for a whole year for the purpose of reorganising the Mathematical Tripos.

In 1873 and 1874 Professor Maxwell was one of the examiners for the Natural Sciences Tripos, and in 1873 he was the first "Additional Examiner" in the Mathematical Tripos under the new regulations which then came into force. This was the fifth time that he had examined for the Mathematical Tripos in the course of seven years. He was president of the Cambridge Philosophical Society during the session 1876-77.[1]

---

[1] An account of the last years of Maxwell's life would not be complete without a reference to his acquaintance with Professor H. A. Rowland, formerly of Troy, and now of the Johns Hopkins University, Baltimore. Professor Rowland visited Maxwell more than once, and on these occasions much time was spent in comparing notes on electrical questions. Some instruments which Professor Rowland designed were not only identical with Maxwell's in the relative dimensions of the several parts, but their

Besides many contributions to *Nature* and other similar publications during his residence in Cambridge, Maxwell wrote several articles for the Ninth Edition of the *Encyclopædia Britannica*. The last scientific paper he ever wrote was the very brief article on Harmonic Analysis, the proof of which was sent for correction when its author was too weak to read it.

Although the publication of the *Treatise on Heat* and of the *Electricity and Magnetism* falls within this period, they were mainly written during the time of his retirement at Glenlair. The "small book on a great subject," entitled *Matter and Motion*, was merely the concise expression of his most habitual thoughts. But his chief literary work during the last seven years of his life was the editing of the *Electrical Researches of the Hon. Henry Cavendish, F.R.S.*

Henry Cavendish was son of Lord Charles Cavendish and great uncle to the present Duke of Devonshire. He published only two papers relating to electricity—"An Attempt to Explain some of the Phenomena of Electricity by means of an Elastic Fluid" (*Phil. Trans.* 1771), and "An Account of some Attempts to Imitate the Effects of the Torpedo by Electricity" (*Phil. Trans.* 1776). He had prepared, however, some twenty packets of manuscript on Mathematical and Experimental Electricity. These, after his death, were placed by the then Earl of Burlington, now Duke of Devonshire, in the hands of the late Sir William Snow Harris, who appears to have made an abstract of them, with a commentary of great value on their contents.

---

absolute dimensions also were very nearly the same. After Maxwell's death Professor Rowland pointed out some sources of error in the experimental determination of the Ohm as carried out at King's College, and in the recent redetermination made by Lord Rayleigh in the Cavendish Laboratory these sources of error have been removed. Maxwell's opinion of Professor Rowland was very high, and he frequently alludes to him in his correspondence, and more than once "Rowland of Troy, that doughty knight," appears in his verses, where, as the American investigator in a certain branch of magnetic science studied here by Professor Oliver Lodge and Mr. Oliver Heaviside, he is in one place referred to as "One Rowland for two Olivers." I well remember the interest with which Maxwell looked forward to Mr. Rowland's first visit, and the meeting of "Greek and Trojan" on that occasion at Glenlair.

Of this abstract and commentary Professor Maxwell was
unable to gain possession, but the Cavendish Manuscripts
were placed in his hands by the Duke of Devonshire in
1874. The manner in which the contents of these manuscripts were investigated by Professor Maxwell, and the
series of experiments he conducted in order to test
Cavendish's results, have a permanent interest for students.
The final proof-sheets were returned to press during the
summer of 1879, and the book was published in
October of the same year. The letters on this subject, which will be found below, are types of very many
that were written by Maxwell respecting the Cavendish
papers.

The title of the book, as published in October 1879,
(one thick volume, 8vo) is, *An Account of the Electrical
Researches of the Honourable Henry Cavendish, F.R.S., between*
1771 *and* 1781. Few or none could have performed
that task as Maxwell has performed it. And yet some
may wish that these precious years had been given rather
to the unimpeded prosecution of his own original researches.[1]

At my last meeting with him,—it was in his house at
Cambridge, in the year 1877,—in the midst of some
discursive talk, he took the MS. of this book out of a
cabinet, and began showing it to me, and discoursing about
it in the old eager, playful, affectionate way, just as with
the magic discs in boyhood, or the register of the colour-
box observations at a later time, in the little study at
Glenlair. "And what," I said, " of your own investigations
in various ways ?" "I have to give up so many things,"
he answered, with a sad look, which till then I had never
seen in his eyes. Even before this, as it now appears, he
had felt the first symptoms of the inexorable malady, which
in the spring of 1879 assumed a dangerous aspect, and
killed him in the autumn of that year.

[1] An unfinished fragment of a new work on Electricity, in which he
treads more closely than ever in the steps of Faraday, has been edited
since his death by Mr. Garnett and published in 1881.

LETTERS, 1871 TO 1879—ÆT. 39-48.

FROM C. J. MONRO, Esq.

Hadley, Barnet, 3d March 1871.

The Hon. J. W. Strutt, son of Lord Rayleigh, and senior wrangler in 1865, has been meddling with your colours, and has given occasion also to me to do so again. I send a selection of *Natures* containing him and me, and my old contributions of last year, which, or one of which, you say met Mr. Benson's approval. Strutt's last letter ends with a sentence which obliged me to write to him personally ; and I could not help saying, with regard to the sentence which begins it, p. 264, that I thought you would object to inferences founded on comparison by *contrast*, and that the proper way was to compare by matching recognised browns with a compound.

Listing's paper, mentioned in p. 102, was to me rather a paradox,—I had got to regard the subdivisions of the colour-scale which are assumed in language, as something so arbitrary. If you cared to see it, I have that number of Poggendorff ; I think he would hardly agree with your J. J. Müller. I wish you or Benson could eradicate the insane trick of reasoning about colours *as identified by their names*. People seem to think that blue is blue, and one blue as good as another. Benson's book I have seen (since I heard of it from you), but not read. His way of mixing by means of a prism is very happy. . . . I wish, with your new set up box, you would just put the prism observations into relation with the disk ones. It would be very easy. White we have got ; and it would only be *strictly* necessary to determine *two* other standard colours, such as vermilion or emerald, by reference to the spectrum primaries. You don't say whether your dwellers in Mesopotamia and elsewhere agree on the whole better or worse than " J " and " K," who, I suppose, agree for better and for worse. To judge by their case, the discrepancy would be a little diminished by taking as units of colour co-ordinates for any given pair of eyes, not the intensities of the primaries as they appear in the spectrum, but their intensities as they appear in the combination which to that pair of eyes makes (say) *white*. This amounts to transforming from trilinear to Hamilton's anharmonic co-ordinates with white for the fourth point,—in the language of " scientific metaphor."

On the other hand, ought not all your co-ordinates to be cooked by multiplying by $\dfrac{d \,.\, \text{scale, page 68}}{d \,.\, \text{wave-length}}$?

You know where I learnt *scientific metaphor*. I have read the address in Section A more than once with much pleasure, and, I hope, profit in proportion. The pleasure, I confess, was with me, as I found it was with Litchfield, partly that of recognising an old well-remembered style, and reflecting that here at least was something which might be "thought to be beyond the reach of change." . . . By the way, Boole is "one of the profoundest mathematicians of our time;" but how about "thinkers"? Certainly his expositions of the principle of a piece of mathematics are beautiful up to and, I don't doubt, beyond my appreciating. But that last chapter of the *Laws*, etc., from which you quote, with Empedocles and Pseudo-Origen and the rest of them, always seems to me to render a sound as of a largish internal cavity ; and the whole book, taken together with his R.S.E. paper on testimony and least squares, presents, I think, too many instances of a particular class of fallacy—I know I am speaking blasphemies, but there would be a strike among the postmen if I put in all the necessary qualifications— too many instances to be got over, not in absolute number if they were of different kinds, for anybody may make mistakes, but too many of one kind. The kind is *insufficient interpretation, i.e.* letting your equations lead you by the nose. The most serious example,—I maintain it *is* an example,—is his insisting that his theory of logic is not founded on quantity, so that it furnishes (he holds) an independent foundation for probabilities, independent of the usual quantitative foundation. That this is a fallacy, and that in particular it is an example of the fallacy of insufficient interpretation, is evident surely when you find that, even in the higher case of "secondary" propositions, the elective symbols represent in his own opinion *quantities* of "time" after all. With regard to the sentence you quote, I am always suspicious of any inclination I may feel to find a question too easy ; and, independently of that, your quoting it is itself a staggerer. But the difficulty I confess does strike me as a rather artificial one. There is nothing, scarcely, in which I think Mill is so right and the Hamiltonians so wrong as that question about logic being the laws of thought. Hamilton says *as thought*, Mill says *as valid*, and so does Boole and so do you ; but if Mill is right, where is the difficulty ? Why *should* the conditions of

thinking correctly be inviolable in the sense of not preventing
you from thinking incorrectly, provided they are inviolable in
the sense of ensuring that you take the consequences if you do ?
The laws of projection in geometry are inviolable, but nobody
ever thought it a paradox that it is possible for a picture to be
out of drawing in spite of them, nor is it a paradox that in un-
familiar classes of cases a rigorously accurate piece of perspective
looks out of drawing. Perhaps you meant, for I suppose the
report in *Nature* is incomplete, that it was a difficulty to say in
what sense mathematical propositions could be said to be *certain*,
considering that one may make mistakes about them. Perhaps
something else, which for the above reason or others, is hidden
from me.

    . . . By the way, I hope it is true that you are to profess
experimental physics at Cambridge, or what I hope comes to the
same thing, that you are a candidate.

To C. J. Monro, Esq.

Glenlair, Dalbeattie, 15th March 1871.

I have been so busy writing a sermon on Colour, and Tyn-
dalising my imagination up to the lecture point, that along with
other business I have had no leisure to write to any one.

I think a good deal may be learned from the *names* of colours ;
not about colours, of course, but about names ; and I think it
is remarkable that the rhematic instinct has been so much more
active, at least in modern times, on the less refrangible side of
primary green ($\lambda = 510 \times 10^{-9}$ inches).

I am not up in ancient colours, but my recollection of the
interpretations of the lexicographers is of considerable confusion
of hues between red and yellow, and rather more discrimination
on the blue side. Qu. If this is true, has the red sensation
become better developed since those days ? Benson has a new
book, Chapman & Hall, 1871, called *Manual of Colour*.

I think it is a great improvement on the Quarto, both in size
and quality. It is the size of this paper I write on.

I have not asked you if you wish to go to sermon on Colour,
for I do not think the R. I.[1] a good place to go to of nights,
even for strong men. I have, however, some tickets to spare.

---

[1] Royal Institution.

The peculiarity of our space is that of its three dimensions, none is before or after another. As is x, so is y and so is z.

If you have 4 dimensions this becomes a puzzle, for—first, if three of them are in our space, then which three? Also, if we lived in space of m dimensions, but were only capable of thinking n of them, then 1st, Which n? 2d, If so, things would happen requiring the rest to explain them, and so we should either be stultified or made wiser.

I am quite sure that the kind of continuity which has four dimensions all co-equal is not to be discovered by merely generalising Cartesian space equations. (I don't mean by Cartesian space that which Spinoza worked from Extension the one essential property of matter, and Quiet the best glue to stick bodies together.) I think it was Jacob Steiner who considered the final cause of space to be the suggestion of new forms of continuity.

I hope you will continue to trail clouds of glory after you, and tropical air, and be as it were a climate to yourself. I am glad to see you occasionally in *Nature.* I shall be in London for a few days next week,—address Athenæum Club.

I think Strutt on sky-blue is very good. It settles Clausius's vesicular theory,

> " for, putting all his words together,
> 'tis 3 blue beans in 1 blue bladder."—*Mat. Prior.*

The Exp. Phys. at Cambridge is not built yet, but we are going to try.

The desideratum is to set a Don and a Freshman to observe and register (say) the vibrations of a magnet together, or the Don to turn a winch, and the Freshman to observe and govern him.

FROM PROFESSOR TYNDALL.

Monday.

MY DEAR MAXWELL—Why . . . did you run away so rapidly? I wished to shake your hand before parting.—Yours ever, JOHN TYNDALL.

TO MRS. MAXWELL.

20th March 1871.

There are two parties about the professorship. One wants popular lectures, and the other cares more for experimental work. I think there should be a gradation—popular lectures and rough experiments for the masses ; real experiments for real students ; and laborious experiments for first-rate men like Trotter and Stuart and Strutt.

FROM C. J. MONRO, Esq.

Hadley, 21st March 1871.

. . . I never observed before that ancient colour-nomenclature was more discriminate than ours for the more "violently" refracted tints as compared with the less ; but I think there must be something in it. But I have always suspected that they referred colour to a positively distinct set of co-ordinates from ours. Gladstone says something of this sort in *Homer ;* who put it into his head I can't think ; if he made it out for himself I should be very sorry to agree with a man who does not believe in spectrum analysis, and does believe that Leto is the Virgin Mary. Such queer applications of words of colour one does find. You know the " pale " horse of the Apocalypse (vi. 8) ; well, that is χλωρός, which is usually "green," you know. General Daumas says the Arabs call " vert " what the French call " louvet " in horses ; and *louvet,* in Littré, "Se dit, chez le cheval, d'une robe caractérisée par la présence de la nuance jaune et du noir, qui lui donne une certaine ressemblance avec le poil du loup. . . . Substantivement," he continues, " Le louvet n'est, à proprement parler, qu'un isabelle charbonné." The Arabic for green, and (I have no doubt) the word Daumas speaks of, is akhdár, kh as ch in Scotch, and the dot marking a modification which, it happens, is imitated by interpolating an L in Spanish and Portuguese ; so χλωρός may have been supposed to have something to do with the Semitic word. However, according to dictionaries, "the three greens" in Arabic are "gold, wine, and meat," which beats the green horse. I suppose the Revisionists will leave "pale," and certainly χλωρόν δέος is the Homeric for a blue funk. But χλωρός, and akhdár, too, are certainly the colour of chlorophyll, and Daumas's remark is a note on a line in a translation from a poet, which runs " Ces chevaux verts comme le roseau qui croît au bord des fleuves."

I am glad you are going to preach, and I should like to sit under you, but, as you assume, it would not do. Thanks all the same.

To Mrs. Maxwell.

Athenæum, 22d March 1871.

I also got a first-rate letter from Monro about colour, and the Arab words for it (I suppose he studied them in Algeria). They call horses of a smutty yellow colour "green." The "pale" horse in Revelation is generally transcribed green elsewhere, the word being applied to grass, etc. But the three green things in the Arabic dictionary are "gold, wine, and meat," which is a very hard saying.

From C. J. Monro, Esq.

Hadley, Barnet, 10th September 1871.

. . . Of your own things, the *Classification of Quantities* and the *Hills and Dales*, are all I have read to much purpose. Nor them either, you may say, if I go on to ask why you say that "in the pure theory of surfaces there is no method of determining a line of water-shed or water-course, except as therein is excepted, that is in page 6 ? Why does not this determine them ? to wit—

$$\left(\frac{dz}{dx}\right)^2 + \left(\frac{dz}{dy}\right)^2 \text{maximum, } \& \left\{ \begin{array}{l} z \text{ max. for a shed.} \\ z \text{ min. for a course.} \end{array} \right.$$

Or if this does determine them, how does it resolve itself into "*first* finding," etc. ?

I am glad you like Strutt on sky-blue. You see he sees his way now to a new theory of double refraction. Looking at your old letter again, I don't quite see the force of either of your objections to space of more than three dimensions. First, you ask if we can think some of the dimensions and not others, then which ? Surely one might answer, that depends — depends namely on your circumstances — on circumstances which in your circumstances you cannot expect to judge of.

" I can easily believe," as Darwin would say, that before we were tidal ascidians we were a slimy sheet of cells floating on the surface of the sea. Well, in those days, the missing dimension, and the two forthcoming ones respectively, kept changing with the rotation of the earth,—we *now* know how, but could not guess then. So, now, the missing dimension or dimensions, if any, might be determined by circumstances which we could not tell unless we knew all about the said dimension or dimensions.

To Dr. Huggins, F.R.S.

11 Scroope Terrace, Cambridge, 2d May 1872.

My dear Sir—Toby and I enclose our photographs with our best regards to you and Kepler.[1]   I had intended to be in London to-morrow, but I am busy here.   I hope the air-pump has recovered its cohesion.   There seemed to be a solution of continuity between the mercury and the glass.—Yours very truly,   J. C. M.

To Professor Lewis Campbell.

Glenlair, Dalbeattie, 19th October 1872.

. . . Lectures begin 24th.   Laboratory rising, I hear ; but I have no place to erect my chair, but move about like the cuckoo, depositing my notions in the chemical lecture-room 1st term ; in the Botanical in Lent, and in Comparative Anatomy in Easter.

I am continually engaged in stirring up the Clarendon Press, but they have been tolerably regular for two months.   I find nine sheets in thirteen weeks is their average.   Tait gives me great help in detecting absurdities.   I am getting converted to Quaternions, and have put some in my book, in a heretical form, however, for as the Greek alphabet was used up, I have used German capitals from $\mathfrak{A}$ to $\mathfrak{J}$ to stand for Vectors, and, of course, ∇ occurs continually.   This letter is called "Nabla,"[2] and the investigation a Nablody.   You will be glad to hear that the theory of gases is being experimented on by Profs. Loschmidt and Stefan of Vienna, and that the conductivity of air and hydrogen are within 2 per cent of the value calculated from my experiments on friction of gases, though the diffusion of one gas into another is "*in erglänzender ubereinstimmung mit $\frac{dp}{dt}$schen Theorie.*"

---

[1] The following scrap from a letter written five years after this may be inserted here :—

Dear Dr. Huggins—We were very sorry to hear about poor Kepler. . . . We can quite enter into the feeling of the melancholy home it makes when a dear doggie dies.   Of course you have buried him in your own garden. . . .

[2] The name of an Assyrian harp of the shape ∇.

To Professor W. G. Adams.

Natural Science Tripos,
3d December 1873.

I got Professor Guthrie's circular some time ago. I do not approve of the plan of a physical society considered as an instrument for the improvement of natural knowledge. If it is to publish papers on physical subjects which would not find their place in the transactions of existing societies, or in scientific journals, I think the progress towards dissolution will be very rapid. But if there is sufficient liveliness and leisure among persons interested in experiments to maintain a series of stated meetings to show experiments, and talk about them as some of the Ray Club do here, then I wish them all joy; only the manners and customs of London, and the distances at which people live from any convenient centre, are very much against the vitality of such sociability.

To make the meeting a dinner supplies that solid ground to which the formers of societies must trust if they would build for aye. A dinner has the advantage over mere scientific communications, that it can always be had when certain conditions are satisfied, and that no one can doubt its existence. On the other hand, it completely excludes any scientific matter which cannot be expressed in the form of conversation with your two chance neighbours, or else by a formal speech on your legs; and during its whole continuance it reduces the Society to the form of a closed curve, the elements of which are incapable of changing their relative position.

For the evolution of science by societies the main requisite is the perfect freedom of communication between each member and any one of the others who may act as a reagent.

The gaseous condition is exemplified in the soiree, where the members rush about confusedly, and the only communication is during a collision, which in some instances may be prolonged by button-holing.

The opposite condition, the crystalline, is shown in the lecture, where the members sit in rows, while science flows in an uninterrupted stream from a source which we take as the origin. This is radiation of science.

Conduction takes place along the series of members seated round a dinner table, and fixed there for several hours, with flowers in the middle to prevent any cross currents.

The condition most favourable to life is an intermediate plastic or colloïdal condition, where the order of business is (1) Greetings and confused talk ; (2) A short communication from one who has something to say and to show ; (3) Remarks on the communication addressed to the Chair, introducing matters irrelevant to the communication but interesting to the members ; (4) This lets each member see who is interested in his special hobby, and who is likely to help him ; and leads to (5) Confused conversation and examination of objects on the table.

I have not indicated how this programme is to be combined with eating. It is more easily carried out in a small town than in London, and more easily in Faraday's young days (see his life by B. Jones) than now. It might answer in some London district where there happen to be several clubbable senior men who could attract the juniors from a distance.

To Professor Lewis Campbell.

Glenlair, Dalbeattie, 3d April 1873.

The roof of the Devonshire Laboratory is being put on, and we hope to have some floors in by May, and the contractors cleared out by October. We are busy electing School Boards here. The religious difficulty is unknown here. The chief party is that which insists on keeping down the rates ; no other platform will do. All candidates must show the retrenchment ticket.

The Cambridge Philosophical Society have been entertained by Mr. Paley on Solar Myths, Odusseus as the Setting Sun, etc. Your Trachiniæ is rather in that style, but I think Middlemarch is not a mere unconscious myth, as the Odyssey was to its author, but an elaborately conscious one, in which all the characters are intended to be astronomical or meteorological.

Rosamond is evidently the Dawn. By her fascinations she draws up into her embrace the rising sun, represented as the Healer from one point of view, and the Opener of Mysteries from another ; his name, Lyd Gate, being compounded of two nouns, both of which signify something which opens, as the eye-lids of the morn, and the gates of day. But as the sun-god ascends, the same clouds which emblazoned his rising, absorb all his beams, and put a stop to the early promise of enlightenment, so that he, the ascending sun, disappears from the heavens. But the Rosa Munda of the dawn (see Vision of Sin) reappears as the Rosa Mundi in the evening, along with her daughters ♀ and ☿, in the chariot of the setting sun, who is also a healer, but not an enlightener.

Dorothea, on the other hand, the goddess of gifts, represents the other half of the revolution. She is at first attracted by and united to the fading glories of the days that are no more, but after passing, as the title of the last book expressly tells us, " from sunset to sunrise," we find her in union with the pioneer of the coming age, the editor.

Her sister Celia, the Hollow One, represents the vault of the midnight sky, and the nothingness of things.

There is no need to refer to Nicolas Bulstrode, who evidently represents the Mithraic mystery, or to the kindly family of Garth, representing the work of nature under the rays of the sun, or to the various clergymen and doctors, who are all planets. The whole thing is, and is intended to be, a solar myth from beginning to end.

To Mrs. Maxwell.

December 1873.

I am always with you in spirit, but there is One who is nearer to you and to me than we ever can be to each other, and it is only through Him and in Him that we can ever really get to know each other. Let us try to realise the great mystery in Ephesians v., and then we shall be in our right position with respect to the world outside, the men and women whom Christ came to save from their sins.

To Professor Lewis Campbell.

11 Scroope Terrace,
Cambridge, 26th February 1874.

Jackson has sent me a MS. of yours about the mechanism of the heavens.[1] After the interpretation of $\epsilon i\lambda\lambda o\mu\acute{e}\nu\eta\nu$, about which Greek appears to meet Greek as to whether it expresses motion or only configuration, the main point seems to be, What is the motion and function of $\tau\grave{o}\nu$ $\delta\iota\grave{a}$ $\pi\alpha\nu\tau\grave{o}s$ $\pi\acute{o}\lambda o\nu$?

(α) Is it in one piece with the sphere of the stars ? or (β) with that of the sun ? or (γ) is it fixed in the earth ?

It is evidently a good stout axle, not a mere geometrical line, and it has some stiff work to do.

---

[1] See the *Cambridge Journal of Philology*, vol. v., No. 10, pp. 206, foll.

What is this work ?

If the earth is fixed, and the great shaft has its bearings in a hole in the earth, then she (the earth) may, in virtue of her dignity and office, cause the axle to revolve, carrying with it the stars according to a, or the sun according to β. Thus the earth may be the cause of the motion of the Same without moving herself, as a spinster is the cause of the whirling of the spindle, though she does not herself pirouette.

Or we may suppose the earth to act as one who twirls an expanded umbrella over his head about its stick as an axis, the holes in the same representing the stars. The objection to this view (which seems to me to be Jowett's) is, that in stating the relation between the earth and the axis, the earth is said to be related to the axis (packed or whirling as the case may be), and not the axis to the earth. Now, I suppose that without all contradiction the less is related to the better. Here the earth is like a ball of clay packed round a graft on the branch of a tree, rather than like a field in which, by means of a rotatory boring tool, men bore for water.

But the business of the earth is not so much to keep the stars in motion as to effect the changes of night and day. This she may do either by rotating herself from W. to E., or by controlling the motion of the sun by the help of the great shaft.

Now, if you always observe at the same time of night (a common practice), you find the eastern stars higher every day, and the western lower. All have the *same* motion, which carries them round from E. to W. in a *year*.

Mars, Jupiter, and Saturn, in spite of their wanderings, go on the whole in the same direction, but slower. Venus and Mercury oscillate about the sun, and the moon goes the opposite way—from W. to E.

That this way of viewing the matter was really prevalent at one time is plain, from the expression the rising of such a star to denote not a time of night but a time of year. It means either (1) the day when the star rises, just before it is lost in the brightness of the sun who follows it, or (2) the day when the star is rising, when it just becomes visible after sunset.

Virgil, who speaks of stars rising, evidently had no practical knowledge of what he meant. Plato, if he sometimes gets hazy, is far clearer than Virgil. Grote would place him far below Mr. Jellinger Symons, who denied the rotation of the moon, because Grote makes Plato say that both the heavens and the earth rotate both in the same direction and with the same angular velocity.

I think I understand you to make Plato make the earth sit still and preside over the heavenly motions, and so become the artificer of day and night, like a policeman who swings his bull's-eye round to his back. But his words are capable of being used by the movers of the earth, as Milton says,

> If earth, *industrious of herself*, fetch day
> Travelling east.

I hope you will let me know whether I have not misunderstood both you, Plato, and the Truth. I have never thanked you for your Œdipus, etc., which I have enjoyed. But at present I am all day at the Laboratory, which is emerging from chaos, but is not yet cleared of gas-men, who are the laziest and most permanent of all the gods who have been hatched under heaven.[1]

Mrs. Maxwell joins me in kind regards to Mrs. Campbell and yourself.—Your afft. friend.

To W. Garnett, Esq.

Glenlair, 8th July 1874.

. . . In the MS. he [Cavendish] appears to be familiar with the theory of divided currents, and also of conductors in series, but some reference to his printed paper [on the Torpedo] is required to throw light on what he says. He made a most extensive series of experiments on the conductivity of saline solutions in tubes compared with wires of different metals, and it seems as if more marks were wanted for him if he cut out G. S. Ohm long before constant currents were invented. His measurements of capacity will give us some work at the Cavendish Lab., before we work up to the point where he left it. His only defect is not having Thomson's electrometer. He found out inductive capacity of glass, resin, wax, etc.

To Professor Lewis Campbell.

Glenlair, Dalbeattie, 26th September 1874.

Æt. 43.   Yours of the 29th instant is to hand. Whether your

---

[1] Alluding to the passage of Plato's *Timæus*, p. 40, which had given rise to the previous discussion.

devotion to Michael Angelo has urged you to anticipate his day, or whether Time gallops with those who sit to view Necessity, with her weary pund o' tow massed round her rock, being all the remains of the stane o' lint with which she was originally endowed, those who may be set to construe this sentence will be apt to lose much time.

With regard to atoms, I am preparing a hash of them for Baynes of the *Britannica*. The easiest way of showing what atoms can't do is to get some sort of notion of what they can do. If atoms are finite in number, each of them being of a certain weight, then it becomes impossible that the germ from which a man is developed should contain (actually, of course, not potentially, for potentiality is nonsense in materialism unless it is expressed as configuration and motion) gemmules of everything which the man is to inherit, and by which he is differentiated from other animals and men,—his father's temper, his mother's memory, his grandfather's way of blowing his nose, his arboreal ancestor's arrangement of hair on his arms, and his more remote littoral ancestor's devotion to the tide-swaying moon. Francis Galton, whose mission it seems to be to ride other men's hobbies to death, has invented the felicitous expression " structureless germs." Now, if a germ, or anything else, contains in itself a power of development into some distinct thing, and if this power is purely physical, arising from the configuration and motion of parts of the germ, it is nonsense to call it structureless because the microscope does not show the structure ; the germ of a rat *must* contain more separable parts and organs than there are drops in the sea. But if we are sure that there are not more than a few million molecules in it, each molecule being composed of component molecules, identical with those of carbon, oxygen, nitrogen, hydrogen, etc., there is no room left for the sort of structure which is required for pangenesis on purely physical principles. Again, suppose that a great many individual atoms take part in a disturbance in my brain, to whom does this signify anything ? As for the atoms, they have been in far worse rows before they become naturalised in my brain, but they forget the days before, etc.[1] At any rate the atoms are a very tough lot, and can stand a great deal of knocking about, and it is strange to find a number of them combining to form a man of feeling.

---

[1] Tennyson's *In Memoriam*, xliii.

In your letter you apply the word imponderable to a molecule.   Don't do that again.   It may also be worth knowing that
the æther cannot be molecular.   If it were, it would be a gas,
and a pint of it would have the same properties as regards heat,
etc., as a pint of air, except that it would not be so heavy.

Under what form (right or light) can an atom be imagined?
Bezonian! speak or die!   Now I must go to post with two
dogs in the rain.—Your afft. friend.

To the Same.

11 Scroope Terrace,
Cambridge, 4th March 1876.

Æt. 44.   Aias arrived here about a week ago.   I read him with
pleasure.   He recalled the year 1851, when I got him up.
The outline of the play seems very bare and unpromising compared with some others, but this is relieved by other features
which are not in the "argument," as *e.g.* the loyalty of the
chorus and of Tecmessa to Aias under all circumstances (for the
chorus in general veers about, and backs occasionally, according
as the wind blows or the cat jumps).   This contrasts favourably
with the character of Athena, who is but so so, only not so
comic as the Atreidæ.

But why do Ulysses and Aias not name each other in the
same language?   I suppose the last syllable of Odysseus, pronounced Anglicé, is somewhat unpleasant in verse, and Ajax,
though familiarised by Pope, has lost the interjectional sound
of your hero's name.

Two Aberdonians, Chrystal and Mollison, are working at the
Cavendish Laboratory.   I think Chrystal's work is of a kind
not comparable with that done in "a third-class German university," which was the charitable hope of *Nature* as to what
we might aspire to in ten years' time.   He has worked steadily
at the testing of Ohm's Law since October, and Ohm has come
out triumphant, though in some experiments the wire was kept
bright red-hot by the current.—Your afft. friend.

From the Right Rev. C. J. Ellicott, D.D., Lord Bishop of Gloucester and Bristol.

Palace, Gloucester, 21st Nov. 1876.
My dear Sir—Will you kindly pardon a great liberty?   I

have quoted in a forthcoming charge a remarkable expression of yours that atoms are "manufactured articles." Could you in your kindness give me the proper title and reference to the paper and the page ? I am now, alas, far from libraries, and have, in matters scientific especially, to ask the aid of others. Will you excuse me asking this further question ?

Are you, as a scientific man, able to accept the statement that is often made on the theological side, viz., that the creation of the sun posterior to light involves no serious difficulty,—the creation of light being the establishment of the primal vibrations, generally ; the creation of the sun, the primal formation of an origin, whence vibrations would be propagated earthward ?

My own mind,—far from a scientific one,—is not clear on this point. I surmise, then, that the scientific mind might not only not be clear as to the explanation, but equitably bound to say that it was no explanation at all. Excuse the trouble I am giving you, for the truth's sake, and believe me, very faithfully yours,   C. J. GLOUCESTER AND BRISTOL.

Maxwell replied as follows by return of post :—

11 Scroope Terrace, Cambridge,
22d Nov. 1876.

MY LORD BISHOP—The comparison of atoms or of molecules to "manufactured articles," was originally made by Sir J. F. D. Herschel in his "Preliminary Discourse on the Study of Natural Philosophy," Art. 28, p. 38 (ed. 1851, Longmans).

I send you by book post several papers in which I have directed attention to certain kinds of equality among all molecules of the same substance, and to the bearing of this fact on speculations as to their origin.

The comparison to "manufactured articles" was criticised (I think in a letter to *Nature*) by Mr. C. J. Monro [*Nature*, x. 481, 15th October 1874], and the latter part of the *Encyc. Brit.*, Article "Atom," is intended to meet this criticism, which points out that in some cases the uniformity among manufactured articles is evidence of want of power in the manufacturer to adapt each article to its special use.

What I thought of was not so much that uniformity of result which is due to uniformity in the process of formation, as a uniformity intended and accomplished by the same wisdom and power of which uniformity, accuracy, symmetry, consistency, and continuity of plan are as important attributes as the contrivance of the special utility of each individual thing.

With respect to your second question, there is a statement printed in most commentaries that the fact of light being created before the sun is in striking agreement with the last results of science (I quote from memory).

I have often wished to ascertain the date of the original appearance of this statement, as this would be the only way of finding what "last result of science" it referred to. It is certainly older than the time when any notions of the undulatory theory became prevalent among men of science or commentators.

If it were necessary to provide an interpretation of the text in accordance with the science of 1876 (which may not agree with that of 1896), it would be very tempting to say that the light of the first day means the all-embracing æther, the vehicle of radiation, and not actual light, whether from the sun or from any other source. But I cannot suppose that this was the very idea meant to be conveyed by the original author of the book to those for whom he was writing. He tells us of a previous darkness. Both light and darkness imply a being who can see if there is light, but not if it is dark, and the words are always understood so. That light and darkness are terms relative to the creature only is recognised in Ps. cxxxix. 12.

As a mere matter of conjectural cosmogony, however, we naturally suppose those things most primeval which we find least subject to change.

Now the æther or material substance which fills all the interspace between world and world, without a gap or flaw of $\frac{1}{100000}$ inch anywhere, and which probably penetrates through all grosser matters, is the largest, most uniform, and apparently most permanent object we know, and we are therefore inclined to suppose that it existed before the formation of the systems of gross matter which now exist within it, just as we suppose the sea older than the individual fishes in it.

But I should be very sorry if an interpretation founded on a most conjectural scientific hypothesis were to get fastened to the text in Genesis, even if by so doing it got rid of the old statement of the commentators which has long ceased to be intelligible. The rate of change of scientific hypothesis is naturally much more rapid than that of Biblical interpretations, so that if an interpretation is founded on such an hypothesis, it may help to keep the hypothesis above ground long after it ought to be buried and forgotten.

At the same time I think that each individual man should do all he can to impress his own mind with the extent, the order, and the unity of the universe, and should carry these ideas with him as he reads such passages as the 1st Chap. of the Ep. to Colossians (see Lightfoot on Colossians, p. 182), just as enlarged conceptions of the extent and unity of the world of life may be of service to us in reading Psalm viii.; Heb. ii. 6, etc. Believe me, yours faithfully,

J. CLERK MAXWELL.

FROM THE BISHOP OF GLOUCESTER AND BRISTOL.

Palace, Gloucester,
24th Nov. 1876.

DEAR PROFESSOR CLERK MAXWELL—Allow me not to lose a post in thanking you most warmly for your most kind letter and for the packet of pamphlets,—for which I hardly know how enough to express my gratitude. They are exactly what I needed,—yet I fear I may be taking from your stock more than I ought to take. I have already read a good deal of the *Encyc. Brit.* article on atoms; so pray, if you are short of copies, don't hesitate to drop me a line. The paper on attraction was also most welcome. I am ashamed to own (for bishops should not enter into these pleasures) that I have of late been speculating a good deal on the physical explanation of gravitation. I seem to feel it must be in the Ether,—and yet how, I see not. In the case of a body near the earth, I can conceive a vast amount of elastic ether behind it, and possibly urging it on, while a small quantity is under it, being excluded by the earth.

I seem also to see how this might be applied to the case of the heavy bodies that fell nearer to the steep side of Schehallion than they ought to have done by calculation; but then, when I attempt to go further, I find the theory break down.

It seems to me that we want for several things, *e.g.* light, the conception of an ether-beach all round the visible universe from which waves might be reflexively started, and at which the particles might be more closely packed; but then again I see not what it is that keeps up the beach.

But I am really ashamed of troubling you, a scientific man,

with such wanderings.   It will only show that your kindness is thoroughly appreciated.

I cordially agree with you as to the light question.   Theologians are a great deal too fond of using up the last scientific hypothesis they can get hold of.   The Christian Knowledge Society are publishing my charge.   When it is published I shall ask you to do me the favour to accept a copy.   You will then see that the best note in the little volume is due to your kindness and aid.   I remain, with all good wishes, and sincere thanks, very faithfully yours,

C. J. GLOUCESTER AND BRISTOL.

(*P.S.*)—If you are in London in the spring and near the Athenæum, do me the kindness of looking in on me, as I shall be very glad to make your personal acquaintance.   I am commonly in town regularly after Easter.

To PROFESSOR LEWIS CAMPBELL.

Glenlair, Dalbeattie, Christmas 1876.

. . . I hope that when this severe weather is past you will be able to derive benefit from a moderate use of Plato and Sophocles.

Æt. 45.

We intended to have gone round by Edinburgh to pay Aunt Jane a visit ; but we both had such bad colds that we came home to nurse them, and are now snowed up, and enjoying the artificial heat of coals, peats, and sticks, judiciously intermingled.

The demonstrator at the Cavendish Laboratory has been out of sorts all this term, and has had to go home about a month ago, so we have not been in full force there.   I hope he will be well in February, to absorb the energy of the new B.A.'s set free from the Tripos and its attendant anxieties.

As we get richer in apparatus, mathematical lectures give way to experimental, and the black board to the lamp and scale.   I have had a pupil quite innocent of mathematics who has learned to measure focal lengths of lenses, and has found the electro-motive force from the water-pipes to the gas-pipes, and from either set of pipes to the lightning-conductor.

I have been making a mechanical model of an induction coil, in which the primary and secondary currents are represented by the motion of wheels, and in which I can symbolise all the effects of putting in more or less of the iron core, or more or less resistance and Leyden jars in either circuit.

I have also been making a clay model of Prof. W. Gibb's thermodynamic surface, representing the relations of the solid, liquid and gaseous states, and the different paths by which a body may get from the one to the other.—Your afft. friend,

J. CLERK MAXWELL.

To W. GARNETT, Esq.

Glenlair, 4th January 1877.

By all means take the Groves and coils for your lecture. Are you aware that the electric flash is entirely due to the resinous particles of electricity? This is well known on the stage, where they blow the particles through a tube over a candle to make stage lightning. The vitreous electricity has nothing to do with it, as you may prove by using pounded glass.

In a letter to Mr. Garnett, dated Glenlair, 9th July 1877, Professor Maxwell gave the following suggestions respecting a projected article on Dynamics, and the letter, like those which follow it, is a good illustration of the help he was constantly rendering to his students and others who asked his advice :—

I think it a pity that the old historical word Dynamics should, for mere considerations of time, be split up into Kinematics, Kinetics, and Statics. With respect to the divisions of the subject, I think they fall thus :—

1. Early attempts at founding the science, ancient Kinematics (mechanical description of curves, etc.) generally correct.

Ancient Statics.—Archimedes.

Modern Dynamics.—Galileo, first founder. Descartes, good up to Kinematics and Statics, failed in Kinetics.

Promoters—

WREN, WALLIS, HUYGHENS, HOOKE.

Laws of collision established, and motion in a circle.

X

NEWTON.

Three laws of motion.   Form suggested by the laws of Descartes.   Meaning established by Newton's own copious and complete examples of using them.

Second statement of Newton's third Law.

My notions on the three laws are in " Matter and Motion."

NEWTONIANS.

Cambridge School.	*Popularisers.*	*Scotch School.*
Roger Cotes.	D. Gregory.	Colin Maclaurin.[1]
Robert Smith, etc.	Desaguliers.	James Gregory.
Attwood.	Mme. du Chatelet	J. Playfair.
Whewell.	and Voltaire.	Ivory.

Leibnitz and the Vis Viva Controversy.

Methods of dealing with connected systems.

Example of correct methods by Newton and others before D'Alembert.

D'Alembert's enunciation.—Its historical importance.

Euler.   The Bernoullis, etc.   Laplace, the flower of this stage of development.

Lagrange and Virtual Velocity.

This is the germ of the method of energy which was fully developed in mathematical form in the *Mecanique Analytique*, but very little appreciated outside the inner circle of mathematicians till the physical theory of energy became generally known.

Mathematical development of higher dynamics.   (See Cayley's *Brit. Ass. Report*, 1857 and 1862 ? specially Hamilton and Jacobi.)

Effect of T and T' since 1867.

Kirchoff's notions in *beginning* of Vorlesungen (not equal to Lagrange, but worth noticing).

I also think that Clausius's equation and definition of "Virial" is important.

The dynamics of other varieties of space than our own requires very brief notice indeed.—Yours truly,

J. CLERK MAXWELL.

---

[1] Introduces $M \frac{d^2x}{dt^2} = X$, etc.   See Maclaurin's *Fluxions*.

To W. Garnett, Esq.

Glenlair, Dalbeattie, 24th July 1877.

. . . There is a great slur over the word mechanics since a few poets and biologists have misused it. Pratt thought it a fine word.

The result of motion without reference to time I call Displacement. Kinematics must involve the idea of time if it treats of continuous displacements, velocities, and accelerations, though it does not contain within itself materials for comparing different intervals of time. For this we must go to the science which deals with matter; call it Kinetics, Dynamics, or Mechanics.

But I consider that Statics also deserves a place on the same level as Kinematics, as it deals with the equivalence of different systems of forces. But I do not agree with Whewell that Statics is more elementary than Kinematics. . . .

To the Same.

Glenlair, 11th August 1877.

Your experiments on electrified paraffin oil are excellent, and may lead to increase of knowledge.

If the fluid dielectric and also the air are perfect insulators, nothing can get electrified, but the equation at the surface, instead of being $P = P_0$, will be

$$P + \frac{1}{8n} (K^2 - 1) \left. \frac{\overline{dV^2}}{dv} \right| = P_0$$

(excluding capillary action) where $\dfrac{dV}{dv}$ is the resultant electric force normal to the surface and just outside it. This causes the surface to rise wherever the normal force is great, or close to the electrodes.

· · · · · ·

The science of displacements is in Euc. I. 4, etc., and wherever one figure is placed upon another. It belongs to the method of contemplating the relations of two figures which may be supposed to co-exist, though we may also suppose that they are copies of the same figure in different positions.

But just as we assume that distance is a continuous quantity capable of measurement, though all our attempts at measurement are made with instruments made of non-rigid and discontinuous matter, so we may assume that time is a continuously flowing quantity capable of measurement, though we have not yet found out any accurate method of comparing distant intervals of time.

Now Kinematics requires no more than this notion of time, as the common independent variable t. If we suppose that τ is that (unknown) which flows uniformly, then for kinematical purposes it is enough that t is a function of τ; but when we come to Kinetics proper we must have $\dfrac{d^2t}{d\tau^2}$ very small.

Have you read Julius in *Nature*, about the beginning of June? [14th June].

The most constant things we know are the properties of bodies. For instance, water in equilibrium with ice and vapour gives us a good deal.

I. A unit of density (not the orthodox one) $\dfrac{M}{L^3} = D.$

II. A unit of pressure (too small for practical use) $\dfrac{M}{LT^2} = P.$

III. A unit of time (namely, the time of revolution of a satellite just grazing a sphere of water) $= T.$

These three quantities being independent of each other give M, L, and T.

$\dfrac{P}{D}$ gives a (velocity)^2 which could also be got from the $\dfrac{P}{D}$ of the vapour (a different one).   .

Then this gives also a standard temperature; all that we want is to get pure water.

To the Same.

Glenlair, 23d August 1877.

I have been copying Cavendish on the resistance of electrolytes. If there is any one who would try a few of them roughly in the U tube, it might be interesting to compare with Cavendish's results. For weak solutions Kohlrausch may be referred to.

Sea Salt (Chloride of Sodium).

Experiments in January 1781.

Watered to 1 of Salt.		Resistance.	Resistance × quantity of Salt.
Saturated sol.	3·78	1	
	12	1·91	·602
	30	3·97	·500
	70	8·8	·475
	143	15·75	·416
	1,000	93·02	·352
	20,000	18·23	·345

Salt in 20,000 conducts about 7 times better than distilled water.

Salt in 69 of water conducts 1·97 times better at 105° F. than at 58½°.

If Professor Liveing is in Cambridge could you ask him to put me in the way of finding the best book on chemistry for the year 1777, so as to obtain the equivalents and the names of salts used by Cavendish ?

The numbers in the first columns are the quantities which were equivalent to the " acid " in solution of 1 of salt in 29 of water.

3·2 Sal Sylvii (potassium chloride).

2·3 Sal Amm. (ammonium chloride).

14·10 Calc. S.S.A. (?)

2·21 Calcined Glauber's Salt (sodium sulphate).

3·17 Quadrangular Nitre (sodium nitrate).

5·19 Salt D. (?)

The solutions were 3, 10, 12.

I am going to try if this is Troy or Apothecaries' weight.

Saturated solution (1 in 3·78) of common salt has 437,000 the resistance of iron wire. New distilled water has more resistance than distilled water kept a year.

All these results and many more were got by comparison of the strength of shocks taken through Cavendish's body. I think this series of experiments is the most wonderful of them all, and well worth verification.

. . . . .

Cavendish is the first verifier of Ohm's Law, for he finds by successive series of experiments that the resistance is as the following power of the velocity, 1·08, 1·03, ·980, and concludes that it is as the first power. All this by the physiological galvanometer.

. . . Can you solve the equation

$$\frac{dz}{dx}\left(\frac{d^2z}{dy^2} - 2\ \frac{d^2z}{dxdy}\right) + \frac{dz}{dy}\left(\frac{d^2z}{dx^2} - 2\ \frac{d^2z}{dxdy}\right) = 0\ ?$$

$z = \dfrac{\mathrm{A}}{xy}$ is a solution. Find the general ditto.

To Professor Lewis Campbell.

11 Scroope Terrace,
Cambridge, 5th January 1878.

Æt. 46.   It is more than a month that I have had your letter lying by me. I am glad you like Chrystal. His departure is a great loss to the laboratory, as it is difficult to find any one to take up heavy work. W. D. Niven (brother of the competitor) is going in for a heavy piece of work on conduction of heat in gases. I am no judge of Greek plays, but I think that your success in choruses is fully equal to that in dialogue, considering the greater difficulty, not only in the interpretation but in guessing the kind of effect, musical, rhythmical, rhetorical, poetical, and pictorial, which was aimed at in the delivery of the chorus.

We have all been conversing on the telephone. Garnett recognised the voice of a man who called by chance. But the phonograph will preserve to posterity the voices of our best speakers and singers. See *Nature* of Jan. 3d.

To W. Garnett, Esq.

Glenlair, 20th September 1878.

. . . Cavendish would speak of the *pressure* of a ·voltaic battery (only he hadn't one), but we require to be educated up to his mark.

To the Librarian of the Royal Society.

Glenlair, Dalbeattie, 23d June 1879.

Dear Sir — Your information about FF.R.S. has been so

useful to me that I now ask about Dr. G. Knight, F.R.S., librarian to the British Museum.

(1.) Is his name Gowan, Gowen, Gowin, or Godwin, for I find all four spellings current?

(2.) Who is the author of the paper in *Phil. Trans.* for 1776 (near the end of the vol.) describing his great magazines of magnets?

(3.) Are the magazines [sketch shown] mounted like great guns still in the possession of the R.S. ?

(4.) Is the portrait of Gowin Knight, by Benjamin Wilson, F.R.S., among the pictures of the R.S.?

I have got from the Meteorological Office some Cavendish MSS. on Magnetism which prompt these inquiries, and also this—

When the R. S. was at Crane Court had it a garden adjoining? Also, where was Crane Court?

Henry Cavendish and his father Lord Charles worked together at observations of the variation compass and dipping needle in the R. S. room and garden. Are the variation compass and dipping needle still in the R. S. collection?

Cavendish wrote out directions for using the dipping needle for Captain Pickersgill, Captain Bayley, Dalrymple.

Dalrymple, I find from Poggendorff, was hydrographer to the H.E.I.C. If Cavendish apportioned his instructions according to the capacity of the recipients, then their capacities would be in descending order, Dalrymple, Pickersgill, Bayley. Were any of these F.R.S. ?

Also, was John Walsh, F.R.S., also M.P. ?

Do not answer any of these questions which would involve trouble, but I have not here any means of answering them except by the aid of those who are among the records of the past. None of the questions are of vital importance, because I can leave out any statements I have made which are doubtful.

—Yours very truly,   J. CLERK MAXWELL.

Professor Maxwell was frequently invited to join the Victoria Institute, and in March 1875 he received a letter from the secretary conveying the special invitation of the President and Council to join the Society, "among whose members are his Grace the Archbishop of Canterbury, and other prelates and leading ministers, several professors of

Oxford and Cambridge and other universities, and many literary and scientific men." The following is all that has been found of a rough draft of his reply :—

SIR—I do not think it my duty to become a candidate for admission into the Victoria Institute. Among the objects of the Society are some of which I think very highly. I think men of science as well as other men need to learn from Christ, and I think Christians whose minds are scientific are bound to study science that their view of the glory of God may be as extensive as their being is capable of. But I think that the results which each man arrives at in his attempts to harmonise his science with his Christianity ought not to be regarded as having any significance except to the man himself, and to him only for a time, and should not receive the stamp of a society. For it is of the nature of science, especially of those branches of science which are spreading into unknown regions to be continually ——[here the MS. ends].

CHAPTER XII.

ILLNESS AND DEATH—1879—ÆT. 47, 48.

AFTER his recovery from the attack of erysipelas at Glenlair in 1865, Maxwell's health appears to have been fairly good until the spring of 1877. He then began to be troubled with dyspeptic symptoms, especially with a painful choking sensation after taking meat. He consulted no one for about two years. But one day in 1877, on coming into the Laboratory after his luncheon, he dissolved a crystal of carbonate of soda in a small beaker of water, and drank it off. A little while after this he said he had found how to manage so as to avoid pain. The trouble proved obstinate, however, and at last, on the 21st of April 1879, he mentioned it when writing to Dr. Paget about Mrs. Maxwell.

By this time his friends at Cambridge had begun to observe a change in his appearance, and some failure of the old superabundant energy. They missed the elasticity of step, and the well-known sparkle in his eye. During the Easter Term of 1879 he attended the Laboratory daily, but only stayed a very short time. At the end of the term he remarked that he had been unable to do much more than to give his lectures. And before leaving Cambridge for the vacation he was more than once very seriously unwell.

In June he returned, as usual, to Glenlair. His letters continued to be marked by humorous cheerfulness, and, as was always the case, contained information about everything and everybody except himself. He was still unwearied in his exertions for those to whom his services could be of use. But some casual remarks gave cause for apprehension that he was not gaining strength, and after he had been in Scotland for a few weeks he wrote that " he felt like a child, as for some time he had been allowed no food but milk." By and by the reports were more encouraging, and in September, according to appointment, Mr. and Mrs. Garnett were received at Glenlair. On Maxwell's coming out of the house to welcome them, Mr. Garnett saw a great change in him, and was for the first time seriously alarmed.

In the evening, however, the master of the house conducted family worship as usual for the assembled household. And the days passed much in the same kindly fashion as of old, linking the present to the past in "natural piety." There were the drawings of the oval curves of 1846 ; the family scrap-book, with Mrs. Blackburn's water-colour sketches from the earliest time ; the Glenlair autograph book ; the bagpipes which saved the life of Captain Clerk in the Hooghly ; and a host of other treasures which Maxwell took delight in showing. He led his guests down to the river, and accompanied them a little way along its wooded banks, pointing out where the stepping-stones used to be, where he bathed when a boy, and where the exploit of tub-navigation had been performed. This was the longest walk he had taken for some time. He was unable to drive with them in the afternoon, because he could not bear the shaking of the carriage.

On the 2d of October 1879, in the midst of great weakness and of great pain, he was told by the late Dr. Sanders of Edinburgh, who had been summoned to Glenlair, that he had not a month to live. From that moment he had only one anxiety, the same which had for so long been his chief care—to provide for *her* comfort, whom he now saw that he must leave behind.

The following letter, probably the last that Maxwell penned, was written on the day after Dr. Sanders's visit :—

Glenlair, Dalbeattie, 3d October 1879.

DEAR GARNETT—We were glad to hear from Mrs. Garnett

of your arrival in Cambridge. We intend to travel through by the Rugby and Bletchley route on Monday the 6th, arriving at the Cambridge Station at 10 P.M. If Pullin is well enough, please tell him to get a fly from Curwain (or if not, from some one else), and so be ready to help us.

I have had some relief from some of the things which troubled me, so I am not in such pain; but, on the whole, I am getting weaker, and we had Dr. Sanders from Edinburgh on Wednesday, who recommended us to go to Cambridge as soon as we could. So we mean to come on Monday; but if we have to change I will write or telegraph to Pullin at the Laboratory, as I do not know where you are between the nest and the rookery.[1] I address this to the rookery.

Mrs. Maxwell has done wonderfully since I have been so much laid up, but she will be very tired when she gets to Cambridge, and I shall not be much better.—Yours very truly,

J. CLERK MAXWELL.

He returned to Cambridge; but he was so weak as to be hardly able to walk from the train to a carriage. Under the diligent care of Dr. Paget his most painful symptoms were considerably relieved, and his friends began to entertain fond hopes of his recovery. But his strength gradually failed, and at length it was evident to all that the disease could not be stayed.

During the last few weeks his sufferings were very great, but he seldom mentioned them; and, apart from his anxiety for others, his mind was absolutely calm. The one thought which weighed upon him, and to which he constantly referred, was for the future welfare and comfort of Mrs. Maxwell. During the whole period of their married life (twenty-one years) his ever-present watchfulness and sympathy had supported her even in the smallest domestic concerns; his knowledge, his constructiveness, his dexterity of hand, had been ever ready to minister to her slightest need,—and now, unable to nurse him as of old, she seemed more than ever dependent on his care. To the last, he regularly gave the orders that were necessary for her comfort, and endeavoured to see that they were carried out.

---

[1] *i.e.* Home and College.

When too weak to dwell on those scientific inquiries which had been the work of his life, his mind continued active about many of his favourite studies. He remarked one day that he had been wondering why the lines in Shakespeare's *Merchant of Venice*, about the harmony that is in mortal souls (repeating the whole passage) should have been put in the mouth of such a frivolous person as Lorenzo. At another time, when continuous conversation had become impossible, and he had been lying for some time with closed eyes, he looked up and repeated the verse, "Every good gift and every perfect gift is from above," etc., and then added—"Do you know that that is a hexameter? πᾶσα δόσις ἀγαθὴ καὶ πᾶν δώρημα τέλειον. I wonder who composed it?" He frequently quoted Richard Baxter's hymn—

> "Lord, it belongs not to my care,
>   Whether I die or live;
> To love and serve Thee is my share,
>   And that Thy grace must give," etc.

On the Saturday preceding his death he received the Sacrament of the Lord's Supper from Dr. Guillemard, and it was while Dr. G. was putting on his surplice that Maxwell repeated to him George Herbert's lines on the priest's vestments, entitled *Aaron*.[1]   Maxwell's

---

[1] AARON.

Holiness on the head,
   Light and perfections on the breast,
Harmonious bells below, raising the dead
   To lead them unto life and rest :
   Thus are true Aarons drest.

Profaneness in my head,
   Defects and darkness in my breast,
A noise of passions ringing me for dead
   Unto a place where is no rest :
   Poor priest, thus am I drest.

Only another head
   I have, another heart and breast,
Another music, making live, not dead,
   Without whom I could have no rest :
   In Him I am well drest.

mind and memory remained perfectly clear to the very last.

The fortitude with which he bore his sufferings, and the calm self-possession with which he met his end, impressed those most who watched him most narrowly, and had the best reason to know the acuteness of his sufferings.

The end may best be told by those who were nearest to him at the time. I have been favoured with the following communications :—(1) From Dr. Paget ; (2) from the Rev. Dr. Guillemard ; and (3) from his cousin, Mr. Colin Mackenzie, who acted the part of a brother at the last, as he had done many a time before.

(1.) *Dr. Paget's Statement.*

In April 1879 he began to be troubled with some difficulty in swallowing—the first significant symptom of the disease which was to prove fatal. The summer he spent at Glenlair. At the end of July he consulted Prof. Sanders and Prof. Spence of Edinburgh, and while at Glenlair was attended by Dr. Lorraine of Castle-Douglas. But he grew worse, and at the end of September Prof. Sanders was summoned to him from Edinburgh. He was then suffering from attacks of violent pain, had become dropsical, and his strength was rapidly failing. At Glenlair he was seven miles from Dr. Lorraine. It was therefore decided to remove him to Edinburgh or Cambridge. He chose Cambridge, and arrived there on October 8, accompanied by Mrs. Maxwell, and attended during the journey by Dr. Richard Lorraine.

In Cambridge his more severe sufferings were gradually in great measure relieved, but the disease continued its progress.

> Christ is my only head,
>   My alone only heart and breast,
> My only music, striking me e'en dead ;
>   That to the old man I may rest,
>   And be in him new drest.
>
> So holy in my head,
>   Perfect and light in my dear breast,
> My doctrine tuned by Christ (who is not dead,
>   But lives in me while I do rest),
>   Come, people ; Aaron's drest.

It was the disease of which his mother had died at the same age.

As he had been in health, so was he in sickness and in face of death. The calmness of his mind was never once disturbed. His sufferings were acute for some days after his return to Cambridge, and, even after their mitigation, were still of a kind to try severely any ordinary patience and fortitude. But they were never spoken of by him in a complaining tone. In the midst of them his thoughts and consideration were rather for others than for himself.

Neither did the approach of death disturb his habitual composure. Before leaving Glenlair he had learnt from Prof. Sanders that he had not more than about a month to live. A few days before his death he asked me (Dr. Paget) how much longer he could last. The inquiry was made with the most perfect calmness. He wished to live until the expected arrival from Edinburgh of his friend and relative Mr. Colin Mackenzie. His only anxiety seemed to be about his wife, whose health had for a few years been delicate, and had recently become worse. He had been to her for some time the most tender and assiduous of nurses. An hour only before his death, when, through extreme bodily weakness, his voice was reduced to a whisper so feeble that it could be heard only when the ear was held close to his mouth, the words whispered to Dr. Paget related not to himself but to Mrs. Maxwell.

His intellect also remained clear and apparently unimpaired to the last. While his bodily strength was ebbing away to death, his mind never once wandered or wavered, but remained clear to the very end. No man ever met death more consciously or more calmly.[1]

On November 5 he gently passed away.

---

[1] Dr. J. W. Lorraine of Castle-Douglas, in a letter addressed to Dr. Paget, and dated 5th October 1879, remarks as follows concerning his patient :—"I must say he is one of the best men I have ever met, and a greater merit than his scientific attainments is his being, so far as human judgment can discern, a most perfect example of a Christian gentleman." This remark, Dr. Paget observes, "is a *very* unusual one in a letter from one physician to another." Dr. Paget also says in writing to Mr. Garnett: "There is a deep interest in the fact of *how* such a man as Maxwell met the trials of sickness and the approach of death. They are severe tests of amiability and unselfishness, and of the genuineness of religious convictions. It is something to say of a man that his unselfishness and composure remained undisturbed, and it is interesting physiologically and

Dr. Paget's report of Maxwell's composure throughout his illness is very strikingly confirmed by his letter to that physician, dated October 3, which is too confidential to be inserted here, but consists of a simple unadorned description of the facts of the case, and a request for aid which he knew would be forthcoming. A stranger, in reading that letter, would never divine, and indeed might find it hard to believe, that on *the previous day* (Oct. 2) the writer had been told by medical authority that he had only a month to live. Yet such is the fact. The words "for I am really very helpless," however touching as a description of his condition, are merely the statement of a reason why some one should be got "officially to help" Maxwell himself, but really and chiefly to do for Mrs. Maxwell what *he* had done so long as he had any strength in him. Students of history may perhaps recall Nicias's letter to the Athenians :—"You should also send a general to succeed me, for I have a disease, and cannot remain ;"[1] but the words of the unfortunate general, "I claim your indulgence,"[2] though dignified enough, are more than Maxwell would have written.

(2.) The following letter, addressed to me by the Rev. Dr. Guillemard, of St. Mary's the Less, Cambridge, may be left to speak for itself :—

Cambridge, 19th May 1881.

MY DEAR SIR—I shall disappoint you very much in my reminiscences of Maxwell. I never was an INTIMATE FRIEND of his, though we were always on the very best terms, and met not unfrequently, and he was most constant and assiduous in his attendance at church, and interested in all church matters.

But I knew very little about his *inner self* before I was summoned to his dying bed ; and he had been brought very low physically, before his return to Cambridge, and was unequal to much *continuous* thought or conversation. He welcomed me warmly whenever I visited him, joined fervently in all acts of

---

psychologically, that in the very extremity of bodily weakness, when the nourishment of the brain must have become so reduced, the mind remained perfectly clear." Dr. Lorraine's remark on Maxwell's personal character expresses the feelings of all, nurses included, that were about Maxwell in his last illness.   [1] Thuc. 7, 15.   [2] *Ibid.*

prayer, listened with a most intelligent interest to all I read, either out of the Bible (which he knew well-nigh by heart) or out of any of our great devotional writers in prose or poetry; was especially fond of any new hymns, and frequently capped such by reciting from his wonderful memory some parallel passages of his favourite old authors, specially George Herbert.

His faith in the grand cardinal verities was firm, simple, and full ; and he avowed it humbly but unhesitatingly, with the deepest gratitude for the revelation of the truth in Jesus. I do not think he had any doubts or difficulties to cloud his clear mind or shake his peace.

He was calmly and serenely resigned to the will of God, and bowed in meek acquiescence before what he believed to be the Word of God.

I never saw a sign of impatience or fretfulness under all his long suffering, or heard an approach to a murmur. His one and only care was for his wife. It was a grand sight to see him day by day girding himself calmly and resolutely for the last struggle, and he passed through it undismayed. I wish I had preserved any of his last words : they have passed away from my shallow memory.—Yours very truly,   W. H. GUILLEMARD.

I am also permitted to insert the following more circumstantial account, which was written by Dr. Guillemard to the Rev. Isaac Bowman, Vicar of South Creake, Fakenham, Norfolk, on the 9th of December 1879, within five weeks after Maxwell's death :—

He suffered exquisite pain, hardly able to lie still for a minute together, sleepless, and with no appetite for the food which he so required.

He understood his position from the first ; knew what it all meant, and calmly girded himself for the awful struggle. He welcomed me at once as visiting him, not only as a friend, but as the Parish Priest come to assist him and to minister to him, and spoke of our relations with a grave, simple cheerfulness. You know the lightheartedness of the man in ordinary times ; and really it abode on him throughout ; he was never downcast or overburdened, and yet he was the humblest and most diffident of men, with the deepest sense of his own unworthiness, of his many short-comings, of his neglected opportunities. " But he loved much, and love had cast out fear." I used to go to him nearly every day of the five or six weeks he was here, to read and pray with him. He preferred the prayers of the Church, and asked for them, and by the wonderful power of his memory knew them all by heart; but he gladly joined in other devotions, and took special delight in sacred poetry, of which I generally read him two or three short pieces.

He knew all our best writers in that line thoroughly: Milton, Keble, Newman, Wesley, George Herbert—the latter his chief favourite; and he repeated to me the morning after an unusually bad night, the five stanzas of "Aaron" without a mistake. His knowledge of the Bible was remarkable, and he constantly asked for his most deeply-prized passages. Four days before he was removed from us he received the Holy Communion at my hands, with holy, reverent, fervid devotion, and said what strength it gave him.

I saw him only once again; he was too weak and restless and exhausted for much intercourse; but as I rose from my knees he said:—"My dear friend, you have been a true under shepherd to me: read me, before you go, the beautiful prayer out of the Burial Service, 'Suffer me not at my last hour' "— and his grasp of my hand, as we parted, told me all he felt.

I had known but little of his inner self before his illness; he was singularly reticent; and though we occasionally discussed a text critically, we rarely got upon doctrine, or anything that touched upon the spiritual life. He was a constant regular attendant at church, and seldom, if ever, failed to join in our monthly late celebration of Holy Communion, and he was a generous contributor to all our parish charitable institutions. But his illness drew out the whole heart and soul and spirit of the man: his firm and undoubting faith in the Incarnation and all its results; in the full sufficing of the Atonement; in the work of the Holy Spirit. He had gauged and fathomed all the schemes and systems of philosophy, and had found them utterly empty and unsatisfying—"unworkable" was his own word about them—and he turned with simple faith to the Gospel of the Saviour.

(3.) Mr. Colin Mackenzie, who is by this time well known to the reader, was present at the last. He says:—

Y

A few minutes before his death, Professor Clerk Maxwell was being held up in bed, struggling for breath, when he said slowly and distinctly, "God help me! God help my wife!" he then turned to me (Mr. Mackenzie) and said, "Colin, you are strong, lift me up;" He next said, "Lay me down lower, for I am very low myself, and it suits me to lie low." After this he breathed deeply and slowly, and, with a long look at his wife, passed away.

(4.) Another friend who saw him in his last illness, the Rev. Professor Hort, has summed up his recollections of Maxwell, especially of the graver side of his character, in the following letter :—

FROM PROF. F. J. A. HORT TO PROF. L. CAMPBELL.

Feb. 4, 1882.

It is with extreme regret that I find myself powerless to comply with your request that I should contribute to your Memoir of Professor Maxwell a sketch of his position in reference to theology and religion. A competent and faithful account of Maxwell's inner thoughts during manhood would, for several reasons, have been of the highest interest. But his habitual reticence as to all that moved him deeply, and my own bad memory, have together left me without the materials needed for a task in itself most attractive. Though the impression of rare greatness which he left upon me in the first days of our acquaintance became stronger and stronger to the end, I have little to offer but a few vague and scattered reminiscences. Such as they are, I am thankful to be allowed to send them.

My earlier recollections of Maxwell are chiefly associated with a small society at Cambridge to which we both belonged, which used to meet on Saturday evenings for the discussion of literary and speculative questions. The aversion to rhetoric which he found traditional among its members was much to his taste, and he always took an animated and interested part in the conversations. Unfortunately his love of speaking in parables, combined with a certain obscurity of intonation, rendered it often difficult to seize his meaning; but bright and penetrating little sayings, usually whimsical in form, and sometimes accompanied by strange gestures, recurred almost unfailingly at no distant intervals. Whether the tone of his mind was much affected by his participation in our discussions it is difficult to say. During the time that I knew him I can recall no perceptible signs of change other than quiet growth, and suspect that he attained too early and too stable a maturity to receive easily a new direction from any kind of intercourse with his University contemporaries. But it is likely enough that his mind was at least invigorated and consolidated by an influence which others have found reason to count among the strongest and also on the whole most salutary that they have known. The same may probably be said of the influence of Mr. Maurice's writings, which certainly occupied Maxwell at this time. To what extent he was affected by them I do not know ; but the tone in which he used to speak of Mr. Maurice leads me to think that they must have at least given him considerable aid in the adjustment and clearing up of his own beliefs on the highest subjects.

My intercourse with Maxwell dropped when we both left Cambridge. When I returned in 1872, after an absence of fifteen years, he had lately been installed at the new Cavendish Laboratory, and I had the happiness of looking forward to a renewal of friendship with him. I found him, as was natural, a graver man than of old ; but as warm of heart and fresh in mind as ever. Owing to accidental circumstances on both sides, we met seldomer than I had hoped, though certainly there was no diminution of cordiality on the part of either. Strangely enough, it was again to the meetings of a small society, in purpose not unlike the former, that I owe most of my impressions of Maxwell in these later years. Though he was often unable to attend its meetings, and could rarely stay for more than an hour, he seemed to find much satisfaction in thus joining in the discussion of speculative questions with a few friends, chiefly middle-aged men, representing among them great diversity of studies and no less diversity of opinion. The old peculiarities of his manner of speaking remained virtually unchanged. It was still no easy matter to read the course of his thoughts through the humorous veil which they wove for themselves ; and still the obscurity would now and then be lit up by some radiant explosion.

Perhaps the most noteworthy of Maxwell's characteristics was his absolute independence of mind, an independence unsullied by conceit or consciousness. Preserved by his simplicity and humility from any fondness for barren paradox, he endeavoured

always to see things with his own eyes, without regard to the
points of view assumed on one side or another in ordinary controversy : in a word, he was more free from "notionalism" than
any one whom I have known.   The testimony of his unshaken
faith to Christian truth was, I venture to think, of exceptional
value on account of his freedom from the mental dualism often
found in distinguished men who are absorbed chiefly in physical
inquiries.   It would have been alien to his whole nature to
seclude any province of his beliefs from the free exercise of
whatever faculties he possessed ; and in his eyes every subject
had its affinities with the rest of the universal truth.   His
strong sense of the vastness of the world not now accessible to
human powers, and of the partial nature of all human modes of
apprehension, seemed to enlarge for him the domain of reasonable belief.   Thus in later years it was a favourite thought of
his that the relation of parts to wholes pervades the invisible no
less than the visible world, and that beneath the individuality
which accompanies our personal life there lies hidden a deeper
community of being as well as of feeling and action.   But no
one could be less of a dreamer, or less capable of putting either
fancies or wishes in the place of sober reality.   In mind, as in
speech, his veracity was thorough and resolute : he carried into
every thought a perfect fidelity to the divine proverb which
hung beside yet more sacred verses on the wall of his private
room, " The lip of truth shall be established for ever."

During Maxwell's last illness I had the privilege of enjoying
two conversations with him ; and not long afterwards I put on
paper a short and desultory record of some of his words.   These
notes contain nothing that might not with propriety be brought
under other eyes, and therefore I venture to quote them here.
Most of what passed on these two occasions presented nothing
worthy of remark, unless it be the cheerful naturalness with
which Maxwell spoke on all the varied topics that happened
to come up before us.   His thoughts had evidently been mainly
taking a retrospective direction ; and every interest of life
seemed to be hallowed and brightened by the probable nearness
of the Divine summons to a new form of existence.

He told me briefly the story of his illness ; how he had been
ailing all the year, but had gone northward after Easter Term
without apprehending anything worse than transient ill-health.
He had taken with him Professor Clifford's *Lectures and Essays*
which he had been asked to review.   He had read them with

close attention for the purpose, and had then, at some time in the summer, prepared to write his criticism. It was a difficult and delicate task, he said, for "there were many things in the book that wanted trouncing, and yet the trouncing had to be done with extreme care and gentleness, Clifford was such a nice fellow." As soon as he tried to begin, his brain refused its office, and he found himself incapable of composition ; and then he knew that his illness had become serious.

Something, I forget what, led the conversation to the perilousness of strong religious excitement in early youth, on account of the spiritual exhaustion and permanent religious insensibility that are apt to follow the dying-out of the original fervour, and that derive a plausible justification from the premature and fallacious experience. He spoke with thankfulness of his own escape from a similar danger. "The ferment," he said, "about the Free Church movement had one very bad effect. Quite young people were carried away by it ; and when the natural reaction came, they ceased to think about religious matters at all, and became unable to receive fresh impressions. My father was so much afraid of this that he placed me where I should be under the influence of Dean Ramsay, knowing him to be a good and sensible man.

"My father was an advocate. This added much to his usefulness in the country. He was always fond of inventing plans for country houses ; his note-books show that he did this as early as when he was twelve years old. He wanted to build his house on a scale suited to what he thought he would require as sheriff, and had so built a small part of it when he died. We afterwards completed it, as far as possible according to his idea, but on a much smaller scale. He had wished me to be an advocate ; but I never attended law classes, as by that time it had already become apparent that my tastes lay in another direction. Moreover, he looked up greatly to James Forbes, and desired that I should be like him. My father died before my marriage, and before I had been actually elected Professor at Aberdeen. He had been greatly interested in the sending in of offers of application. He much wished me to have a Scottish Professorship, that I might have the long vacation free for living at home.

"My interest is always in things rather than in persons. I cannot help thinking about the immediate circumstances which have brought a thing to pass, rather than about any will setting them in motion. What is done by what is called myself is, I feel, done by something greater than myself in me. My interest in things has always made me care much more for theology than for anthropology ; states of the will only puzzle me. I cannot ascribe so much to a depraved will as some people do, though I do to a certain extent believe in it. Much wrong-doing seems to be no more than not doing the right thing ; and that finite beings should fail in that does not seem to need the supposition of a depraved will." On my saying that, though the immediate cause of the miseries of the world is oftener folly than wickedness, yet men's folly can frequently be traced back to past misdoing on their part, he warmly assented, and then added in a different strain : "They were foolish because they did not ask for wisdom,—not, of course, absolute wisdom, but the wisdom needed for the moment.

"I have been thinking how very gently I have been always dealt with. I have never had a violent shove in all my life.

"The only desire which I can have is like David to serve my own generation by the will of God, and then fall asleep."

The unexampled impression which his death produced at Cambridge was due to other causes besides his scientific eminence. Those who lived so near to him, though they saw little of him, could not fail to have some feeling of the man. Some rumours of his wonderful peacefulness in suffering had gone far enough to touch many hearts. And it was a deep and widely-spread emotion which found a voice that Sunday in St. Mary's Church, through the mouth of one who had known him when both were scholars of Trinity—the Rev. Dr. Butler, the distinguished headmaster of Harrow School :—

It is a solemn thing—even the least thoughtful is touched by it—when a great intellect passes away into the silence, and we see it no more. Such a loss, such a void, is present, I feel certain, to many here to-day. It is not often, even in this great home of thought and knowledge, that so bright a light is extinguished as that which is now mourned by many illustrious mourners, here chiefly, but also far beyond this place. I shall be believed when I say in all simplicity that I wish it had fallen to some more competent tongue to put into words those feelings of reverent affection which are, I am persuaded, uppermost in many hearts on this Sunday. My poor words shall be few, but believe me they come from the heart. You know, brethren, with what an eager pride we follow the fortunes of those whom we have loved and reverenced in our undergraduate days. We may see them but seldom, few letters may pass between us, but their names are never common names. They never become to us only what other men are. When I came up to Trinity twenty-eight years ago, James Clerk Maxwell was just beginning his second year. His position among us—I speak in the presence of many who remember that time—was unique. He was the one acknowledged man of genius among the undergraduates. We understood even then that, though barely of age, he was in his own line of inquiry not a beginner, but a master. His name was already a familiar name to men of science. If he lived, it was certain that he was one of that small but sacred band to whom it would be given to enlarge the bounds of human knowledge. It was a position which might have turned the head of a smaller man ; but the friend of whom we were all so proud, and who seemed, as it were, to link us thus early with the great outside world of the pioneers of knowledge, had one of those rich and lavish natures which no prosperity can impoverish, and which make faith in goodness easy for others. I have often thought that those who never knew the grand old Adam Sedgwick and the then young and ever youthful Clerk Maxwell, had yet to learn the largeness and fulness of the moulds in which some choice natures are framed. Of the scientific greatness of our friend we were most of us unable to judge ; but any one could see and admire the boylike glee, the joyous invention, the wide reading, the eager thirst for truth, the subtle thought, the perfect temper, the unfailing reverence, the singular absence of any taint of the breath of worldliness in any of its thousand forms.

Brethren, you may know such men now among your college friends, though there can be but few in any year, or indeed in any century, that possess the rare genius of the man whom we deplore. If it be so, then, if you will accept the counsel of a stranger, thank God for His gift. Believe me when I tell you that few such blessings will come to you in later life. There are blessings that come once in a lifetime. One of these is the reverence with which we look up to greatness and goodness in a college friend—above us, beyond us, far out of our mental or

moral grasp, but still one of us, near to us, our own. You know
in part, at least, how in this case the promise of youth was more
than fulfilled, and how the man who, but a fortnight ago, was
the ornament of the University, and—shall I be wrong in saying
it ?—almost the discoverer of a new world of knowledge, was
even more loved than he was admired, retaining after twenty
years of fame that mirth, that simplicity, that childlike delight
in all that is fresh and wonderful, which we rejoice to think of
as some of the surest accompaniment of true scientific genius.

You know, also, that he was a devout as well as thoughtful
Christian.   I do not note this in the triumphant spirit of a con-
troversialist.   I will not for a moment assume that there is any
natural opposition between scientific genius and simple Christian
faith.   I will not compare him with others who have had the
genius without the faith.   Christianity, though she thankfully
welcomes and deeply prizes them, does not need now, any more
than when St. Paul first preached the Cross at Corinth, the
speculations of the subtle or the wisdom of the wise.   If I wished
to show men, especially young men, the living force of the
Gospel, I would take them not so much to a learned and devout
Christian man, to whom all stores of knowledge were familiar,
but to some country village, where for fifty years there had been
devout traditions and devout practice.   There they would see
the gospel lived out ; truths, which other men spoke of, seen and
known ; a spirit not of this world visibly, hourly present ;
citizenship in heaven daily assumed, and daily realised.   Such
characters I believe to be the most convincing preachers to those
who ask whether Revelation is a fable and God an unknowable.
Yes, in most cases,—not, I admit in all,—simple faith, even
peradventure more than devout genius, is mighty for removing
doubts and implanting fresh conviction.   But having said this,
we may well give thanks to God that our friend was what he
was, a firm Christian believer, and that his powerful mind, after
ranging at will through the illimitable spaces of Creation, and
almost handling what he called "the foundation stones of the
material universe," found its true rest and happiness in the love
and the mercy of Him whom the humblest Christian calls his
Father.   Of such a man it may be truly said that he had his
citizenship in heaven, and that he looked for, as a Saviour, the
Lord Jesus Christ, through whom the unnumbered worlds were
made, and in the likeness of whose image our new and spiritual
body will be fashioned.

There was a preliminary funeral ceremony in Trinity College Chapel, where the first part of the Burial Service was read, in the presence of all the leading members of the University. The body was then taken home to Glenlair, and buried in Parton Churchyard, the funeral being attended by numbers of his countrymen from far and near.

In these reminiscences I have purposely abstained as much as possible from comment. But, in concluding this biographical narrative, I may be permitted to record a very few general observations or impressions.

The leading note of Maxwell's character is a grand simplicity. But in attempting to analyse it we find a complex of qualities which exist separately in smaller men. Extraordinary gentleness is combined with keen penetration, wonderful activity with a no less wonderful repose, personal humility and modesty with intellectual scorn. His deep reserve in common intercourse was commensurate with the fulness of his occasional outpourings to those he loved. His tenderness for all living things was deep and instinctive ; from earliest childhood he could not hurt a fly. Not less instinctive was the sense of equality amongst all human beings, which underlay the plainness of his address. But, on the other hand, his respect for the actual order of the world and for the wisdom of the past was at least as steadfast as his faith in progress. While fearless in speculation he was strongly conservative in practice.

In his intellectual faculties there was also a balance of powers which are often opposed. His imagination was in the highest sense concrete, grasping the actual reality, and not only the relations of things. No one was ever more impatient of mere abstractions.[1] Yet few have had so firm a hold upon ideas. Once more, while he was continually striving to reduce to greater definiteness men's conceptions of leading physical laws, he seemed habitually to live in a sort of mystical communion with the infinite.

---

[1] He was particularly indignant at the confusion by some would-be philosophers of *facts* with *laws*.

His aunt, Mrs. Wedderburn, who had had the care of
him during so much of his early life, said on the occasion
of his marriage, " James has lived hitherto at the gate of
heaven."

Mr. Colin Mackenzie has repeated to me two sayings of
his during those last days, which may be repeated here—
" Old chap, I have read up many queer religions : there is
nothing like the old thing after all ;" and—" I have looked
into most philosophical systems, and I have seen that none
will work without a God."

Maxwell's humour, which with many passed for mere
eccentricity, and to some was the characteristic by which
he was chiefly known, at least in earlier life, may be passed
over lightly here.   With strangers it was sometimes the
veil of a sensitiveness which but for this would have made
him the victim of his immediate surroundings.   In confidential intercourse it was a perpetual fund of delight, the
vehicle of his exuberant fancy, as it glanced in all directions
from the immediate topic of discourse.

It was his way of acknowledging " the grotesque view "[1]
of everything.   Like other humourists whom I have known,
he was never tired of a joke which had once tickled him ;
only, if retained in employment, it must always be tricked
out with some new livery, and have some fresh turn given
to it.   As late as the summer of 1879, in writing to Professor Baynes about the article on Harmonic Analysis for
the *Encyclopædia Britannica,* he repeated in a novel shape
the well-worn jest [2] about " an Analyser or a Charlatan."
Even on his deathbed at Cambridge, in familiar converse
with his cousin and friend, Mr. Colin Mackenzie, he still

---

[1] P. 179.
[2] " In Preparation
" *The Harmonic Anne Eliza*
" By Charlotte Anne
" 0·001 vol. 4to.
" Edin. A. & C. Black.
$\frac{dp}{dt}$,"
Postmark—" Dalbeattie, July 19/79."

used the old quaint familiar speech :—" No, not that phial!
the little red-headed chap !"

Nor is it necessary to dwell on the rare freshness of
feeling which he carried into middle life. The reader of
his correspondence at any period must feel involuntarily
that he had " the dew of his youth."

In thinking of him in college days, I used often to
associate him in my own mind with Socrates. There is
one point in the resemblance which I had not then realised,
the " Socratic strength " of Antisthenes—his extraordinary
power of moral and physical endurance.—Once at Cambridge, when his wife was lying ill in her room, and a
terrier, who had already shown "a wild trick of his
ancestors," was watching beside the bed, Maxwell happened
to go in for the purpose of moving her. The dog sprang
at him and fastened on his nose. In order not to disturb
Mrs. Maxwell, he went out quietly, holding his arm beneath the creature, which was still hanging to his face.

What had struck me, I suppose, in making the above
comparison, was the eager spirit of inquiry beneath the
ironical shell. I might have added the union of speculation with mysticism, and of conservatism with progressive
thought. But in one essential point, the dialectical cross-
questioning method, the analogy fails. For Maxwell had
not spent his youth in the Athenian agora, but in the
solitudes of Galloway, where he had interrogated Nature
more than Man.

In his conversation he might rather be compared with
the earlier Greek thinkers, "who," says Plato (Soph. 243 B),
" went on their several ways, without caring whether they
took us with them or left us behind." The necessity of
utterance was often stronger with him than the endeavour
to make himself understood, and he would pour out his
ideas in simple affectionateness to those who could not
follow them. His thoughts were often tentative, but his
expression of them was always dogmatic, even in the negative formula " No one knows what is meant by " so and so.

His indirect, allusive way of speaking was not, however,
wilfully assumed, but was the result of idiosyncrasy and

early habit; and it disappeared utterly in the presence of any great occasion—a great joy, a great sorrow, or a great duty. Then his speech resolved itself into statements of fact, brief and unemotional, but absolutely simple and direct. And latterly, at all events, such were generally the characteristics of his style in writing. I have been told by Mr. Huddlestone, a late Fellow of King's College, Cambridge, that when consulted about a lightning conductor for King's College Chapel (a building which he greatly loved) Maxwell called and made a verbal explanation which was unintelligible, but in going away he fortunately left a written statement, and this was perfectly clear.

The Galloway boy was in many ways father to the Cambridge man; and even the "ploys" of his childhood contained a germ of his life-work. Indeed, it may be said that with him, despite the popular adage, "Work when you work," etc., play was always passing into work and work into play. In twirling his magic discs his mind was already busied about the cause of optical phenomena. He plied the devil-on-two-sticks with the same eager industry and with the same simple enjoyment with which he afterwards spun his dynamical top. And amidst his profoundest investigations, whether about the Rings of Saturn or the Lines of Force, or the molecular structure of material things, the playful spirit of his boyhood was ever ready to break forth. Meanwhile, alike beneath the grave and sparkling mood, a spirit of deep PIETY pervaded all he did, whether in the most private relations of life, or in his position as an appointed teacher and investigator, or in his philosophic contemplation of the universe. There is no attribute from which the thought of him is more inseparable.

He had keen sympathy with ideal aspirations, together with an occasional sense of their fruitlessness. "It's no use thinking of the chap ye might have been." When, in their early married life, Mrs. Maxwell was oppressed with a sense of failure in her first attempts at Cottage-visiting, he made her sit down while he read to her Milton's sonnet ending with the line, "They also serve, who only stand and wait."

He appears in early days to have been conscious of

some superficial weaknesses, of a certain excitability of temperament, leading to "preconscious states" and preventing him from at once setting himself right in new surroundings; also of the equal danger of shrinking into himself, and "mystifying" those about him. This difficulty, and many others "within and without," he overcame. But it would be too much to say of him that "his affections never swayed more than his reason," or that he obtained as firm a foothold in practical life as he had by birthright in the region of scientific thought. This great mass of mind was so delicately hung as to be guided sometimes by a silken thread. Few men, if any, would venture to argue or remonstrate with Maxwell when he had decided on a course of action in the council-chamber of his own breast. But he could not consciously hurt any creature, nor permit the possibility of causing pain to those he loved. Nor was his power over others always adequate to the keenness of his perceptions. For while his penetration often reached the secrets of the heart, his generosity sometimes overlooked the most obvious characteristics—especially in the shape of mean or vulgar motives.

His liberality, in every sense of the word, was absolute. People have been disposed to criticise the plainness of his entertainments, without knowing that while this was a matter of taste, the difference between the plain and the luxurious table was uniformly dispensed in charity. He has also been supposed by some who think that science should disown religion, to have been intolerant as well as orthodox. The contrary was true. And, in particular, the mutual admiration and regard for one another of two such men as Maxwell and Clifford, notwithstanding their profound divergence of opinion on subjects of human interest, deserves to be quoted as an honourable exception to the narrow exclusiveness which has been too prevalent alike in the Christian and the anti-Christian world.[1]

---

[1] About the year 1860 I remember discussing with him J. Macleod Campbell's book on the Atonement, which had lately appeared. He made some criticisms, which I have forgotten, but I remember the emphatic tone in which he said, "We want light."

He never sought for fame, but with sacred devotion continued in mature life the labours which had been his spontaneous delight in boyhood. Yet, considering the high region in which he worked, he received a large measure of recognition even in his lifetime. The Rumford Medal, conferred in 1860, was the first of a long list of honours, which up to his last year continued to accumulate from all parts of the civilised world.[1] And some of those who had an eye for genius, though their intellectual interests lay in different spheres from his, could not forbear their testimony. Out of many such expressions it is enough to have selected one. Mr. Frederick Pollock in his work on Spinoza, having occasion to refer to Maxwell's views on matter and space, adds the following note (p. 115):—

Clerk Maxwell was living when these lines were written : I cannot let them pass through the press without adding a word of tribute to a man of profound and original genius, too early lost to England and to Science.

Great as was the range and depth of Maxwell's powers, that which is still more remarkable is the unity of his nature and of his life. This unity came not from circumstance, for there were breaks in his outward career, but from the native strength of the spirit that was in him. In the eyes of those who knew him best, the whole man gained in beauty year by year. As son, friend, lover, husband; in science, in society, in religion; whether buried

---

[1] In 1870 Maxwell received the honorary degree of LL.D. in the University of Edinburgh; on 11th November 1874 he was elected Foreign Honorary Member of the American Academy of Arts and Sciences of Boston; on 15th October 1875, Member of the American Philosophical Society of Philadelphia; on 4th December 1875, Corresponding Member of the Royal Society of Sciences of Göttingen; on 21st June 1876 he received the honorary degree of D.C.L. at Oxford; on 5th December 1876 he was elected Honorary Member of the New York Academy of Science; on 27th April 1877, Member of the Royal Academy of Science of Amsterdam; on 18th August 1877, Foreign Corresponding Member in the Mathematico-Natural-Science Class of the Imperial Academy of Sciences of Vienna; and in the spring of 1878 he received the Volta Medal and degree of Doctor of Physical Science *honoris causâ* in the University of Pavia.

in retirement or immersed in business—he is absolutely
single-hearted. This is true of his mental as well as of his
emotional being, for indeed they were inseparably blended.
And the fixity of his devotion both to persons and ideas
was compatible with all but universal sympathies and the
most fearless openness of thought. There are no "watertight compartments,"[1] there is no "tabooed ground;"[2] in
spite of much natural reserve, he never really lost his
predilection for "a thorough draft."[3] That marvellous
interpenetration of scientific industry, philosophic insight,
poetic feeling and imagination, and overflowing humour,
was closely related to the profound *sincerity* which, after
all is said, is the truest sign alike of his genius and of his
inmost nature, and is most apt to make his life instructive
beyond the limits of the scientific world. He would not
wish to be set up as an authority on subjects (such as
historical criticism) which, however interesting to him, he
had not had leisure to study exhaustively. But our age
has much to learn from his example. And in his life,
regarded as a whole, there is a depth of goodness which
can be but faintly indicated in his biography.

---

[1] P. 148. [2] P. 126.
[3] See the Poem on St. David's Day.

APPENDIX.

A.

ESSAYS AT CAMBRIDGE—1853 to 1856.

THE description of Maxwell's life at Cambridge would be incomplete without some notice of the Essays written by him from time to time for the "Apostles'" Club. These range from the spring of 1853 to the summer of 1856. Thrown off, as such things are, in irresponsible gaiety of heart, mere "gardens of Adonis," as Plato would call them, they contain real indications of the writer's speculative tendencies, and are most characteristic of the activity and fulness of his mind, of his ironical humour, and of his provoking discursiveness and indirectness of expression. He is not "upon his oath," and often throws out tentatively a whole train of arguments or ideas.

1. *"Decision."* Written in February 1853.

After a humorous sketch of the distraction arising from the *Æt.* 21. different associations of term and vacation time, the question is raised whether on the whole a learned education is unfavourable to decision of character and opinion. The answer pointed at, though not distinctly given, is that high education may often unsettle opinion, but ought to strengthen character. It must suffice here to quote a few of the most characteristic passages :—

" . . . In this charitable (holiday) frame of mind, we resolved to try the effect of our learning upon a mixed company.
"Not to dazzle them too much at first, we merely ventured to quote to an elderly lady a passage from Griffin on Presbyopic Vision. She intended to get a new pair of spectacles, and hoped

that optical advice, fresh from College, might assist her in her choice. She was surprised to learn that she must ascertain the distance behind the retina at which the image of a distant object is formed, and that she might then determine from the proper formula the focal lengths of the lenses she required.

"Shocked at the unhesitating way in which we proposed the most barbarous if not impossible operations, she replied that she would rather try several pairs, and take those that suited her best."

" . . . When this indecision" (of opinion) "cannot be traced to hypochondria, we generally find indications of a defective appreciation of quantity and a deceptive memory.

"Its victims measure reasons by their number and not by their weight. They do not say 'so much,' but 'so many things to be said on both sides.' To make the number equal on both sides they will split an argument or state it in several ways. These ingenious self-tormentors have invented a form of reasoning which ought to take its place beside the 'reasoning in a circle.' We may call it reasoning in a corner, or tergiversation. . . . It derives its name from the motion of the imprisoned monarch in a drawn game at draughts, and is resorted to when hard pressed by a disjunctive argument. . . . In this way these clacking metronomes endeavour to transfer their inquietude to their neighbours."

" . . . It is this consciousness of aim that gives to their experience the character of self-education. While other men are drifted hither and thither by conflicting influences, their sails seem to resolve every blast in a favourable direction. To them catastrophes are lessons and mysteries illustrations. Every thing and every person is estimated by its effect in accelerating personal advancement.

"The aims thus adopted may be different in kind and value. One may aim at effective deeds, another at completeness, a third at correctness, a fourth at dignity, while another class estimates its progress by the universality of its sentiments and the comprehensiveness of its sympathy with the varieties of the human mind. Some, in short, attend more to self-government, and some to mental expansion. When these tendencies can be combined and subordinated, there emerges the perfectly educated man, who, in the rigidity of his principles, acts with decision, and in the expansibility of his sympathy tolerates all opinions."

2. "*What is the Nature of Evidence of Design?*"   1853.

"Design! The very word . . . disturbs our quiet discussions about *how* things happen with restless questionings
about the *why* of them all. We seem to have recklessly abandoned the railroad of phenomenology, and the black rocks of
Ontology stiffen their serried brows and frown inevitable
destruction.

" . . . The belief in design is a necessary consequence of
the Laws of Thought acting on the phenomena of perception.

" . . . The essentials then for true evidence of design are
—(1) A phenomenon having significance to us ; (2) Two ascertained chains of physical causes contingently connected, and
both having the same apparent terminations, viz., the phenomenon
itself and some presupposed personality. . . . If the discovery
of a watch awakens my torpid intelligence I perceive a significant end which the watch subserves. It goes, and, considering its locality, it is going well. . . . My young and growing reason points out two sets of phenomena . . . (*a*) the
elasticity of springs, etc. etc., and (*b*) the astronomical facts
which render the mean solar day the unit of civil time combined
with those social habits which require a cognisance of the time
of day.

" . . . It is the business of science to investigate these
causal chains. If they are found not to be independent but to
meet in some ascertained point, we must transfer the evidence
of design from the ultimate fact to the existence of the chain.
Thus, suppose we ascertained that watches are now made by
machinery . . . the machinery including the watch forms one
more complicated and therefore more evident instance of design."

" . . . The only subordinate centres of causation which I
have seen formally investigated are men and animals ; the latter
even are often overlooked. But every well-ascertained law
points to some central cause, and at once constitutes that centre
a *being* in the general sense of the word. Whether that being
be *personal* is a question which may be determined by induction.
The less difficult question whether the *being* be *intelligent* is
more practicable, and should be kept in view in the investigation of organised beings.

"The search for such invisible potencies or wisdoms may
appear novel and unsanctioned. . . . For my part I do not

think that any speculations about the personality or intelligence of subordinate agents in creation could ever be perverted into witchcraft or demonolatry.

"Why should not the Original Creator have shared the pleasure of His work with His creatures and made the morning stars sing together, etc. ?

"I suspect that such a hope has prompted many speculations of natural historians, who would be ashamed to put it into words.[1]

". . . Three fallacies—(1) Putting the final cause in the place of a physical connection, as when Bernoulli saw the propriety of making the curves of isochronous oscillations and of shortest time of descent both cycloids ; (2) The erroneous assertion of a physical relation, as when Bacon supplemented the statement of Socrates about the use of the eyebrows by saying that pilosity is incident to moist places ; (3) (and worst) applying an argument from final causes to wrongly asserted phenomena :—' Because water is incompressible, it cannot transmit sound, and therefore fishes have no ears.' Every fact here stated is erroneous."

In the course of this paper—in which are discernible the traces of early impressions derived through the poetry of Milton —there occurs also incidentally a statement of the Hamiltonian doctrine of Perception,[2] with the following significant corollary :—

"Perception is the ultimate consciousness of self and thing together.

"If we admit, as we must, that this *ultimate* phenomenon is incapable of further analysis, and that subject and object alone are immediately concerned in it, it follows that the fact is strictly private and incommunicable. One only can know it, therefore two cannot agree in a name for it. And since the fact is simple

---

[1] This Neo-platonic fancy (of δημιουργοί), with which the reader may *contrast* the serio-comic lines on "Paradoxical Philosophy," is embodied in the alternative title of the paper—"Ought the discovery of a Plurality of Intelligent Creators to weaken our Belief in an Ultimate First Cause ?" A third title has been added later in the author's hand—"Does the Existence of Causal Chains prove an Astral Entity or a Cosmothetic Idealism ?"

[2] This statement concludes as follows :—"The late superfluity of assertions might have been avoided by simply, unintelligibly, and therefore unanswerably, proclaiming myself a natural dualist, uncontaminated with the heresy of unitarianism or the pollution of cosmothetic idealism."

it cannot be thought of by itself nor *compared alone* with any other *equally simple fact.* We may therefore dismiss all questions about the absolute nature of perception, and all theories of their resemblances and differences. We may next refuse to turn our attention to perception in general, as all perceptions are particular."

3. *Idiotic Imps.* Summer Term, 1853.

Starting from Isaac Taylor's *Physical Theory of another Life,* which Maxwell at this time seems to have regarded as in itself an innocent and rather attractive piece of fancy,—"the perusal of it has a tendency rather to excite speculation than to satisfy curiosity, and the author obtains the approbation of the reader, while he fails to convince him of the soundness of his views,"— he takes occasion from it to characterise the "Dark Sciences" to which Taylor's book may unintentionally lend encouragement— a result to be deprecated.

"The first question I would ask concerning a spiritual theory would be, Is it favourable or adverse to the present developments of Dark Science? The Dark Sciences . . . while they profess to treat of laws which have never been investigated, afford the most conspicuous examples of the operation of the well-known laws of association . . . in imitating the phraseology of science, and in combining its facts with those which must naturally suggest themselves to a mind unnaturally disposed. In the misbegotten science thus produced we have speciously sounding laws of which our first impression is that they are truisms, and the second that they are absurd, and a bewildering mass of experimental proof, of which all the tendencies lie on the surface and all the data turn out when examined to be heaped together as confusedly as the stores of button-makers . . . and those undigested narratives which are said to form the nutriment of the minute philosopher. . . . The most orthodox system of metaphysics may be transformed into a dark science by its phraseology being popularised, while its principles are lost sight of."

Three phases of dark science are described :—
"(1.) At first they were or pretended to be physical sciences. Their language was imitated from popular physics, and their

professed aim was to explain occult phenomena by means of new and still more occult material laws. Experiments in animal magnetism were always performed with the nose carefully turned towards the north. In electrobiology a scrupulous system of insulation was practised at first, and afterwards, when galvanism became more popular than statical electricity, circuits were formed of alternate elements, those of one sex being placed between those of the other. . . . The fluid which in former times circulated through the nerves under the form of animal spirits, is in our day expanded so as to fill the universe, and is the invisible medium through which the communion of the sensitive takes place.

"(2.) The next phase of the dark sciences is that in which . . . the phraseology of physics is exchanged for that of psychology. In this stage we hear much of the power of the will. The verb to will acquires a new and popular sense, so that every one now is able to will a thing without bequeathing it. People can will not to be able to do a thing, then try and not succeed ; while those of stronger minds can will their victims out of their wits and back again.

"(3.) The third or pneumatological phase begins by distrusting, as it well may, the explanations prevalent during the former stages of apparitions, distant intercourse, etc. It suggests that different minds may have some communion though separated by space, through some spiritual medium. Such a suggestion if discreetly followed up might lead to important discoveries, and would certainly give rise to entertaining meditations. But the cultivators of the dark sciences have done as they have ever delighted to do. Their spirits are not content with making themselves present

> ' Where all the nerves of sense are numb,
>   Spirit to spirit, ghost to ghost.'

but they become the familiar spirits of money-making media, and rap out lies for hours together for the amusement of a promiscuous 'circle.' . . . While the believers sit round the table of the medium and form one loop of the figure 8, the spiritual circle enclosing the celestial mahogany forms the upper portion of the curve, the medium herself constituting the double point. But who shall say of the dark sciences that they have reached the maximum of darkness ? Men have listened to the toes of a medium as to the voice of the departed. Let them now stand about her table as about the table of devils. If one spirit can wrap itself in petticoats, why may not another dance with three legs ? A most searching question truly ! And, accordingly, the powerful analysis of Godfrey has led him to the conclusion that a table of which the plane surface is touched by believing fingers may be transformed into a diaboloid of revolution. . . . Will there be an interminable series of such expressions of belief, each more unnatural than its predecessor, and gradually converging towards absolute absurdity ?"

4. *Has everything beautiful in Art its original in Nature?*
   Spring of 1854—shortly after the Tripos Examination.

"As the possibility of working out the question within the time forms no part of our specification, we may glance at heights which mock the attenuated triangle of the mathematician, and throw our pebble into depths which his cord and plummet can never sound."

Maxwell here takes his revenge upon the Senate-house by becoming more discursive than ever.[1]

He begins by deprecating precise definitions and proposing an appeal to facts.

His conclusion is as follows :—" Nothing beautiful can be produced by Man except by the laws of mind acting in him as those of Nature do without him ; and therefore the kind of beauty he can thus evolve must be limited by the very small number of correlative sciences which he has mastered ; but as the Theoretic and imaginative faculty is far in advance of Reason, he can apprehend and artistically reproduce natural beauty of a higher order than his science can attain to ; and as his Moral powers are capable of a still wider range, he may make his work the embodiment of a still higher beauty, which expresses the glory of nature as the instrument by which our spirits are exercised, delighted, and taught. If there is anything more I desire to say it is that while I confess the vastness of nature and the narrowness of our symbolical sciences, yet I fear not any effect which either Science or Knowledge may have on the beauty of that which is beautiful once and for ever."

The following observations occur in the course of the essay :—

---

[1] See above, pp. 115, 117.

" All your analysis is cruelly anatomical, and your separated faculties have all the appearance of preparations. You may retain their names for distinctness, but forbear to tear them asunder for lecture-room demonstration. . . . They separate a faculty by saying it is not intellectual, and then, by reasoning blindfold, every philosopher goes up his own tree, finds a mare's nest and laughs at the eggs, which turn out to be pure intellectual abstractions in spite of every definition.

" With respect to beauty of things audible and visible, we have a firm conviction that the pleasure it affords to any being would be of the same kind by whatever organisation he became conscious of it. . . . Our enjoyment of music is accompanied by an intuitive perception of the relations of sounds, and the agreement of the human race would go far to establish the universality of these conditions of pleasure, though Science had not discovered their physical and numerical significance."

Beauty of Form. — " A mathematician might express his admiration of the Ellipse. Ruskin agrees with him. . . . It is a universal condition of the enjoyable that the mind must believe in the existence of a law, and yet have a mystery to move about in. . . . All things are full of ellipses—bicentral sources of lasting joy, as the wondrous Oken might have said." Beauty of form, then, is—1. Geometrical ; 2. Organic ; 3. " Rivers and mountains have not even an organic symmetry ; the pleasure we derive from their forms is not that of comprehension, but of apprehension of their fitness as the forms of flowing and withstanding matter. When such objects are represented by Art they acquire an additional beauty as the language of Nature understood by Man, the interpreter, although by no means the emendator, of her expressions.

" . . . The power of Making is man's highest power in connexion with Nature."

Beauty of Colour. — " The Science of Colour does, indeed, point out certain arrangements and gradations, which follow as necessarily from first principles as the curves of the second order from their equations. These results of science are, many of them, realised in natural phenomena taking place according to those physical laws of which our mathematical formulæ are symbols ; but it is possible that combinations of colours may be imagined or calculated, which no optical phenomenon we are acquainted with could reproduce. Such a result would no more prove the impropriety of the arrangement than ignorance of the planetary orbits kept the Greeks from admiring the Ellipse."

5. *Envelopment: Can Ideas be developed without Reference to Things as their developing Authorities?* Summer Term, 1854.

Early in 1854 Maxwell had read J. H. Newman's[1] Essay on the Development of Christian Doctrine. He appears to have felt an inconsistency between the tenor of that work and its title, which set him meditating on the difference between true Development—*i.e.* Education—and Envelopment or Self-Involution, as a tendency incident to certain habits of thought.

He traces the working of this tendency in various subjects, ending with theology, and then proceeds as follows :—

"Envelopment is a process by which the human mind, possessed with a preternatural impatience of facts and fascinated by the apparent simplicity of some half-apprehended theory, seeks, by involving the chain of its speculations in hopeless confusion, to round it, as it were, to a separate whole.

"Thus Mr. Newman and his predecessors take up some single practice of Christians, and by means of analogies derived from the practices of Egyptian priests, Roman emperors, or Jewish rabbis, they determine, most precisely, the situation, extent, and exposure of the place of purging by fire, together with all the technicalities, observances, and etiquette of that mysterious region. The convolutions of the brain are very wonderful."

As a further illustration he proceeds to trace the genesis of phreno-mesmerism.

Against the Theory of the Development of Doctrine he sets the fact of the Education of Mankind.

The Essay is highly ironical and full of caustic touches, but it is difficult to detach them for quotation.

"One great art in argument when you have the first move is to divide everything into that which is and that which is not in some assigned class. In this way you make it the business of the opponent to discover what other important things there may be which may be said of the subject in hand.

---

[1] Cardinal Newman.

" . . . These subtle differences when further multiplied by the application of the seven tests of development, would require a seven years' apprenticeship with Thomas Aquinas before anything could be said of them except assent or contempt.

" . . . In every human pursuit there are two courses—one, that which in its lowest form is called the useful, and has for its ultimate object the extension of knowledge, the dominion over Nature, and the welfare of mankind. The objects of the second course are entirely self-contained. Theories are elaborated for theories' sake, difficulties are sought out and treasured as such, and no argument is to be considered perfect unless it lands the reasoner at the point from which he started.

" . . . Some years ago I encountered a gentleman whose main object was to discover the musical relations of the number eleven. I hear on good authority that the question is not only more perplexed but more interesting than ever.

" . . . I have unaccountably passed over that Logic by means of which many a powerful mind has persuaded itself that it was usefully engaged while devoting a life to the defence or attack of the fourth figure of the syllogism, and that Metaphysics which even now seeks to find arguments about the operations of the senses, while it rejects the aid of physiology or any other appeal to facts.

" I now proceed to envelop an argument from one of those dark sciences which seem to have been sent up from Dom Daniel for the special purpose of displaying reasonings of this kind.

" It is well known that the brain is the organ of intellectual activity. It is held by all that the intellect is made up of many distinct faculties. Therefore the brain must be composed of corresponding organs."

The Essay concludes quite seriously—" The education of man is so well provided for in the world around him, and so hopeless in any of the worlds which he makes for himself, that it becomes of the utmost importance to distinguish natural truth from artificial system, the development of a science from the envelopment of a craft."

6. *Morality.* May 1855. (See above, p. 154.) *Is Ethical Truth obtainable from an Individual Point of View ?*

An inquiry concerning the first principles of Moral Philosophy. Of three criteria, fitness, pleasure, and freedom, the last is preferred, but is pronounced incomplete. Adam Smith's use of the principle of sympathy is then considered. " The repeated action of what Smith calls sympathy, calls forth various moral principles, which may be deduced, no doubt, from other theories, as necessary truths, but of which the actual presence is now first accounted for. . . . Instead of supposing the moral action of the mind to be a speculation on fitness, a calculation of happiness, or an effort towards freedom, he makes it depend on a recognition of our relation to others like ourselves." This method (that of self-projection) is pronounced the only true one, but is to be extended so as to embrace other relations than that of mere similarity.

Such is the bare outline of an essay which would fill at least a dozen pages. It touches on various themes, from the origin of law to the religious sanction of morals, and contains no little evidence of the writer's growing power of observing human life.

7. *Language and Speculation.* Autumn of 1855. (See above, p. 159.) *Is the Modern Vocabulary of the English Language the Effect or the Cause of its Speculative State?*

A series of observations on style, original but *very* discursive, chiefly aimed at certain literary affectations which were then beginning to creep in.

". . . The new form of the old thought must be dressed out with words, and must attract attention by bringing forward what should be kept in the background. No wonder the poor fellow thinks his head is turned when he is trying to see over the collar of his coat.

" . . . By all means let us have technical terms belonging to every science and mystery practised by men, but let us not have mere freemasonry or Ziph language by which men of the same cult can secretly combine."

8. *Analogies.* February 1856. *Are there Real Analogies in Nature?*

This essay contains a serious exposition of Maxwell's deliberate views on philosophical questions, and is therefore given here entire, not omitting the playful opening paragraph.

" In the ancient and religious foundation of Peterhouse there is observed this rule, that whoso makes a pun shall be counted the author of it, but that whoso pretends to find it out shall be counted the publisher of it, and that both shall be fined. Now, as in a pun two truths lie hid under one expression, so in an analogy one truth is discovered under two expressions. Every question concerning analogies is therefore the reciprocal of a question concerning puns, and the solutions can be transposed by reciprocation. But since we are still in doubt as to the legitimacy of reasoning by analogy, and as reasoning even by paradox has been pronounced less heinous than reasoning by puns, we must adopt the direct method with respect to analogy, and then, if necessary, deduce by reciprocation the theory of puns.

" That analogies appear to exist is plain in the face of things, for all parables, fables, similes, metaphors, tropes, and figures of speech are analogies, natural or revealed, artificial or concealed. The question is entirely of their reality. Now, no question exists as to the possibility of an analogy without a mind to recognise it—that is rank nonsense. You might as well talk of a demonstration or refutation existing unconditionally. Neither is there any question as to the occurrence of analogies to our minds. They are as plenty as reasons, not to say blackberries. For, not to mention all the things in external nature which men have seen as the projections of things in their own minds, the whole framework of science, up to the very pinnacle of philosophy, seems sometimes a dissected model of nature, and sometimes a natural growth on the inner surface of the mind. Now, if in examining the admitted truths in science and philosophy, we find certain general principles appearing throughout a vast range of subjects, and sometimes re-appearing in some quite distinct part of human knowledge ; and if, on turning to the constitution of the intellect itself, we think we can discern there the reason of this uniformity in the form of a fundamental law of the right action of the intellect, are we to conclude that these various departments of nature in which analogous laws exist, have a real inter-dependence ; or that their relation is only apparent and owing to the necessary conditions of human thought ?

" There is nothing more essential to the right understanding of things than a perception of the relations of *number*. Now the very first notion of number implies a previous act of intelligence. Before we can count any number of things we must

pick them out of the universe, and give each of them a fictitious unity by definition. Until we have done this, the universe
of sense is neither one nor many, but indefinite. But yet, do
what we will, Nature seems to have a certain horror of parti-
tion. Perhaps the most natural thing to count "one" for is a
man or human being, but yet it is very difficult to do so. Some
count by heads, others by souls, others by noses ; still there is
a tendency either to run together into masses or to split up into
limbs. The dimmed outlines of phenomenal things all merge into
one another unless we put on the focussing glass of theory, and
screw it up sometimes to one pitch of definition and sometimes
to another, so as to see down into different depths through the
great millstone of the world.

"As for space and time, any man will tell you that 'it is
now known and ascertained that they are merely modifications
of our own minds.' And yet if we conceive of the mind as
absolutely indivisible and capable of only one state at a time,
we must admit that these states may be arranged in chronological order, and that this is the only real order of these states.
For we have no reason to believe, on the ground of a given
succession of simple sensations, that differences in position, as
well as in order of occurrence, exist among the causes of these
sensations. But yet we are convinced of the co-existence of
different objects at the same time, and of the identity of the
same object at different times. Now if we admit that we can
think of difference independent of sequence, and of sequence
without difference, we have admitted enough on which to found
the possibility of the ideas of space and time.

"But if we come to look more closely into these ideas, as
developed in human beings, we find that *their* space has triple
extension, but is the same in all directions, without behind or
before, whereas time extends only back and forward, and always
goes forward.

"To inquire why these peculiarities of these fundamental
ideas are so would require a most painful if not impossible act
of self-exenteration ; but to determine whether there is anything in Nature corresponding to them, or whether they are
mere projections of our mental machinery on the surface of
external things, is absolutely necessary to appease the cravings
of intelligence. Now it appears to me that when we say that
space has three dimensions, we not only express the impossibility of conceiving a fourth dimension, co-ordinate with the

three known ones, but assert the objective truth that points may differ in position by the independent variation of three variables. Here, therefore, we have a *real* analogy between the constitution of the intellect and that of the external world.

"With respect to time, it is sometimes assumed that the consecution of ideas is a fact precisely the same kind as the sequence of events in time. But it does not appear that there is any closer connection between these than between mental difference and difference of position. No doubt it is possible to assign the accurate date of every act of thought, but I doubt whether a chronological table drawn up in this way would coincide with the sequence of ideas of which we are conscious. There is an analogy, but I think not an identity, between these two orders of thoughts and things. Again, if we know what is at any assigned point of space at any assigned instant of time, we may be said to know all the events in Nature. We cannot conceive any other thing which it would be necessary to know; and, in fact, if any other necessary element does exist, it never enters into any phenomenon so as to make it differ from what it would be on the supposition of space and time being the only necessary elements.

"We cannot, however, think any set of thoughts without conceiving of them as depending on reasons. These reasons, when spoken of with relation to objects, get the name of *causes*, which are reasons, analogically referred to objects instead of thoughts. When the objects are mechanical, or are considered in a mechanical point of view, the causes are still more strictly defined, and are called *forces*.

"Now if we are acquainted not only with the events, but also with the forces, in Nature, we acquire the power of predicting events not previously known.

"This conception of cause, we are informed, has been ascertained to be a notion of invariable sequence. No doubt invariable sequence, if observed, would suggest the notion of cause, just as the end of a poker painted red suggests the notion of heat, but although a cause without its invariable effect is absurd, a cause by its apparent frustration only suggests the notion of an equal and opposite cause.

"Now the analogy between reasons, causes, forces, principles, and moral rules, is glaring, but dazzling.

" A reason or argument is a conductor by which the mind is led from a proposition to a necessary consequence of that proposition. In pure logic reasons must all tend in the same direction. There can be no conflict of reasons. We may lose sight of them or abandon them, but cannot pit them against one another. If our faculties were indefinitely intensified, so that we could see all the consequences of any admission, then all reasons would resolve themselves into one reason, and all demonstrative truth would be one proposition. There would be no room for plurality of reasons, still less for conflict. But when we come to causes of phenomena and not reasons of truths, the conflict of causes, or rather the mutual annihilation of effects, is manifest. Not but what there is a tendency in the human mind to lump up all causes, and give them an aggregate name, or to trace chains of causes up to their knots and asymptotes. Still we see, or seem to see, a plurality of causes at work, and there are some who are content with plurality.

" Those who are thus content with plurality delight in the use of the word force as applied to cause. Cause is a metaphysical word implying something unchangeable and always producing its effect. Force, on the other hand, is a scientific word, signifying something which always meets with opposition, and often with successful opposition, but yet never fails to do what it can in its own favour. Such are the physical forces with which science deals, and their maxim is that might is right, and they call themselves laws of nature. But there are other laws of nature which determine the form and action of organic structure. These are founded on the forces of nature, but they seem to do no work except that of direction. Ought they to be called forces ? A force does work in proportion to its strength. These *direct* forces to work after a model. They are *moulds,* not forces. Now since we have here a standard from which deviation may take place, we have, besides the notion of *strength,* which belongs to force, that of *health,* which belongs to organic law. Organic beings are not conscious of organic laws, and it is not the conscious being that takes part in them, but another set of laws now appear in very close connection with the conscious being. I mean the laws of thought. These may be interfered with by organic laws, or by physical disturbances, and no doubt every such interference is regulated by the laws of the brain and of the connection between that medulla and the process of thought. But the thing to be observed is, that the laws

which regulate the *right* process of the intellect are identical
with the most abstract of all laws, those which are found among
the relations of necessary truths, and that though these are mixed
up with, and modified by, the most complex systems of phenomena in physiology and physics, they must be recognised as
supreme among the other laws of thought.   And this supremacy
does not consist in superior strength, as in physical laws, nor yet,
I think, in reproducing a type as in organic laws, but in being
right and true ; even when other causes have been for a season
masters of the brain.

   " When we consider voluntary actions in general, we think
we see causes acting like forces on the willing being.   Some of
our motions arise from physical necessity, some from irritability
or organic excitement, some are performed by our machinery
without our knowledge, and some evidently are due to us and
our volitions.   Of these, again, some are merely a repetition of
a customary act, some are due to the attractions of pleasure or
the pressure of constrained activity, and a few show some indications of being the results of distinct acts of the will.   Here
again we have a continuation of the analogy of Cause.   Some
had supposed that in will they had found the only true cause,
and that all physical causes are only apparent.   I need not say
that this doctrine is exploded.

   " What we have to observe is, that new elements enter into
the nature of these higher causes, for mere abstract reasons are
simply absolute ; forces are related by their strength ; organic
laws act towards resemblances to types ; animal emotions tend
to that which promotes the enjoyment of life ; and will is in
great measure actually subject to all these, although certain
other laws of *right*, which are abstract and demonstrable, like
those of reason, are *supreme* among the laws of will.

   " Now the question of the reality of analogies in nature
derives most of its interest from its application to the opinion,
that all the phenomena of nature, being varieties of motion, can
only differ in complexity, and therefore the only way of studying
nature, is to master the fundamental laws of motion first, and
then examine what kinds of complication of these laws must be
studied in order to obtain true views of the universe.   If this
theory be true, we must look for indications of these fundamental
laws throughout the whole range of science, and not least among
those remarkable products of organic life, the results of cerebra-

tion (commonly called 'thinking'). In this case, of course, the resemblances between the laws of different classes of phenomena should hardly be called analogies, as they are only transformed identities.

" If, on the other hand, we start from the study of the laws of thought (the abstract, logical laws, not the *physio*-logical), then these apparent analogies become merely repetitions by reflexion of certain necessary modes of action to which our minds are subject. I do not see how, upon either hypothesis, we can account for the existence of one set of laws of which the supremacy is necessary, but to the operation contingent. But we find another set of laws of the same kind, and sometimes coinciding with physical laws, the operation of which is inflexible when once in action, but depends in its beginnings on some act of volition. The theory of the consequences of actions is greatly perplexed by the fact that each act sets in motion many trains of machinery, which react on other agents and come into regions of physical and metaphysical chaos from which it is difficult to disentangle them. But if we could place the telescope of theory in proper adjustment, to see not the physical events which form the subordinate foci of the disturbance propagated through the universe, but the moral foci where the true image of the original act is reproduced, then we shall recognise the fact, that when we clearly see any moral act, then there appears a moral necessity for the trains of consequences of that act, which are spreading through the world to be concentrated on some focus, so as to give a true and complete image of the act in its moral point of view. All that bystanders see, is the physical act, and some of its immediate physical consequences, but as a partial pencil of light, even when not adapted for distinct vision, may enable us to see an *object*, and not merely light, so the partial view we have of any act, though far from perfect, may enable us to see it morally as an act, and not merely physically as an event.

" If we think we see in the diverging trains of physical consequences not only a capability of forming a true image of the act, but also of reacting upon the agent, either directly or after a long circuit, then perhaps we have caught the idea of *necessary* retribution, as the legitimate consequence of all moral action.

" But as this idea of the *necessary* reaction of the consequences of action is derived only from a few instances, in which we have guessed at such a law among the necessary laws of the universe ;

and we have a much more distinct idea of *justice*, derived from those laws which we necessarily recognise as supreme, we connect the idea of retribution much more with that of *justice* than with that of *cause and effect*. We therefore regard retribution as the result of *interference* with the mechanical order of things, and intended to vindicate the supremacy of the right order of things, but still we suspect that the two orders of things will eventually dissolve into one.

"I have been somewhat diffuse and confused on the subject of moral law, in order to show to what length analogy will carry the speculations of men. Whenever they see a relation between two things they know well, and think they see there must be a similar relation between things less known, they reason from the one to the other. This supposes that although pairs of things may differ widely from each other, the *relation* in the one pair may be the same as that in the other. Now, as in a scientific point of view the *relation* is the most important thing to know, a knowledge of the one thing leads us a long way towards a knowledge of the other. If all that we know is *relation*, and if all the relations of one pair of things correspond to those of another pair, it will be difficult to distinguish the one pair from the other, although not presenting a single point of resemblance, unless we have some difference of relation to something else, whereby to distinguish them. Such mistakes can hardly occur except in mathematical and physical analogies, but if we are going to study the constitution of the individual mental man, and draw all our arguments from the laws of society on the one hand, or those of the nervous tissue on the other, we may chance to convert useful helps into Wills-of-the-wisp. Perhaps the 'book,' as it has been called, of nature is regularly paged; if so, no doubt the introductory parts will explain those that follow, and the methods taught in the first chapters will be taken for granted and used as illustrations in the more advanced parts of the course; but if it is not a 'book' at all, but a *magazine*, nothing is more foolish to suppose that one part can throw light on another.

"Perhaps the next most remarkable analogy is between the principle, law, or plan according to which all things are made suitably to what they have to do, and the intention which a man has of making machines which will work. The doctrine of final causes, although productive of barrenness in its exclusive form, has certainly been a great help to inquirers into nature ; and if we only maintain the existence of the analogy, and allow observation to determine its form, we cannot be led far from the truth.

" There is another analogy which seems to be supplanting the other on its own ground, which lies between the principle, law, or plan, according to which the forms of things are made to have a certain community of type, and that which induces human artists to make a set of different things according to varieties of the same model. ˙Here apparently the final cause is analogy or homogeneity, to the exclusion of usefulness.

" And last of all we have the secondary forms of crystals bursting in upon us, and sparkling in the rigidity of mathematical necessity, and telling us neither of harmony of design, usefulness or moral significance,—nothing but spherical trigonometry and Napier's analogies. It is because we have blindly excluded the lessons of these angular bodies from the domain of human knowledge that we are still in doubt about the great doctrine that the only laws of matter are those which our minds must fabricate, and the only laws of mind are fabricated for it by matter."

9. *Autobiography.* (Dated) 8th March 1856.
Is Autobiography possible ?

Under the guise of an ironical paradox, that all biography is (1) impossible, (2) inevitable, Maxwell recommends the simple record of facts, and deprecates the method of introspection. Of many shrewd remarks occurring in the course of this essay, the following are the most noticeable :—

" . . . When a man once begins to make a theory of himself, he generally succeeds in making himself into a theory.

" . . . The truthfulness of the biography depends quite as much upon the relations which subsisted between the author and his subject as upon his fidelity in collecting authentic accounts of his actions.

" . . . It will be found that the motives under which the celebrated characters of history have acted, are, whether good or bad, pretty much of the same order of refinement, as long as we gather them from the same historian. It is when we pass from one historian to another that we discover a new order of motives, both in the good and the bad characters.

" . . . People do not talk of you, or if they do, they make blunders. But they *do* reflect you, and that more faithfully than your looking-glass.

" . . . The stomach-pump of the confessional ought only to be used in cases of manifest poisoning. More gentle remedies are better for the constitution in ordinary cases.

" . . . Every man has a right and is bound to become acquainted with himself; but he will find himself out better by intercourse with well-chosen reagents than by putting on his own thumbscrews, or by sending round to his friends for their opinions. In the choice of reagents, the first thing to be avoided is incapability and insincerity, which generally go together.

" . . . Suppose such a history or biography to exist, where actions are described without comment, but in a spirit faithful to the highest truth. It will be an indestructible picture of life, which cannot be distorted by future accidents, and which, by its clear arrangement and perfect simplicity, is sure to pass into our experience without that opposition which, by the constitution of man, accompanies the forcible administration of moral precept."

10. *Unnecessary Thought.* October (?), 1856. *"Is a horror of Unnecessary Thought natural or unnatural? Which does Nature abhor most, a superplenum or a vacuum of thought"?*

A great part of every life is necessarily unconscious or mechanical. "We have a natural and widespread aversion to the act of thinking, which exists more or less in all men." But, on the other hand, abstract thought needs to be continually checked through contact with reality, and it is more important that our thoughts should have a living root in experience than that they should be perfectly self-consistent at any particular stage of their growth.

" . . . They know the laws by heart, and do the calculations by fingers. . . . When will they begin to think? Then comes active life: What do they do that by? Precedent, wheel-tracks, and finger-posts.

' . . . There is one part of the process at least to which attention is unfavourable. I mean the very important and necessary operation of forgetting useless facts.

" . . . Growth goes on in the mind as in the body by a

process of appropriation and rejection ; and the mental growth is rendered steady and real by its close connection with material and external things."

11 and 12. Two unfinished Essays, on *Sensation*, and on *Reason and Faith*, may be probably assigned to the period of attendance on his father's illness in Edinburgh, in the spring of 1855. See his letter to C. J. Monro, of Feb. 19, on p. 152. "I have a few thoughts on . . . sensation generally, and a kind of dim outline of Cambridge palavers, tending to shadow forth the influence of mathematical training on opinion and speculation."

B.

LAST ESSAYS AT CAMBRIDGE.

AFTER Maxwell's return to Cambridge in 1871, several persons of high standing, some of whom had been "Apostles" together in 1853-57, revived the habit of meeting together for the discussion of speculative questions. This club of seniors (ἀνδρῶν πρεσβυτέρων ἑταιρία), which included such men as Dr. Lightfoot, now Bishop of Durham, and Professors Hort and Westcott, was christened Erănus (see p. 279), and three of Maxwell's contributions, dated by himself, have been preserved. It seems advisable to print these entire,—although not even chips from his workshop, but rather sparks from the whetstone of his mind, —since what he thought worthy of detaining the attention of such listeners in those ripe years cannot fail to be of interest to many readers.

I.

Does the progress of Physical Science tend to give any advantage to the opinion of Necessity (or Determinism) over that of the Contingency of Events and the Freedom of the Will ?

11th February 1873.   *Æt.* 41

The general character and téndency of human thought is a topic the interest of which is not confined to professional philosophers. Though every one of us must, each for himself, accept some sort of a philosophy, good or bad, and though the whole virtue of this philosophy depends on it being our own, yet none of us thinks it out entirely for himself. It is essential to our comfort that we should know whether we are going with the general stream of human thought or against it, and if it should turn out that the general stream flows in a direction different from the current of our private thought, though we may endeavour to explain it as the result of a widespread aberration of intellect, we would be more satisfied if we could obtain some evidence that it is not ourselves who are going astray.

In such an inquiry we need some fiducial point or standard of reference, by which we may ascertain the direction in which we are drifting. The books written by men of former ages who thought about the same questions would be of great use, if it were not that we are apt to derive a wrong impression from them if we approach them by a course of reading unknown to those for whom they were written.

There are certain questions, however, which form the *pièces de résistance* of philosophy, on which men of all ages have exhausted their arguments, and which are perfectly certain to furnish matter of debate to generations to come, and which may therefore serve to show how we are drifting. At a certain epoch of our adolescence those of us who are good for anything begin to get anxious about these questions, and unless the cares of this world utterly choke our metaphysical anxieties, we become developed into advocates of necessity or of free-will. What it is which determines for us which side we shall take must for the purpose of this essay be regarded as contingent. According to Mr. F. Galton, it is derived from structureless elements in our parents, which were probably never developed in their earthly existence, and which may have been handed down to them, still in the latent state, through untold generations. Much might be said in favour of such a congenital bias towards a particular scheme of philosophy ; at the same time we must acknowledge that much of a man's mental history depends upon events occurring after his birth in time, and that he is on the whole more likely to espouse doctrines which harmonise with the particular set of ideas to which he is induced, by the process of education, to confine his attention. What will be the probable effect if these ideas happen mainly to be those of modern physical science ?

The intimate connection between physical and metaphysical science is indicated even by their names. What are the chief requisites of a physical laboratory ? Facilities for measuring space, time, and mass. What is the occupation of a metaphysi-

cian ? Speculating on the modes of difference of co-existent
things, on invariable sequences, and on the existence of matter.

He is nothing but a physicist disarmed of all his weapons,—
a disembodied spirit trying to measure distances in terms of his
own cubit, to form a chronology in which intervals of time are
measured by the number of thoughts which they include, and
to evolve a standard pound out of his own self-consciousness.
Taking metaphysicians singly, we find again that as is their
physics, so is their metaphysics. Descartes, with his perfect
insight into geometrical truth, and his wonderful ingenuity in
the imagination of mechanical contrivances, was far behind the
other great men of his time with respect to the conception of
matter as a receptacle of momentum and energy. His doctrine
of the collision of bodies is ludicrously absurd. He admits,
indeed, that the facts are against him, but explains them as the
result either of the want of perfect hardness in the bodies, or of
the action of the surrounding air. His inability to form that
notion which we now call force is exemplified in his explanation
of the hardness of bodies as the result of the quiescence of their
parts.

"Neque profecto ullum glutinum possumus excogitare, quod
particulas durorum corporum firmius inter se conjungat, quàm
ipsarum quies."—*Princip., Pars* II. LV.

Descartes, in fact, was a firm believer that matter has but
one essential property, namely extension, and his influence in
preserving this pernicious heresy in existence extends even to
very recent times. Spinoza's idea of matter, as he receives it
from the authorities, is exactly that of Descartes ; and if he has
added to it another essential function, namely thought, the new
ingredient does not interfere with the old, and certainly does
not bring the matter of Descartes into closer resemblance with
that of Newton.

The influence of the physical ideas of Newton on philosophical thought deserves a careful study. It may be traced in
a very direct way through Maclaurin and the Stewarts to the
Scotch School, the members of which had all listened to the
popular expositions of the Newtonian Philosophy in their
respective colleges. In England, Boyle and Locke reflect
Newtonian ideas with tolerable distinctness, though both have
ideas of their own. Berkeley, on the other hand, though he
is a master of the language of his time, is quite impervious to
its ideas. Samuel Clarke is perhaps one of the best examples

of the influence of Newton ; while Roger Cotes, in spite of his clever exposition of Newton's doctrines, must be condemned as one of the earliest heretics bred in the bosom of Newtonianism.

It is absolutely manifest from these and other instances that any development of physical science is likely to produce some modification of the methods and ideas of philosophers, provided that the physical ideas are expounded in such a way that the philosophers can understand them.

The principal developments of physical ideas in modern times have been—

1st. The idea of matter as the receptacle of momentum and energy. This we may attribute to Galileo and some of his contemporaries. This idea is fully expressed by Newton, under the form of Laws of Motion.

2d. The discussion of the relation between the fact of gravitation and the maxim that matter cannot act where it is not.

3d. The discoveries in Physical Optics, at the beginning of this century. These have produced much less effect outside the scientific world than might be expected. There are two reasons for this. In the first place it is difficult, especially in these days of the separation of technical from popular knowledge, to expound physical optics to persons not professedly mathematicians. The second reason is, that it is extremely easy to show such persons the phenomena, which are very beautiful in themselves, and this is often accepted as instruction in physical optics.

4th. The development of the doctrine of the Conservation of Energy. This has produced a far greater effect on the thinking world outside that of technical thermodynamics.

As the doctrine of the conservation of matter gave a definiteness to statements regarding the immateriality of the soul, so the doctrine of the conservation of energy, when applied to living beings, leads to the conclusion that the soul of an animal is not, like the mainspring of a watch, the motive power of the body, but that its function is rather that of a steersman of a vessel,—not to produce, but to regulate and direct the animal powers.

5th. The discoveries in Electricity and Magnetism labour under the same disadvantages as those in Light. It is difficult to present the ideas in an adequate manner to laymen, and it is easy to show them wonderful experiments.

6th. On the other hand, recent developments of Molecular

Science seem likely to have a powerful effect on the world of thought. The doctrine that visible bodies apparently at rest are made up of parts, each of which is moving with the velocity of a cannon ball, and yet never departing to a visible extent from its mean place, is sufficiently startling to attract the attention of an unprofessional man.

But I think the most important effect of molecular science on our way of thinking will be that it forces on our attention the distinction between two kinds of knowledge, which we may call for convenience the Dynamical and Statistical.

The statistical method of investigating social questions has Laplace for its most scientific and Buckle for its most popular expounder. Persons are grouped according to some characteristic, and the number of persons forming the group is set down under that characteristic. This is the raw material from which the statist endeavours to deduce general theorems in sociology. Other students of human nature proceed on a different plan. They observe individual men, ascertain their history, analyse their motives, and compare their expectation of what they will do with their actual conduct. This may be called the dynamical method of study as applied to man. However imperfect the dynamical study of man may be in practice, it evidently is the only perfect method in principle, and its shortcomings arise from the limitation of our powers rather than from a faulty method of procedure. If we betake ourselves to the statistical method, we do so confessing that we are unable to follow the details of each individual case, and expecting that the effects of widespread causes, though very different in each individual, will produce an average result on the whole nation, from a study of which we may estimate the character and propensities of an imaginary being called the Mean Man.

Now, if the molecular theory of the constitution of bodies is true, all our knowledge of matter is of the statistical kind. A constituent molecule of a body has properties very different from those of the body to which it belongs. Besides its immutability and other recondite properties, it has a velocity which is different from that which we attribute to the body as a whole.

The smallest portion of a body which we can discern consists of a vast number of such molecules, and all that we can learn about this group of molecules is statistical information. We can determine the motion of the centre of gravity of the group, but not that of any one of its members for the time being, and these members themselves are continually passing from one group to another in a manner confessedly beyond our power of tracing them.

Hence those uniformities which we observe in our experiments with quantities of matter containing millions of millions of molecules are uniformities of the same kind as those explained by Laplace and wondered at by Buckle, arising from the slumping together of multitudes of cases, each of which is by no means uniform with the others.

The discussion of statistical matter is within the province of human reason, and valid consequences may be deduced from it by legitimate methods ; but there are certain peculiarities in the very form of the results which indicate that they belong to a different department of knowledge from the domain of exact science. They are not symmetrical functions of the time. It makes all the difference in the world whether we suppose the inquiry to be historical or prophetical—whether our object is to deduce the past state or the future state of things from the known present state. In astronomy, the two problems differ only in the sign of t, the time ; in the theory of the diffusion of matter, heat, or motion, the prophetical problem is always capable of solution ; but the historical one, except in singular cases, is insoluble. There may be other cases in which the past, but not the future, may be deducible from the present. Perhaps the process by which we remember past events, by submitting our memory to analysis, may be a case of this kind.

Much light may be thrown on some of these questions by the consideration of stability and instability. When the state of things is such that an infinitely small variation of the present state will alter only by an infinitely small quantity the state at some future time, the condition of the system, whether at rest or in motion, is said to be stable ; but when an infinitely small variation in the present state may bring about a finite difference in the state of the system in a finite time, the condition of the system is said to be unstable.

It is manifest that the existence of unstable conditions renders impossible the prediction of future events, if our knowledge of the present state is only approximate and not accurate.

It has been well pointed out by Professor Balfour Stewart that physical stability is the characteristic of those systems from the contemplation of which determinists draw their arguments, and physical instability that of those living bodies, and moral instability that of those developable souls, which furnish to consciousness the conviction of free will.

Having thus pointed out some of the relations of physical science to the question, we are the better prepared to inquire what is meant by determination and what by free will.

No one, I suppose, would assign to free will a more than infinitesimal range. No leopard can change his spots, nor can any one by merely wishing it, or, as some say, *willing* it, introduce discontinuity into his course of existence. Our free will at the best is like that of Lucretius's atoms,—which at quite uncertain times and places deviate in an uncertain manner from their course. In the course of this our moral life we more or less frequently find ourselves on a physical or moral watershed, where an imperceptible deviation is sufficient to determine into which of two valleys we shall descend. The doctrine of free will asserts that in some such cases the Ego alone is the determining cause. The doctrine of Determinism asserts that in every case, without exception, the result is determined by the previous conditions of the subject, whether bodily or mental, and that Ego is mistaken in supposing himself in any way the cause of the actual result, as both what he is pleased to call decisions and the resultant action are corresponding events due to the same fixed laws. Now, when we speak of causes and effects, we always imply some person who knows the causes and deduces the effects. Who is this person? Is he a man, or is he the Deity?

If he is man,—that is to say, a person who can make observations with a certain finite degree of accuracy,—we have seen that it is only in certain cases that he can predict results with even approximate correctness.

If he is the Deity, I object to any argument founded on a supposed acquaintance with the conditions of Divine foreknowledge.

The subject of the essay is the relation to determinism, not of theology, metaphysics, or mathematics, but of physical science, —the science which depends for its material on the observation and measurement of visible things, but which aims at the development of doctrines whose consistency with each other shall be apparent to our reason.

It is a metaphysical doctrine that from the same antecedents follow the same consequents. No one can gainsay this. But it

is not of much use in a world like this, in which the same antecedents never again concur, and nothing ever happens twice.
Indeed, for aught we know, one of the antecedents might be the
precise date and place of the event, in which case experience
would go for nothing.   The metaphysical axiom would be of
use only to a being possessed of the knowledge of contingent
events, *scientia simplicis intelligentiæ*,—a degree of knowledge to
which mere omniscience of all facts, *scientia visionis*, is but
ignorance.

The physical axiom which has a somewhat similar aspect is
" That from like antecedents follow like consequents."   But
here we have passed from sameness to likeness, from absolute
accuracy to a more or less rough approximation.   There are
certain classes of phenomena, as I have said, in which a small
error in the data only introduces a small error in the result.
Such are, among others, the larger phenomena of the Solar
System, and those in which the more elementary laws in
Dynamics contribute the greater part of the result.   The course
of events in these cases is stable.

There are other classes of phenomena which are more complicated, and in which cases of instability may occur, the number
of such cases increasing, in an exceedingly rapid manner, as the
number of variables increases.   Thus, to take a case from a
branch of science which comes next to astronomy itself as a
manifestation of order :   In the refraction of light, the direction
of the refracted ray depends on that of the incident ray, so that
in general, if the one direction be slightly altered, the other
also will be slightly altered.   In doubly refracting media there
are two refracting rays, but it is true of each of them that like
causes produce like effects.   But if the direction of the ray
within a biaxal crystal is nearly but not exactly coincident with
that of the ray-axis of the crystal, a small change in direction
will produce a great change in the direction of the emergent ray.
Of course, this arises from a singularity in the properties of the
ray-axis, and there are only two ray-axes among the infinite
number of possible directions of lines in the crystal ; but it is to
be expected that in phenomena of higher complexity there will
be a far greater number of singularities, near which the axiom
about like causes producing like effects ceases to be true.   Thus
the conditions under which gun-cotton explodes are far from
being well known ; but the aim of chemists is not so much to
predict the time at which gun-cotton will go off of itself, as to

find a kind of gun-cotton which, when placed in certain circumstances, has never yet exploded, and this even when slight irregularities both in the manufacture and in the storage are taken account of by trying numerous and long-continued experiments.

In all such cases there is one common circumstance,—the system has a quantity of potential energy, which is capable of being transformed into motion, but which cannot begin to be so transformed till the system has reached a certain configuration, to attain which requires an expenditure of work, which in certain cases may be infinitesimally small, and in general bears no definite proportion to the energy developed in consequence thereof. For example, the rock loosed by frost and balanced on a singular point of the mountain-side, the little spark which kindles the great forest, the little word which sets the world a fighting, the little scruple which prevents a man from doing his will, the little spore which blights all the potatoes, the little gemmule which makes us philosophers or idiots. Every existence above a certain rank has its singular points : the higher the rank the more of them. At these points, influences whose physical magnitude is too small to be taken account of by a finite being, may produce results of the greatest importance. All great results produced by human endeavour depend on taking advantage of these singular states when they occur.

> There is a tide in the affairs of men
> Which, taken at the flood, leads on to fortune.

The man of tact says "the right word at the right time," and, "a word spoken in due season how good is it!" The man of no tact is like vinegar upon nitre when he sings his songs to a heavy heart. The ill-timed admonition hardens the heart, and the good resolution, taken when it is sure to be broken, becomes macadamised into pavement for the abyss.

It appears then that in our own nature there are more singular points,—where prediction, except from absolutely perfect data, and guided by the omniscience of contingency, becomes impossible,—than there are in any lower organisation. But singular points are by their very nature isolated, and form no appreciable fraction of the continuous course of our existence. Hence predictions of human conduct may be made in many cases. First, with respect to those who have no character at all, especially when considered in crowds, after the statistical method.

Second, with respect to individuals of confirmed character, with respect to actions of the kind for which their character is confirmed.

If, therefore, those cultivators of physical science from whom the intelligent public deduce their conception of the physicist, and whose style is recognised as marking with a scientific stamp the doctrines they promulgate, are led in pursuit of the arcana of science to the study of the singularities and instabilities, rather than the continuities and stabilities of things, the promotion of natural knowledge may tend to remove that prejudice in favour of determinism which seems to arise from assuming that the physical science of the future is a mere magnified image of that of the past.

II.

ON MODIFIED ASPECTS OF PAIN.

31st October 1876.

Æt. 45.   We often make sensation in general the subject of discussion, but it does not appear that we think much about particular sensations.   If we did, we should have had more names for them. Most of the words which seem at first sight to be names of sensations are really used as names of objects which we suppose to be associated with the sensation, and to be indicated by it.   All such words as hot and cold, flat and sharp, green, bright, bitter, frouzy, and so on, though they may sometimes excite in a very sympathetic mind a faint image of some actual sensation, call up much more vividly the idea of some external object or phenomenon.   Language, in fact, has become far more an instrument for conveying information and for recording facts than for awakening sympathy ; and even thought, in articulately speaking men, is occupied rather in methodising our perceptions than in chewing the cud of our sensations.

Of the few words which we have left to distinguish states of feeling, most of the better sort, such as pleasure, joy, happiness, are remarkably vague, so that the only available part of the vocabulary of sensations consists of the names of pains.

Such words as toothache, headache, heartache, certainly fulfil the condition of suggesting, at least to non-medical persons, a state of feeling rather than an objective phenomenon.

Now, whatever we may think, each for ourselves, at the

time when we feel a pain or an ache, about consciousness or subjectivity, we are compelled, when we have to speak about it, or even to think about it, to view it from the outside, and to adopt the objective method of treatment.

A pain, then, in a sentient being other than ourselves is a condition which that being ordinarily endeavours to put a stop to, and the recurrence of which it tries to prevent ; just as a pleasurable sensation is one which it endeavours to prolong, and afterwards to reproduce.

The psychologist has therefore to study pleasures and pains in their effects on a sentient being, just as the naturalist studies forces in their effects on the motion of a material system. The motion of the material system would go on in a determinate manner though no forces were in action. The actions of a living being, when not in a state of conscious effort, and often, indeed, even when it supposes itself to be exercising what it would call its will, go on in a manner determined by habits established by long custom, and transmitted from generation to generation, though varying slightly from individual to individual.

According to the simplest form of the Evolution theory, those individuals, tribes, or species, which have habits unfavourable to their success in the battle of life, die out, and help to improve the average quality of the remainder. This good old rule, however, this simple plan, though it might suffice for beings of great fecundity, would involve a great waste of life among higher and less prolific forms. Hence if any of these should come to have tastes and feelings, and if these should happen to be such as to repel them from pernicious courses and attract them into salutary ones, this would give them an advantage in the struggle for existence. Of course, there would be an equal chance that the tastes and feelings, when first developed, would be in favour of courses leading to destruction ; but the individuals possessed by these tastes and feelings would be all the quicker exterminated for the good—that is to say, the more vigorous continuation—of the species.

The susceptibility to pleasure and pain must therefore be regarded as permitting a certain mitigation of the first covenant of the evolutionists, "This do and live ;" the original severity of which was all the greater since the word "this" could be interpreted only by observing what actions were not followed by death.

By pursuing what we feel to be pleasant, and avoiding what we feel to be painful, we are following a course which was probably followed by many of our ancestors, and of which we know at least this much—that it did not bring them to such speedy destruction as to prevent them from leaving us as their descendants ; and this is more than we can say for any absolutely new rule of life struck out by ourselves.

But it must be confessed that the monitions of pleasure and pain are not held in such high esteem by all men, as the view which we have just taken would seem to warrant. For though here and there we may find an isolated teacher who has inculcated the cultivation of all forms of pleasurable sensation, and the elimination of whatever is disagreeable, yet there has never been a state of society in which it has not been reckoned more honourable

> To scorn delights and live laborious days,

than to run after pleasure and to shrink from pain.

And this brings me to the main point for our consideration. Why is it that in all times and countries the endurance of pain has been looked upon with great respect, and has been considered necessary, salutary, honourable, or meritorious ?   There is no difficulty, of course, about those cases in which a person undertakes some enterprise, good in itself, and in pursuance of this enterprise meets with various forms of suffering.   These are only instances of the general maxim to despise evils of a lower order when they stand in the way of some good of a higher order.

The ability to endure suffering while engaged in a good work being recognised as a species of excellence, it is only natural that this kind of ability should become the subject of special cultivation.   The aspirant to this form of virtue, therefore, voluntarily submits himself to suffering, not for the sake of any visible benefit to himself and others to be obtained by enduring that particular pain, but for the sake of discipline.

The aim of discipline is that he himself, and still more that others, may have confidence that he is able to endure suffering in a good cause, because he has already endured suffering merely to justify this confidence.

Practices of this kind have in some countries been developed to an extravagant degree, and may have given rise to various abnormal sentiments and maxims ; but in the principle of educational discipline there is nothing but the soundest wisdom, for the only way in which an individual can acquire confidence that he can perform a given act when he wishes to do so is by previous practice ; and when it is necessary for the public good that there should be a body of men, of each of whom we can be sure that he will act in a particular manner when the occasion for it arrives, it is absolutely necessary that they should be drilled to an exercise as like as possible to the action which is expected of them. But in all this the inconvenience or suffering which has to be endured is by no means regarded as good in itself. It is treated as a necessary concomitant of the act to be performed, just as muscular effort, which may sometimes arise to the intensity of a pain, is a necessary concomitant of an athletic exercise in which we may find pleasure.

Indeed the pleasurable or painful character of an elementary sensation or thought cannot be determined without taking into account all its surroundings. A sensation or a thought when separated from its surroundings may be disagreeable or painful ; but when it occurs as a part of an act of perception, we may not recognise it as painful.

There may even be a pleasurable complex emotion into which the painful elementary sensation enters as an essential ingredient, so that if on any occasion the painful sensation is deficient, we feel that the pleasurable emotion is thereby marred and rendered incomplete.

There is another class of cases, however, in which the pain itself is the essential element. I mean penal suffering. The aim of punishment, when not vindictive, is to prevent the repetition of certain acts by associating with them penal consequences.

The painful consequences of an act may be associated with it by the way of natural consequence, or through the medium of some external punishing authority, or by the determination of the actor to punish himself.

When painful effects follow an act by way of natural consequence, they are not generally called punishment, because we do not attribute to nature any intention of punishing the particular act. But there can be no better instances of the conditions of efficacious punishment than those in which an act is so immediately and so certainly followed by a painful sensation, that the sensation becomes inseparably associated with the act, as in the case in which we touch red-hot iron. In such cases the act is hardly ever repeated.

When the connection between the act and the sensation is not so immediate, but has to be traced through the action of a voluntary punisher, as when an act of a boy or a dog is followed by an unpleasant skin-sensation inflicted by the master, the efficacy of the punishment still depends in a great degree on its promptness and certainty, for these are the conditions under which a permanent association can be effected between the act and the sensation.

Let us now consider the feelings with which punishment may be regarded by the recipient.

There may be beings in whom the feeling is simple—pure repugnance. There is a beast called the Tasmanian Devil, which is said to fight against any odds, however overpowering, as long as any of him can stick together. There is no hope of taming or subduing such a beast by force, and it is probable that he will soon become extinct.

But in the case of less indomitable beings, punishment may soon assume a less hateful aspect.

For even if it is not efficacious in changing the habits, as soon as it is recognised as a certain consequence of transgression, the execution of the punishment may be welcomed as a relief from the expectation of it, and the culprit may have a satisfaction in getting it over, as an honest man has when he pays his debts.

If, however, he is really cured of the habit, he may look on the punishment as an operation by which he has not only paid in full for his past transgression, but has been freed from the danger of falling into future transgressions.

Lastly, if his moral perceptions have been so far improved that he recognises that the action for which he was punished was really bad, he will sympathise more with the punisher than with his former self, and will admit not only the justice of his punishment as being according to law, but the justice of the law according to which he was punished.

We come next to those cases in which there is no external punisher, but in which grief or sorrow is awakened within ourselves on account of what we have done.

Here, again, the effect may be very different, according to

the mode in which the sensation of grief is applied, and the result is rendered complicated on account of the identity between the punisher and the punished.

The legitimate application of the emotion of grief is of course to the wrong act, so as to associate the act and all that belongs to it with this painful emotion, and so diminish the tendency to repeat the act.

But the association may not be strong enough, or the emotion of grief may altogether miss its mark, and may concentrate attention on itself, and so become transformed into self-pity,—a very complex emotion, in which the sweet is so mingled with the bitter that its ultimate effect on our conduct becomes very uncertain ; the most probable result, however, being that on future occasions what should have been contrition passes still more easily into self-pity, and the whole performance assumes the character of a graceful play of feelings which we enjoy rather than suffer.

But though such perversions of feeling may occur, there is no doubt that men do make successful use of self-inflicted discipline as a means of influencing their own conduct. The lower degrees of such discipline are put in practice whenever we have to change our habits in the most minute particular. Without it we could not improve our pronunciation or our handwriting.

The great difficulty, however, in providing for the punishment being applied in the right quarter, when the punisher is identical with the punished person, has led to the adoption of various imperfect solutions of the problem of penance, in some of which the discipline is inflicted by the arms on some other part of the body, and in others hunger is brought into play by abstaining from food. But in no sacrament is the intention of the administrator of such vital importance as in self-penance. Spenser tells us how the Red-Cross Knight underwent discipline under the directions of Patience :

> But yet the cause and root of all his ill,
>   Inward corruption and infected sin,
> Not purged nor healed, behind remained still,
>   And fest'ring sore, did ranckle yet within,
> Close creeping 'twixt the marrow and the skin ;
>   Which to extirpe, he laid him privily
>   Down in a darksome lowly place far in,
> Whereas he meant his corrosives to apply,
> And with streight diet tame his stubborn malady.

In ashes and sackcloth he did array
  His daintie corse, proud humours to abate
And dieted with fasting every day
  The swelling of his wounds to mitigate ;
And made him pray both early and eke late.
And ever as superfluous flesh did rot,
  Amendment ready still at hand did wayt,
To pluck it out with pincers fiery whott
That soon in him was left no one corrupted iott.

Here we see the advantage of allegory. In real life the
poor man, instead of having Patience and Amendment as his
good friends standing by his side, would have to conjure them
up inside of him, and to apply the pincers with his own hand.
But setting allegory aside, we can find here no exaltation of
pain in itself. The pain is a necessary concomitant of the
extirpation of evil habits from a conscious being. Amendment
is the aim and end of the discipline, and the sole reason that he
has to heat his pincers fiery whott is, that the evil which he has
to extirpe has crept close betwixt the marrow and the skin, and
requires the actual cautery to prevent its creeping further.

Again, in the Collect for the first Sunday in Lent, we pray
for "grace to use such abstinence," that, our flesh being subdued
to the spirit, we may ever obey "the godly motions" of Christ.
Abstinence is to be used only as a help towards the subjugation
of our lower nature, and the opening up of our higher nature to
divine influence.

I have said nothing of the aspect of penal suffering as a
satisfaction either of justice from the point of view of a ruler, or
of vengeance from the point of view of an aggrieved person.

Nor have I attempted to discuss the process by which the
suffering, real or apparent, of one may be a direct source of
pleasure to another who has cultivated the spirit of cruelty.
For I cannot think that pure cruelty, as distinct from com-
bativeness, anger, and love of power, is anything but a morbid
growth of feeling, subject, of course, to the general laws of the
growth of feeling, whatever they may be ; but no more to be
regarded as a subject for our discussion here than those forms
of perverted feeling which induce dogs to gnaw off their own
toes, or devotees to hold their arms above their heads till they
can no longer bring them down again.

III.

(PSYCHOPHYSIK.)

5th February 1878.

Whence came we? whither are we going? and what should we do now? are three questions of some celebrity. We have come from somewhere between this and Orion; we are going at   kilomètres per second towards Hercules; and we must therefore observe stars in a direction at right angles to our path; —are the answers suggested twenty-five years ago. It seems to me that a change has come over the questions, so that they now read, What used I to believe about myself? what is it likely I shall have to believe about myself? and what should I believe about myself now?

I used to believe myself to be the Conscious Ego. I am told I shall have soon to believe myself to be a congeries of plastidule souls, and that I must at once study psychophysik in order to obtain a true knowledge of myself.

I propose, therefore, to talk of the Conscious Ego, of Plastidule souls, and of Psychophysik.

(1.) What is your name? is a still more celebrated question. The suggested answer, N. or M., recalls to the mathematician ideas and operations of the most heterogeneous kind. Let us consider some of them. The instructors of my youth would have expected me to answer—My name is the Conscious Ego, one and indivisible, the Subject, in relation to whom all other beings, material, human, or divine, are mere Objects. Whether the being of such Objects can be maintained or upheld apart from my continuous perception of them is the great question of Metaphysic.

Though nothing can rise to the dignity even of an Object, except in so far as it is perceived by me, I regard certain Objects as nearer in rank to me, the Subject, than others, because it is through them that other Objects are perceived. Indeed, I often catch myself, when thinking about my body or my mind, supposing that I am thinking about myself.

There are other objects within the sphere of our perceptions which resemble our bodies, though they are not ours. The actions of these objects are so far like our own that we not only attribute to these objects the power of thinking, but also the consciousness of knowing, feeling, desiring and willing. In short, we suppose that each of these objects, when he asserts himself to be the Conscious Ego, means what we do when we make a similar statement.

The late Professor Ferrier, in his " Metaphysic," makes great use of this Alter Ego, and for his own purposes he treats him as a true Ego, whereas in Metaphysic he can never be more than an Object. This, however, is only a confusion of persons, not an actual division of the substance of the Ego. Our business to-night lies in the abysmal depths of Personality, and relates to the Unity of the Ego.

A great deal of what has been written on this subject relates to the continuity of the Ego in space and time, or in what corresponds in metaphysic to the space and time of physic. And first of Space. Has the Ego anything corresponding to Extension ? Has he parts ? and, if so, are these parts separable in fact or even in idea ?

It has been maintained that he has no parts ; that his state of consciousness at any instant is an inseparable whole, comparable, in respect of extension, to a mathematical point. According to this view, when I think I see an extensive prospect all at once before me, I am in reality either actually rolling my eye in an unconscious frenzy, or without any bodily motion I, —that is, the perceptive Ego,—am attending first to one *minimum visibile*, and then to another, so that what is presented to me is like the idea which a blind man forms of the shape of an object by stroking it with the end of his stick. The evidence relates only to the position of points in the line traced by the end of his stick, but he fills in the rest of the surface in accordance with his notions of continuity and probability.

There is no department of psychophysik which has been so successfully studied as that which relates to vision. When we keep not only our eyes, but our attention, fixed on one small object, the field of conscious vision seems to contract, till only that object remains visible, and even it seems about to disappear. It generally happens, however, that the feeling of uneasiness which grows upon us causes at last a slight displacement of the eye, when suddenly a large extent of the field starts into visibility, and the edges of objects, especially those normal to the line of displacement, become obtrusively prominent. This experiment seems at first sight to indicate that the central spot of the retina has some exclusive privilege in the economy of vision. What it really shows is that changes in the mode of excitation are essential to perfect vision, and that vision cannot be maintained under an absolute sameness of excitation. On the other hand, by means of the instantaneous light of a single electric spark, we may read a whole sentence of print. Here we know that though the illumination lasts only for a few millionths of a second, the image on the retina lasts for a time amply sufficient for an expert reader to go over it letter by letter, and even to detect misprints. This experiment suggests certain speculations about memory, a faculty which is often supposed to be essential to the continuity of the Ego in time.

When men wish to have things remembered they set up monuments, and write inscriptions and books,—they draw pictures and take photographs,—in order that these material things may help them, in time to come, to call up the thought of that which they were intended to commemorate.

In our own bodies we have records of past events. Old wounds may remind us of impressions made years ago, and ocular spectra remind us of impressions made seconds ago. Even in quiet meditation we sometimes find the ideas of visible objects accompanied with sensations hardly less vivid than those produced by real objects, and the memory of spoken words passes in a continuous manner, as the condition of our nerves becomes more exalted, first into a silent straining of the organs of speech, and then into an audible voice.

Beginners in music may practise on a dumb piano, and there is a silent process by which we may improve our pronunciation of foreign words.

We can thus trace a continuous series of the instruments of memory, beginning at the tables of stone and going on to the tables of the heart ; and we are tempted to ask whether all memorials are not of the same kind—a physical impression on a material system.

The last American invention of the past year is Edison's Talking Phonograph. This instrument has an ear of its own, into which you may say your lesson, and a mouth of its own, which at any future time is ready to repeat that lesson.

The memory of this machine consists of tinfoil thin enough to be impressionable by the metal style which is set in motion by the voice, and yet thick enough to be retentive of these impressions, and at a proper time to communicate a corresponding motion to the style of the talking part of the machine.

Such is the heart of this instrument, by which it gets its speeches. Are our own hearts essentially different? We know what damage can be done to our memory by physical disturbances. We find ourselves quite unable to recall what we had often perused and reperused on the pages of memory. The page is lost out of our consciousness. Time goes on, and some day we find that the page with all that it contained has been restored to its place. Where was that page when it was out of our consciousness? Not surely in the Ego, unless there be an unconscious Ego. It must be out of the Ego, and therefore an Object. If this be so, it is of no great consequence to the dignity of the Ego whether this particular object is purely spiritual or has a material substratum, just as history is history whether or not it has a material substratum of paper and ink.

Memory is sometimes spoken of as if it were essential to individuality. When I wish to convince myself that I am the same person as a certain baby, I may do so by remembering as my own certain acts done by that baby. It may happen, however, that I cannot ascertain whether my present memory of these acts is due entirely to the direct impression made by these acts on me, or whether it is not mainly due to the frequent repetition of the story of these acts, as told to me afterwards by older persons.

But even if I were to find my memory to be all wrong, and that I am not that baby but a changeling, this would not touch my conviction that I who now am, am one.

The phenomenon of double consciousness, though not common, seems to be well established. A person has a double series of alternate states. In one the memory, education, accomplishments, and temper, are quite different from what they are in the other.

Instances have even been adduced of a man believing himself to be two or even three different individuals at the same time. But when we come to examine any particular case we find that the man has nothing more than an erroneous opinion that he is entitled to the position and rights of the King, or of some other person, as well as his own, so that even in his own imagination he is no more than a person who holds several different offices at the same time.

(2.) The theory of Plastidule souls has been hinted at by several persons, of whom Dr. Tyndall has spoken loudest. A much clearer utterance is that of Professor von Nägeli, of

Munich, in an address delivered at the Munich meeting of the German Association in 1877.

Du Bois Reymond, in an address to the same body at Leipzig in 1872, had asserted—

"That in the first trace of pleasure which was felt by one of the simplest beings in the beginning of animal life upon our earth, an insuperable limit was marked ; while upwards from this, to the most elevated mental activity, and downwards from the vital force of the organic to the simple physical force, he nowhere finds another limit."

To this Professor Nägeli replies—

"Experience shows that from the clearest consciousness of the thinker downwards, through the more imperfect consciousness of the child, to the unconsciousness of the embryo, and to the insensibility of the human ovum,—or through the more imperfect consciousness of undeveloped human races and of higher animals to the unconsciousness of lower animals and of sensitive plants, and to the insensibility of all other plants,—there exists a continuous gradation without definable limit, and that the same gradation continues from the life of the animal ovum and the vegetable cell downwards, through organised elementary and more or less lifeless forms (parts of the cell), to crystals and chemical molecules."

Professor von Nägeli accepts the fact of sensation, appetency, and thought, in the higher forms of life ; but instead of trying to resolve it into a mechanical process, he levels up the discontinuity of the chain of being by attributing sensation not only to all organisms, but also to all cells, molecules, and atoms. This is what he says—

"Now, if the molecules possess anything which is ever so distantly related to sensation, and we cannot doubt it, since each one feels the presence, the certain condition, the peculiar forces of the other, and, accordingly, has the inclination to move, and under circumstances really begins to move—becomes alive as it were ; moreover, since such molecules are the elements which cause pleasure and pain ; if, therefore, the molecules feel something that is related to sensation, then this must be pleasure, if they can respond to attraction and repulsion, *i.e.* follow their inclination or disinclination ; it must be displeasure if they are forced to execute some opposite movement, and it must be neither pleasure nor displeasure if they remain at rest."

Professor von Nägeli is what Professor Huxley would call a

mere biologist, or he would have known that the molecules, like the planets, move along like blessed gods. They cannot be disturbed from the path of their choice by the action of any forces, for they have a constant and perpetual will to render to every force precisely the amount of deflexion which is due to it. They must therefore enjoy a perpetuity of the highest and most unmixed pleasure, even when, as Professor Nägeli says, they are the cause of pain to us.

To attribute life, sensation, and thought to objects in which these attributes are not established by sufficient evidence is nothing more than the good old figure of Personification.

If certain bodies, like the sun and stars, move in a regular manner, which we can predict, we may, if it pleases us, suppose that their nature is like that of the just man whom nothing can turn from the path of rectitude. If the motion of other bodies is less simple, so that we cannot account for it, we may suppose their nature to be tainted with that capriciousness which we observe in our fellow men, and of which we are occasionally conscious in ourselves.

But the study of nature has always tended to show that what we formerly attributed to the caprice of bodies is only an instance of a regularity which is unbroken, but which cannot be traced by us till we acquire the requisite skill.

But granting that the mental powers of atoms may be, for anything we know, of the very highest order, what step have we made towards linking our own mental powers with those of lower orders of being ?

(3.) Let us suppose that a thinking man is built up of a number of thinking atoms. Have the thoughts of the man any relation to the thoughts of atoms or of one or more of them ? Those who try to account by means of atoms for mental processes do so not by the thoughts of the atoms but by their motions.

Hobbes, in the frontispiece of his *Leviathan*, shows us a monster like the wicker images of our British antecessors stuffed with men, and the whole method of his book is founded on an analogy between the body politic and the individual man.

Herbert Spencer has pushed the analogy both upwards and downwards as far as it will go, and further than it can go on all fours. He shows us how a society is an organism, and how an organism is a society,—how the lower forms of societies and organisms consist of a multitude of homogeneous parts, the functions of which are imperfectly differentiated, so that each can at a pinch undertake the office of any other ; whereas the parts of higher forms of organisms and societies are exceedingly heterogeneous, and discharge more perfectly differentiated functions.   Hence to the lower forms a breaking up may be a multiplication of the species, whereas to the higher forms it is death.

In a society, as in an organism, both the working and the thinking will be better done if undertaken by different members, provided that the thinking members can guide the working members, while [the working members support the thinking members,—the workers retaining just enough intelligence to enable them to receive the guidance, and the thinkers retaining just enough working power to enable them to appropriate the pabulum presented to them by the workers.

Hence, in the more highly developed systems, the guiding powers may be concentrated into a smaller portion of the whole system, and may exercise a more undisputed power of guiding the rest, till in the highest organism we arrive at what is called Personal Government, and the organism may bear without abuse the grand old name of Individual.   This result is brought about by all the members except one bartering their right of guiding themselves for the privilege of being guided, and so delegating to the one ruling member the functions of government.   When the human society has lapsed into the condition of personal government, the consciousness of the head of the state may be expressed by him in the phrase, "L'état c'est moi ;" but though the other members of the society may delegate to the head all their political powers, they cannot delegate their sensations or any other fact of consciousness, for these are the incommunicable attributes of that Ego to whom they belong.

I have now to confess that up to the present moment I have remained in ignorance of how I came to be, or, in the Spencerian language, how consciousness must arise. . I was dimly aware that somewhere in the vast System of Philosophy this question had been settled, because the Evolutionists are all so calm about it ; but in a hasty search for it I never suspected in how quiet and unostentatious a manner the origin of myself would be accounted for.   I am indebted to Mr. Kirkman for pointing it

out in his *Philosophy without Assumptions*. Here it is with Mr.
Kirkman's comment.   *Principles of Psychology*, § 179, p. 403 :—
" These separate impressions are received by the senses—by
different parts of the body. If they go no further than the
places at which they are received, they are useless.   Or if only
some of them are brought into relation with one another, they
are useless.   That an effectual adjustment may be made, they
must all be brought into relation with one another.   But this
implies some centre of communication common to them all,
through which they severally pass ; and, as they cannot pass
through it simultaneously, they must pass through it in succession.   So that as the external phenomena responded to become
greater in number and more complicated in kind, the variety and
rapidity of the changes to which this common centre of communication is subject must increase—there must result an unbroken
series of these changes—there must arise a consciousness."

On this Kirkman remarks : " He knew he could do it, and
he did it !"—What was the evolution of light to this ?   The
next Longinus will put that in before γενέσθω φῶς καὶ
ἐγένετο φῶς.

The opinions about my origin are as various as those about
my nature.   Canon Liddon tells me that I was created out of
nothing in the year 1831, though I cannot make out from what
he says on what day of that year the event took place, or why
my parents and not some one else found me under a gooseberry bush ; or, indeed, why I should have any part or lot
in family matters, from Adam's first sin down to my father's
last name.

Mr. Francis Galton tells me that I am developed from
structureless germs contributed not only by my two parents
but by their remotest ancestors centuries ago.   My existence,
therefore, does not begin abruptly, but tails off as an exponential function of t does for negative values of that variable.
My local existence, however, though at present confined within
the periphractic region of my skin, was in former times discontinuous as regards space, being carried about by two, four, or
more, distinct human beings.

Dr. Julius Müller tells me that by an analysis of my conscience I shall come to a very different result, namely, that I
existed (if, indeed, the fact can be expressed by a past tense
and not a pure aorist), in an extra-temporal state, and that in

that state I freely determined myself to choose evil rather than good.

He does not say I can remember this transaction. The conviction I am to acquire of it is not to be an experimental or empirical consciousness, but a speculative or philosophical knowledge.

Since, according to Müller's theory, this extra-temporal decision is perfectly free, and since it would be difficult to predicate freedom of a choice which is invariably on one side, he is obliged to assert that, in the extra-temporal state, some of our species must have chosen the better part. But he has also to maintain that all of us who are born into this world by ordinary generation have already chosen the worse part.

Hence, though he does not say so, he makes the extra-temporal fall a condition of our being born into this world. Whether those of us who make the better choice are born into some other world, or whether, so long as they remain unfallen, they continue in the extra-temporal state—a state certainly not higher but rather more undeveloped than that of time—Müller does not say.

Dr. John Henry Newman has shown us how the doctrine of post-baptismal sin became developed into the discovery of Purgatory, with all its geographical details. It would seem as if the doctrine of original sin, in the hands of speculative theologians, might open up to our view a far more transcendental region, compared with which the stairs and terraces and fires of purgatory are as familiar as those of our own hearths and homes.

As to my present state, Du Bois Reymond tells me that not only my bodily but a large part of my mental functions are performed by the motion of atoms under fixed laws, and his result is that the finite mind, as it has developed itself through the animal world up to man, is a double one,—on the one side the acting, inventing, unconscious, material mind, which puts the muscles into motion and determines the world's history: this is nothing else but the mechanics of atoms, and is subject to the causal law; and on the other side the inactive, contemplative, remembering, fancying, conscious, immaterial mind, which feels pleasure and pain, love and hate: this one lies outside of the mechanics of matter and cares nothing for cause and effect.

Dr. Drysdale tells me that not only my thinking powers but

my feelings are functions of the material organism, and that I myself am such a function. He admits that I am not material —no function can be material, for matter is a substance, and a function is not a being at all. Dr. Drysdale, as a Christian materialist, follows his master Fletcher, who says—

"As often as it shall be said that mind or the faculty of thinking is a property of living matter,—that it is born with the body, is developed with the body, decays with the body, and dies with the body,—it is to be understood of the mind only, not the soul. The soul is something not material indeed, but substantial—a divine gift to the highest alone of God's creatures, responsible for all the actions of mind, but as totally distinct from it as one thing can be from another, or rather as something is from nothing."

Dr. Drysdale, however, in order to save the dynamical theory of life and mind, says that this soul or spirit must either, if now existing, be a passive spectator of the action of the living being connected with it, or else that he has no existence during this present life, but is to be constituted by a divine act after the death of the living being.

In either case, I cannot identify this soul with myself, for I know that I exist now, and that I act, and that what I do may be right or wrong ; and that, whether right or wrong, it is my act, which I cannot repudiate.

In this search for information about myself from eminent thinkers of different types, I seem to have learnt one lesson, that all science and philosophy, and every form of human speech, is about objects capable of being perceived by the speaker and the hearer ; and that when our thought pretends to deal with the Subject it is really only dealing with an Object under a false name. The only proposition about the Subject, namely, "I am," cannot be used in the same sense by any two of us, and, therefore, it can never become science at all.

JUVENILE VERSES.

THE VAMPYRE.[1]

Compylt into Meeter by James Clerk Maxwell. [1845.]

THAIR is a knichte rydis through the wood,
    And a douchty knichte is hee,
And sure hee is on a message sent,
    He rydis sae hastilie.
Hee passit the aik, and hee passit the birk,
    And hee passit monie a tre,
Bot plesant to him was the saugh sae slim,
    For beneath it hee did see
The boniest ladye that ever he saw,
    Scho was sae schyn and fair.
And there scho sat, beneath the saugh,
    Kaiming hir gowden hair.
And then the knichte—" Oh ladye brichte,
    What chance hes broucht you here,
But say the word, and ye schall gang
    Back to your kindred dear."
Then up and spok the Ladye fair—
    " I have nae friends or kin,
Bot in a littel boat I live,
    Amidst the waves' loud din."
Then answered thus the douchty knichte—
    " I'll follow you through all,
For gin ye bee in a littel boat,
    The world to it seemis small."
They gaed through the wood, and through the wood
    To the end of the wood they came :
And when they came to the end of the wood
    They saw the salt sea faem.
And then they saw the wee, wee boat,
    That daunced on the top of the wave,
And first got in the ladye fair,
    And then the knichte sae brave ;
They got into the wee, wee boat,
    And rowed wi' a' their micht ;

---

[1] P. 48.

When the knichte sae brave, he turnit about,
   And lookit at the ladye brichte ;
He lookit at her bonie cheik,
   And hee lookit at hir twa brichte eyne,
Bot hir rosie cheik growe ghaistly pale,
   And scho seymit as scho deid had been.
The fause fause knichte growe pale wi' frichte,
   And his hair rose up on end,
For gane-by days cam to his mynde,
   And his former luve he kenned.
Then spake the ladye,—" Thou, fause knichte,
   Hast done to mee much ill,
Thou didst forsake me long ago,
   Bot I am constant still ;
For though I ligg in the woods sae cauld,
   At rest I canna bee
Until I sucke the gude lyfe blude
   Of the man that gart me dee."
Hee saw hir lipps were wet wi' blude,
   And hee saw hir lyfelesse eyne,
And loud hee cry'd, " Get frae my syde,
   Thou vampyr corps uncleane !"
Bot no, hee is in hir magic boat,
   And on the wyde wyde sea ;
And the vampyr suckis his gude lyfe blude
   Sho suckis hym till hee dee.
So now beware, whoe're you are,
   That walkis in this lone wood ;
Beware of that deceitfull spright,
   The ghaist that suckis the blude.

(Song of the Edinburgh Academician
[1848.]

If ony here has got an ear,
   He'd better tak' a haud o' me
Or I'll begin, wi' roarin' din,
   To cheer our old Academy.

Dear old Academy,
Queer old Academy,
A merry lot we were, I wot,
When at the old Academy.

There's some may think me crouse wi' drink,
And some may think it mad o' me,
But ither some will gladly come
And cheer our old Academy.

Some set their hopes on Kings and Popes,
But, o' the sons of Adam, he
Was first, without the smallest doubt,
That built the first Academy.

Let Pedants seek for scraps of Greek,
Their lingo to Macadamize ;
Gie me the sense, without pretence,
That comes o' Scots Academies.

Let scholars all, both grit and small,
Of Learning mourn the sad demise ;
That's as they think, but we will drink
Good luck to Scots Academies.

OCCASIONAL PIECES.

REFLEX MUSINGS :

REFLECTION FROM VARIOUS SURFACES.

18th April 1853.

IN the dense entangled street,
    Where the web of Trade is weaving,
Forms unknown in crowds I meet
    Much of each and all believing ;
    Each his small designs achieving
Hurries on with restless feet,
    While, through Fancy's power deceiving,
Self in every form I greet.

2 C

Oft in yonder rocky dell
  'Neath the birches' shadow seated,
I have watched the darksome well,
  Where my stooping form, repeated,
  Now advanced and now retreated
With the spring's alternate swell,
  Till destroyed before completed
As the big drops grew and fell.

By the hollow mountain-side
  Questions strange I shout for ever,
While the echoes far and wide
  Seem to mock my vain endeavour;
  Still I shout, for though they never
Cast my borrowed voice aside,
  Words from empty words they sever—
Words of Truth from words of Pride.

Yes, the faces in the crowd,
  And the wakened echoes, glancing
From the mountain, rocky browed,
  And the lights in water dancing—
  Each, my wandering sense entrancing,
Tells me back my thoughts aloud,
  All the joys of Truth enhancing,
Crushing all that makes me proud.

A STUDENT'S EVENING HYMN.

Cambridge, April 25, 1853.

I.

Now no more the slanting rays
  With the mountain summits dally,
Now no more in crimson blaze
  Evening's fleecy cloudlets rally,
  Soon shall Night from off the valley
Sweep that bright yet earthly haze,
  And the stars most musically
Move in endless rounds of praise.

II.

While the world is growing dim,
   And the Sun is slow descending
Past the far horizon's rim,
   Earth's low sky to heaven extending,
   Let my feeble earth-notes, blending
With the songs of cherubim,
   Through the same expanse ascending,
Thus renew my evening hymn.

III.

Thou that fill'st our waiting eyes
   With the food of contemplation,
Setting in thy darkened skies
   Signs of infinite creation,
   Grant to nightly meditation
What the toilsome day denies—
   Teach me in this earthly station
Heavenly Truth to realise.

IV.

Give me wisdom so to use
   These brief hours of thoughtful leisure,
That I may no instant lose
   In mere meditative pleasure,
   But with strictest justice measure
All the ends my life pursues,
   Lies to crush and truths to treasure,
Wrong to shun and Right to choose.

V.

Then, when unexpected Sleep,
   O'er my long-closed eyelids stealing,
Opens up that lower deep
   Where Existence has no feeling,
   May sweet Calm, my languor healing,
Lend me strength at dawn to reap
   All that Shadows, world-concealing,
For the bold inquirer keep.

VI.

Through the creatures Thou hast made
  Show the brightness of Thy glory,
Be eternal Truth displayed
  In their substance transitory,
  Till green Earth and Ocean hoary,
Massy rock and tender blade
  Tell the same unending story—
" We are Truth in Form arrayed."

VII.

When to study I retire,
  And from books of ancient sages
Glean fresh sparks of buried fire
  Lurking in their ample pages—
  While the task my mind engages
Let old words new truths inspire—
  Truths that to all after-ages
Prompt the Thoughts that never tire.

VIII.

Yet if, led by shadows fair,
  I have uttered words of folly,
Let the kind absorbing air
  Stifle every sound unholy.
  So when Saints with Angels lowly
Join in heaven's unceasing prayer,
  Mine as certainly, though slowly,
May ascend and mingle there.

*Two stanzas omitted, the Author knows where, but not to be inserted
till he knows how.*

Teach me so Thy works to read
  That my faith,—new strength accruing,—
May from world to world proceed,
  Wisdom's fruitful search pursuing ;
  Till, thy truth my mind imbuing,
I proclaim the Eternal Creed,
  Oft the glorious theme renewing
God our Lord is God indeed.

Give me love aright to trace
        Thine to everything created,
Preaching to a ransomed race
        By Thy mercy renovated,
        Till with all thy fulness sated
I behold thee face to face
        And with Ardour unabated
Sing the glories of thy grace.

(On St. David's Day.[1] To Mrs. E. C. Morrieson.)

1st March 1854.

'Twas not chance but deep design,
Tho' of whom I can't divine
Made the courtly Valentine
        (Corpulent saint and bishop)
Such a time with Bob to stay :—
Let me now in bardish way
On your own St. David's day
        Toss you a simple dish up.

'Tis a tale we learnt at school,—
Oft we broke domestic rule,
Standing till our brows were cool
        In the forbidden lobby.[2]
There we talked and there we laughed,
Till the townsfolk thought us daft,
What of that ? a thorough draft
        Was and is still my hobby.

To my tale : In ancient days,
Ere men left the good old ways,
Lived a lady whose just praise
        Passes all fancied glory.
Rich was she in field and store,
Richer in the sons she bore,
How could she be honoured more ?
        Listen and hear the story.

---

[1] See p. 150.   [2] P. 48, l. 10.

On a high and festive day
When the chariots bright and gay
To the temple far away
　　　Passed in majestic order,—
When the hour was nigh at hand,
She who should have led the band
Found no oxen at command,
　　　Searching through all her border.[1]

Then her two sons brave and strong
Girt their limbs with band and thong,
And before the wondering throng
　　　Drew their exulting mother.
Swift and steady, on they came ;
At the temple loud acclaim
Greeted that illustrious dame,
　　　Blest above every other.

Then, while triumph filled her breast,
Loud she prayed above the rest,
Give my sons whatever best
　　　Man may receive from heaven.
To the shrine the brothers stept,
Low they bowed, they sunk, they slept,
Stillness o'er their brave limbs crept :—
　　　Rest was the guerdon given.

Such the simple story told,
By a sage renowned of old,[2]
To a king [3] whose fabled gold
　　　Could not procure him learning.
Heathen was the sage indeed,
Yet his tale we gladly read,
Thro' his dark and doubtful creed
　　　Glimpses of Truth discerning.

Now no more the altar's blaze
Glares athwart our worldly haze,
Warning men how evil ways
　　　Lead to just tribulation.

---

[1] Herodotus, i. 31.　　　[2] Solon.　　　[3] Crœsus.

Now no more the temple stands,
Pointing out to godless lands
That which is not made with hands,
    Even the whole Creation.

Ask no more, then, " what is best,
How shall those you love be blest,"
Ask at once, eternal Rest,
    Peace and assurance giving.
Rest of Life and not of death,
Rest in Love and Hope and Faith,
Till the God who gives their breath
    Calls them to rest from living.

RECOLLECTIONS OF DREAMLAND.

Cambridge, June ? 1856.[1]

ROUSE ye! torpid daylight-dreamers, cast your carking cares
    away!
As calm air to troubled water, so my night is to your day;
All the dreary day you labour, groping after common sense,
And your eyes ye will not open on the night's magnificence.
Ye would scoff were I to tell you how a guiding radiance gleams
On the outer world of action from my inner world of dreams.

When, with mind released from study, late I lay me down to
    sleep,
From the midst of facts and figures, into boundless space I leap;
For the inner world grows wider as the outer disappears,
And the soul, retiring inward, finds itself beyond the spheres.
Then, to this unbroken sameness, some fantastic dream succeeds,
Vague emotions rise and ripen into thoughts and words and
    deeds.
Old impressions, long forgotten, range themselves in Time and
    Space,
Till I recollect the features of some once familiar place.
Then from valley into valley in my dreaming course I roam,
Till the wanderings of my fancy end, where they began, at home.

---

[1] See p. 165.

Calm it lies in morning twilight, while each streamlet far and
wide
Still retains its hazy mantle, borrowed from the mountain's side;
Every knoll is now an island, every wooded bank a shore,
To the lake of quiet vapour that has spread the valley o'er.
Sheep are couched on every hillock, waiting till the morning
dawns,
Hares are on their early rambles, limping o'er the dewy lawns.
All within the house is silent, darkened all the chambers
seem,
As with noiseless step I enter, gliding onwards in my dream.

What! has Time run out his cycle, do the years return again?
Are there treasure-caves in Dreamland where departed days
remain?
I have leapt the bars of distance—left the life that late I led—
I remember years and labours as a tale that I have read;
Yet my heart is hot within me, for I feel the gentle power
Of the spirits that still love me, waiting for this sacred hour.
Yes,—I know the forms that meet me are but phantoms of the
brain,
For they walk in mortal bodies, and they have not ceased from
pain.
Oh! those signs of human weakness, left behind for ever now,
Dearer far to me than glories round a fancied seraph's brow.
Oh! the old familiar voices! Oh! the patient waiting eyes!
Let me live with them in dreamland, while the world in slumber
lies!
For by bonds of sacred honour will they guard my soul in sleep
From the spells of aimless fancies, that around my senses creep.
They will link the past and present into one continuous life,
While I feel their hope, their patience, nerve me for the daily
strife.

For it is not all a fancy that our lives and theirs are one,
And we know that all we see is but an endless work begun.
Part is left in Nature's keeping, part is entered into rest,
Part remains to grow and ripen, hidden in some living breast.
What is ours we know not, either when we wake or when we
sleep,
But we know that Love and Honour, day and night, are ours
to keep.

What though Dreams be wandering fancies, by some lawless force entwined,

Empty bubbles, floating upwards through the current of the mind ?

There are powers and thoughts within us, that we know not, till they rise

Through the stream of conscious action from where Self in secret lies.

But when Will and Sense are silent, by the thoughts that come and go,

We may trace the rocks and eddies in the hidden depths below.

Let me dream my dream till morning ; let my mind run slow and clear,

Free from all the world's distraction, feeling that the Dead are near,

Let me wake, and see my duty lie before me straight and plain.

Let me rise refreshed, and ready to begin my work again.

To the Air of " Lörelei."

Aberdeen, January 1858.

I.

Alone on a hillside of heather,
 I lay with dark thoughts in my mind,
In the midst of the beautiful weather
 I was deaf, I was dumb, I was blind.
I knew not the glories around me,
 I counted the world as it seems,
Till a spirit of melody found me,
 And taught me in visions and dreams.

II.

For the sound of a chorus of voices
 Came gathering up from below,
And I heard how all Nature rejoices,
 And moves with a musical flow.

O strange ! we are lost in delusion,
    Our ways and doings are wrong,
We are drowning in[1] wilful confusion
    The notes of that[2] wonderful song.

III.

But listen, what harmony holy
    Is mingling its notes with our own !
The discord is vanishing slowly,
    And melts in that dominant tone.
And they that have heard it can never
    Return to confusion again,
Their voices are music for ever,
    And join in the mystical strain.

IV.

No mortal can[3] utter the beauty
    That dwells in[4] the song that they sing ;
They move in the pathway of duty,
    They follow the steps of their King.
I would barter the world and its glory,
    That vision of joy to prolong,
Or to hear and remember the story
    That lies in the heart of their song.

"I'VE HEARD THE RUSHING."

Aberdeen, 1858.

I'VE heard the rushing of mountain torrents, gushing
    Down through the rocks, in a cataract of spray,
        Onward to the ocean ;
        Swift seemed their motion,
Till, lost in the desert, they dwindled away.

I've learnt the story of all human glory,
    I've felt high resolves growing weaker every day,

---

[1] *v.r.* marring with.   [2] *v.r.* the.
[3] *v.r.* may.   [4] *v.r.* breathes through.

Till cares, springing round me,
With creeping tendrils bound me,
And all I once hoped for was wearing fast away.

I've seen the river rolling on for ever,
    Silent and strong, without tumult or display.
            In the desert arid,
            Its waters never tarried,
Till far out at sea we still found them on their way.

Now no more weary we faint in deserts dreary,
    Toiling alone till the closing of the day;
            All now is righted,
            Our souls flow on united,
Till the years and their sorrows have all died away.

"WILL YOU COME ALONG WITH ME?"

Aberdeen, 1858.

I.

WILL you come along with me,
    In the fresh spring-tide,
My comforter to be
    Through the world so wide?
Will you come and learn the ways
A student spends his days,
On the bonny, bonny braes
    Of our ain burnside?

II.

For the lambs will soon be here,
    In the fresh spring-tide;
As lambs come every year
    On our ain burnside.
Poor things, they will not stay,
But we will keep the day
When first we saw them play
    On our ain burnside.

III.

We will watch the budding trees
    In the fresh spring-tide,

While the murmurs of the breeze
    Through the branches glide.
Where the mavis builds her nest,
And finds both work and rest,
In the bush she loves the best,
    On our ain burnside.

IV.

And the life we then shall lead
    In the fresh spring-tide,
Will make thee mine indeed,
    Though the world be wide.
No stranger's blame or praise
Shall turn us from the ways
That brought us happy days
    On our ain burnside.

"WHY, WHEN OUR SUN SHINES CLEAREST."

1858.

WHY, when our sun shines clearest,
Why, when our hopes seem nearest,
Why, when our life feels dearest,
    Rises a secret pain—
Hope's perfect mirror broken—
Shadows of things unspoken—
Why will not some sure token
    Calm us to rest again ?

Mixed with all earthly blessing
Lingers the fear distressing—
Conscience within confessing
    Nothing of ours is pure.
Still must such thoughts upbraid us,
Seeking our own to aid us ;
God, not ourselves, hath made us ;
    Trusting in Him we're sure.

Thus, from our sorrows gleaning
Thoughts of the world's deep meaning,
Let us rejoice while leaning
    Firm on our Father's arm.
Now are we one for ever,
Joined so that none may sever,
Souls, so united, never
    Faint through mischance or harm.

To K. M. D.

Aberdeen, 1858.

In the buds, before they burst,
    Leaves and flowers are moulded ;
Closely pressed they lie at first,
    Exquisitely folded.

Though no hope of change they felt,
    Folded hard together,
Soon their sap begins to melt
    In the warmer weather.

Till, when Life returns with Spring,
    Through them softly stealing,
All their freshness forth they fling,
    Hidden forms revealing.

Who can fold those flowers again,
    In the way he found them ?
Or those spreading leaves restrain,
    In the buds that bound them ?

Trust me, Spring is very near,
    All the buds are swelling ;
All the glory of the year
    In those buds is dwelling.

What the opened buds reveal
    Tells us—Life is flowing ;
What the buds, still shut, conceal,
    We shall end in knowing.

Long I lingered in the bud,
　　Doubting of the season,
Winter's cold had chilled my blood—
　　I was ripe for treason.

Now no more I doubt or wait,
　　All my fears are vanished,
Summer's coming, dear, though late,
　　Fogs and frosts are banished.

Tune, *Il Segreto per esser felice.*

24th March 1858.

I.

THERE are some folks that say,
They have found out a way,
　　To be healthy and wealthy and wise—
" Let your thoughts be but few,
Do as other folk do,
　　And never be caught by surprise.
Let your motto be—Follow the fashion,
　　But let other people alone ;
Do not love them, nor hate them, nor care for their fate,
　　But keep a look out for your own.
Then what though the world may run riot,
　　Still playing at catch who catch can ;
You may just eat your dinner in quiet,
　　And live like a sensible man."

II.

'Twere a beautiful thing,
Thus to sit like a king,
　　And talk of the world turning round,
If it were not that we,
Like all things that we see,
　　Are standing on movable ground.
While we boast of our tranquil enjoyments,
　　The means of enjoyment are flown,

Both our joys and our pains, till there's nothing remains,
   But the tranquil repose of a stone.
The world may be utterly crazy,
   And life may be labour in vain ;
But I'd rather be silly than lazy,
   And would not quit life for its pain.

III.

In Nature I read
Quite a different creed,
   There everything lives in the rest ;
Each feels the same force,
As it moves in its course,
   And all by one blessing are blest.
The end that we live for is single,
   But we labour not therefore alone,
For together we feel how by wheel within wheel,
   We are helped by a force not our own.
o we flee not the world and its dangers,
   For He that has made it is wise,
He knows we are pilgrims and strangers,
   And He will enlighten our eyes.

(To HIS WIFE.)

1864.

OFT in the night, from this lone room
   I long to fly o'er land and sea,
To pierce the dark, dividing gloom,
   And join myself to thee.

And thou to me wouldst gladly fly,
   I know thee well, my own true wife !
We feel, that when we live not nigh,
   We lose the crown of life.

Yet soon I hope, at dead of night,
   To meet where all is strange beside,
And 'mid the train's resounding flight
   To have thee by my side.

Then shall I feel that thou art near,
  Joined hand to hand and soul to soul ;
Short will that happy night appear,
  As through the dark we roll.

Then shall the secret of the will,
  That dares not enter into bliss ;
That longs for love, yet lingers still,
  Be solved in one long kiss.

I, drinking deep of thy rich love,
  Thou feeling all the strength of mine,
Our souls will rise in faith above
  The cares which make us pine.

Till I give thee, thou giving me,
  As that which either loves the best,
To Him that loved us both, that He
  May take us to His rest.

Wandering and weak are all our prayers,
  And fleeting half the gifts we crave ;
Love only, cleansed from sins and cares,
  Shall live beyond the grave.

Strengthen our love, O Lord, that we
  May in Thine own great love believe
And, opening all our soul to Thee,
  May Thy free gift receive.

All powers of mind, all force of will,
  May lie in dust when we are dead,
But love is ours, and shall be still,
  When earth and seas are fled.

SERIO-COMIC VERSE.

LINES *written under the conviction that it is not wise to read Mathematics in November after one's fire is out.*

10th Nov. 1853.

In the sad November time,
When the leaf has left the lime,
And the Cam, with sludge and slime,
 Plasters his ugly channel,
While, with sober step and slow,
Round about the marshes low,
Stiffening students stumping go
 Shivering through their flannel.

Then to me in doleful mood
Rises up a question rude,
Asking what sufficient good
 Comes of this mode of living?
Moping on from day to day,
Grinding up what will not "pay,"
Till the jaded brain gives way
 Under its own misgiving.

Why should wretched Man employ
Years which Nature meant for joy,
Striving vainly to destroy
 Freedom of thought and feeling?
Still the injured powers remain
Endless stores of hopeless pain,
When at last the vanquished brain
 Languishes past all healing.

Where is then his wealth of mind—
All the schemes that Hope designed?
Gone, like spring, to leave behind
 Indolent melancholy.
Thus he ends his helpless days,
Vex't with thoughts of former praise—
Tell me, how are Wisdom's ways
 Better than senseless Folly?

2 D

Happier those whom trifles please,
Dreaming out a life of ease,
Sinking by unfelt degrees
      Into annihilation.
Or the slave, to labour born,
Heedless of the freeman's scorn,
Destined to be slowly worn
      Down to the brute creation.

Thus a tempting spirit spoke,
As from troubled sleep I woke
To a morning thick with smoke,
      Sunless and damp and chilly.
Then to sleep I turned once more,
Eyes inflamed and windpipe sore,
Dreaming dreams I dreamt before,
      Only not quite so silly.

In my dream methought I strayed
Where a learned-looking maid
Stores of flimsy goods displayed,
      Articles not worth wearing.
" These," she said, with solemn air,
" Are the robes that sages wear,
  Warranted, when kept with care,
      Never to need repairing."

Then unnumbered witlings, caught
By her wiles, the trappings bought,
And by labour, not by thought,
      Honour and fame were earning.
While the men of wiser mind
Passed for blind among the blind ;
Pedants left them far behind
      In the career of learning.

" Those that fix their eager eyes
  Ever on the nearest prize
  Well may venture to despise
      Loftier aspirations.

Pedantry is in demand !
Buy it up at second-hand,
Seek no more to understand
    Profitless speculations."

Thus the gaudy gowns were sold,
Cast off sloughs of pedants old ;
Proudly marched the students bold
    Through the domain of error,
Till their trappings, false though fair,
Mouldered off and left them bare,
Clustering close in blank despair,
    Nakedness, cold, and terror.

Then, I said, " These haughty Schools
Boast that by their formal rules
They produce more learned fools
    Than could be well expected.
Learned fools they are indeed,
Learned in the books they read ;
Fools whene'er they come to need
    Wisdom, too long neglected.

" Oh ! that men indeed were wise,
  And would raise their purblind eyes
  To the opening mysteries
    Scattered around them ever.
  Truth should spring from sterile ground,
  Beauty beam from all around,
  Right should then at last be found
    Joining what none may sever."

A Problem in Dynamics.

19th Feb. 1854.

> An inextensible heavy chain
> Lies on a smooth horizontal plane,
> An impulsive force is applied at A,
> Required the initial motion of K.

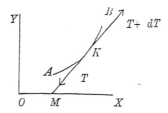

> Let ds be the *infinitesimal* link,
> Of which for the present we've only to think;
> Let T be the tension, and $T + dT$
> The same for the end that is nearest to B.
> Let a be put, by a common convention,
> For the angle at M 'twixt OX and the tension;
> Let V_t and V_n be ds's velocities,
> Of which V_t along and V_n across it is;
> Then $\dfrac{V_n}{V_t}$ the tangent will equal,
> Of the angle of starting worked out in the sequel.

> In working the problem the first thing of course is
> To equate the impressed and effectual forces.
> K is tugged by two tensions, whose difference dT
> (1) Must equal the element's mass into V_t.
> V_n must be due to the force perpendicular
> To ds's direction, which shows the particular
> Advantage of using da to serve at your
> Pleasure to estimate ds's curvature.
> For V_n into mass of a unit of chain
> (2) Must equal the curvature into the strain.

Thus managing cause and effect to discriminate,
The student must fruitlessly try to eliminate,
And painfully learn, that in order to do it, he
Must find the Equation of Continuity.
The reason is this, that the tough little element,
Which the force of impulsion to beat to a jelly meant,
Was endowed with a property incomprehensible,
And was " given," in the language of *Shop*, " inextensible."
It therefore with such pertinacity odd defied
The force which the length of the chain would have modified,
That its stubborn example may possibly yet recall
These overgrown rhymes to their prosody metrical.
The condition is got by resolving again,
According to axes assumed in the plane.
If then you reduce to the tangent and normal,
(3) You will find the equation more neat tho' less formal.
(4) The condition thus found after these preparations,
When duly combined with the former equations,
Will give you another, in which differentials
(5) (When the chain forms a circle), become in essentials
No harder than those that we easily solve
(6) In the time a T totum would take to revolve.

Now joyfully leaving *ds* to itself, a-
Ttend to the values of T and of a.
The chain undergoes a distorting convulsion,
Produced first at A by the force of impulsion.
In magnitude R, in direction tangential,
(7) Equating this R to the form exponential,
Obtained for the tension when a is zero,
It will measure the tug, such a tug as the " hero
Plume-waving" experienced, tied to the chariot.
But when dragged by the heels his grim head could not
carry aught,
(8) So give a its due at the end of the chain,
And the tension ought there to be zero again.
From these two conditions we get three equations,
Which serve to determine the proper relations
Between the first impulse and each coefficient
In the form for the tension, and this is sufficient
To work out the problem, and then, if you choose,
You may turn it and twist it the Dons to amuse.

Equations referred to.

$$(1) \quad d\mathrm{T} = m\mathrm{V}_t\, ds$$

$$(2) \quad m\mathrm{V}_n = \mathrm{T}\frac{da}{ds}$$

$$(3) \quad \frac{d\mathrm{V}_t}{ds} = \mathrm{V}_n\frac{da}{ds}$$

$$(4) \quad \frac{d^2\mathrm{T}}{ds^2} - \mathrm{T}\left(\frac{da}{ds}\right)^2 = 0$$

$$(5) \quad \frac{d^2\mathrm{T}}{da^2} - \mathrm{T} = 0$$

$$(6) \quad \mathrm{T} = \mathrm{C}_1 e^{a} + \mathrm{C}_2\, e^{-a}$$

$$(7) \quad \mathrm{R} = \mathrm{C}_1 + \mathrm{C}_2$$

$$(8) \quad 0 = \mathrm{C}_1 e^{a_1} + \mathrm{C}_2 e^{-a_1}$$

$$\frac{\mathrm{V}_n}{\mathrm{V}_t} = \tan\beta = -\frac{e^{(a_1-a)} - e^{-(a_1-a)}}{e^{(a_1-a)} + e^{-(a_1-a)}}$$

VALEDICTORY ADDRESS TO THE D—N.

May 1854.

JOHN Alexander Frere, John,
　　When we were first acquent,
You lectured us as Freshmen
　　In the holy term of Lent ;
But now you're gettin' bald, John,
　　Your end is drawing near,
And I think we'd better say " Goodbye,
　　John Alexander Frere."

John Alexander Frere, John,
　　How swiftly Time has flown !
The weeks that you refused us
　　Are now no more your own ;
Tho' Time was in your hand, John,
　　You lingered out the year,
That Grace might more abound unto
　　John Alexander Frere.[1]

---

[1] Mr. Frere had accepted the living of Shillington, but retained his fellowship for the customary " year of grace."

There's young Monro of Trinity,
　And Hunter bold of Queen's,
Who spurn the chapel system,
　And " vex the souls of Deans."
But all their petty squabbles
　More ludicrous appear,
When we muse on thy departed form,
　John Alexander Frere.

There's many a better man, John,
　That scorns the scoffing crew,
But keeps with fond affection
　The notes he got from you—
" Why he was out of College,
　Till two o'clock or near,
The Senior Dean requests to know,
　Yours truly, J. A. Frere."

John Alexander Frere, John,
　I wonder what you mean
By mixing up your name so
　With me, and with " The Dean."
Another Don may dean us,
　But ne'er again, we fear,
Shall we receive such notes as yours,
　John Alexander Frere.

The Lecture Room no more, John,
　Shall hear thy drowsy tone,
No more shall men in Chapel
　Bow down before thy throne.
But Shillington with meekness
　The oracle shall hear,
That set St. Mary's all to sleep—
　John Alexander Frere.

Then once before we part, John,
　Let all be clean forgot,
Our scandalous inventions,
　[Thy note-lets, prized or not].

For under all conventions,
    The small man lived sincere,
The kernel of the Senior Dean,
    John Alexander Frere.[1]

IN MEMORY OF EDWARD WILSON,

Who repented of what was in his mind to write after section.

Rigid Body (sings).

GIN a body meet a body
    Flyin' through the air,
Gin a body hit a body,
    Will it fly ? and where ?
Ilka impact has its measure,
    Ne'er a ane hae I,
Yet a' the lads they measure me,
    Or, at least, they try.

Gin a body meet a body
    Altogether free,
How they travel afterwards
    We do not always see.
Ilka problem has its method
    By analytics high ;
For me, I ken na ane o' them,
    But what the waur am I ?

VALENTINE BY A TELEGRAPH CLERK ♂ TO A TELEGRAPH
                CLERK ♀.

" THE tendrils of my soul are twined
    With thine, though many a mile apart,
And thine in close-coiled circuits wind
    Around the needle of my heart.

---

[1] The genuine esteem expressed in the concluding words, which alone
in this youthful pasquinade are to be taken seriously, must be the apology
for inserting what Maxwell himself would not have printed.

" Constant as Daniell, strong as Grove,
  Ebullient through its depths like Smee,
My heart pours forth its tide of love,
  And all its circuits close in thee.

" O tell me, when along the line
  From my full heart the message flows,
What currents are induced in thine ?
  One click from thee will end my woes."

Through many an Ohm the Weber flew,
  And clicked this answer back to me,—
" I am thy Farad, staunch[1] and true,
  Charged to a Volt with love for thee."

LECTURES TO WOMEN ON PHYSICAL SCIENCE.

I.

PLACE.—*A small alcove with dark curtains.*

The Class consists of one member.

SUBJECT.—*Thomson's Mirror Galvanometer.*

THE lamp-light falls on blackened walls,
  And streams through narrow perforations,
The long beam trails o'er pasteboard scales,
  With slow-decaying oscillations.
Flow, current, flow, set the quick light-spot flying,
Flow current, answer light-spot, flashing, quivering, dying.

O look ! how queer ! how thin and clear,
  And thinner, clearer, sharper growing
The gliding fire ! with central wire,
  The fine degrees distinctly showing.
Swing, magnet, swing, advancing and receding,
Swing magnet ! Answer dearest, What's your final reading ?

---

[1] *v.r.* Stout.

O love ! you fail to read the scale
    Correct to tenths of a division.
To mirror heaven those eyes were given,
    And not for methods of precision.
Break contact, break, set the free light-spot flying ;
Break contact, rest thee, magnet, swinging, creeping, dying.

LECTURES TO WOMEN ON PHYSICAL SCIENCE.

July 1874.

II.

*Professor Chrschtschonovitsch, Ph.D., " On the C. G. S.[1] system
of Units."*

Remarks submitted to the Lecturer by a student.

PRIM Doctor of Philosophy
    From academic Heidelberg !
Your sum of vital energy
    Is not the millionth of an erg.[2]
Your liveliest motion might be reckoned
At one-tenth metre[3] in a second.

" The air," you said, in language fine,
    Which scientific thought expresses,
" The air—which with a megadyne,[4]
    On each square centimetre presses—
The air, and I may add the ocean,
Are nought but molecules in motion."

Atoms, you told me, were discrete,
    Than you they could not be discreter,
Who know how many Millions meet
    Within a cubic millimetre.

---

[1] C. G. S. system—the system of units founded on the centimetre, gramme, and second. See report of Committee on units.—*Brit. Ass. Report* for 1873, p. 222.

[2] Erg—the energy communicated by a dyne, acting through a centimetre. See p. 411, note 1.

[3] Tenth-metre = 1 metre $\times$ 10^{-10}.

[4] Megadyne = 1 dyne $\times$ 10^6. It is somewhat more than the weight of a kilogramme.

They clash together as they fly,
But *you !*—you cannot tell me why.

And when in tuning my guitar
    The interval would *not* come right,
" This string," you said, " is strained too far,
    'Tis forty dynes,[1] at least too tight !"
And then you told me, as I sang,
    What overtones were in my clang.[2]

You gabbled on, but every phrase
    Was stiff with scientific shoddy,
The only song you deigned to praise
    Was " Gin a body meet a body,"
" And even there," you said, " collision
Was not described with due precision."

" In the invariable plane,"
    You told me, " lay the impulsive couple."[3]
You seized my hand—you gave me pain,
    By torsion of a wrist so supple ;
You told me what that wrench would do,—
" 'Twould set me twisting round a screw."[4]

Were every hair of every tress
    (Which you, no doubt, imagine mine),
Drawn towards you with its breaking stress—
    A stress, say, of a megadyne,
That tension I would sooner suffer
Than meet again with such a duffer !

---

[1] Dyne—the force which, acting on a gramme for a second, would give a velocity of a centimetre per second. The weight of a gramme is about 980 dynes.

[2] See *Sound and Music*, by Sedley Taylor, p. 89.

[3] See Poinsot, *Théorie nouvelle de la rotation des corps.*

[4] See Prof. Ball on the Theory of Screws, *Phil. Trans.*, 1873.

To the Chief Musician upon Nabla.[1]

A Tyndallic Ode.

I.

I come from fields of fractured ice,
　　Whose wounds are cured by squeezing,
Melting[2] they cool, but in a trice,
　　Get[3] warm again by freezing.
Here, in the frosty air, the sprays
　　With fern-like hoar-frost bristle,
There, liquid stars their watery rays
　　Shoot through the solid crystal.

II.

I come from empyrean fires—
　　From microscopic spaces,
Where molecules with fierce desires,
　　Shiver in hot embraces.
The atoms clash, the spectra flash,
　　Projected on the screen,
The double D, magnesian *b*,
　　And Thallium's living green.

III.

We place our eye where these dark rays
　　Unite in this dark focus,
Right on the source of power we gaze,
　　Without a screen to cloak us.
Then, where the eye was placed at first,
　　We place a disc[4] of platinum,
It glows, it puckers ! will it[5] burst ?
　　How ever shall we[6] flatten him !

---

[1] Nabla was the name of an Assyrian harp of the shape ∇. ∇ is a quaternion operator $\left(i \dfrac{d}{dx} + j \dfrac{d}{dy} + k \dfrac{d}{dz} \right)$ invented by Sir W. R. Hamilton, whose use and properties were first fully discussed by Professor Tait, who is therefore called the " Chief Musician upon Nabla."

[2] *v.r.* They melt.　　　　[3] *v.r.* Grow.　　　　[4] *v.r.* dish.
[5] *v.r.* like to.　　　　[6] *v.r.* By Jove, I'll have to.

IV.

This crystal tube the electric ray
  Shows optically clean,
No dust or haze within, but stay!
  All has not yet been seen.
What gleams are these of heavenly blue?
  What air-drawn form appearing,
What mystic fish, that, ghostlike, through [1]
  The empty [2] space is steering?

V.

I light this sympathetic flame,
  My faintest wish that answers,
I sing, it sweetly sings the same,
  It dances with the dancers.
I shout, I whistle, clap my hands,
  And [3] stamp upon [4] the platform,
The flame responds [5] to my commands,
  In this form and in that form.

VI.

What means that thrilling, drilling scream,
  Protect me! 'tis the siren:
Her heart is fire, her breath is steam,
  Her larynx is of iron.
Sun! dart thy beams! in tepid streams,
  Rise, viewless exhalations!
And lap me round, that no rude sound
  May mar my meditations.

VII.

Here let me pause.—These transient facts,
  These fugitive impressions,
Must be transformed by mental acts,
  To permanent possessions.

---

[1] *v.r.* What fish, what whale is this, that through.   [2] *v.r.* vacuous.
    [3] *v.r.* I.   [4] *v.r.* about.   [5] *v.r.* bows down.

Then summon up your grasp of mind,
　　Your fancy scientific,
Till[1] sights and sounds with thought combine
　　Become[2] of truth prolific.

VIII.

Go to ! prepare your mental bricks,
　　Fetch them from every quarter,
Firm on the sand your basement fix
　　With best sensation mortar.
The top[3] shall rise to heaven on high—
　　Or such an elevation,
That the swift whirl with which we fly
　　Shall conquer gravitation.

To the Committee of the Cayley Portrait Fund.

1874

O WRETCHED race of men, to space confined !
What honour can ye pay to him, whose mind
To that which lies beyond hath penetrated ?
The symbols he hath formed shall sound his praise,
And lead him on through unimagined ways
To conquests new, in worlds not yet created.

First, ye Determinants ! in ordered row
And massive column ranged, before him go,
To form a phalanx for his safe protection.
Ye powers of the nth roots of -1 !
Around his head in ceaseless[4] cycles run,
As unembodied spirits of direction.

And you, ye undevelopable scrolls !
Above the host wave your emblazoned rolls,
Ruled for the record of his bright inventions.
Ye Cubic surfaces ! by threes and nines
Draw round his camp your seven-and-twenty lines—
The seal of Solomon in three dimensions.

---

[1] *v.r.* That.　　[2] *v.r.* May be.　　[3] *v.r.* tower.　　[4] *v.r.* endless.

March on, symbolic host ! with step sublime,
Up to the flaming bounds of Space and Time !
There pause, until by Dickenson depicted,
In two dimensions, we the form may trace
Of him whose soul, too large for vulgar space,
In n dimensions flourished unrestricted.

BRITISH ASSOCIATION, 1874.

Notes of the President's Address.

In the very beginnings of science, the parsons, who managed
things then,
Being handy with hammer and chisel, made gods in the likeness
of men ;
Till Commerce arose, and at length some men of exceptional
power
Supplanted both demons and gods by the atoms, which last to
this hour.
Yet they did not abolish the gods, but they sent them well out
of the way,
With the rarest of nectar to drink, and blue fields of nothing to
sway.
From nothing comes nothing, they told us, nought happens
by chance, but by fate ;
There is nothing but atoms and void, all else is mere whims
out of date.
Then why should a man curry favour with beings who cannot
exist,
To compass some petty promotion in nebulous kingdoms of
mist ?
But not by the rays of the sun, nor the glittering shafts of the
day,
Must the fear of the gods be dispelled, but by words, and their
wonderful play.
So treading a path all untrod, the poet-philosopher sings
Of the seeds of the mighty world—the first beginnings of
things ;
How freely he scatters his atoms before the beginning of years ;
How he clothes them with force as a garment, those small in-
compressible spheres !

Nor yet does he leave them hard-hearted—he dowers them with
    love and with hate,
Like spherical small British Asses in infinitesimal state ;
Till just as that living Plato, whom foreigners nickname
    Plateau,[1]
Drops oil in his whisky-and-water (for foreigners sweeten
    it so),
Each drop keeps apart from the other, enclosed in a flexible
    skin,
Till touched by the gentle emotion evolved by the prick of a
    pin :
Thus in atoms a simple collision excites a sensational thrill,
Evolved through all sorts of emotion, as sense, understanding,
    and will ;
(For by laying their heads all together, the atoms, as councillors
    do,
May combine to express an opinion to every one of them new.)
There is nobody here, I should say, has felt true indignation at
    all,
Till an indignation meeting is held in the Ulster Hall ;
Then gathers the wave of emotion, then noble feelings arise,
Till you all pass a resolution which takes every man by surprise.
Thus the pure elementary atom, the unit of mass and of thought,
By force of mere juxtaposition to life and sensation is brought ;
So, down through untold generations, transmission of structure-
    less germs
Enables our race to inherit the thoughts of beasts, fishes, and
    worms.
We honour our fathers and mothers, grandfathers and grand-
    mothers too ;
But how shall we honour the vista of ancestors now in our
    view ?
First, then, let us honour the atom, so lively, so wise, and so
    small ;
The atomists next let us praise, Epicurus, Lucretius, and all ;
Let us damn with faint praise Bishop Butler, in whom many
    atoms combined
To form that remarkable structure, it pleased him to call—his
    mind.

---

[1] *Statique Expérimentale et Théorique des Liquides soumis aux seules
Forces Moléculaires.* Par J. Plateau, Professeur à l'Université de Gaud.

Last, praise we the noble body to which, for the time, we
    belong,
Ere yet the swift whirl of the atoms has hurried us, ruthless,
    along,
The British Association — like Leviathan worshipped by
    Hobbes,
The incarnation of wisdom, built up of our witless nobs,
Which will carry on endless discussions, when I, and probably
    you,
Have melted in infinite azure—in English, till all is blue.

REPORT ON TAIT'S LECTURE ON FORCE :—B.A., 1876.

YE British Asses, who expect to hear
        Ever some new thing,
I've nothing new to tell, but what, I fear,
        May be a true thing.
For Tait comes with his plummet and his line,
        Quick to detect your
Old bosh new dressed in what you call a fine
        Popular lecture.

Whence comes that most peculiar smattering,
        Heard in our section ?
Pure nonsense, to a scientific swing
        Drilled to perfection ?
That small word "Force," they make[1] a barber's block,
        Ready to put on
Meanings most strange and various, fit to shock
        Pupils of Newton.

Ancient and foreign ignorance they throw
        Into the bargain ;
The shade of Leibnitz[2] mutters from below
        Horrible jargon.
The phrases of last century in this
        Linger to play tricks—
Vis Viva and *Vis Mortua* and *Vis*
        Acceleratrix :—

---

[1] *v.r.* is made.　　　　　　　[2] *v.r.* sage of Leipzig.

Those long-nebbed words that to our text books still
        Cling by their titles,
And from them creep, as entozoa will,
        Into our vitals.
But see ! Tait writes in lucid symbols clear
        One small equation ;
And Force becomes of Energy a mere
        Space-variation.

Force, then, is Force, but mark you ! not a thing,
        Only a Vector ;
Thy barbèd arrows now have lost their sting,
        Impotent spectre !
Thy reign, O Force ! is over.   Now no more
        Heed we thine action ;
Repulsion leaves us where we were before,
        So does attraction.

Both Action and Reaction now are gone.
        Just ere they vanished,
Stress joined their hands in peace, and made them one :
        Then they were banished.
The Universe is free from pole to pole,
        Free from all forces.
Rejoice ! ye stars—like blessed gods ye roll
        On in your courses.

No more the arrows of the Wrangler race,
        Piercing shall wound you.
Forces no more, those symbols of disgrace,
        Dare to surround you :
But those whose statements baffle all attacks,
        Safe by evasion,—
Whose definitions, like a nose of wax,
        Suit each occasion,—

Whose unreflected rainbow far surpassed
        All our inventions,
Whose very energy appears at last
        Scant of dimensions :—

Are these the gods in whom ye put your trust.
　　Lordlings and ladies ?
The hidden[1] potency of cosmic dust
　　Drives them to Hades.

While you, brave Tait ! who know so well the way
　　Forces to scatter,
Calmly await the slow but sure decay,
　　Even of Matter.

(CATS) CRADLE SONG.

By a Babe in Knots.

PETER the Repeater,
　　Platted round a platter
Slips of slivered paper,
　　Basting them with batter.

Flype 'em, slit 'em, twist 'em,
　　Lop-looped laps of paper ;
Setting out the system
　　By the bones of Neper.

Clear your coil of kinkings
　　Into perfect plaiting,
Locking loops and linkings
　　Interpenetrating.

Why should a man benighted,
　　Beduped, befooled, besotted,
Call knotful knittings plighted,
　　Not knotty but beknotted ?

It's monstrous, horrid, shocking,
　　Beyond the power of thinking,
Not to know, interlocking
　　Is no mere form of linking.

---

[1] *v.r.* secret.

But little Jacky Horner
  Will teach you what is proper,
So pitch him, in his corner,
  Your silver and your copper.

To HERMANN STOFFKRAFT, Ph.D., the Hero of a recent work
called " Paradoxical Philosophy."

A Paradoxical Ode.

[After Shelley.]

1878.

I.

My soul is an entangled[1] knot,
  Upon a liquid vortex wrought
By Intellect, in the Unseen residing,
  And thine doth like a convict sit,
  With marlinspike untwisting it,
Only to find its knottiness abiding ;
  Since all the tools for its untying
  In four-dimensioned space are lying,
  Wherein thy fancy intersperses
  Long[2] avenues of universes,
  While Klein and Clifford fill the void
  With one finite, unbounded homaloid,
And think the Infinite is now at last destroyed.

II.

But when thy Science lifts her pinions
  In Speculation's wild dominions,
We treasure every dictum thou emittest,
  While down the stream of Evolution
  We drift, expecting no solution
But that of the survival of the fittest.
  Till, in the twilight of the gods,
  When earth and sun are frozen clods,
  When, all its energy degraded,
  Matter to æther shall have faded ;

---

[1] *v.r.* 's an amphicheiral.   [2] *v.r.* Whole.

We, that is, all the work we've done,
As waves in æther, shall for ever run
In ever-widening[1] spheres through heavens beyond the sun.

III.

Great Principle of all we see,
Unending Continuity !
By thee are all our angles sweetly rounded,
By thee are our misfits adjusted,
And as I still in thee have trusted,
So trusting, let me never be confounded !
Oh never may direct Creation
Break in upon my contemplation ;
Still may thy causal chain, ascending,
Appear unbroken and unending,
While Residents in the Unseen—
Æons and Emanations—intervene,
And from my shrinking soul the Unconditioned screen.[2]

---

[1] *v.r.* swift expanding.
[2] *v.r.* And where that chain is lost to sight
     Let viewless fancies guide my darkling flight,
   Through atom-haunted worlds in series infinite.

THE END.

Printed by R. & R. CLARK, *Edinburgh.*

SOME OPINIONS OF THE PRESS

ON THE ORIGINAL EDITION OF

A LIFE OF CLERK MAXWELL

WITH

A Selection from his Correspondence and Occasional Writings,
and a Sketch of his Contributions to Science,

By LEWIS CAMPBELL, M.A., LL.D.,

AND

WILLIAM GARNETT, M.A.

With Three Portraits, Illustrations, etc. 8vo. 18s.

Now out of Print.

———————

"To those who knew him, especially those who had the rare privilege of counting him friend, the mention of the name of Clerk Maxwell will induce a strange mixture of feeling—tenderness at the memory of a love of rare unselfishness, and a devout faith whose serenity no science could ruffle; admiration for an intellect of such scope and elasticity that it could with equal ease throw off a song of grotesque humour, or give mathematical expression to the most complicated physical problem; reverence for a genius that seemed actually to see the ultra-microscopic workings of the ultimate molecules of matter. Those who desire to make the acquaintance of one of the rarest and most original spirits of our time will read this biography."—*The Times.*

"A large circle of readers will turn with much interest to these memorials of one of the leaders of physical science. . . . Maxwell's own letters are very numerous, and always readable, for it was not in his nature to be dry; and the account of the more important parts of his scientific work by Mr. Garnett is eminently clear and judicious."—*The Athenæum.*

"The history of Clerk Maxwell's life, as it is now presented to us, in a finished literary form, by the sympathetic hand of one of his earliest friends, Professor Lewis Campbell, will probably have an attraction for many readers besides those who are drawn to it by Maxwell's reputation as a mathematician and a physicist. Few biographies give a more elaborately truthful account of the growth, development, and final activity of a powerful and persistently-employed intelligence; and fewer still contain the portraiture of a moral character so wholly exempt from every taint of the world, the flesh, and the devil."—*The Academy.*

"Certain it is that we have here an unusually complete delineation of a man's life, internal as well as external. This is partly due to Maxwell's own letters and other writings, but much more to the very lively recollection of him at different periods of his life preserved by friends, including Professor Campbell himself; and the subject thus carefully portrayed is one of unusual attractiveness. Maxwell was a man of strongly-marked individuality. . . . It was the combination of this exceptional mechanical ingenuity with exact theoretic conceptions which enabled him to make such important additions to our knowledge of physical phenomena. But his work is probably too well known to find lengthy description here. In this interesting volume the general reader will find an excellent summary of his researches. Rarely has it been our lot to find a work and a worker alike so attractive."—*Saturday Review.*

"This volume will be heartily welcomed by all who knew Clerk Maxwell, and who cherish his memory, and by the still wider circle of those who derive pleasure and new vigour from the study of the lives and work of the great men that have gone before them."—*Nature.*

"The present volume will do much more than confirm the good impression which he produced during his lifetime. The biographical portion of the book is by Mr. Campbell; and a more interesting account of a contemporary writer we have not read for a very long time. By means of an unpretending narrative and a judicious selection from Clerk Maxwell's correspondence, Mr. Campbell has succeeded in presenting a remarkably vivid picture of the facts of his friend's life, and of the essential qualities of his character."—*St. James's Gazette.*

"Clerk Maxwell's name stands, by the unanimous consent of all who have any voice in such matters, in the very foremost rank of British men of science. He possessed not only eminent power in his own field of work, but that still rarer genius which makes itself felt in manifold ways, even to those who can appreciate but a small part of its results. He shared this quality with Faraday in an earlier generation, a discoverer whose conquests Maxwell followed up by other methods; and with Clifford, a fellow-mathematician, younger by several years, whose intellect was in more ways than one akin to Maxwell's own."—*Pall Mall Gazette.*

MACMILLAN AND CO., LONDON.